1970/1979

Here are seven representative plays from the seventies—a decade of theatre characterized as much by a continuation of traditional patterns as by new forms of the art. The award-winning plays collected here attest to a new vitality and affirm the distinguished abilities of their creators.

TED HOFFMAN is a theatre scholar, actor, director, and administrator. He was editor of *The Drama Review* and *Alternative Theatre*. He has taught at Bard College, Stanford University, and Carnegie-Mellon University, and is director of the Theatre Program at New York University.

D0089620

FAMOUS
AMERICAN PLAYS
OF THE
1970s

with an Introduction by
TED HOFFMAN

THE LAUREL DRAMA SERIES

Published by
Dell Publishing Co., Inc.
1 Dag Hammarskjold Plaza
New York, New York 10017

Laurel ® TM 674623, Dell Publishing Co., Inc.

ISBN: 0-440-32537-4

Printed in the United States of America
First printing—February 1981

Contents

Acknowledgments

The author of the Introduction wishes to thank Agnes Wilcox for her role as catalyst and Gareth Esersky for her initiative and editorial enthusiasm.

Famous American Plays
of the 1970s

INTRODUCTION

The Famous American Plays series now spans six decades. Our theatre may not change perceptively every tenth New Year's Day, but when the representative plays of the decade are gathered, on the basis of their individual merits and varied trends, their common qualities demonstrate that the playwriting of each age has a newness readily distinguishable from the newness of the previous age.

The people whose lives animate these plays command instant attention because they represent a break with past drama. The plays collected in the *Famous American Plays of the 1960s* pitted sympathetic but losing characters against destructive forces of war, corruption, violence, discrimination, crime, and racism. Through various dramatic means, each play dealt with human aspiration in diverse American times and social situations. Each play ended in despair, as did the 1960s. But the characters in the *Famous American Plays of the 1970s* seem to be survivors of an Apocalypse. The playwrights ask "what happened?" more often that "what will happen?" They may be elegaic, hysterical, or in mourning, but they move through the residual life of a world that no longer works. They improvise their lives amid skewed human communications systems, sometimes with hilarious ingenuity and sometimes with desperate foreboding, obliged to take themselves for normal in a society gone mad.

Even in the most serious of these plays the characters present behavior that previously might have been considered bizarre or eccentric. Pick a central character from each play and you get: a bookworm who logically extends the war protest activities of his friends into cop-killing and self-immolation; a mooncalf soldier whose efforts to make everyone like him alienates them into aggression against him; a certified public accountant who methodically prorates a weekend affair into a twenty-five-year annual adultery; a one-legged man with a compulsion to clip his sleeping father's hair; a militant black nationalist checking the gumbo for pork at a mixed cocktail party; and a Radcliffe language major trying to speak Florentine Italian to a family of South Philadelphia Neopolitans.

If drama depends on empathetic characters and lofty themes, the plays of the 1970s might be dismissed with a derisive "What's so famous about a bunch of convictionless zombies?" The answer is simply "Keep reading! Keep seeing! Keep thinking!" Plays get dismissed in their own times and accepted later. Henry Hewes found Tennessee Williams' *Glass Menagerie* "less a play than a character sketch." Brooks Atkinson asked of *Pal Joey*, "Can you draw sweet water out of a foul well?" Each of these responses might be elicited from a reading of the plays in this volume.

Looking backwards, we see that the "famous" plays of the 1930s might be characterized as bittersweet indulgence in discovering that life is ironic, and the 1940s would reveal an ethical nostalgia for a pre-war world, but that would not be doing justice to the plays themselves. There may be more depth in the ironic and ethical and more meaning in the bittersweet and nostalgic than an easy summation provides, just as the zombielike survivors of an Apocalypse may yet be perceived by later critics as magnificent characters shaped by memorable playwrights into a penetrating vision of human existence.

Then, again, maybe not. How do we decide what may become "famous" in the immediately previous decade when what used to be famous isn't any more? Literary criticism still treats Eugene O'Neill as a living classic, but the two plays of his that get revived, *Long Day's Journey Into Night* and *The Iceman Cometh*, are late naturalistic regressions unlike the main body of work that made him "famous" in his lifetime. And his famous contemporaries are all more famous in the textbook than onstage or are subject to musical theatre adaptation.

If longevity in the theatre, the sensibility of one age responding to that of an earlier age, makes for "famous," then farce is the great American dramatic tradition. *You Can't Take It with You, The Time of Your Life, Room Service, Arsenic and Old Lace, The Front Page, Once in a Lifetime, Boy Meets Girl,* and *Harvey* not only get revived but get received as meaningful while a revival of Lillian Hellman's *Watch on the Rhine* nobly fails. Add to this the staying power of American comic film and American theatre history needs rewriting. This, however, is no reason to conclude right now that *Same Time, Next Year* and *Gemini* will outlive *Buried Child* and *The Basic Training of Pavlo Hummel.* Future taste is unpredictable. The historians also guess and wait.

If contemporary plays deserve lasting survival, we can best measure their chances by the breadth of their appeal to audiences, which includes both those who see and those who study plays. The standards that have guided the selection of plays for this volume require that a play uniquely express American experience, that it demonstrate the kind of high skill in playwriting which invites imaginative performance craft, and that it influence American theatre through commanding the concern of theatre artists, critics, scholars, and students. A "hit" need not be identified solely as a profitable Broadway run. The long life of a play, as with most of these works, may begin with a minor production and travel the whole range of American and world theatre until the awards it receives have been validated through international prestige.

The plays in this anthology most fully meet the selection standards. Others of merit can fit the discussion of the 1970s as aptly and miss inclusion through no fault of their own. There has been a "wave" of new playwrights with impressive imagination and achievement in the 1970s including John Guare, Jason Miller, Mark Medoff, Lanford Wilson, Ntozake Shange, Terrence McNally, Miguel Pinero, David Mamet, Preston Jones, Joseph Walker, and Michael Christopher, some of whom may produce more impressive plays in the 1980s.

A group of equally gifted, outstanding women playwrights must not be overlooked despite the fact that their work has not yet been accepted and promoted by the masculine production apparatus that leads to popular success. Megan Terry, Rochelle Owens, Eve Merriam, Alice Childress, Rosalyn Drexler, Adrienne Kennedy, Wendy Wasserstein, Tina Howe, Corinne Jacker, Myrna Lamb, Marsha Norman, and Susan Miller are among them. *Fefu and Her Friends* by Maria Irene Fornes deserved to move up the production ladder from its 1977 Off-Off Broadway success to a more prominent status and will survive as hardily as many of the plays offered here.

When Robert Brustein returned to reviewing in 1979, after ten years at Yale, he perceived little change in American theatre. In both 1969 and 1979, Broadway announced the most prosperous season in decades, *The Fantasticks* was still the longest running show, Joe Papp's Public Theatre was doing a rock musical, Neil Simon had a hit, and Albee and Williams and Miller were still represented. He accordingly quoted Walt Whitman on New York as the place you go to sell fruit, not to grow it, and leaned back to see if "the new season will produce fresh nourishment or the same old frozen produce."

The Broadway decade Brustein sat out actually had a roller coaster existence. By the mid-1970s, its economic state had become so perilous that a high level First American Theatre Congress (F.A.C.T.) was convened at Princeton to persuade non-profit theatre to embrace the commercial theatre in a joint quest for subsidy. By 1980, new facts had reversed the projected poverty trend, and a Second Congress was stillborn. Broadway's conscience had shifted to driving vice and porn to other neighborhoods to make Times Square safe for conventions, tourists, and real estate developers. No one cried havoc when $500,000 straight shows fizzled and megabuck musical theatre vanities were benignly laughed into oblivion. Life had become so miraculously sweet again that friendly computerized TKTS booths in Times Square and on Wall Street served unsold tickets at half price—just about what they had cost a decade ago.

A new generation of producers had learned how to run roadhouses for London hits, to package musicals and other extravaganzas with the methods of conglomerate investment diversification for delivery to film and television. They had also learned how to use regional, Off-Off Broadway, and experimental theatres as minor league sources to develop star properties. Three of these plays came up by that process: *Moonchildren, The Basic Training of Pavlo Hummel*, and *Gemini*. Only *Same Time, Next Year* originated on Broadway. Although *Buried Child* won the Pulitzer Prize and *The Taking Of Miss Janie* the Critics' Circle Award, neither made it to Broadway. That, however, is growth. The most imaginative and provocative American plays are no longer discovered through script reading by Broadway producers. Only one of the works in *Famous American Plays of the 1960s* got to Broadway, *We Bombed in New Haven*, and it didn't last long.

The problem is that when a play succeeds today, it gets promoted as a property and the playwright's identity gets submerged. Newspaper advertisements blaze "Critics' Circle" or "Tony Best Play" without mention of the playwright. Even the most creative theatre artist of the 1970s, Stephen Sondheim, suffered the same fate in 1979 in the splashy ads for the spectacular *Sweeney Todd*. Yet the talented American playwright lives, if frugally. We have developed a subsidy apparatus which enables non-profit theatres to produce new plays but not at a production level that can afford adequate royalties. The playwrights get coddling, recognition, earnest but economical production, but no decent income. Meanwhile, they hang onto the ultimate tease of the occasional thrust to wealth through workshop to Off-Off Broadway to regional theatre to Broadway and beyond, which Michael Weller, David Rabe, Albert Innaurato, and David Mamet, worthies all, have consummated. The work of some fifty American playwrights of skill and imagination can be seen regularly in New York, usually in union-restricted, Off-Off Broadway three week runs, excellently performed by actors as underpaid as the playwrights, equally in need of a showcase.

Since few achieve success on Broadway, and Broadway continues to accommodate only a handful of original plays a year, what do the developmental grants to theatres prepare our playwrights for? Film and television! The Los Angeles market, where the promising playwrights of the 1940s, 1950s, and 1960s are also found in differing degrees of comfort and sanity. Film and television now guide the profession and eventually absorb all the top theatre talent. Fair enough. Even those who confess to a lingering addiction to live performance must admit that during the 1970s the dramatic imagination migrated west. The daring artistic invention and finesse that was formerly restricted to European and art films is now budgeted as a staple in routine films which have become more inviting in scope, freedom, and challenge than the limited narrative and scenic iconography of the decreasingly small cast, single-set Broadway straight play. The commanding and stimulating *auteur* work of commercial film often looks like an outgrowth of those theatre talents who didn't make it to Broadway, and it very frequently is.

Film and television in America, despite all the cynical manipulation and junk that dominate, now produce a complex mass art worthy of serious critical and scholarly study. At the same time, theatre, for all its growth, still reached only 3% of the population. Broadway has become a product testing laboratory for film and television, and has lost its research capability. To find new trends and originality in the theatre of the 1970s, one must turn to the theatrical equivalent of the boutiques, gourmet outfits, and home crafts services that offer custom quality within the American mass consumer market.

The American theatre is surprisingly and refreshingly national once again, reprising its state before 1900 when resident production units were displaced by package tours, vaudeville, and the movies. Some sixty non-profit professional theatres across the country offer old and new plays that one hardly sees on Broadway while employing the same pool of actors, directors, and designers. They have their perpetual fund-raising problems, but few fold and some dazzle. *Moonchildren* originated in 1971 at Washington, D.C.'s, Arena Stage. *Gemini* gathered impetus in 1977 at the Huntington, Long Island, PAF Playhouse en route to Broadway through the Circle Rep. The pattern is long endemic and playwrights who were once reluctant to release their new plays to such theatre have since learned that productions at Los Angeles' Mark Taper Forum, New Haven's Long Wharf, Louisville's Actors' Theatre, The Dallas Theatre Center, and other venues make a play read better in a producer's head and also define the perspicacity of the regional audiences.

If Off-Off Broadway and the national threatres have become sources for new plays, the experimental theatre, which charged full tilt out of the 1960s and has only recently lost momentum (and perhaps its targets), has influenced the playwrights and the performance modes their plays require. The process is strangely traditional. The history of the past century of modern drama is best traced as an anti-naturalist avant garde application of new modes of performance and design to new forms of playwriting, with the results assimilated into the commercial theatre. 1970s experimental theatre came out of a "total theatre" vision traceable to the Wagnerian idea of integrating the separate processes of all the arts into a unified performance. If the unified art work has yet to appear, the experimentalists have helped change design, acting, and directing in ways playwrights have absorbed.

Scene designers of the 1970s determined to tear down the "fourth wall" of proscenium illusion and the low slung decor of the open stage by creating "environments" which included not only the audience, lovingly or aggressively, but also, through performer involvement, became a dynamic element in the meaning of the performance. The new playwrights, even when they write for the proscenium theatre, design idiosyncratic and surreal environmental scenery into their work. The *Pavlo Hummel* set provides conventional multiple playing areas and a constructivist landscape of a distant war that conveys real and fantastic shifts of time and focus. The facade of the adjoining backyards in *Gemini* is not just the functional backdrop of *Street Scene* or *Picnic*; it demands the weird light and grubby feeling of a Hopper painting, closing out the external world which intrudes selectively and incongruously as the campers' tent pitched in the yard and a telephone pole that is climbed by a lusty, suicidal woman.

From the "happenings" of the 1950s, which spawned the environmental concepts of design and staging, and also demolished narrative by arranging fixed and accidental actions in serial form, to the experimental theatre groups of the 1960s which responded to the manifesto against "plays," theatre practitioners were soon creating their own "texts" in rehearsal out of their own experiences, documentary materials, and fragments of reshaped literature. This mode of prepared improvisation has influenced the most recent decade of playwrights. Their plays have carefully and complexly ordered plots but do not fill the well-made-play prescription. Scenes take on their own shape, frequently as variations on themes, as if the playwright had permitted the characters to shape structure out of *their* experience and perception, rather than forcing action into the symmetrical "slice of life" sequence of previous drama. The wise director today seeks to realize the inherent structures in a play but is more likely to treat the "text" as a score and conduct it accordingly.

Acting, as well as directing, changed in the 1970s. Vocal and prosody demands increased. Longer speeches were treated more as arias than as emotional rumination or motivated declamation. Pauses and pitch of successive lines distributed among several characters need to be genuinely responsive in character but they also must make musical sense and require orchestration. In plays that seem to consist mainly of talk, gestures, acrobatics, and choreography accompany the conversation. *Gemini* and *Buried Child* define character in terms of appearance and gesture so completely that the performers must constantly work out their lines in conjunction with the action flow. *Pavlo Hummel, Miss Janie,* and *Moonchildren* call for ensemble movement of a kind that obliges the director to deal simultaneously with each performer and to orchestrate constantly shifting focus and tempo. Acting is now livelier. Character quirks, shifting focus, and intrusive thought contribute to a new "truthful" virtuosity.

The source of this eccentric variation is traced most readily to the cabaret improvisation of Chicago's Second City troupe, where it was developed by Paul Sills, and made most famous by Mike Nichols and Elaine May, although their colleagues and successors continue to emerge from that tradition—Alda, Arkin, Asner, and down through the alphabet to their popular offspring, the performers on *Saturday Night Live*. In a radical intellectual ambience, Second City took on the manners of the middle depths of American society with skeptical affection and a sense of existential absurdity, becoming adept at social role playing, rationalizing bizarre behavior, and capturing the nuances of spoken language in all its coded transactional pretense. The satiric flavor is evident in much of the 1970s drama where playwrights continued to investigate the social milieus Second City exposed and parodied.

But there is a difference between the characters who people these plays and the send-ups of Second City. The difference is that the sense of life experienced by people living in the dramatic environments has been altered by external events. An existential shift can be seen in the work of playwrights who straddle the 1960s and 1970s. Sam Shepard's characters from the 1960s come across as maladjusted refugees from a society they find insufferably paradoxical. After 1970, all appear isolated and trapped within the disaster areas of a Beckett *Endgame*. *Moonchildren* deals with the defiant hopes of a generation trying to change society, but it ends with a key figure sobbing a lamentation that "All the human beings are headed west," something like the hero of Brecht's *In the Jungle* who, after every conceivable disaster has struck him, observes, "And those were the good days."

These plays of the 1970s reflect the failure of nerve that characterized post-Vietnam America. The Kent State and Jackson State assassinations demonstrated to anyone playing the game of protest revolution that the Establishment holds the cards and can escalate the stakes at will, which leaves two choices: apathy or violence. Watergate simply proved that anyone's wildest paranoid fears of government are likely to become literal. No central character in any of these plays espouses a cause or offers any hopeful vision for society. Any glimpse backward in time takes on a nostalgic aura, but the Americana evoked is identified as corrupt, decayed, self-destructive, and at best, redolent, like collectibles of ingenious bad taste.

Walter Kerr, whose three decades of criticism calls for an American drama based on the imaginative power of popular forms and the positive verities of American life, observed in his column "Confrontations with Mortality" (*The New York Times,* July 2, 1978), that the 1970s drama was preoccupied with the themes of illness, death and dying, and despair. In a society where people live longer and in which many more people die of wasting disease, the subject is much on our minds. It seems as if the characters of the sum of the outstanding plays of the second half of the decade, including *The Shadow Box, Wings, Ashes, Cold Storage,* and *The Gin Game,* had congregated with us for one long last drink at "The Last Chance Saloon" where "we hoist glasses, clink them, and do our broken but earnest best to probe for the conversation we were told we couldn't have, the conversation we'd never had time for, the conversation we know we were born to."

Search beyond the paralysis of death and despair for more positive themes and you find sex and myth, perhaps attributable to the experimental theatre which advocated not just low budgets but the performer's body and soul as a prime medium of theatre. As performers shed their "autobiographical" selves to unearth a deeper archetypal responsive self, inhibitions were renounced, leading to a theatre of exhibitionism. Serious efforts to liberate the polymorphous perverse nature of modern society enticed commercial theatre to cut loose with explicit sexual skits like those in the indistinguishable sleazy routines of *Oh! Calcutta!,* leaving porn and the erotic to film. Theatre found a new openness and frankness about sex that permitted more full probing of characters and the extension of performance into actions upon which curtains used to fall. Casual nudity is now accepted. Witness the near stripping in *Same Time, Next Year* and *The Taking of Miss Janie.* Note how a full-term pregnant woman proposing to cure her part-time lover's impotence in *Same Time, Next Year*, hardly a sensational play, is meant to be understandably endearing.

More important is the new dispensation to deal with sex and sexuality without resorting to melodrama or symbolism. Homosexuality has become an almost honest subject. The whole scope of women's issues, expanded Off-Off Broadway during the 1970s, is now so critically examined by audiences that female characters in the plays by male playwrights often appear to have been thoroughly researched in life or in books and pretested for consumer reaction to the degree that fairness and conscience produces some female characters that are too good to be true.

Another element of the contemporary theatre passed to the 1970s playwrights from the experimentalists, notably Grotowski, is the playable mystic, mythic character. The 1960s' rearrangement of classical and modern archtypal experience and a tendency in theatre to present life as a dream has given way in the 1970s to characters who lead other lives, dealing with their own mythic existence, however colloquially they put it. The plays of Shepard, Bullins, and Innaurato in particular are shaped by mythic moods, time warps, and anthropological constructs of experience which have already attracted serious critical attention.

The central ethos of these plays, the perceived world, is easily identified among the British imports and among the Broadway successes that filled the 1970s. It is evident in the Victorian perversity of *Sweeney Todd*, the snide semiotics of *Dracula*, the contrived amoralism of *Evita*, and the reduction of grit and danger to absurdity in *Annie*. Whatever the differences in form, concern, style, however varied the sensibilities of the playwrights, these representative plays together constitute a Theatre of the Grotesque. Their historic mode is Gothic Romance, in jeans. Their language is that of mocking gallows humor, in the kitchen or bedroom. Hallie, in *Buried Child*, murmurs "A bad omen. Our youth becoming monsters." The characters keep feeling strange transformations in themselves, or seeing strange transformations in others. All, even the most comic, are filled with an eerie fatalism about life, a dance before the Grim Reaper with many faces. Again and again, the characters convert their threatening dilemmas into a frenetic search for the next improvised masquerade that will make them feel dead or alive.

When *The Basic Training of Pavlo Hummel* opened at the Public Theater in 1971, critics and audiences recognized that the "basic training" of its title was still going on at home in the post-Vietnam period, that the experience of our soldiers in the war was only an extension of the conditioning of our society. The 1976 Broadway version with Al Pacino revealed that the situation had not changed, and playwright David Rabe contributed two other award-winning Vietnam "hits" in the interim: *Sticks and Bones*, which plunged a blind veteran into his more horrifying and destructive home life, and *Streamers*, set in the Army but through its major metaphor of a non-functioning parachute, replete with the reality of American life.

The plot of *Pavlo* suggests a fable, an epic tale recited so endlessly that whoever tells it takes it for granted and is free to emphasize its parts disproportionately, to add or enlarge characters, to set the mind puzzling over the meaning of the obvious, to apply virtuosity of language or action to scenes at will. Reconstructed, the plot is traditional. The dumb army recruit becomes the butt of everyone's jokes and anger until he learns to be a man just before he dies. So Pavlo Hummel, the innocent in Vietnam, tries to act big, misconstrues the regulations, antagonizes everyone, finally wins a fight over a "whore," and is blown up by his victim. The tale is told as if Pavlo were experiencing his life over and over, until the details become illuminating.

Two black soldiers accompany him constantly. Sgt. Tower, who stands on a tower and whose first name is Sergeant, unctuously drill-trains Pavlo in the ways of warfare which Pavlo continually misinterprets. Ardell appears to mock him gently with serious saving advice Pavlo never quite masters.

Pavlo isn't the innocent lower-class bumpkin. As Rabe points out, he is actually trying to replace middle class conditioning with street smarts. "I'm not an asshole anymore," he vaunts to his affluent stepbrother only to learn that when he seeks to make it in the exotic world of violence he is an inveterate loser. Rabe characterizes Pavlo, noting that "his talent is for leaping into the fire." In Rabe's plays, characters reared in the passing tradition of American values confront, or try to confront, the new to discover that if they are not destroyed and return to the old it will destroy them. Rabe is not a "protest" playwright. Neither is he an affirmer. He is mordant and paradoxical, committed, in a large scale or small, to witnessing human decomposition during a time of upheaval.

Moonchildren ushered in the new drama about youth that actually reached a youth audience. Its 1971 Arena Stage production was transferred to Broadway in 1972 with a cast of relatively unknown performers all of whom have since become established. It failed on Broadway but was soon resurrected into a long Off-Broadway run and continued wide revival, proving that its power extended beyond its summation of an already submerged period. Its form has surprisingly ancient roots in comedy, that of ebullient youth imbued with new values confronting a resistent, traditional society. Aristophanes used it against the younger generation, Shakespeare's "light" comedies and early tragedies (*As You Like It* and *Romeo and Juliet*) employed it, and in the 1920s, Katayev's *Squaring the Circle* reflected it in a Soviet context.

Moonchildren is about learning. It tests the involvement of a seemingly typical bunch of semi-communal 1965 kids in education, in political action, and in their own identities over the course of their last year in college. The whole play occurs within the environment of their shared kitchen, but the form is kaleidoscopic, even novelistic, full of switches and changes as the focus shifts constantly, revealing the interactions among the eight students.

There is no plot. Events occur. Relationships are experienced. Characters evolve. The Kathy-Bob-Dick love triangle becomes destructive. Norman turns from bookworm grind to manic idealist and perhaps back again. The war protest and a parent's death make their feeling about each other unreal. Graduation comes with the shock of eviction from a golden age which they had treated as temporary and hostile.

Weller creates an authenticity of manners, minds, and emotions through a constant character combination of seriousness and disbelief. The two intervening choral characters, Mel and Cootie, twist language and ideas into a sort of vaudeville routine which forces all of them to perceive and interpret events and feelings differently. But the kind of skeptical self-mockery which characterizes the language of the play reveals more vulnerability than it conceals. Maturity arrives with the sadness of wisdom. They have all come through academically. Careers are open to them. But knowledge has grown frightening. They knowingly promise to challenge the validity of whatever later experiences they will encounter. Their joyful wit has been transformed into a lonely survival weapon. All of them, not just Bob, might at the end announce to an empty and unlistening world, "Hey, everyone, let me tell you about this really incredible thing that has happened to me."

Ed Bullins' consummate craft suggests that his talent is traditional. In an earlier time, with proper deference and manipulation, he might have made a fortune writing conventional plays with flair and sensation. But Bullins' imagination is emphatically committed to black experience. Critics and scholars who take his plays for a black Yoknapatawpha cycle miss the point that his work was shaped in an effort to reach black audiences during the 1960s at the New Lafayette Theatre in Harlem. His trenchant objectivity is neither liberal nor propagandistic. He is the most Brechtian of American playwrights, not in derivation but in his didactic confidence that if life as it operates is approached with insatiable curiosity and earnest compassion, audiences will learn how to see and act in society out of their own experience and determination.

He celebrates the ordinary and extraordinary in every

character, willingly charts just how anyone fares in the world, and records the complexity of black-white transactions in disturbing depth. His white characters sound more verbatim, and perhaps expose themselves more thoroughly than their equivalents limned by white playwrights. He has no need to romanticize or editorialize his black characters. They exhibit the voluble frustration, idiosyncratic compulsive appetites, the pervasive will found in other black plays, but such character traits are examined as part of the given circumstances in the confrontation of imposed social order which literally alienates them, an existential state white characters have to improvise.

The Taking of Miss Janie looks like another representative youth-growing-disillusioned-in-the-1960s play centered on a thirteen year courtship. It isn't. Neither is it a symbolic rape melodrama. Bullins' Janie is neither white womanhood nor any other white institution. Nor is Monty black manhood or any other black institution. The "taking," when it occurs, is almost accidental, and it happens in a context of long-term mutual illusion, deception, and slow, if inevitable, discovery within an environment loaded against both parties. Rape is transformed into a more grotesque metaphor of social collision. "I've wanted to be friends with you, Monty. Friends, that's all," Janie declares. "You've always understood, Miss Janie," is Monty's view.

The Broadway hit formula has always included a peep show into the manners of improper social life, featuring characters with whom the audiences can identify. *Same Time, Next Year* fills the prescription with discriminating wit, a supersensitive ear, and a sardonic overtone that doesn't mask the "this *is* your life" implications of the story. It masquerades as fantasy, the daydream outlet for comfortable dull marriages, and, for all we know, it may have provided some people with new life experiments.

Its two-character chronologically episodic single set plot seems bittersweet and conventional. George is a variant of the old Expressionist Everyman Mr. Zero, the middle class loser trapped in a system while searching for his soul. Doris's personal and career growth is charted with suspicious gallantry. The play explores the margins of new sexual openness. In 1971, *Moonchildren* seemed daring because women used four letter words freely and actually mentioned fellatio. *Same Time, Next Year* casually and humorously presents a respectable woman evaluating an evening's three orgasms, discusses Trojans, erections, adolescent making out, male tension under rectal examination by a woman doctor, and uses "fucking" as an active personal verb and noun as well as an adjective.

The end is ironically arbitrary. George announces that "I'm going to keep coming back every year until our bones are too brittle to risk contact . . . Because I love happy endings." *Same Time, Next Year* can be taken as escape, but it also suggests that once a year is as far as sexual liberation works for some people, or that love today occurs only in selected isolation. The venerable Mendocino cottage is yet another last chance oasis, a collapsing citadel of ambition and hope. Bernard Slade may be a slick playwright, but he has a knack for making the contemporary experience of courting despair attractive, and making a serious view of life palatable. *Same Time, Next Year* will enjoy production whenever two adroit performers and a meticulous director get together.

Albert Innaurato's earlier plays have been acknowledged as powerful but sadly beyond practical production. As such, *Gemini* seems an ingenious cop-out, with Innaurato a potential Büchner purging himself with a dose of Pollyanna. *Gemini* got promoted as an ethnic goof-off, a family problem comedy about an intelligent young man's surge into the real world. It was cast with performers far more attractive and ingratiating than the character descriptions. Up close on the page, *Gemini* reveals the troubled heartache of aging elders and hopelessly confused youngsters burning out their life energies. The irony of its happy ending in which plump, intellectual Francis resolves a momentary passion for his Radcliffe girlfriend's brother in favor of her, thereby validating the lusty values of his family, is that Innaurato offers his characters before the Fall.

What will happen to them? And is it pre-ordained? The characters don't ask, but the play sets them up. Herschel, the genius fat boy obsessed with transportation, may no more survive science than Francis will survive his sexual preference problem and his opera records. Lucille, the prurient widow, will go on wasting her empty gentility on Fran, the slob father and his "wheezin', coughin', goin' to the bathroom, scratchin', gettin' rashes," while pathetically celebrating "good people" and good food. What fate for Bunny, the decayed earth mother, descrying in her "fat and wrinkles . . . a nineteen-year-old filly hot to trot"? Innaurato's plays are painfully funny, so much so that he seems the screwball adulator of ethnic defiance while administering extreme unction at the dying gasps of still devout terminal patients.

Sam Shepard won a Pulitzer Prize for *Buried Child* and might top any serious critics' poll for Best American Playwright. But he hasn't made Broadway. His plays are considered imperfectly structured, incompletely resolved, dependent on some private musical concept that by commercial standards is in need of endless rewrite. So he has become the Johnny Appleseed of playwriting, an itinerant who plants his plays in odd venues, ever seeking the right performance growth matrix. Any production of his plays seems both committed and incomplete. His works disarmingly offer the identifiable elements of both experimental and orthodox theatre, but they invite a synthesis of performance mode no one has perfected. They demand performers with total vocal instrumentation, not just empathic rhythm, movement skills to oscillate the real and the mythic, and the instincts to play the scenery. Shepard is a playwright in search of a theatre, but as things go, the director who puts him best on stage may prove as unsatisfactory to his own dramatic vision as Stanislavski was for Chekhov's.

Shepard's dramatic mode is the All-American Nightmare. Nightmares take many forms. Shepard holds his own with novelists but he deals with experience on a scale of intensity few novelists manage. His characters also laboriously try to consume the world, get lost in its mysteries, and discover you can't go home again because the mutant cells of the image you left behind have multiplied into cancerous growths. There's a Huckleberry Finn in every Shepard character who, like Huck, acquires an innocent sensibility in one social context and journeys to the splendors and miseries of a larger heritage. Each encountered environment is marvelously strange and documented with comic freshness but turns into horror and danger through the character's own presence.

Shepard is a philosopher-poet—he has a consistent private vision of the condition of life, an insatiable urge to make all sorts of characters encounter it, and an equal compulsion to confront different artistic forms. In *Buried Child* he applies the "hidden scandal" theme of his own work to an Ibsen theme with the assurance of one master who absorbs another's work while leaving it intact.

With *Buried Child*, the play itself is buried in conventional form, as if Shepard were demonstrating that he can handle that, too. The innocent grandson, with accompanying ingenue, returns to an ancestral home transferred by some mysterious family curse, and step by dangerous step unravels the mystery and is himself transformed. In the process, moral perceptions also become mysteries, as in all thrillers. The hints and clues seem obvious. Vince, the grandson, is treated as a surrogate buried child. His father and grandparents refuse to acknowledge him. His lover abandons him. He loses his sense of identity until the real buried child is unearthed. Only then is he free—by a deus ex machina device—to cast off his befouled heritage and cultivate the primeval condition of fertility it miraculously produces. Vince winds up maniacally trapped without resources in the sterile Garden of Eden, a vision Shepard repeatedly evokes in his plays.

All these plays take place after the Fall, after an irrevocable expulsion from Paradise. The lives of the characters are presented as over, and, in some sense, so is the theatre in which they are performed. Each playwright readily demonstrates the abilities to create plausible characters in plausible circumstances. Each proves his knowledge of dramaturgy, of how plays have been and can be written. Each also pulls dramatic switches that throw away convention.

In all these plays, the endings are grotesque, designed to frustrate the audience expectations they ostensibly satisfy. The fully fleshed and rounded characters turn at some point into puppets, puzzled at discovering the strings that control them, resigned to embody some macabre dance of death.

Throughout, we encounter dreams of a forbidden golden age, of the mind, of the world, which cannot be regained, but must be sought and studied and accounted for. The plays themselves take on patterns of disruption, of seeking impossibly to put life experiences back together, of examining some terrible accident. Within the compassionate flowing humor of each are disembodied voices, sardonic and seductive in tone, offering invitations to metaphysical despair, a recurring litany of "that's the way it was. That's the way it really was."

THE BASIC TRAINING OF PAVLO HUMMEL

by David Rabe

FOR MY PARENTS AND JOE PAPP

Acknowledgment is made to Charles E. Tuttle Co., Inc.
for a selection from *Vietnamese Legends*
by George F. Schultz

THE SONG OF TRANG TU

Alas! This life is like a flower that forms, then fades.
My wife is dead, so I bury her; if I were dead, she would
    remarry.
If I had been the first to depart, what a great burst of
    laughter would have poured forth.
In my fields a new laborer would work; on my horse a
    strange rider would appear.
My wife would belong to another; my children would have
    to bear anger and insults.
When I think of her, my heart tightens; but I look at her
    without weeping.
The world accuses me of insensibility and remorselessness;
I scoff at the world for nourishing vain griefs.
If I could restore the course of things by weeping,
My tears would flow for a thousand autumns without ceas-
    ing.

                —Vietnamese legend

Life a funny thing.

                  —Sonny Liston

AUTHOR'S NOTE

If the character of Pavlo Hummel does not have a certain eagerness and wide-eyed spontaneity along with a true, real, and complete inability to grasp the implications of what he does, the play will not work as it can. Pavlo is in fact lost. He has, for a long time, no idea that he is lost. His own perceptions define the world. He never understands that he provokes Kress or anybody else. When in the furnace room he responds to Kress's having told him he has his head up his ass, there is no cleverness in his response. He meant it to be clever but could not manage the words. He must make do with less than the situation demands; yet he is proud of having come as close as he did and is sure his quip will do. There must be something of the clinical neurotic in what he is and does. Nor can he be a street kid: this is what he *is not,* but wants to be. He is from middle income. Even with no father and with the mother he has, he was raised among middle-class kids. He has romanticized the street-kid tough guy and hopes to find himself in that image. It is Pavlo's body that changes. His physical efficiency, even his mental efficiency increases, but real insight never comes. Toughness and cynicism replace open eagerness, but he will learn only that he is lost, not how, why, or even where. His talent is for leaping into the fire.

The Basic Training of Pavlo Hummel *was first produced by Joseph Papp, May 20, 1971, at the New York Shakespeare Festival Public Theater, under the direction of Jeff Bleckner, with the following cast (listed in order of appearance):*

PAVLO HUMMEL	*William Atherton*
YEN	*Victoria Racimo*
ARDELL	*Albert Hall*
SERGEANT TOWER	*Joe Fields*
CAPTAIN (ALL OFFICERS)	*Edward Cannan*
CORPORAL	*Anthony R. Charnota*
KRESS	*Earl Hindman*
PARKER	*Peter Cameron*
PIERCE	*Robert Lehman*
BURNS	*Stephen Clarke*
HENDRIX	*D. Franklyn Lenthall*
HINKLE	*Edward Herrmann*
RYAN	*John Walter Davis*
MICKEY	*Frederick Coffin*
VOICE OF MRS. SORRENTINO	*Victoria Racimo*
MRS. HUMMEL	*Sloane Shelton*
SERGEANT BRISBEY	*Lee Wallace*
JONES	*Garrett Morris*
SERGEANT WALL	*John Benson*
MAMASAN	*Christal Kim*
SMALL BOY	*Hoshin Seki*
GRENNEL	*Tom Harris*
PARHAM	*Bob Delegall*
FIRST VIETCONG	*Hoshin Seki*
SECOND VIETCONG	*Victoria Racimo*

Associate Producer, Bernard Gersten; set by David Mitchell; costumes by Theoni V. Aldredge; lighting by Martin Aronstein.

Place and time: The United States Army, 1965–1967

ACT ONE

(The set is a space, a platform slanting upward from the downstage area. The floor is nothing more than slats that run in various directions with a military precision. It has a brownish color. The backdrop is dark with touches of green. Along the back of the set runs a ramp elevated about two feet off the floor. Stage left and a little down from the ramp stands the drill sergeant's tower. This element is stark and as realistic as possible. Farther downstage and stage left the floor opens into a pit two feet deep. There is an old furnace partly visible. Downstage and stage right are three army cots with footlockers at their base. Upstage and stage right there is a bar area: an army ammunition crate and an army oil drum set as a table and chair before a fragment of sheet-metal wall partly covered with beer-can labels. All elements of the set should have some military tone to them, some echo of basic training.)

To start the play, pop American music is heard for an instant in the dark. Then lights up on the bar area: evening. A drunken GI sits slumped on the crate, leaning forward on the drum. YEN *(pronounced "Ing"), a Vietnamese girl dressed in purple silk pajamas—slacks and pullover top—moves about with a beer, trying to settle* PAVLO *down.)*

PAVLO: (*Dressed in fatigues, moving with the music, dealing somehow with the other two in the room as he speaks.*) Did I do it to him? The triple-Hummel. Can you hear your boy? (*A sort of shudder runs through his shoulders; he punches.*) A little shuffle and then a triple boom-boom-boom. Ain't I bad, man? Gonna eat up Cleveland. Gonna piss on Chicago. (*Banging with his palms on the sides of the oil drum.*)

YEN: Creezy, creezy.

PAVLO: Dinky dow!

SOLDIER: (*Disturbed by the banging, looking up, deeply drunk.*) Les . . . go . . . home. . . .

YEN: Paablo creezy.

PAVLO: Dinky dow.

YEN: Paablo boocoup love. Sleep me all time . . .

PAVLO: Did I ever tell you?—thirteen months a my life ago—Joanna was her name. Sorrentino, a little bit a guinea-wop made outa all the pins and sticks all bitches are made a. And now I'm the guy who's been with the Aussies. *I had tea with 'em. It was me they called to—* "Hummel!" "MEDIC!" (*With a fairly good Australian accent.*) "The dirty little blighters blew me bloody arm off." (YEN *brings a beer.*) Yeh, girl, in a little bit a time. (*And back to the air.*) We had a cat, you know? So we had a kitty box, which is a place for the cat to shit.

YEN: Talk "shit." I can talk "shit." Numba-ten talk.

PAVLO: Ohhh, damn that Sorrentino, what she couldn't be taught. And that's what I'd like to do—look her up and explain a few things like, "Your face, Sorrentino, I don't like your ugly face." Did I ever tell you about the ole lady? Did I ever speak her name, me mudda.

YEN: Mudda you, huh, Paablo? Very nice.

PAVLO: To be seen by her now, oh, she would shit her jeans to see me now, uptight with this little odd-lookin' whore, feelin' good and tall, ready to bed down. Ohhh, Jesus Mahoney. You see what she did, she wrote Joanna a letter. My mother. She called Joanna a dirty little slut, and when I found out, I cried, I wailed, baby, big tears. I screamed and threw kitty litter; I threw it in the air. I screamed over and over, "Happy Birthday, Happy Birthday," and then one day there was Joanna in the subway, and she said, "Hello," and told me my favorite jacket I was wearing made me look ugly, didn't fit, made me look fat.

(*A grenade, thrown by a hand that merely flashes between the curtains, hits with a loud clump in the room, and everyone looks without moving.*)

GRENA-A-ADE!

(PAVLO *drops to his knees, seizing the grenade, and has it in his hands in his lap when the explosion comes, loud, shattering, and the lights go black, go red or blue. The girl screams. The bodies are strewn about. The radio plays. And a black soldier,* ARDELL, *now appears, his uniform strangely unreal with black ribbons and medals; he wears sunglasses, bloused boots.* [ARDELL *will drift throughout the play, present only when specifically a part of the action, appearing, disappearing, without prominent entrances and exits.*] *A body detail is also entering, two men with a stretcher to remove the dead.*)

ARDELL: (*Moving to turn the radio off.*) You want me, Pavlo? You callin'? Don't I hear you? Yeh, that the way it happen sometimes. Everybody hit, everybody hurtin', but the radio ain't been touched, the dog didn't feel a thing; the engine's good as new, but all the people dead and the chassis a wreck, man. (*Bowing a little toward* PAVLO.) Yeh, yeh, some mean motherfucker you don't even see blow you away. Don't I hear you callin'? (*Pivoting, moving swiftly down center stage.*) Get off it. Bounce on up here.

(PAVLO *leaps to his feet, runs to join* ARDELL.)

PAVLO: PFC Pavlo Hummel, sir. RA seven four, three one three, two two six.

ARDELL: We gonna get you your shit straight. No need to call me sir.

PAVLO: Ardell!

ARDELL: Now what's your unit? Now shout it out.

PAVLO: Second of the Sixteenth, First Division, BIG RED ONE!

ARDELL: Company.

PAVLO: Bravo.

ARDELL: CO?

PAVLO: My company commander is Captain M. W. Henderson. My battalion commander is Lieutenant Colonel Roy J. S. Tully.

ARDELL: Platoon?

PAVLO: Third.

ARDELL: Squad.

PAVLO: Third.

ARDELL: Squad and platoon leaders.

PAVLO: My platoon leader is First Lieutenant David R. Barnes; my squad leader is Staff Sergeant Peter T. Collins.

ARDELL: You got family?

PAVLO: No.

ARDELL: You lyin', boy.

PAVLO: One mother; one half brother.

ARDELL: All right.

PAVLO: Yes.

ARDELL: Soldier, what you think a the war?

PAVLO: It's being fought.

ARDELL: Ain't no doubt about that.

PAVLO: No.

ARDELL: You kill anybody?

PAVLO: Yes.

ARDELL: Like it?

PAVLO: Yes.

ARDELL: Have nightmares?

PAVLO: Pardon?

ARDELL: What we talkin' about, boy?

PAVLO: No.

ARDELL: How tall you? you lyin' motherfucker.

PAVLO: Five-ten.

ARDELL: Eyes.

PAVLO: Green.

ARDELL: Hair.

PAVLO: Red.

ARDELL: Weight.

PAVLO: One-five-two.

ARDELL: What you get hit with?

PAVLO: Hand grenade. Fragmentation-type.

ARDELL: Where about it get you?

PAVLO: (*Touching gently his stomach and crotch.*) Here. And here. Mostly in the abdominal and groin areas.

ARDELL: Who you talkin' to? Don't you talk that shit to me, man. Abdominal and groin areas, that shit. It hit you in the stomach, man, like a ten-ton truck, and it hit you in the balls, blew 'em away. Am I lyin'?

PAVLO: (*Able to grin: glad to grin.*) No, man.

ARDELL: Hurt you bad.

PAVLO: Killed me.

ARDELL: That right. Made you dead. You dead man; how you feel about that?

PAVLO: Well . . .

ARDELL: *Don't you know? I think you know!* I think it piss you off. I think you lyin' you say it don't. Make you wanna scream.

PAVLO: Yes.

ARDELL: You had that thing in your hand, didn't you? What was you thinkin' on, you had that thing in your hand?

PAVLO: About throwin' it. About a man I saw when I was eight years old who came through the neighborhood with a softball team called the Demons, and he could do anything with a softball underhand that most big leaguers could do with a hardball overhand. He was fantastic.

ARDELL: That all?

PAVLO: Yes.

ARDELL: You ain't lyin'.

PAVLO: No.

(*A whistle blows loudly and figures run about behind* PAVLO *and* ARDELL, *a large group of men in fatigues without markings other than their name tags and U.S. Army. And on the high drill instructor's tower, which is dimly lit at the moment, stands a large Negro sergeant. A captain observes from the distance. A corporal prowls among the gathering troopers, checking buttons, etc.*)

PAVLO: (*Looking about.*) Who're they?

ARDELL: Man, don't you jive me. You know who they are. That Fort Gordon, man. They Echo Company, Eighth Battalion, Third Training Regiment. They basic training, baby.

PAVLO: —(*Removes PFC stripes and 1st Division patch.*) Am I . . . really . . . dead . . . ?

ARDELL: Damn near, man; real soon. Comin' on. Eight more weeks. Got wings as big as streets. Got large, large wings.

PAVLO: It happened . . . to me. . . .

ARDELL: Whatever you say, Pavlo.

PAVLO: Sure . . . that grenade come flyin', I caught it, held it.

   (*Pause.*)

ARDELL: New York, huh?

PAVLO: Manhattan. Two thirty-one East Forty-fifth. I—

ARDELL: Now we know who we talkin' about. Somebody say "Pavlo Hummel," we know who they mean.

SGT. TOWER: GEN'LMEN! (*As the men standing in ranks below the tower snap to parade rest and* PAVLO, *startled, runs to find his place among them.*) You all lookin' up here and can you see me? Can you see me well? Can you hear and comprehend my words? Can you see what is written here? Over my right tit-tee, can you read it? Tower. My name. And I am bigger than my name. And can you see what is sewn here upon the muscle of my arm? Can you see it? ANSWER!

THE MEN: —(*Yell.*) NO.

SGT. TOWER: No, what? WHAT?

THE MEN: NO, SERGEANT.

SGT. TOWER: It is also my name. It is my first name. *Sergeant.* That who I am. I you Field First. And you gonna see a lot a me. You gonna see so much a me, let me tell you, you gonna think I you mother, father, sisters, brothers, aunts, uncles, nephews, nieces, and children—if-you-got-'em—all rolled into one big black man. Yeh, Gen'lmen. And you gonna become me. You gonna learn to stand tall and be proud and you gonna run as far and shoot as good. Or else you gonna be ashamed; I am one old man, and you can't outdo no thirty-eight-year-old man, you ashamed. AM I GONNA MAKE YOU ASHAMED? WHAT DO YOU SAY?

THE MEN: Yes, Sergeant! .

SGT. TOWER: NO! NO, GEN'LMEN. No, I am not gonna make you ashamed. SERGEANT, YOU ARE NOT GONNA MAKE US ASHAMED.

THE MEN: SERGEANT, YOU ARE NOT GONNA MAKE US ASHAMED.

SGT. TOWER: WE ARE GONNA DO EVERYTHING YOU CAN DO AND DO YOU ONE BETTER!

THE MEN: WE ARE GONNA DO EVERYTHING YOU CAN DO AND DO YOU ONE BETTER!

SGT. TOWER: YOU A BUNCH A LIARS. YOU A BUNCH A FOOLS! Now you listen up; you listen to me. No one does me one better. And especially no people like you. Don't you know what you are? *Trainees!* And there ain't nothin' lower on this earth except for one thing, and we all know what that is, do we not, Gen'lmen?

THE MEN: *Yes . . . Sergeant. . . .*

SGT. TOWER: And what is that? (*Pause.*) And you told me you knew! Did you lie to me? Oh, no, nooo, I can't believe that; please, please, don't lie. Gen'lmen, did you lie?

THE MEN: —(*They are sorry.*) Yes, Sergeant.

SGT. TOWER: No, no, please. If there something you don't know, you tell me. If I ask you something and you do not know the answer, let me know. Civilians. That the answer to my question. The only creatures in this world lower than trainees is civilians, and we hate them all. All. (*Quick pause.*) And now . . . and finally . . . and most important, do you see what is written here? Over my heart; over my left tit-tee, do you see? U.S. Army. Which is where I live. Which is where we all live. Can you, Gen'lmen, can you tell me you first name now, do you know it? (*Quick pause as he looks about in dismay.*) Don't you know? I think you do, yes, I do, but you just too shy to say it. Like little girls watchin' that thing just get bigger and bigger for the first time, you

shy. And what did I tell you to do when you don't know
the answer I have asked?

THE MEN: What is our first name?

SGT. TOWER: You! You there! (*Suddenly pointing into the
ranks of men.*) You! Ugly! Yeah, you. That right. You
ugly. Ain't you. YOU TAKE ONE BIG STEP FOR-
WARD.

(*And it is* PAVLO *stepping hesitantly forward. He does
not know what he has done or what is expected from
him.*)

I think I saw you were not in harmony with the rest of
these men. I think I saw that you were looking about at
the air like some kinda fool, and that malingering,
Trainee, and that intol'able. So you drop, you hear me.
You drop down on your ugly little hands and knees and
lift up you butt and knees from off that beautiful Georgia clay and you give me TEN, and that's push-ups of
which I am speaking.

(PAVLO, *having obeyed the orders step by step, now
begins the push-ups.* TOWER *goes back to the men.*)

NOW YOU ARE TRAINEES, ALL YOU PEOPLE,
AND YOU LISTEN UP. I ASK YOU WHAT IS
YOUR FIRST NAMES, YOU TELL ME "TRAIN-
EES"!

THE MEN: (*Yell.*) TRAINEE!

SGT. TOWER: TRAINEE, SERGEANT!

THE MEN: TRAINEE, SERGE—

SGT. TOWER: I CAN'T HEAR YOU!

THE MEN: *TRAINEE, SERGEANT!*

SGT. TOWER: AND WHAT IS YOUR LAST NAMES?
YOU OWN LAST FUCKING NAMES?

THE MEN: (*A chorus of American names.*)

SGT. TOWER: AND YOU LIVE IN THE ARMY OF THE
UNITED STATES OF AMERICA.

THE MEN: AND WE LIVE IN THE ARMY OF THE
UNITED STATES OF AMERICA.

SGT. TOWER: WITH BALLS BETWEEN YOU LEGS!
YOU HAVE BALLS! NO SLITS! BUT BALLS, AND
YOU—

(*Having risen,* PAVLO *is getting back into ranks.*)

THE MEN: AND WE HAVE BALLS BETWEEN OUR LEGS! NO SLITS, BUT BALLS!

SGT. TOWER: (*Suddenly back at* PAVLO.) UGLY! Now who tole you to stand? Who you think you are, you standin', nobody tole you to stand. You drop. You drop, you hear me.

(*And* PAVLO *goes back into the push-up position.*) What your name, boy?

PAVLO: Yes, sir.

SGT. TOWER: Your name, boy!

PAVLO: Trainee Hummel, sir!

SGT. TOWER: Sergeant.

PAVLO: Yes, sir.

SGT. TOWER: Sergeant. I AM A SERGEANT!

PAVLO: SERGEANT: YOU ARE A SERGEANT!

SGT. TOWER: All right. That nice; all right, only in the future you doin' push-ups, i want you countin' and that countin' so loud it scare me so I think there some kinda terrible, terrible man comin' to get me. Am I understood?

PAVLO: Yes, Sergeant.

SGT. TOWER: I can't hear you!

PAVLO: Yes, Sergeant! Yes, Sergeant!

SGT. TOWER: All right! You get up and fall back where you was. Gen'lmen. You are gonna fall out. By platoon. Which is how you gonna be doin' most everything from now on—by platoon and by the numbers—includin' takin' a shit. Somebody say to you, "One!" you down; "two!" you doin' it; "three!" you wipin' and you ain't finished, you cuttin' it off. I CAN'T HEAR YOU!

THE MEN: YES, SERGEANT.

SGT. TOWER: I say to you "squat!" and you all hunkered down and got nothin' to say to anybody but "How much?" and "What color, Sergeant?"

THE MEN: Yes, Sergeant.

SGT. TOWER: You good people. You a good group. Now I gonna call you to attention and you gonna snap to. That's heels on a line or as near it as the conformation of your body permit; head up, chin in, knees not locked; you relaxed. Am I understood?

THE MEN: Yes—

SGT. TOWER: AM I UNDERSTOOD, GODDAMNIT, OR DO YOU WANT TO ALL DROP FOR TWENTY OR—

(ARDELL, *off to the side, is drifting nearer.*)

THE MEN: YES, SERGEANT, YES, SERGEANT!

ARDELL: Pavlo, my man, you on your way!

CORPORAL: PLATOOOON! PLATOOOON!

SGT. TOWER: I GONNA DO SOME SINGIN', GEN'L-MEN, I WANT IT COMIN' BACK TO ME LIKE WE IN GRAND CANYON—

CORPORAL: TEN–HUT!

ARDELL: DO IT, GET IT!

SGT. TOWER: —AND YOU MY MOTHERFUCKIN' ECHO!

SQUAD LEADERS: RIGHT FACE!

CORPORAL: FORWARD HARCH!

SGT. TOWER: (*Singing.*) LIFT YOUR HEAD AND LIFT IT HIGH . . .

THE MEN: LIFT YOUR HEAD AND LIFT IT HIGH . . .

SGT. TOWER: ECHO COMPANY PASSIN' BY!

THE MEN: ECHO COMPANY PASSIN' BY!

(*They start going off in groups, marching and singing.*)

ARDELL: MOTHER, MOTHER, WHAT'D I DO?

THE MEN: MOTHER, MOTHER, WHAT'D I DO?

ARDELL: THIS ARMY TREATIN' ME WORSE THAN YOU!

THE MEN: THIS ARMY TREATIN' ME WORSE THAN YOU!

SGT. TOWER: LORD HAVE MERCY I'M SO BLUE!

THE MEN: LORD HAVE MERCY I'M SO BLUE! IT EIGHT MORE WEEKS TILL WE BE THROUGH! IT EIGHT MORE WEEKS TILL WE BE THROUGH! IT EIGHT MORE WEEKS TILL WE BE THROUGH!

(*And all the men have marched off in lines in different directions, giving a sense of large numbers, a larger space, and now out of this movement comes a spin-off of two men,* KRESS *and* PARKER, *drilling down the center of the stage, yelling the last of the song, marching, stomping, then breaking and running stage left and into the furnace room, where there is the hulk of the belly of the furnace, the flickering of the fire.* KRESS *is large, muscular, with a constant manner of small confusion as if he feels always that something is going on that he nearly, but not quite, understands. Yet there is something seemingly friendly about him.* PARKER *is smaller; he wears glasses.*)

KRESS: I can't stand it, Parker, bein' so cold all the time, and they're all insane, Parker. Waxin' and buffin' the floor at five-thirty in the morning is insane. And then you can't eat till you go down the monkey bars and you gotta eat in ten minutes and can't talk to nobody, and no place in Georgia is warm. I'm from Jersey. I can jump up in the air, if there's a good wind, I'll land in Fort Dix. Am I right so far? So Sam gets me. What's he do? Fort Dix? Uh-uh. Fort Gordon, Georgia. So I can be warm right? Down South, man. Daffodils and daisies. Year round. (*Hollering.*) BUT AM I WARM? DO YOU THINK I'M WARM? DO I LOOK LIKE I'M WARM? JESUS H! EVEN IN THE GODDAMN FURNACE ROOM I'M FREEZIN' TA DEATH!

PARKER: So, what the hell is hollerin' like a stupid ape gonna do except to let 'em know where we're at?

KRESS: (*As* PAVLO *enters upstage, moving slowly in awe toward the tower, looking.*) Heat up my blood!

ARDELL: (*To* PAVLO.) What you doin' strollin' about like a fool, man? You gonna have people comin' down all over you, don't you know—

OFFICER: (*Having just entered.*) What're you doin' walkin' in this company area? Don't you know you run in this company area? Hummel, you drop, you hear me. You drop!

(PAVLO *drops and begins the push-ups.*)

ARDELL: (*Over him.*) Do 'em right, do 'em right!

KRESS: Why can't I be warm? I wanna be warm.

PARKER: Okay, man, you're warm.

KRESS: No; I'm not; I'm cold, Parker. Where's our god-damn fireman; don't he ever do nothin' but push-ups? Don't he ever do nothin' but trouble!

PARKER: Don't knock that ole boy, Kress; I'm tellin' you Hummel's gonna keep us laughin'!

KRESS: Yesterday I was laughin' so hard. I mean, I'm stu-pid, Parker, but Hummel's *stupid*. I mean, he volunteers to be fireman 'cause he thinks it means you ride in a raincoat on a big red truck and when there's nothin' to do you play cards.

PARKER: Yeah! He don't know it means you gotta baby-sit the goddamn furnace all night, every night. And end up lookin' like a stupid chimney sweep!

KRESS: Lookin' what?

PARKER: (*As* PIERCE *enters at a jog, moving across the stage toward* ARDELL *and* PAVLO.) Like a goddamn chimney sweep!

PAVLO: Where you goin'?

PIERCE: (*Without hesitating.*) Weapons room and furnace room.

PAVLO: (*Getting to his feet.*) Can I come along?

PIERCE: (*Still running, without looking back.*) I don't give a shit.

   (*He exits,* PAVLO, *following, as* ARDELL *is drifting the opposite direction.*)

PAVLO: . . . great . . .

KRESS: Yeh? Yeh, Parker, that's good. Chimney sweeps!

PARKER: Yeh, they were these weird little men always crawlin' around, and they used to do this weird shit to chimneys.

   (PIERCE *and* PAVLO *enter. They have their rifles.* PIERCE *is a trainee acting as a squad leader. He has a cloth marked with corporal's stripes tied on his left sleeve.*)

PIERCE: At ease!

KRESS: Hey, the chimney shit. Hey, what's happenin', Chimney Shit?

PAVLO: How you doin', Kress?

KRESS: Where's your red hat, man?

PAVLO: What?

PARKER: Ain't you got no red fireman's hat?

PAVLO: I'm just with Pierce, that's all. He's my squad leader and I'm with him.

PARKER: Mr. Squad Leader.

PAVLO: Isn't that right, Pierce?

PARKER: Whose ass you kiss to get that job anyway, Pierce?

PIERCE: At ease, Trainees.

KRESS: He's RA, man. Regular Army. Him and Hummel. Lifer morons. Whata they gonna do to us today anyway, Mr. Actin' Sergeant, Corporal. What's the lesson for the day: first aid or bayonet? I love this fuckin' army.

PIERCE: The schedule's posted, Kress!

KRESS: You know I don't read, man; hurts my eyes; makes 'em water.

PAVLO: When's the gas chamber, that's what I wanna know.

KRESS: For you, Chimney Shit, in about ten seconds when I fart in your face.

PAVLO: I'm all right. I do all right.

KRESS: Sure you do, except you got your head up your ass.

PAVLO: Yeh? Well maybe I'd rather have it up my ass than where you got it.

(*Slight pause: it has made no sense to* KRESS *at all.*)

KRESS: What?

PAVLO: You heard me, Kress.

KRESS: What'd he say, Parker? (*There is frenzy in this.*) I heard him, but I don't know what he said. WHAT'D YOU SAY TO ME, HUMMEL?

PAVLO: Just never you mind, Kress.

KRESS: I DON'T KNOW WHAT YOU SAID TO ME, YOU WEIRD PERSON!

PARKER: (*Patting* KRESS.) Easy, man, easy; be cool.

KRESS: But I don't like weird people, Parker. I don't like them. How come I gotta be around him? I don't wanna be around you, Hummel!

PAVLO: Don't you worry about it, I'm just here with Pierce. I just wanna know about the gas chamber.

KRESS: It's got gas in it! Ain't that right, Parker! It's like this goddamn giant asshole, it farts on you. THHPPBBBZZZZZZZZ!

(*Silence.*)

PAVLO: When is it, Pierce?

KRESS: Ohhhhh, Jesus, I'm cold.

PAVLO: This ain't cold, Kress.

KRESS: I know if I'm cold.

PAVLO: I been colder than this. This ain't cold. I been a lot colder than—

KRESS: DON'T TELL ME IT AIN'T COLD OR I'LL KILL YOU! JESUS GOD ALMIGHTY I HATE THIS MOTHER ARMY STICKIN' ME IN WITH WEIRD PEOPLE! DIE, HUMMEL! Will you please do me that favor! Oh, God, let me close my eyes and when I open them, Hummel is dead. Please. Please.

(*He squeezes his eyes shut, clenches his hands, and then looks at* PAVLO, *who is grinning.*)

PAVLO: Boy, I sure do dread that gas chamber.

KRESS: He hates me, Parker. He truly hates me.

PAVLO: No, I don't.

KRESS: What'd I ever do to him, you suppose.

PARKER: I don't know, Kress.

PAVLO: I don't hate you.

PARKER: How come he's so worried about that gas chamber, that's what I wonder.

PAVLO: Well, see, I had an uncle die in San Quentin.

(KRESS *screams.*)

That's the truth, Kress.

(KRESS *screams again.*)

I don't care if you believe it. He killed four people in a fight in a bar.

PARKER: Usin' his bare hands, right?

PAVLO: You know how many people are executed every damn day in San Quentin? One hell of a lot. And every one of 'em just about is somebody's uncle and one of 'em was my Uncle Roy. He killed four people in a barroom brawl usin' broken bottles and table legs and screamin', jus' screamin'. He was mean, man. He was rotten; and my folks been scared the same thing might happen to me; all their lives they been scared. I got that same look in my eyes like him.

PARKER: What kinda look is that?

KRESS: That really rotten look, man. He got that really rotten look. Can't you see it?

PAVLO: You ever steal a car, Kress? You know how many cars I stole?

KRESS: Shut up Hummel! You're a goddamn chimney sweep and I don't wanna talk to you because you don't talk American, you talk Hummel! Some goddamn foreign language!

PARKER: How many cars you stole?

PAVLO: Twenty-three.

KRESS: Twenty-three!

(PARKER *whistles.*)

PAVLO: That's a lotta cars, huh?

PARKER: You damn betcha, man. How long'd it take you, for chrissake? Ten years?

PAVLO: Two.

PARKER: Workin' off and on, you mean.

PAVLO: Sure. Not every night, or they'd catch you. And not always from the same part of town. Man, sometimes I'd hit lower Manhattan and then the next night The Bronx or Queens, and sometimes I'd even cut right on outa town. One time, in fact, I went all the way to New Haven. Boy that was some night because they almost caught me. Can you imagine that. Huh? Parker? Huh? Pierce? All the way to New Haven and cops on my tail every inch a the way, roadblocks closin' up behind me, bang, bang, and then some highway patrolman, just as I was wheelin' into New Haven, he come roarin' outa this side road. See, they must a called ahead or somethin' and he come hot on my ass. I kicked it, man, arrrrggggggghhhhh . . . ! Eighty-two per. Had a Porsche; he didn't know who he was after; that stupid fuzz, eighty-two per, straight down the gut, people jumpin' outa my way, kids and businessmen and little old ladies, all of 'em, and me kickin' ass, up to ninety-seven now, roarin' baby sirens all around me, so I cut into this alley and jump. Oh, Jesus, Christ, just lettin' the car go,

I hit, roll, I'm up and runnin' down for this board fence, up and over, sirens all over now, I mean, *all over*, but I'm walkin' calm, I'm cool. Cops are goin' this way and that way. One of 'em asks me if I seen a Porsche go by real fast. Did *I* see—

KRESS: *Jesus-goddamn*—the furnace room's smellin' like the gas chamber!

(*He rises to leave,* PARKER *following.*)

PARKER: Right, Hummel. That's right. I mean I liked your story about your really rotten uncle Roy better than the one about all the cars.

KRESS: Gotta go get our weapons.

PARKER: Defend our fuckin' selves.

PAVLO: I'll see you guys later.

(*They are gone. Silence*)

Hey, Pierce, you wanna hear my General Orders; make sure I know 'em, okay! Like we're on guard mount and you're the OD . . . You wanna see if I'm sharp enough to be one a your boys. Okay? (*Snapping to attention.*) Sir! My first general order is to take charge of this post and all government property in view, keeping always on the alert and . . .

PIERCE: Gimme your eighth, Hummel.

PAVLO: Eighth? No, no, lemme do 'em one, two, three. You'll mess me up I don't do them one, two, three.

PIERCE: That's the way it's gonna be, Hummel. The man comes up to you on guard mount he's gonna be all over you—right on top a you yellin' down your throat. You understand me? He won't be standin' back polite and pretty lettin' you run your mouth.

PAVLO: Just to practice, Pierce. I just wanna practice.

PIERCE: You don't wanna practice shit. You just wanna stand there and have me pat your goddamned head for bein' a good boy. Don't you know we stood here laughin' at you lyin' outa your ass? Don't you have any pride, man?

PAVLO: I got pride. And anyway, they didn't know I was lyin'.

PIERCE: Shit.

PAVLO: And anyway, I wasn't lyin'; it was storytelling.

They was just messin' with me a little, pickin' on me. My mom used to always tell my dad not to be so hard on me, but he knew.

(*Whistle blows loudly from off.*)

PIERCE: Let's go.

PAVLO: See, he was hard on me 'cause he loved me. I'm RA, Pierce.

PIERCE: You got an RA prefix, man, but you ain't Regular Army.

PAVLO: They was just jumpin' on me a little; pickin' on me.

(*Again the whistle.*)

PIERCE: That whistle means formation, man.

PAVLO: They're just gonna draw weapons and I already got mine.

PIERCE: That ain't what I said, jerkoff!

PAVLO: Well, I ain't goin' out there to stand around doin' nothin' when I can stay right here and put the time to good use practicin' D and D.

(*Again the whistle. The men are gathering; we hear their murmuring.*)

PIERCE: You ain't no motherin' exception to that whistle!

PAVLO: You ain't any real corporal anyway, Pierce. So don't get so big with me just because you got that hunk a thing wrapped around you—

PIERCE: Don't you mess up my squad, Hummel! Don't you make me look bad or I'll get you your legs broken.

PAVLO: (*As whistle blows and Pierce is running and gone.*) I bet you never heard a individual initiative.

(*Whistle again as soldiers rush in to line up in formation at parade rest while* SGT. TOWER *climbs to stand atop the platform.*)

ARDELL: They don't know, do they? They don't know who they talkin' to.

PAVLO: No.

ARDELL: You gonna be so straight.

PAVLO: So clean.

(*As* SGT. TOWER, *noticing that someone is missing from formation, turns, descends, exits.*)

Port Harms!

(*And he does the move with only a slight and quickly corrected error.*)

ARDELL: Good, Pavlo. Good (*Slight pause*) Order Harms!
(*There is some skill in the move.*)

PAVLO: Okay . . .

ARDELL: RIGHT SHOULDER . . . HARMS!
(PAVLO's *head flinches, the rifle nicking the top of his helmet. His back is toward the group.* SGT. TOWER *enters, watches for a time.*)

PAVLO: Goddamnit. Shit.
(*Again the rifle back to order arms.*)

ARDELL: RIGHT SHOULDER . . .

PAVLO: HARMS!
(*Again it is not good.*)
You mother rifle. You stupid fucking rifle. RIGHT SHOULDER, HARMS. (*He tries.*) Mother! Stupid mother, whatsamatter with you? I'll kill you! (*And he has it high above his head. He is looking up.*) Rifle, please. Work for me, do it for me. I know what to do, just do it.

ARDELL: Just go easy. Man . . . just easy. It don't mean that much. What's it matter?

SGT. TOWER: What you doin', Trainee?

PAVLO: (*Snapping to attention.*) Yes, sir! Trainee Pavlo Hummel, sir.

SGT. TOWER: I didn't ask you your name, boy. I asked you what you doin' in here when you supposed to be out on that formation?

PAVLO: Yes, sir.

SGT. TOWER: No, I don't have no bars on my collar; do you see any bars on my collar?

PAVLO: (*Looking.*) No . . . No . . .

SGT. TOWER: But what do you see on my sleeve at about the height a my shoulder less a little, what do you see?

PAVLO: Stripes, Sergeant. Sergeant stripes.

SGT. TOWER: So how come you call me sir? I ain't no sir. I don't want to be no sir. I am a sergeant. Now do we know one another?

PAVLO: Yes, Sergeant.

SGT. TOWER: That mean you can answer my question in the proper manner, do it not?

PAVLO: I was practicin' D and D, Sergeant, to make me a good soldier.

SGT. TOWER: Ohhhhhhh! I think you tryin' to jive this ole man, that what you doin'. Or else you awful stupid, because all the good soldiers is out there in that formation like they supposed to when they hear that whistle. Now which?

PAVLO: Pardon, Sergeant?

SGT. TOWER: Which is it? You jivin' on me or you awful stupid, you take your pick. And lemme tell you why you can't put no jive on the old sarge. Because long time ago this ole sarge was one brand-new, baby-soft, smart-assed recruit. So I see you and I say, "What that young recruit doin' in that furnace room this whole company out there bein' talked at by the CO?" And the answer come to me like a blast a thunder and this voice sayin' to me in my head, "This here young recruit jerkin' off, that what he doin'," and then into my head come this picture and we ain't in no furnace room, we in that jungle catchin' hell from this one little yellow man and his automatic weapon that he chained to up on top of this hill. "Get on up that hill!" I tell my young recruit. And he tell me, "Yes, Sergeant," like he been taught, and then he start thinkin' to hisself, "What that ole sarge talkin' about, 'run on up that hill'? Ah git my ass blown clean away. I think maybe he got hit on his head, he don't know what he talkin' about no more—maybe I go on over behind that ole rock—practice me a little D and D." Ain't that some shit the way them young recruits wanna carry on? So what I think we do, you and me, long about twenty-two hundred hours we do a little D and D and PT and all them kinda alphabetical things. Make you a good soldier.

PAVLO: (*Thinking he wants to work with* SGT. TOWER.) I don't think I can. That's nighttime, Sergeant, and I'm a fireman. I got to watch the furnace.

SGT. TOWER: That don't make me no never mind. We jus' work it in between your shifts. You see? Ain't it a won-

der how you let the old sarge do the worrin' and fig-
urin' and he find a way?

(*Turns, starting to leave.*)

PAVLO: Sergeant, I was wondering how many push-ups you
can do. How many you can do, that's how many I want
to be able to do before I ever leave.

SGT. TOWER: Boy, don't you go sayin' no shit like that, you
won't ever get out. You be an ole bearded blind fuckin'
man pushin' up all over Georgia.

(SGT. TOWER *moves to leave, and* PAVLO, *speaking immediately and rapidly in a single rush of breath, again
stops him. Incredulously* SGT. TOWER *watches, starts
to leave, watches.*)

PAVLO: And I was wondering also, Sergeant Tower, and
wanted to ask you—when I was leaving home, my
mother wanted to come along to the train station, but I
lied to her about the time. She would have wanted to
hug me right in front of everybody. She would have
waved a handkerchief at the train. It would have been
awful.

(SGT. TOWER *turns; now he is leaving.*)

She would have stood there waving. Was I wrong?

CORPORAL: TEN-HUT! FORWARD HARCH!

(*And the men begin to march in place while* PAVLO,
without joining them, also marches.)

SGT. TOWER: AIN'T NO USE IN GOIN' HOME.

THE MEN: (*Beginning to exit.*) AIN'T NO USE IN GOIN'
HOME.

SGT. TOWER: (*At the side of the stage.*) JODY GOT
YOUR GAL AND GONE.

THE MEN: JODY HUMPIN' ON AND ON.

SGT. TOWER: AIN'T NO USE IN GOIN' BACK.

(*And* PAVLO, *in his own area, is marching away.*)

THE MEN: JODY GOT OUR CADILLAC.

CORPORAL: AIN'T NO MATTER WHAT WE DO.

ALL: JODY DOIN' OUR SISTER TOO.

CORPORAL: Count cadence, delayed cadence, count cadence, count!

ALL: One—two—three—four—One, two, three, four. One,
two, three, four. *Hey!*

(*All are now gone except* PAVLO, *who spins out of his marching pattern to come stomping to a halt in the furnace-room area while* ARDELL *drifts toward him.*)

ARDELL: Oh, yeh; army train you, shape you up, teach you all kinds a good stuff. Like Bayonet. It all about what you do you got no more bullets and this man after you. So you put this knife on the end a your rifle, start yellin' and carryin' on. Then there Hand to Hand. Hand to Hand cool.

(PAVLO *is watching, listening.*)

It all about hittin' and kickin'. What you do when you got no gun and no knife. Then there CBR. CBR: Chemical, Biological, and Radiological Warfare. What you do when some mean motherfucker hit you with some kinda chemical. You

(ARDELL *mimes throwing a grenade at* PAVLO.)

got green fuckin' killin' smoke all around you. What you gonna do? You gotta git on your protective mask. You ain't got it?

PAVLO: (*Choking.*) But I'm too beautiful to die. (*Rummages about in the furnace room.*)

ARDELL: (*Throwing a mask to him.*) But you the only one who believe that, Pavlo. You gotta be hollerin' loud as you know how, "Gas!" And then, sweet Lord almighty, little bit later you walkin' along, somebody else hit you with some kinda biological jive. But you know your shit. Mask on.

(*And* PAVLO, *having put the mask on, is waving his arms.*)

PAVLO: GAS! GAS! GAS!

ARDELL: You gettin' it, Pavlo. All right. Lookin' real good. But now you tired and you still walkin' and you come up on somebody bad—this boy mean—he hit you with radiation.

(PAVLO *goes into a tense, defensive posture.*)

PAVLO: (*Realizing his helplessness.*) Awww.

ARDELL: That right. You know what you do? You kinda stand there, that what you do, whimperin' and talkin' to yourself, 'cause he got you. You gotta be some kinda fool, somebody hit you with radiation, man, you put on a mask, start hollerin', "Gas." Am I lyin'? Pavlo. What do you say?

PAVLO: Aww, no. . . . No man—No, No—No, no. No, no. Oh . . .

(There has been, toward the end of this, a gathering of a group of soldiers in the barracks area. PAVLO, *muttering in denial of the radiation, crosses the stage hurriedly fleeing the radiation, and runs into* PARKER, *who grabs him, spins him.)*

I did not.

KRESS: The hell you didn't.

PARKER: *(Kneeling behind* PAVLO *to take a billfold from his pocket.)* You been found out, jerkoff.

PAVLO: No.

KRESS: We got people saw you. Straight, honest guys.

PARKER: Get that thing *(Meaning the mask.)* off your face.

BURNS: The shit I didn't see you.

PARKER: You never saw a billfold before in your life, is that what you're tryin' to say? You didn't even know what it was?

KRESS: Is that what you're tryin' to say, Hummel?

PAVLO: No.

KRESS: What are you tryin' to say?

PAVLO: I'm goin' to bed. *(Moves toward his bed but is stopped by* KRESS.)

KRESS: We already had two guys lose money to some thief around here, shitbird, and we got people sayin' they saw you with Hinkle's billfold in your pudgy little paws.

HINKLE: *(In a deep Southern drawl [as* PARKER *hands him the billfold he found on* PAVLO]) Is that right, Hummel?

PAVLO: I was just testin' you, Hinkle, to see how stupid you were leavin' your billfold layin' out like that when somebody's been stealin' right in our own platoon. What kinda army is this anyway, you're supposed to trust people with your life, you can't even trust 'em not to steal your money.

PARKER: Listen to him.

PAVLO: That's the truth, Parker. I was just makin' a little

test experiment to see how long it'd be before he'd notice it was gone. I don't steal

KRESS: What about all them cars?

PAVLO: What cars?

PARKER: The New Haven caper, jerkoff. You know.

PAVLO: Ohhh, that was different, you guys. That was altogether different.

KRESS: Yeh, they were cars and you couldn't fit them in your pocket.

PAVLO: Those people weren't my friends.

PARKER: You don't steal from your friends. That what you're sayin'? Kress, Hummel says he don't steal from his friends.

KRESS: (*Jumping up on* PAVLO's *bed, standing, walking about.*) Don't that make his prospects pretty damn near unlimited.

PAVLO: Hey! Kress; what're you doin'?

KRESS: What?

PAVLO: I said, "What're you up to?" You're on my bed.

KRESS: Who is?

PAVLO: You are. You are.

KRESS: Where?

PAVLO: Right here. You're on my bed. That's my bed.

KRESS: No it isn't. It's not anybody's. It's not yours, Hummel.

PAVLO: It is too.

KRESS: Did you buy it?

PAVLO: Get off my bed, Kress!

KRESS: If you didn't buy it, then how is it yours, ugly!

PAVLO: It was given to me.

KRESS: By who?

PAVLO: You know by who, Kress. The army gave it to me. Get off it.

KRESS: Are you going to take it with you when you leave here? If it's yours, you ought to be planning on taking it with you; are you?

PAVLO: I can't do that.

KRESS: You're taking people's billfolds; you're taking their money; why can't you take this bed?

PAVLO: Because it was just loaned to me.

KRESS: Do you have any kind of papers to prove that? Do you have papers to prove that this is your bed?

PAVLO: There's proof in the orderly room; in the orderly room or maybe the supply room, and you know it. That bed's got a number on it somewhere, and that number is like its name and that name is by my name on some papers somewhere in the supply room or the orderly room.

KRESS: Go get them.

PAVLO: What do you mean?

KRESS: Go get them. Bring them here.

PAVLO: I can't.

KRESS: If they're yours, you can.

PAVLO: They're not my papers, it's my bed. Get off my bed, Kress.

    (KRESS *kneels, taking a more total possession of the bed.*)

Goddamnit, Kress. GODDAMNIT!

    (*Silence as* KRESS *seems in fact about to lie down.*)

All right. Okay. You sleep in my bed, I'm gonna sleep in yours.

    (PAVLO *charges toward* KRESS's *bed.* KRESS *rises a little, tense, as all stand watching* PAVLO.)

KRESS: No, Hummel.

PAVLO: (*Yelling.*) The hell I ain't, Kress.

KRESS: No, no, I strongly advise against it. I do strongly so advise. Or something awful might happen. I might get up in the middle of the night to take a leak and stagger back to my old bed. Lord knows what I might think you are . . . laying there. Lord knows what I might do.

PAVLO: (*Yelling.*) Then get out of my bed.

KRESS: You don't understand at all, do you, shitbird! I'm sleeping here. This is where I'm going to sleep. You're not going to sleep anywhere. You're going to sit up, or sleep on the floor, whatever. And in the morning you're going to make this bed. This one. Because if you don't, it'll be unmade when Sergeant Tower comes to inspect in the morning, and as we've already discussed, there's papers somewhere in one room or another and they show whose bed this is.

PAVLO: (*Rushing back, stomping, raging.*) GODDAMN YOU, KRESS, GET OUT OF MY BED! GET OFF MY BED! GET OUT OF IT!

(*Whistle blows and everyone scrambles. There is the popping of many rifles firing as on the ramp across the back three or four men are in firing position; others stand behind them at port arms until* SGT. TOWER *calls, "Cease fire!" and the firing stops. The men who have been firing put their rifles on their shoulders to be cleared.* SGT. TOWER *walks behind them, tapping each on the head when he has seen the weapon is clear. The men leap to their feet.* SGT. TOWER *then steps out in front of them, begins to pace up and down.*)

SGT. TOWER: GEN'LMEN! IT GETTIN' TOWARD DARK NOW AND WE GOT TO GET HOME. IT A LONG LONG WAYS TO HOME AND OUR MOTHERS GOT SUPPER READY WAITIN' FOR US. WHAT CAN WE DO? WE GOT TO GET HOME FAST AS WE CAN, WHAT CAN WE DO? DO ANYBODY HAVE AN IDEA? LET ME HEAR YOU SPEAK IF YOU DO. . . . I HAVE AN IDEA. ANYBODY KNOW MY IDEA, LET ME HEAR IF YOU DO.

PAVLO: Run . . .

BURNS: Run?

SGT. TOWER: WHAT?

MORE MEN: RUN!

SGT. TOWER: I CAN'T HEAR YOU.

THE MEN: WHAT?

SGT. TOWER: RUN!

THE MEN: RUN!

SGT. TOWER and THE MEN: RUN! RUN! RUN! RUN! RUN!

SGT. TOWER: (*As the men still yell, "Run, run."*) PORT HARMS . . . WHOOO! DOUBLE TIME . . . WHOOOOO!

(*They have been running in place. Now* SGT. TOWER *leads them off. They exit, running, reappear, exit, and reappear, spreading out now, though* PAVLO *is fairly close behind* SGT. TOWER, *who enters once again to run to a point downstage where he turns to* PAVLO *entering staggering, leading.*)

FALL OUT!

(*And* PAVLO *collapses. The others struggle in, fall down.*)

PIERCE: FIVE GODDAMN MILES!

(*All are in extreme pain.*)

KRESS: MOTHER-GODDAMN-BITCH—I NEVER RAN NO FIVE GODDAMN MILES IN MY LIFE. YOU GOTTA BE CRAZY TO RUN FIVE GODDAMN MILES. . . .

PARKER: I hurt. I hurt all over. I hurt, Kress. Oh, Christ.

PIERCE: There are guys spread from here to Range Two. You can be proud you made it, Parker. The whole company, man—they're gonna be comin' in for the next ten days.

(*And* PARKER *yells in pain.*)

KRESS: Pierce, what's wrong with Parker?

PARKER: SHIT TOO, YOU MOTHER!

KRESS: It'll pass, Parker. Don't worry. Just stay easy.

(*While a little separate from the others,* PAVLO *is about to begin doing push-ups. He is very tired; it hurts him to do what he's doing.*)

Oh, Hummel, no. Hummel, please.

(PAVLO *is doing the push-ups, breathing the count, wheezing, gasping.*)

Hummel, you're crazy. You really are. He really is, Parker. Look at him. I hate crazy people. I hate 'em. YOU ARE REALLY CRAZY, HUMMEL. STOP IT OR I'LL KILL YOU. (*As* PAVLO *pivots into a sit-up position.*) I mean, I wanna know how much money this platoon lost to that thief we got among us.

PIERCE: Three hundred and twelve dollars.

KRESS: What're you gonna do with all that money?

PAVLO: Spend it. Spend it.

KRESS: Something gonna be done to you! You hear me, weird face? You know what's wrong with you? You wouldn't know cunt if your nose was in it. You never had a piece a ass in your life.

(*There is a loud blast on a whistle.*)

PAVLO: Joanna Sorrentino ga' me so much ass my mother called her a slut.

KRESS: YOU FUCKING IDIOT!

(*Again the whistle.*)

PIERCE: Oh, Christ . . .

PAVLO: Let's go. LET'S GO. LET'S GET IT.

KRESS: Shut up.

PAVLO: (*Moving.*) Let's GO, GO, GO—

(*All start to exit.*)

KRESS: SHUT YOUR MOUTH, ASSHOLE!

PAVLO: LET'S—GO, GO, GO, GO, GO, GO, GO . . .

(*Yelling, leading, yelling, as all ran off stage.*)

(*Simultaneously, in the light on the opposite side of the stage two soldiers—the corporal and* HENDRIX—*are seen with pool cues at a pool table. There are no pool balls; the game will be pantomime; they use a cue ball to shoot and work with.*)

HENDRIX: You break.

CORPORAL: Naw, man, I shoot break on your say so, when I whip your ass, you'll come cryin'. You call.

(*He flips a coin as* PAVLO *comes running back to get his helmet, which lies near where he was doing the push-ups.*)

HENDRIX: Heads.

CORPORAL: You got it.

(PAVLO, *scurrying off with his helmet, meets* SGT. TOWER *entering from opposite side.*)

SGT. TOWER: Trainee, go clean the dayroom. Sweep it up.

PAVLO: Pardon, Sergeant? I forgot my helmet . . .

SGT. TOWER: Go clean the dayroom, Trainee.

(PAVLO *runs off as at the pool game* HENDRIX *shoots break.*)

CORPORAL: My . . . my . . . my. . . . Yes sir. You're gonna be tough all right. That was a pretty damn break all right. (*Moving now to position himself for his shot.*) Except you missed all the holes. Didn't nobody tell you you were supposed to knock the little balls in the little holes?

PAVLO: (*Entering.*) Sergeant Tower said for me to sweep up the dayroom.

HENDRIX: And that's what you do—you don't smile, laugh, or talk; you sweep.

CORPORAL: You know what "buck a ball" means, Trainee?

PAVLO: What?

CORPORAL: Trainee's rich, Hendrix. Can't go to town, got money up the ass.

PAVLO: Sure I know what "buck a ball" means.

CORPORAL: Ohh, you hustlin' trainee motherfucker. New game. Right now. Rack 'em up!

    (HENDRIX *moves as if to rerack the balls.*)

PAVLO: You sayin' I can play?

CORPORAL: Hendrix, you keep an eye out for anybody who might not agree Trainee can relax a bit. You break, man.

PAVLO: I'll break.

CORPORAL: That's right.

PAVLO: You been to the war, huh? That's a First Division patch you got there, ain't it? (*Shooting first shot, missing, not too good.*)

CORPORAL: That's right.

PAVLO: Where at?

CORPORAL: How many wars we got?

PAVLO: I mean exactly where.

CORPORAL: (*Lining up his shot.*) Di An. Ever hear of it?

PAVLO: Sure.

CORPORAL: Not much of a place, but real close to Da Nang. (*He shoots, watches, moves for the next shot.*)

PAVLO: You up there too?

CORPORAL: Where's that?

PAVLO: By Da Nang.

    (*The corporal is startled by* PAVLO *knowing this. He shoots and misses.*)

I mean, I thought Di An was more down by Saigon. D Zone. Down there. They call that D Zone, don't they?

CORPORAL: You're right, man; you know your shit. We got us a map-readin' motherfucker, Hendrix. Yeh, I was by Saigon, Hummel.

PAVLO: I thought so.

CORPORAL: Your shot.

    (*He has moved off to the side where* HENDRIX *has a hip flask of whiskey.*)

PAVLO: (*Moving for his shot.*) Big Red One, man, I'd be proud wearin' that. (*He shoots and misses.*) Shit.

CORPORAL: (*Moving again to the table.*) Good outfit. Top kinda outfit. Mean bastards, all of 'em. Every place we went, man, we used ta tear 'em a new asshole, you can believe me. (*Shooting, making it, he moves on.*) I'm gonna win all your damn money, man. You got your orders yet for where you go when you're finished with basic?

PAVLO: No.

CORPORAL: Maybe if you're lucky, you'll get infantry, huh? Yeh, yeh, I seen some shit, you can believe me (*And he moves about the table, shooting, shooting, as he speaks.*) But you go over there, that's what you're goin' for. To mess with them people, because they don't know nothin'. Them slopes; man they're the stupidest bunch a people anybody ever saw. It don't matter what you do to 'em or what you say, man they just look at you. They're some kinda goddamn phenomenon, man. Can of bug spray buy you all the ass you can handle in some places. Insect repellent, man. You ready for that? You give 'em can a bug spray, you can lay their fourteen-year-old daughter. Not that any of 'em screw worth a shit. (*He thinks it all interesting.*)

    You hear a lot of people talkin' Airborne, One Seventy-third, Hundred and First, Marines, but you gotta go some to beat the First Division. I had a squad leader, Sergeant Tinden. He'd been there two goddamn years when I got there so he knew the road, man; he knew his way. So we was comin' into this village once, the whole company, and it was supposed to be secure. We was Charlie Company and Alpha'd been through already, left a guard. And we was lead platoon and lead squad, and comin' toward us on the path is this old man, he musta been a hundred, about three foot tall, and he's got this little girl by the hand and she's maybe a half-step behind him. He's wavin' at us, "Okay, okay, GI."

And she's wavin', too, but she ain't sayin' nothin', but there's this funny noise you can hear, a kind of cryin' like. (*He still moves about, shooting.*) Anyway, I'm next to the Sarge and he tells this old boy to stop; but they keep comin' like they don't understand, smilin' and wavin', so the Sarge says for 'em to stop in Vietnamese and then I can see that the kid is cryin'; she's got big tears runnin' outa her eyes, and her eyes are gettin' bigger and bigger and I can see she's tuggin' at the old man's hand to run away, but he holds her and he hollers at her and I'm thinkin', "Damn, ain't that a bitch, she's so scared of us." And Tinden, right then, man he dropped to his knees and let go two bursts—first the old man, then the kid—cuttin' them both right across the face, man you could see the bullets walkin'. It was somethin'.

(*He sets and takes his shot. He flops the cue onto the table.*)

You owe me, man; thirteen bucks. But I'm superstitious, so we'll make it twelve.

(PAVLO *pulls out a wad of money to pay.*)

That's right. My ole daddy—the last day he saw me—he tole me good—"Don't you ever run on nobody, boy, or if you do I hope there's somebody there got sense enough to shoot you down. Or if I hear you got away, I'll kill you myself." There's folks like that runnin' loose, Hummel. My ole man. You dig it.

(*But* PAVLO *doesn't and he stares.*)

What the fuck are you lookin' at?

PAVLO: I don't know why he shot . . . them.

CORPORAL: Satchel charges, man. The both of them, front and back. They had enough TNT on 'em to blow up this whole damn state and the kid got scared. They was wearing it under their clothes.

PAVLO: And he knew . . .

CORPORAL: That's right. Been around, so he knew. You ready, Hendrix?

(*They are moving to exit.*)

HENDRIX: Ain't that some shit, Hummel? Ain't that the way to be?

(PARKER *can be seen far across the stage in dimness. Near him* KRESS *and three or four other soldiers crouch among the beds.*)

PARKER: Dear Mother. It was the oddest thing last night. I sat near my bunk, half awake, half asleep . . .

CORPORAL: You keep your ear to the ground, Hummel, you're gonna be all right. (*Exiting*) We'll see you around.

PAVLO: Just to see and to move; just to move

(*He mimes with his broom the firing of a rifle while* ARDELL *stares and lunges suddenly backward, rapidly hauling the table off.*)

PARKER: (*Loudly and flamboyantly.*) Yes, yes, good Mother, I could not sleep, I don't know why. And then for further reasons that I do not know, I happened to look behind me and there . . . was a spaceship, yes a spaceship, green and golden, good Mother, come down to the sand of our Georgia home. A spaceship . . .

(PAVLO *wanders nearer.* PARKER *glances toward* KRESS—*who is kneeling with a blanket—and the others.*)

And out of it, leaping they came, little green men no larger than pins. "Good Lord in heaven," said I to myself, "what do they want? Sneaking among us, ever in silence, ever in stealth." Then I saw Hummel. "Hummel is coming," said I. "I will ask Hummel," said I to myself. "Hummel is coming."

(PAVLO *enters.*)

THIEF!

(*And the blanket is thrown over him. He is dragged to the floor. They beat and kick him. Call him "thief." He cries out. Squirms. A second blanket is thrown upon him, a mattress—it is his own bedding. As they beat and kick him, a whistle blows. All go running out, grabbing rifles and helmets, to form up for bayonet practice where* SGT. TOWER *awaits them.*

PAVLO *emerges from beneath the blankets and no one is there but* ARDELL.)

PAVLO: Didn't I do enough push-ups? How many do you have to do, Ardell?

ARDELL: You got to understand, Pavlo, it fun sometimes to get a man the way they got you. Come down on him, maybe pivot kick. Break his fuckin' spine. Do him, man. Do . . . him . . . good.

SGT. TOWER: (*Atop his platform, bayonet in hand.*) You got to know this bayonet shit, Gen'lmen, else you get recycled, you be back to learn it all again. Eight more beautiful weeks in the armpit a the nation. Else you don't get recycled, you get killed. Then you wish for maybe half a second you been recycled. Do you know the spirit of the bayonet is to kill? What is the spirit of the bayonet?

THE MEN: To kill!

(*While PAVLO stirs about, PIERCE enters the barracks. He is disheveled, a little drunk.*)

SGT. TOWER: You sound like pussies. You sound like slits.

THE MEN: TO KILL!

SGT. TOWER: You sound like pussies.

THE MEN: TO KILL!

(*PAVLO, sensing PIERCE, hurriedly opens his footlocker, digs out a book, which he tries to pretend to read.*)

PIERCE: Look at you. Ohhh, you know how much beer I hadda drink to get fucked up on three-two beer? Hummel, look at me. You think it's neat to be a squad leader? It's not neat to be a squad leader.

(*PAVLO reads from the little book.*)

I hear you got beat up this afternoon.

PAVLO: I got a blanket party.

PIERCE: You're in my squad and other guys in my squad beat you, man; I feel like I oughta do somethin'. I'm older, see. Been to college a little; got a wife. And I'm here to tell you, even with all I seen, sometimes you are unbelievable, Hummel.

PAVLO: I don't care. I don't care.

PIERCE: I mean, I worry about you and the shit you do, man.

PAVLO: You do what you want, Pierce.

PIERCE: I mean, that's why people are after you, Hummel. That's why they fuck with you.

PAVLO: I'm trying to study my Code a Conduct, Pierce,

you mind? It's just not too damn long to the proficiency test. Maybe you oughta be studyin' your Code a Conduct too, insteada sneakin' off to drink at the PX.

PIERCE: I wanna know how you got those rocks down your rifle. It's a two-mile walk out to the rifle range, and you got rocks in your barrel when we get there. That's what I'm talkin' about.

PAVLO: I don't know how that happened.

PIERCE: And every fight you get into, you do nothin' but dance, man. Round in a circle, bobbin' and weavin' and gettin' smacked in the mouth. Man, you oughta at least try and hit somebody. (*And then, suddenly, strangely, he is laughing.*) *Jesus Christ*, Hummel, what's wrong with you? We're in the shower and I tell you to maybe throw a punch once in a while, step with it, pivot, so you try it right there on that wet floor and damn near kill yourself smashin' into a wall.

PAVLO: Fuck you, Pierce.

PIERCE: Fuck you, Hummel.

(*Silence.*)

PAVLO: You know somethin', Pierce. My name ain't even really Pavlo Hummel. It's Michael Hummel. I had it legally changed. I had my name changed.

PIERCE: You're puttin' me on.

PAVLO: No, no, and someday, see, my father's gonna say to me, "Michael, I'm so sorry I ran out on you," and I'm gonna say, "I'm not Michael, asshole. I'm not Michael anymore." Pierce? You weren't with those guys who beat up on me, were you?

PIERCE: No.

(PAVLO *begins making his bunk.*)

ARDELL: Sometimes I look at you, I don't know what I think I'm seein', but it sooo simple. You black on the inside. In there where you live, you that awful hurtin' black so you can't see yourself no way. Not up or down or in or out.

SGT. TOWER—(*Down from the platform, he moves among the men.*) There ain't no army in the world got a shorter bayonet than this one we got. Maneuverability. It the only virtue. You got to get inside that big long knife that other man got. What is the spirit of the bayonet?

THE MEN: TO KILL!

SGT. TOWER: You sound like pussies.

THE MEN: TO KILL!

SGT. TOWER: You sound like slits.

THE MEN: TO KILL!

SGT. TOWER: EN GARDE!

THE MEN: AGGGH!

SGT. TOWER: LONG THRUST, PARRY LEFT . . . WHOOOOOO!

> (*And the men growl and move, one of them stumbling, falling down, clumsy, embarrassed.*)

Where you think you are? You think you in the movies? This here real life, Gen'lmen. You actin' like there ain't never been a war in this world. Don't you know what I'm sayin'? You got to want to put this steel into a man. You got to want to cut him, hurt him, make him die. You got to want to feel the skin and muscle come apart with the push you give. It come to you in the wood. RECOVER AND HOLD!

THE MEN: AGGGH!

> (*They yell and growl with each thrust. Another falls, gets up.*)

SGT. TOWER: EN GARDE!

THE MEN: AGGGH!

SGT. TOWER: Lookin' good, lookin' good. Only you ain't mean.

> (*The men growl.*)

How come you ain't mean?

> (*The men growl.*)

HORIZONTAL BUTT-STROKE SERIES, WHOOO!

> (*And they move, making the thrust, recovery, upper-cutting butt-stroke, horizontal butt-stroke, and downward slash. The growling and yelling get louder.*)

Look at you; look at you. Ohhh, but you men put into my mind one German I saw in the war. I got one bullet left, don't think I want to shoot it, and here come this goddamned, big-assed German. "Agggghhhh," I yell to him, and it a challenge and he accept. "Agggghhhh," he

say to me and set hisself, and I just shoot him. Boom!
Ohhh, he got a look on his face like I never saw before
in my life. He one baffled motherfucker, Jim.
(*Without command the men begin to march.*)

ARDELL: (*Singing.*) ONCE A WEEK I GET TO
TOWN) . . .

THE MEN: THEY SEE ME COMIN', THEY ALL LAY
DOWN.

ARDELL: IF I HAD A LOWER IQ . . .
(*All are marching, exiting.*)

THE MEN: I COULD BE A SERGEANT TOO.

SGT. TOWER: LORD HAVE MERCY, I'M SO BLUE. . . .

THE MEN: LORD HAVE MERCY, I'M SO BLUE. . . .

SGT. TOWER: IT SIX MORE WEEKS TILL I BE
THROUGH. . . .

THE MEN: IT SIX MORE WEEKS TILL I BE
THROUGH.

SGT. TOWER: SOUND OFF!

THE MEN: ONE—TWO.
(BURNS, PIERCE, *and another soldier enter the barracks area still singing as others are exiting, and these
three men set up a crap game on a footlocker.*)

SGT. TOWER: SOUND AGAIN!

THE MEN: THREE—FOUR.
(PAVLO, HINKLE, *and others enter.*)

SGT. TOWER: COUNT CADENCE, COUNT.

THE MEN: ONE, TWO, THREE, FOUR. ONE, TWO,
THREE, FOUR. ONE, TWO, THREE, FOUR.
(*And they are all spread about the barracks, reading,
sleeping.*)

PAVLO: (*To* HINKLE [*as the crap game goes on nearby*].)
Can you imagine that, Hinkle? Just knowin'. Seein'
nothin' but bein' sure enough to gun down two people.
They had TNT on 'em; they was stupid slopeheads. That
Sergeant Tinden saved everybody's life. I get made anything but infantry, I'm gonna fight it, man. I'm gonna
fight it. You wanna go infantry with me, Hinkle? You're
infantry and good at it too, you're your own man, I'm
gonna wear my uniform everywhere when I'm home,
Hinkle. My mother's gonna be so excited when she sees

me. She's just gonna yell. I get nervous when I think about if she should hug me. You gonna hug your mother when you get home?

PAVLO: My mom's a little bitty skinny woman.

PAVLO: I don't know if I should or shouldn't.

HINKLE: What's your mom like?

PIERCE: You tellin' him about your barnhouse exploits, Hinkle?

HINKLE: Oh, no.

PIERCE: Hinkle says he screwed sheep. He tellin' you that, Hummel?

PARKER: How about pigs, Hinkle?

HINKLE: Oh, yeh.

KRESS: I'm tellin' you, Parker, it was too much; all that writin' and shit, and runnin' around. They ain't got no right to test you; proficiency test, proficiency test; I don't even know what a proficiency is—goddamn people—crawlin' and writin'—I'm tellin' you, they ain't got no right to test you. They get you here, they mess with you—they let you go. Who says they gotta test you?

PIERCE: (*Who has the dice and is laying down money.*) Who's back, man? I'm shootin' five.

KRESS: I got so nervous in hand-to-hand, I threw a guy against the wall. They flunked me for bein' too rough.

PIERCE: Who's back, man?

KRESS: I'll take three.

(*He puts down money while* PARKER *drops a couple of ones.*)

I get recycled, I'll kill myself, I swear it.

(*As* PIERCE *is shaking the dice, saying over and over,* "Karen loves me, Karen loves me.")

I'll cut off my ear.

PIERCE: (*Throwing the dice.*) Karen says I'm *good!*

KRESS: Goddamn! Shit! How they do it again, Parker?

PARKER: Pierce, you're incredible.

KRESS: Parker!

PARKER: They add up your scores, man; your PT, plus your rifle, plus the score they got today. Then they divide by three. (*Throwing down a five.*) You lettin' it ride, Pierce?

PIERCE: Karen loves me.

KRESS: (*Putting in money.*) Where they get the three?

PARKER: There's three events, man.

PIERCE: (*Throwing the dice.*) Karen says, "I know the road!"

KRESS: You fucking asshole.

PARKER: Goddamnit, Pierce!

PIERCE: Who wants me? Back man's got no heart. Shootin' twenty I come seven or eleven—double or nothin'. Whose twenty says I can't come for all out of the gate? . . .

(*A soldier enters on the run.*)

SOLDIER: Tower's right behind me; he's got the scores.

(*General commotion as they hide the dice and the money, and* SGT. TOWER *strides across the stage and enters their area.*)

PIERCE: TENHUT!

(*All come to attention before their bunks.*)

SGT. TOWER: AT EASE!

(*Men to parade rest.*)

Gen'lmen. It's truth-and-consequences time. The sad tidings and (*handing a paper to Pierce for him to post.*) the glad tidings. You got two men in this platoon didn't make it. They Burn and Kress. They gonna have to stay here eight more weeks, and if they as dumb as it look, maybe eight more after that and eight fuckin' more. The rest a you people, maybe you ain't got no spectacular qualities been endowed upon my mind, but you goin' home when you figured. (*He turns, leaving.*)

PIERCE: TENHUT!

SGT. TOWER: Carry on.

(*They are silent. Kress stands. All start talking and yelling at once.*)

PIERCE: Lemme holler . . . just one . . . time, lemme holler . . .

HINKLE: Mother, mother, make my bed!

A SOLDIER: (*At the bulletin board.*) Me! My name! Me!

PIERCE: AGGGGGGGGGHHHIIHHHHHHHHHHHHHH-
AAAA!

PARKER: Lemme just pack my bags!

HENDRIX: (*Entering with civilian clothes, shirt and trousers on a hanger, hat on his head.*) Lookee—lookee—

HINKLE: What're them funny clothes?

PIERCE: CIVILIAN CLOTHES! CIVILIAN—

HINKLE: CI-WHO-LIAN?

PIERCE: PEOPLE OUTSIDE, MAN! THAT'S WHY THEY AIN'T ALL FUNNY AND GREEN, BECAUSE YOU'RE OUTSIDE WHEN YOU WEAR 'EM. YOU'RE BACK ON THE BLOCK, BACK IN THE WORLD!

PAVLO: (*Standing on his bed.*) DON'T NOBODY HEAR ME CALLIN' "KRESS!" (*He has said the name during the yelling.*) I think we oughta tell him how sorry we are he didn't make it. I'm gonna. I'm gonna tell him. I'm sorry Kress, that you're gonna be recycled and you're not goin' home. I think we're all sorry. I bet it's kinda like gettin' your head caught in a blanket, the way you feel. It's a bad feelin', I bet, and I think I understand it even if I am goin' back where there's lights and it's pretty. I feel sorry for you, Kress, I just wanna laugh, I feel so sorry—

(*And* KRESS, *leaping, pushes him.* PAVLO *staggers backward.*)

Sonofabitch, what're you—SONOFABITCH!

(*He swings a wild right hand. They flail and crash about.* KRESS *grabs* PAVLO's *wrist, drawing him forward into a hammerlock.*)

KRESS: Down. (*Then lifting.*) Don't you hear me? Down, I'm sayin'. Don't you hear me? Thata boy. . . . Called crawlin'. . . .

(*And* PAVLO *is thrown to the floor,* KRESS *on top of him.*)

You got the hang of it . . . now. . . . Crawlin'. . . . Yeh. Now I'm gonna ask you something? Okay?

PAVLO: . . . okay . . .

KRESS: What I'd like to know is who is it in this platoon steals money from his buddies? Who is it don't know how to talk decent to nobody? and don't have one goddamn friend? Who is that person? You tell me, Hummel? The name a that person passed his test today by cheatin'.

PAVLO: I don't . . . know . . .

KRESS: (*Working the arm.*) Who?

PAVLO: No—

(*And the arm is twisted again.*)

Stop him, somebody. Pierce. You're my squad leader, Pierce. Ohhhh . . . Pierce, please . . . Aggghhhh . . . Pierce . . .

KRESS: WHO?

(*And* PAVLO *yells*)

PIERCE: Ease off a little. . . .

KRESS: I CAN'T HEAR YOU!

PIERCE: Kress, I—

PAVLO: HUMMEL!

KRESS: WHAT? WHAT?

PAVLO: HUMMEL! HUMMEL!

KRESS WHAT?

PAVLO: HUMMEL! HUMMEL! He did 'em. All of those things. All of 'em. He cheated. He cheated. HUMMEL! HUM—

PIERCE: Kress, goddamnit. GODDAMNIT! (*Leaping, he lifts* KRESS *away from* PAVLO *and throws him sideways.*)

KRESS: What? What you want, Corporal? Don't mess with me, man. (*Staring at* PIERCE, *who is between him and* PAVLO, KRESS *backs away, yet he rages.*) Don't mess with Kress. Not when he's feelin' bad. He'll kill ya, honest to God. He'll pee in your dead mouth.

(*And* PAVLO *rushes at* KRESS, *howling.*)

PIERCE: Noooooooooo. (*Seizes* PAVLO, *pushing him back.*)

PAVLO: (*As* KRESS *storms out and the other soldiers follow in an effort to console him.*) I'm all right. I'm all right. I do all right!

PIERCE: Will you listen to me, man; you're goin' home; not Kress. You got him.

PAVLO: Fucking asshole!

PIERCE: Will you listen? (*Shoving* PAVLO, *scolding him.*) You gotta learn to think, Hummel. You gotta start puttin' two and two together so they fit. You beat him; you had old Kress beat and then you fixed it so you hadda lose. You went after him so he hadda be able to put you down.

PAVLO: I just wanted to let him know what I thought.

PIERCE: No, no!

PAVLO: He had no call to hit me like that. I was just talkin'—

PIERCE: You dared him, man.

PAVLO: You shoulda stopped him, that's the problem. You're the squad leader. That's just this whole damn army messin' with me, and it ain't ever gonna end but in shit. How come you're a squad leader? Who the fuck are you? I'm not gonna get a chance at what I want. Not ever. Nothin' but shit. They're gonna mess with me— make a clerk outta me or a medic or truck driver, a goddamn moron—or a medic—a nurse—a fuckin' Wac with no tits—or a clerk, some little goddamn twerp of a guy with glasses and no guts at all. So don't gimme shit about what I done, Pierce, it's what you done and done and done and didn't—

(*During this whole thing* PIERCE *has moved about straightening the bunks and footlockers, and* PAVLO, *in growing desperation, has followed him. Now* PIERCE, *in disgust, starts to leave.*)

That's right; keep on walkin' away from your duties, keep—

PIERCE: You're happy as a pig in shit, I don't know why I keep thinkin' you ain't.

PAVLO: I am not.

PIERCE: Up to your eyeballs!

PAVLO: I'm gonna kill myself, Pierce! (*It bursts out of him.*)

PIERCE: If you weren't in my squad, I'd spit in your face. . . .

(*He pivots and goes off after* KRESS *and the other soldiers.*)

PAVLO: (*Rocking backward, then bowing forward.*) Fuck you, fuck you.

(*He is alone and yelling after them as* ARDELL *enters.*)

I hate you goddamn people!

ARDELL: I know.

PAVLO: Ardell.

> (*At his footlocker* PAVLO *rummages.*)

ARDELL: I know. I know. All you life like a river and there's no water all around—this emptiness—you gotta fill it. Gotta get water. You dive, man, you dive off a stone wall

> (PAVLO *has a canteen and paper bag in his hands.*)

into the Hudson River waitin' down dark under you. For a second it's all air . . . so free. . . . Do you know the distance you got to fall? You think you goin' up. Don't nobody fall up, man. Nobody.

PAVLO: What is it? I want to know what it is. The thing that sergeant saw to make him know to shoot that kid and old man. I want to have it, know it, be it

ARDELL: I know.

PAVLO: When?

ARDELL: Soon.

PAVLO: If I could be bone, Ardell; if I could be bone. In my deepest part or center, if I could be bone.

> (*Taking a bottle from the bag, he takes pills, washes them down with water, and crawls under the covers of his bunk while* SGT. TOWER, *already on the platform, speaks.*)

SGT. TOWER: Now I'm gonna tell you gen'lmen how you find you way when you lost. You better listen up. What you do, you find the North Star and the North Star show you true north accurate all year round. You look for the Big Dipper, and there are two stars at the end a that place in the stars that look like the bowl on the dipper and they called the pointer. They them two stars at where the water would come out the dipper if it had some water and out from them on a straight line you gonna see this big damn star and that the North Star and it show you north and once you know that, Gen'l-men, you can figure the rest. You ain't lost no more.

THE MEN: (*Beginning to enter to position themselves for the next scene.*) YESSSS, SERGEANT!

SGT. TOWER: I hope so. I do hope so. . . .

> (PIERCE, PARKER, *and others set up a card game on a footlocker.*)

KRESS: (*Passing the bunk where* PAVLO *is a lump beneath his blanket.*) I wonder what the fuckin', chimney-shittin' shit is doin' now?

  (HINKLE *settles curiously on the bunk next to* PAVLO.)

PARKER: You gonna see me, Pierce?

PIERCE: And raise you.

PARKER: Ten ta one he's under there jerkin' off!

HINKLE: (*Bending near to* PAVLO.) No, no, he's got this paper bag and everything smells funny. Y'all some kind of acrobat, Hummel?

KRESS: He's got some chick's bicycle seat in a bag, man.

HINKLE: And the noises he's makin'.

PIERCE: Poor pathetic motherfucker.

KRESS: He ain't pathetic.

PIERCE: He is too.

PARKER: Under there pounding his pud.

KRESS: You musta not seen many pathetic people, you think he's pathetic.

PIERCE: I seen plenty.

PARKER: Call.

PIERCE: (*Laying down his cards.*) Full boat. Jacks and threes!

PARKER: Jesus Goddamn Christ.

HINKLE: I was wonderin' can ah look in you all's bag, Hummel? (*He reaches under the blanket.*)

PARKER: Jesus Goddamn Christ.

HINKLE: Ohhhh . . . it's . . . you been sniffin' airplane glue. . . . (*And he laughs, turns toward the others.*) Hummel's been sniffin' airplane glue.

KRESS: ATTAWAY TO GO, HUMMEL.

HINKLE: (*Holding the bottle*). An' where's all the asp'rins . . . ?

PAVLO: Tumtum Pavlo.

HINKLE: You all kiddin' me.

PAVLO: No.

HINKLE: Y'all ate 'em?

PAVLO: Yeah!

HINKLE: Hey y'all. . . . (*To* PAVLO.) Was it full?

  (PAVLO *attempts to sit up, flops back down.*)

PAVLO: Tippy top.

HINKLE: Hummel just ate—(*Examining the bottle.*) one hundred asp'rins. Hummel just ate 'em.

KRESS: Attaway to go, Hummel.

PARKER: Nighty-night.

HINKLE: Won't it hurt him, Pierce?

KRESS: Kill him probably.

PARKER: Hopefully.

KRESS: Hinkle, ask him did he use chocolate syrup?

HINKLE: He's breathin' kinda funny, Pierce, don't you think?

KRESS: Hummel does everything funny.

PIERCE: (*Beginning to deal.*) Five cards, Gen'lmen; jacks or better.

HINKLE: Pierce.

PIERCE: Hummel, you stop worryin' that boy. Tell him no headache big enough in the world, you're gonna take a hundred asp'rins.

> (*Slight pause.* KRESS *begins imitating* PAVLO's *odd breathing.*)

How come everybody's all the time bustin' up my good luck.

BURNS: Shit, man, he took a hundred asp'rins, he wouldn't be breathin' period.

RYAN: Sounds like a goddamn tire pump.

BURNS: Hummel, TENHUT!

PIERCE: Hummel, you just jivin' cause you don't know what else to do, or did you eat them pills?

BURNS: Tryin' to blow himself up like a balloon . . . drift away. Float outa the fort.

> (PARKER *begins to imitate* KRESS *imitating* PAVLO's *breathing.*)

RYAN: He's fakin', man.

BURNS: How you know?

RYAN: They'd kill you like a bullet.

HINKLE: Get over here, Pierce!

KRESS: How come the army don't thrown him out, Parker?

PARKER: Army likes weird people, Kress.

KRESS: I hate weird people.

PARKER: Sure you do.

KRESS: Weird, chimney-shittin', friendless, gutless, cheatin' . . .

(*PIERCE is examining* PAVLO. PAVLO *makes a sound and then begins to cough.*)

PIERCE: NOOO! NOT IN MY SQUAD, YOU MOTHER. GET UP!

(*He is trying to get* PAVLO *to his feet; another soldier is helping.*)

YOU SILLY SONOFABITCH. We got to walk him.

(*PAVLO is feebly resisting.*)

Hinkle, double-time it over the orderly room.

HINKLE: Right.

PIERCE: Tell 'em we got a guy over here took a hundred asp'rins, they should get an ambulance.

HINKLE: (*Turning to head for the door.*) Right.

KRESS: Hinkle!

HINKLE: (*Hesitating.*) Yeh!

KRESS: Pick me up a Coke on your way back.

PIERCE: Hold him steady. I think we oughta get him outside, more air.

ARDELL: (*Standing over near the base of the tower.*) Pavlo. You gonna have ambulances and sirens and all kinds of good shit. Ain't you somethin'? It gonna be a celebration. C'mon over here.

(*As if* ARDELL's *voice draws them,* PIERCE *and the other soldier lug* PAVLO *toward the tower: they lay him down, remove all clothes from him but his underwear and T-shirt.*)

Pavlo! Look at you. You got people runnin' around like a bunch a fools. That what you wanted? Yeah, that what you want! They sayin' "Move him. Lift him. Take his shirt off." They walkin' you around in the air. They all thinkin' about you, anyway. But what you doin' but cryin'? You always think you signifyin' on everybody else, but all you doin' is showin' your own fool self. You don't know nothin' about showboatin', Pavlo. You hear me? Now you get on up off that floor. You don't get up, man, I blow a motherfuckin' whistle up side you head. I blow it loud. YOU THINK YOU GOT A MOTHER-FUCKIN' WHISTLE IN YOUR BRAIN.

(PIERCE *and the other man have turned away. Every-thing* PAVLO *does is performed in the manner of a person alone: as if* ARDELL *is a voice in his head. The light perhaps suggests this.* KRESS, *all others, are frozen.*)

I'm tellin' you how to be. That right.

(PAVLO *slumps back down.*)

Ohhh, don't act so bad; you actin', man. What you expect, you go out get you head smokin' on all kinds a shit sniffin' that goddamn glue, then fallin' down all over yourself. Man, you lucky you alive, carryin' on like that.

(PAVLO *is doubled over.*)

Ain't doin' you no good you wish you dead, 'cause you ain't, man. Get on up.

(PAVLO *takes a deep breath and stands.*)

You go in the latrine now, get you a bromo, you wash off you face . . .

(PAVLO *exits, staggering.*)

Then get you ass right back out here. And you don't need no shave, man, you ain't got no beard no ways. (*Sees* PAVLO'*s uniform lying on the floor.*) What kinda shit this? Your poor ole Sarge see this, he sit down on the ground and he cry, man. Poor ole Sarge, he work himself like he crazy tryin' ta teach you so you can act like a man. An' what you do? (*Turning suddenly, yelling after* PAVLO.) Pavlo! You diddlin' in there, you take this long. And you bring out you other uniform. We gonna shape you up.

(PAVLO *enters carrying military dress uniform in a clothing bag, which he hangs on the tower.*)

It daytime, man, you goin' out struttin'. You goin' out standin' tall. You tear it open. Trousers first, man. Dig 'em out.

(PAVLO, *having selected the trousers, moves as if to put them on.*)

NOOOO! Damnit, ain't you got no sense at all?

(*He rushed to* PAVLO, *lifted the trouser bottoms off the floor.*)

You drag 'em all over the floor like that, man, they gonna look like shit. Get up on this footlocker!

(*Now* PIERCE *and the other soldier move in to help* PAVLO *dress. All is ease now.*)

That right, that it. Make 'em look like they got no notion at all what it like to be dirty. Be clean, man. Yeh. Now the shirt.

(*It is a ritual now:* PAVLO *must exert no effort whatsoever as he is transformed.*)

Lemme look you brass over. Ain't too bad. It do. Lemme just touch 'em up a little. (*He brushes with his handkerchief at the brass.*) You put on you tie. Make you a big knot. Big knot make you look tall. Where you boots?

(*And, finished with the jacket,* PIERCE *and the other soldier move to the boots.*)

Where you boots? An' you got some shades? Lemme get you some shades. (*Walking backward.*) And tuck that tie square. Give her little loop, she come off you throat high and pretty.

(*As* ARDELL *exits,* PAVLO *sits on the footlocker.* PIERCE *and the other soldier kneel to put the boots onto him.*)

HUT . . . HOO . . . HEE . . . HAW . . . (*Singing.*) IF I HAD A LOWER IQ.

ALL THE MEN: IF I HAD A LOWER IQ.

ARDELL: I COULD BE A SERGEANT TOO.

THE MEN: I COULD BE A SERGEANT TOO!

(*Across the back of the stage two men march.*)

ARDELL: LORD HAVE MERCY, I'M SO BLUE.

(*The two men do an intricate drill-team step.*)

THE MEN: IT FOUR MORE WEEKS TILL I BE THROUGH.

(*The two men spin their rifles and strike the ground smartly with the butts as* ARDELL *returns, carrying a pair of sunglasses.*)

ARDELL: You gonna be over, man, I finish with you.

(PAVLO *stands up fully dressed.*)

You gonna be the fat rat, man; you eatin' cheese.

(ARDELL *moves about* PAVLO, *examining him, guiding him toward the tower. As* ARDELL *talks,* PAVLO *climbs the tower and stands on it;* ARDELL *joins him.*)

OVER, BABY! Ardell can make you straight; you startin' ta look good now; you finish up, you gonna be the fattest rat, man, eatin' the finest cheese. Put you in good company, you wear that uniform. You go out walkin' on the street, people know you, they say, "Who that?" Somebody else say, "Man, he straight. He look good." Somebody else say, "That boy got pride." Yeh, baby, Pavlo, you gonna be over, man. You gonna be that fat fat rat, eatin' cheese, down on his knees, yeh, baby, doffin' his red cap, sayin', "Yes, Massa." You lookee out there.

(*Both are atop the tower.* ARDELL *is a little behind* PAVLO *and gesturing outward.* PAVLO *stands. He has sunglasses on.*)

Who you see in that mirror, man? Who you see? That ain't no Pavlo Hummel. Noooo, man. That somebody else. An' he somethin' else.

(PAVLO *is looking.*)

Ohhh, you goin' out on the street, they gonna see you. Ardell tellin' you and Ardell know. You back on the block an' you goin' out struttin'. An' they gonna cry when they see you. You so pretty, baby, you gonna make 'em cry. You tell me you name, you pretty baby!

PAVLO: (*Snapping to attention.*) PAVLO MOTHER-IIUMPIN' HUMMEL!

(*Blackout.*)

ACT TWO

(*Set changes: The debris of the bar wall remains up-stage and stage right, though the barrel and crate are gone. Downstage and stage right there is a larger, more detailed version of the bar: metal wall, barrel used as table, two crates used as chairs, a footlocker off to the side, beer cans and bottles scattered about. The drill sergeant's tower remains. Far downstage and just a little left of center a telephone sits on the floor near another footlocker. Stage left of the tower there is an army cot with a green but nonmilitary bed-spread.*)

(*The lights come up on the men in formation. PAVLO is still atop the tower, standing, looking out as he was. The men face upstage. Standing at the rear of the set are the captain and SGT. TOWER. They face the men. Downstage stands MICKEY, PAVLO's half brother. MICKEY wears slacks, T-shirt, shoes. He is standing as if looking into a mirror about to comb his hair; how-ever he does not move. The captain, stiffly formal, ad-dresses the troops.*)

CAPTAIN: As we enter now the final weeks of your basic training, I feel a certain obligation as your company commander to speak to you of the final purpose of what we have done here. Normally this is more difficult to make clear. Pleiku, Vietnam, is the purpose of what we have done here. A few nights ago mortar and machine-gun fire in a sneak attack in the highlands killed nine Americans and wounded a hundred and forty serving at our camp there in Pleiku. In retaliation a bombing of the North has begun, and it will continue until the government of Hanoi, battered and reeling, goes back to the North.

SGT. TOWER: Company, fall out!

(*And the troops scatter. Music starts from* MICKEY'S *radio.* PAVLO *descends, picks up duffle bag and* AWOL *bag.* MICKEY *starts combing his hair.*)

PAVLO: Hey Mickey, it's me. I'm home! It's me. I'm home, I'm home.

MICKEY: Pavlo. Whata you say, huh? Hey, hey, what happened? You took so long. You took a wrong turn, huh? Missed your stop and now you come home all dressed up like a conductor. What happened? You were down in that subway so long they put you to work? Huh? Man, you look good though; you look good. Where were you again?

PAVLO: Georgia.

MICKEY: Hot as a bitch, right?

PAVLO: No. Cold.

MICKEY: In Georgia?

PAVLO: Yeh, it was real cold; we used to hide out in the furnace room every damn chance we ever got.

MICKEY: Hey, you want a drink? Damn that don't make much sense, does it?

PAVLO: What?

MICKEY: They send you to Georgia for the winter and it's like a witch's tit. Can you imagine that? A witch's tit? Eeeeeeggggggg. Puts ice on your tongue. That ever happened to me, man, I'd turn in my tool. Ain't you gonna ask about the ole lady? How's she doin' and all that, cause she's doin' fine. Pickin' and plantin' daisies. Doin' fine.

(*And* PAVLO *laughs, shaking his head, taking the drink* MICKEY *has made him.*)

Whatsa matter? You don't believe yo-yos can be happy?

Psychotics have fun, man. You oughta know that.

PAVLO: I just bet she's climbin' some kinda wall. Some kinda wall and she's pregnant again, she thinks, or you are or me or somebody.

MICKEY: Noo, man, noo, it's everybody else now. Only nonfamily.

PAVLO: (*Laughing, loudly.*) THAT'S ME AND YOU! NONFAMILY MOTHERFUCKERS!

MICKEY: All the dogs and women of the world!

PAVLO: Yeh, yeh, all the guys in the barracks used to think I was a little weird, so I'd—

MICKEY: You *are* a little weird—

PAVLO: Yeh, yeh, I'd tell 'em, "You think I'm weird, you oughta see my brother, Mickey. He don't give a big rat's ass for nothin' or nobody."

MICKEY: And did you tell 'em about his brains, too. And his wit and charm. The way his dick hangs to his knees—about his eighteen thou a year? Did you tell 'em all that sweet shit?

PAVLO: They said they hoped you died of all you got.

(MICKEY *has been dressing as they speak, and now he wears a shirt and tie and suit coat.*)

MICKEY: How come the troops were thinkin' you weird? You doin' that weird stuff again. You say "Georgia" and "the army." For all I know you been downtown in the movies for the last three months and you bought that goddamn uniform at some junk shop.

PAVLO: I am in the army.

MICKEY: How do I know?

PAVLO: I'm tellin' you.

MICKEY: But you're a fuckin' liar; you're a fuckin' myth-maker.

PAVLO: I gotta go to Vietnam, Mickey.

MICKEY: Vietnam don't even exist.

PAVLO: I gotta go to it.

MICKEY: Arizona, man; that's where you're goin'. Wyoming.

PAVLO: Look at me! I'm different! I'm different than I was! (*This is with fury.*) I'm not the same anymore. I was an asshole. I'm not an asshole anymore. I'm not an asshole

anymore (*Silence as he stares in anguish.*) I came here
to forgive you. I don't need you anymore.

MICKEY: You're a goddamn cartoon, you know that.

PAVLO: (*Rapidly, in a rush of words.*) I'm happier now
than I ever was, I got people who respect me. Lots of
'em. There was this guy Kress in my outfit. We didn't
hit it off . . . and he called me out . . . he was gonna
kill me, he said. Everybody tried to stop me because this
guy had hurt a lot of people already and he had this
uncle who'd taught him all about fightin' and this uncle
has been executed in San Quentin for killing people. We
went out back of the barracks. It went on and on, hitting
and kicking. It went on and on; all around the barracks.
The crowd right with us. And then . . . all of a sudden . . this look came into his eye . . . and he just
stopped . . . and reached down to me and hugged me.
He just hugged and hugged me. And that look was in all
their eyes. All the soldiers. I don't need you anymore,
Mickey. I got real brothers now.

MICKEY: You know . . . if my father hadn't died, you
wouldn't even exist.

PAVLO: No big thing! We got the same mother; that's shit
enough. I'm gonna shower and shave, okay? Then we
can go out drinkin'.

MICKEY: All those one-night stands. You ever think of
that? Ghostly pricks. I used to hear 'em humpin' the ole
whore. I probably had my ear against the wall the night
they got you goin'.

PAVLO: (*After a slight silence.*) You seen Joanna lately?

MICKEY: Joanna?

PAVLO: Joanna. My ole girl. I thought maybe she probably
killed herself and it was in the papers. You know, on
account of my absence. But she probably did it in secret.

MICKEY: No doubt.

PAVLO: No doubt.

MICKEY: Ain't she the one who got married? I think the
ole lady tole me Joanna got married and she was gonna
write you a big letter all about it. Sure she was. Anyway,
since we're speaking of old girls and pregnant people,
I've got to go to this little party tonight. Got a good new

sweet young thing and she thinks I'm better than her daddy. I've had a run of chicks lately you wouldn't believe, Pavlo. They give away ass like Red Cross girls dealin' out doughnuts. I don't understand how I get half a what I get. Oh, yeh, old lady comes and goes around here. She's the same old witch.

PAVLO: I'm gonna go see Joanna. I'll call her up. Use the magic fuckin' phone to call her up.

MICKEY: I'll give you call later on.

PAVLO: I'll be out, man. I'll be out on the street.

MICKEY: (*Exiting.*) You make yourself at home.

> (*And soldiers appear far upstage, marching forward as* ARDELL, *off to the side, counts cadence, and other soldiers appear at various points about the stage.*)

ARDELL: HUT . . . HOO . . . HEE . . .

SGT. TOWER: (*Entering as* PAVLO, *glancing at him, exits.*) SAW SOME STOCKIN'S ON THE STREET . . .

THE MEN: WISHED I WAS BETWEEN THOSE FEET.

SGT. TOWER: WISHED I WAS BETWEEN THOSE FEET. HONEY, HONEY, DON'T YOU FROWN.

THE MEN: I LOVE YOU DRUNK AND LAYIN' DOWN.

SGT. TOWER: STANDIN' TALL AND LOOKIN' GOOD. WE BELONG IN HOLLYWOOD.

> (*He is atop the tower as the men come to a stomping halt.*)

THE MEN: WE BELONG IN HOLLYWOOD.

SGT. TOWER: Take five, Gen'lmen, but the smokin' lamp is not lit.

> (PAVLO *is there, off to the side, disheveled, carrying a pint whiskey bottle. He undresses, speaking his anger, throwing his uniform down. The men are relaxing a little.*)

PAVLO: Stupid fuckin' uniform. Miserable hunk a green shit. Don't we go to good bars—why don't you work for me? And there's this really neat girl there sayin' to me how do I like bein' a robot? How do I like bein' one in a hundred million robots all marchin' in a row? Don't anybody understand about uniforms? I ain't no robot. You gotta have braid . . . ribbons and patches all about what you did. I got nothin'. What's so complicated? I look like nothin' cause I done nothin'. (*In his T-shirt and underwear, he kneels now with the bottle.*)

SGT. TOWER: Gen'lmen, you best listen up real close now even though you restin'. Gonna tell you little bit about what you do you comin' through the woods, you find a man wounded in his chest. You gotta seal it off. That wound workin' like a valve, pullin' in air, makin' pressure to collapse that man's lung; you get him to breathe out and hold his breath. You apply the metal-foil side a the waterproof wrapping of the first-aid dressing, tie it off. Gonna hafta tie it extra; you use your poncho, his poncho, you get strips of cloth. You tear up you own damn shirt. I don't care. You let that boy have his lung. You let him breathe. AM I UNDERSTOOD?

THE MEN: YES, SERGEANT!

SGT. TOWER: FALL IN!

(*The men leap to attention.*)

DISMISSED!

(*And the troops run off, leaving* PAVLO *alone in his underwear near the bed.*)

PAVLO: I wanna get laid . . . Bed . . . Bottle. (*Pause.*) I wanna get laid! I wanna get laid, Phone! You goddamn stuck-up motherin' phone. Need a piece of ass, Bed. Lemme walk on over to that phone. Lemme crawl on over to that phone. Lemme get there. Gonna outflank you. Goddamn army ant. Thas right. Thas right. Hello. (*He has crawled drunkenly to the phone and is dialing now.*) This is Pavlo, Joanna. Hello. Certainly of course. I'd be glad to screw your thingy with my thingy. BSZZZZZZZ . . .

WOMAN'S VOICE: (*Over the phone.*) Hello?

PAVLO: BSZZZZZZZZZZZZZZZZZZZZZZZ . . .

WOMAN'S VOICE: Hello?

PAVLO: Little bitty creature . . . hello, hello. . . .

WOMAN'S VOICE: Who is this?

PAVLO: Hollering . . . hollering . . . poor creature . . . locked inside, can't get out, can't—

WOMAN'S VOICE: Pavlo?

PAVLO: Do you know me? Yes. Yes, it is me, Pavlo. Pavlo

Hummel. . . . Joanna . . . And I am calling to ask how can you have lived to this day away from me?

WOMAN'S VOICE: Pavlo, listen.

PAVLO: Yes. I am. I do.

WOMAN'S VOICE: This isn't Joanna.

PAVLO: What?

WOMAN'S VOICE: This is Mrs. Sorrentino, Pavlo. Joanna isn't here.

PAVLO: What?

WOMAN'S VOICE: I said "Joanna isn't here," Pavlo. This is her mother; may I have her call you?

PAVLO: What?

WOMAN'S VOICE: I said, "May I have her call you? Or did you just call to say hello?

PAVLO: Who is this?

WOMAN'S VOICE: Pavlo, what's wrong with you?

PAVLO: Who are you? I don't know who this is. You get off the line, goddamnit, you hear me, or I'll report you to the telephone company. I'll report you to Bell Telephone. And GE, too. And the Coke Company and General Motors.

(*The woman hangs up the phone.*)

You'll be hurtin' baby. I report you to all those people. Now you tell me where she is. Where is she?

(*And behind him a light pops on, a table lamp. His mother, a small, dark-haired woman, plump, fashionably dressed, has been there for some time, sitting in the dark, listening. She begins to speak almost at the same instant the light goes on.*)

MRS. HUMMEL: In Stratford, Connecticut, Pavlo. Pregnant more than likely. Vomiting in the morning. Yes . . . trying to . . . get . . . rid of . . . it . . . Hello, Pavlo . . . I wrote you that. . . . I wrote you.

(*Silence.*)

Hello . . . Pavlo. I wrote you she was married. Why are you calling? Why?

(*Silence.*)

Pavlo? Listen, are you finished on the phone and could we talk a minute? I don't want to interrupt. . . . I only have a few . . . few things to say. They won't take long. I've been working since you've been gone. Did you know?

(*As she continues to talk,* PAVLO *slowly hangs up the telephone and places it on the footlocker.*)

Doing quite well. Quite well indeed. In a department store. Yes. One of the smaller ones. Yes. And we had an awful, awful shock there the other day, and that's what I want to tell you about. There's a woman, Sally Kelly, and Ken was her son, in the army like you now, and he went overseas last August. Well, I talked to Sally when I went in at noon and she was in the lunchroom writing a little card to Ken and she let me read it. She knew that you were in the army so she said she was sure I knew the way it was consolation to write a little note. Then about five forty-five I was working on the shoes and I saw two army officers come up the escalator and talk to one of the other clerks. I never gave them another thought and at six o'clock Sally came through and went down the escalator and made a remark to me and laughed a little and went on down. In about fifteen more minutes I was waiting on a lady and she said to me, "Isn't that terrible about the lady's son who works downstairs?" I said, "Who?" She said, "The lady who works at your candy department just got word her son was killed in Vietnam." Well, I was really shook when I heard that and I said, "Oh, you must be mistaken. She just went downstairs from her supper hour and I talked to her and she was fine." She said, "Well, that's what I heard on the main floor." Well, I went right to the phone and called the reception desk and they said it was true. This is what happened, this is what I want to tell you. The officers had gone to Sally's house, but no one was home so they talked to the neighbors and found out Sally worked at the store. So they went up to our receptionist and asked for our manager. He wasn't in so they asked for one of the men and Tommy Bottle came and they told him they needed his help because they had to tell one of the employees that her son was killed in Vietnam. Tommy really got shook, as you can imagine, and he took the officers to Mr. Brenner's office and closed the door. While they were in there, Sally came out of the lunchroom and came downstairs. Joyce, the girl who is the receptionist, knew by this time and Sally laughed when she went by and said that she better get to work or something like that. Joyce said later on that she could hardly look at her. Anyway, Tommy called the floorman from first floor to come up and he told him what had happened and then he had to go back down to first floor and tell Sally she was wanted in Mr. Brenner's office. She said, "Oh boy, what have I done now?" By the time she got to the fourth floor, the office door was open and she saw the two army men and said, "Oh, dear God, not Kenny." (*Pause.*) A mother . . . and her children should be as a tree and her branches. . . . A mother spends . . . but she gets . . . change. You think me a fool . . . don't you. There are many who do. (*Pause.*) He joined to be a mechanic and they transferred him to Infantry so he was killed on December first. So you see . . . I know what to expect. I know . . . what you're trying to do.

PAVLO: Who . . . was . . . my father? Where is he?

MRS. HUMMEL: You know that.

PAVLO: No, I want you to tell me.

MRS. HUMMEL: I've already told you.

PAVLO: No, where is he now? What did he look like?

MRS. HUMMEL: I wrote it all in a letter. I put it all in an envelope, I sealed it, mailed it.

PAVLO: I never got it.

MRS. HUMMEL: I think you did.

PAVLO: No!

MRS. HUMMEL: No, you had many fathers, many men, movie men, filmdom's great—all of them, those grand old men of yesteryear, they were your father. The Fighting Seventy-sixth, do you remember, oh, I remember, little Jimmy, what a tough little mite he was, and how he leaped upon that grenade, did you see, my God what a glory, what a glorious thing with his little tin hat.

PAVLO: My real father!

MRS. HUMMEL: He was like them, the ones I showed you in movies, I pointed them out.

PAVLO: What was his name?

MRS. HUMMEL: I've told you.

PAVLO: No. What was his name? I don't know what it was.

MRS. HUMMEL: Is it my fault you've forgotten?

PAVLO: You never told me.

MRS. HUMMEL: I did. I whispered it in your ear. You were three. I whispered the whole thing in your ear!

PAVLO: Lunatic!

MRS. HUMMEL: Nooooo!

PAVLO: Insane, hideous person!

MRS. HUMMEL: I've got to go to bed now. I have to get my rest.

(*Her back is turned. She is walking to leave him.*)

PAVLO: (*Yelling.*) I picked this girl up in this bar tonight, and when I took her home and got her to the door and kissed her, her tongue went into my mouth. I thought that meant she was going to let me into her apartment. "Don't get hurt," she said, "and get in touch when you get back; I'd love to see you." She knew I was going overseas; did you? And then the door was shut and all I wanted to say was, "What are you doing sticking your tongue in my mouth and then leaving me, you goddamn stuck-up motherin' bitch." But I didn't say anything.

MRS. HUMMEL: (*As she leaves.*) Yes . . . well . . . I'll . . . see you in the morning.

ARDELL: (*Who has been watching.*) Oh, man, how come? You wanted to get laid, how come you didn't do like the ole Sarge told you steada gettin' all tore up with them walkin' blues? Take you a little money, the ole Sarge say, roll it up longways, put it in your fly, man, so it stickin' out. Then go on walkin' up and down the street, that green stickin' right outa your fly. You get laid. You got that money stickin' outa your fly, you get laid. You get your nut! How come you didn't do that?

OFFICER: (*Who has been standing on the rear platform at parade rest.*) And the following will depart CONUS twelve August nineteen sixty-six for the Republic of Vietnam on assignment to the Twenty-third Field Hospital. Thomas. Simpson. Horner. Hinkle. Hummel.

PAVLO: I don't wanna be no medic!

(*And the bar music starts.* YEN *and* MAMASAN, *an older Vietnamese woman, enter from one side of the stage,* SGT. BRISBEY *is calling from the other, and then his hospital bed on wheels is pushed on by two soldiers. Meanwhile* ARDELL *has hauled off the footlocker with the telephone. Now visible on the floor is a pile of clothes,* PAVLO's *jungle fatigues, which he immediately starts getting into.* YEN *is at the bar. All this happens nearly simultaneously.* MAMASAN, *scurrying about, exits.*)

YEN: Hey, GI cheap Charlie, you want one more beer?

JONES: (*Offstage.*) One Bomniba, one beer.

SGT. BRISBEY: Pavlo.

YEN: (*As* JONES, *in a bright-colored walking suit, enters.*) EEEEEEaaaaaa? What you talk? One Bomniba, one beer. Same-same, huh? I no stand. What you want?

JONES: (*Pursuing her* [*both are playing, yet both have real anger*].) You gimme boocoup now?

YEN: Boocoup what? I don't know what you want. Crazy GI, you dinky dow.

SGT. BRISBEY: *Pavlo!*

PAVLO: (*Who is still putting on the fatigues.*) I'm in the can, Brisbey. I'll be there in a minute.

ARDELL: He be there, Brisbey.

JONES: You got lips as fat as mine, you know that, Ho?

YEN: Tôi không biêt.

JONES: Shit, you don't know.

YEN: Shit. I can say, too. I know. Shit.
(*And he is reaching for her.*)
No. We fini. Fini. You no talk me no more, you numba fuckin' ten.
(*She bounces away to sit on a crate and look at sheet music.*)

SGT BRISBEY: Do you know, Pavlo? I saw the metal point of that mine sticking up from the ground just under my foot—I said, "That's a mine. I'm stepping on a mine." And my foot went right on down and I felt the pin sink and heard the first small . . . pop. I jumped . . . like a fool. And up she came right outa the ground. I hit at it with my hand as if to push it away, it came up so slow against my hand. . . . Steel . . . bits . . . of dirt . . .

PAVLO: I'm off duty now, Brisbey.

ARDELL: Ole Brisbey got himself hit by a Bouncin' Betty. That a kind of land mine; you step on it, she jump up to about right here (*Indicating his waist.*). . . . Then she blow you in half. That why she got that name. Little yellow man dug a hole, put it in, hoped he'd come around. He an old man, damn near; got seventeen years in the army; no legs no more, no balls, one arm.

(*A small Vietnamese boy comes running by and grabs* PAVLO's *hand.*)

BOY: Hey, GI, show you numba one! (*He guides him into the whorehouse-bar and leaves him there.*)

PAVLO: (*To* JONES, *who is sitting there drinking a beer.*) Hey, what's goin' on?

JONES: What's happenin', man?

MAMASAN: (*Returning.*) Hello, hello! You come my house, I am glad. Do you want a beer? I have. Do you want a girl? I have. Numba one girl. Numba one. You want?

PAVLO: (*Pointing to* MAMASAN.) You?

MAMASAN: No, no, I am Mamasan. But I have many girl. You see, maybe you like. Maybe you want short-time, huh? Maybe you want long time. I don't know, you tell me. All numba one.

JONES: (*Laughs.*) Man, don't you believe that ole lady, yo just gotta get on and ride. (*Indicating* YEN) Like her. I been. And I'm restin' to go again; an' I don't think it any kinda numba one; but I been outa the world so *damn* long. I jus' close my eyes an' jive my own self— "That ain't no dead person," I say, "that ain't no dead Ho jus' 'cause she layin' so still. I saw her walk in here." I mean, man they so screwed up over here. They got no nature. You understand me, Bro? They got no nature, these women. You—how long you been over here?

PAVLO: Not long; couple a weeks.

JONES: You new then, huh?

PAVLO: Yeh.

JONES: You wanna go? (*Reaching out toward* YEN, *who is*

across the room, calling to her.) Hey, Ho! C'mon over
here!

YEN: You talk me?

JONES: Yeh, Baby, you. C'mon over here. You wanna go,
man?

PAVLO: (*Taking a seat.*) What about the VD?

JONES: (—*Big laugh.*) What about it?

YEN: (*Approaching with a beer.*) I no have. I no sick. No.
No sweat, GI. You want short-time me, no sweat.

JONES: Shit, Ho, you insides rotten. You Vietnamee, ain't
you? Vietnamee same-same VD.

YEN: No! No sick! (*As* JONES *grabs her, sets her down on*
PAVLO's *lap*) What you do? No.

JONES: I'm jus' tryin' ta help you get some money, Baby. I
be you Sportsman. Okay. (*Holding her in place.*) You
just sit on down an' be nice on the man's lap, pretty
soon he ain't gonna be worried 'bout no VD. if you
jus' . . . sorta shift (*He demonstrates.*) every now and
then. Okay. . . .

   (*She is still now and he turns his attention to* PAVLO.)
Now, lemme tell you 'bout it, lemme tell you how it is.
It be hot, man. I come from Georgia, and it get hot in
Georgia, but it ain't ever been this kinda hot, am I lyin'?
An' you gonna be here one year, and that three hundred
sixty-five days, so you gonna sweat. Now do you think
I'm lyin'?

   (YEN *is touching* PAVLO, *rubbing under his shirt.*)

PAVLO: I ain't never sweat so much.

JONES: So that's what I'm sayin'. You gonna be here and
you gonna sweat. And you gonna be here and you
gonna get VD! You worried about sweatin'? Ahhhhh.
You grinnin'. So I see I have made my meanin' clear.

   (YEN *has been rubbing* PAVLO's *thigh.*)
How you feelin' now? She kinda nice, huh? She kinda
soft and nice.

PAVLO: Where you work?

JONES: (—*Laughs.*) Don't you be askin' me where I work.
That ain't what you wanna know. I gotta get you
straight, my man, gotta get outa here, buy myself some
supplies. My ole mom all the time tellin' me, "Don't you

go near that PX. You get blown away for sure. Them VCs gotta wanna get that PX." Ain't it a world of trouble?

PAVLO: (*To* YEN.) What's your name?

YEN: Name me Yen.

PAVLO: Name me Pavlo. Pavlo.

YEN: Paaa-blo.

PAVLO: How much?

JONES: Lord, she says his name, he loves her.

YEN: You want short-time: I ask Mamasan.

(*But* MAMASAN *has been watching.*)

MAMASAN: (*Approaching.*) Okay. Okay. Yen numba one. I am happy. Five hundred P's.

JONES: Two hundred.

MAMASAN: She very beautiful.

JONES: Two fifty.

MAMASAN: Four hundred, can do. No sweat.

JONES: Mamasan, who you think you jivin'?

MAMASAN: Yen boocoup boyfriend! She very love!

JONES: Two fifty.

MAMASAN: (*To* PAVLO.) Three hundred twenty. You, huh? Three hundred twenty.

JONES: Pavlo, give her three hundred; tell her things is tough at home, she don't know.

MAMASAN: (*As* PAVLO *hands her the money.*) No, no, I talk you three hundred twenty!

JONES: And I talk him three hundred, Mamasan, three hundred!

MAMASAN: (*Softly, whiny, to* PAVLO.) GI, you be nice; you give Mamasan ten P's more. GI? Ten P's very easy you!

PAVLO: (*To* JONES.) How much *is* ten P's, man?

JONES: Eight cents, or about—

PAVLO: Eight cents! Eight cents. Over eight goddamn stupid cents I'm standin' here!

JONES: (*As* PAVLO *is giving more money to* MAMASAN.) Man, no!

MAMASAN: (*Patting* PAVLO *on the back.*) Okay, okay. You numba one—

YEN: (*Taking* PAVLO *by the hand toward the bed.*) I show you.

JONES: (*As he leaves.*) Oh man, deliver me from these green troops; they makin' everybody fat but me.
  (*The whistle blows loudly, and the troops come roaring on and into formation, facing the tower.*)
SGT. TOWER: GEN'LMEN!
  (*And his voice stops* PAVLO, *who comes to attention kneeling on the bed.* YEN *has jumped onto the bed. As* SGT. TOWER *continues his speech, she unbuttons* PAVLO's *pants, unbuttons his shirt, takes his pants down—all this as* SGT. TOWER *gives instructions.*)
(*Holding up a rifle.*) This an M-sixteen rifle, this the best you country got. Now we got to make you good enough to have it. You got to have feelin' for it, like it a good woman to you, like it you arm, like it you rib. The command is "Right shoulder . . . *harms!*" At the command "harms," raise and carry the rifle diagonally across the body, at the same time grasping it at the balance with the left hand, trigger guard in the hollow of the bone. Then carry the left hand, thumb and fingers extended, to the small of the stock, and cut away smartly, and everything about . . . you, Trainee, is at the position of attention. RIGHT SHOULDER . . . HARMS!
THE men: (*Performing the drill* [*as* PAVLO *also yells and performs it in pantomime with them*].) ONE, TWO, THREE, FOUR.
SGT. TOWER: You got to love this rifle, Gen'lmen, like it you pecker and you love to make love. You got to care about how it is and what can it do and what can it not do, what do it want and need. ORDER HARMS!
THE MEN and PAVLO: ONE, TWO, THREE, FOUR.
SGT. TOWER: RIGHT SHOULDER . . . HARMS!
THE MEN and PAVLO: ONE, TWO, THREE, FOUR.
CORPORAL: FORWARD HARCH!
  (*And* PAVLO *pulls up his trousers and marches.*)
SGT. TOWER: AIN'T NO USE IN GOIN' HOME . . .
THE MEN: AIN'T NO USE IN GOIN' HOME . . .
  (PAVLO's *marching is joyous.*)
SGT. TOWER: JODY GOT YOUR GAL AND GONE . . .
THE MEN: JODY HUMPIN' ON AND ON.

(*Something of* PAVLO's *making love to* YEN *is in his marching.*)

SGT. TOWER: AIN'T NO USE IN GOIN' BACK . . .

THE MEN: JODY GOT OUR CADILLAC.

CORPORAL: LORD HAVE MERCY, I'M SO BLUE . . .

THE MEN: IT TWO MORE WEEKS TILL I BE THROUGH.

CORPORAL: Count cadence, delayed cadence, count cadence—count!

(*And the men, performing delayed cadence, exit.* PAVLO *counts with them, marching away beside the bed, around the bed, leaping upon the bed as the counting comes to its loud end.*)

SGT. BRISBEY: ([*Who has been onstage in his bed all this while*], *calling.*) Pavlo!

PAVLO: Just a second, Brisbey!

SGT. BRISBEY: Pavlo!

PAVLO: (*Crossing toward* BRISBEY.) Whatta you want, Brisbey?

SGT. BRISBEY: Pavlo, can I talk to you a little?

PAVLO: Sure.

SGT. BRISBEY: You're a medic, right?

PAVLO: Yeh.

SGT. TOWER: But you're not a conscientious objector, are you? So you got a rifle.

PAVLO: Sure.

(PAVLO *is busy now with* BRISBEY's *pulse and chart, straightening the bed, preparing the shot he must give.*)

SGT. BRISBEY: I like the feel of 'em. I like to hold 'em.

PAVLO: I'm not gonna get my rifle for you, Brisbey.

SGT. BRISBEY: Just as a favor.

PAVLO: No.

SGT. BRISBEY: It's the only pleasure I got anymore.

PAVLO: Lemme give you a hypo; you got a visitor; you can see him before you sleep.

SGT. BRISBEY: The egg that slept, that's what I am. You think I look like an egg with a head?

(PAVLO *is preparing the needle. There is a figure off in the shadows.*)

Or else I'm a stump. Some guys, they get hit, they have a stump. I am a stump.

PAVLO: What about your visitor; you wanna see him?

(*And the figure,* SGT. WALL, *steps forward. He is middle-aged, gray-haired, chunky.*)

SGT. BRISBEY: Henry?

SGT. WALL: It's me, Brisbey, how you doin'?

SGT. BRISBEY: Henry, Henry, who was the first man round the world, Henry? That's what I want to know. Where's the deepest pit in the ocean? You carryin'? What do you have? Forty-five? You must have a blade. Magellan. Threw out a rope. I ever tell you that story? Gonna go sleepy-bye. Been tryin' to get young Pavlo Hummel to put me away, but he prefers to break needles on me. How's the unit? You tell 'em I'll be back. You tell 'em, soon as I'm well, I'll be back.

SGT. WALL: I'm off the line . . . now, Brisbey. No more boonies. I'm in Supply now.

SGT. BRISBEY: Supply? What . . . do you supply? (*Slight pause, as if bewildered. Thinking, yet with bitterness.*) If I promise to tell you the secret of life, Henry, will you slit my throat? You can do it while I'm sleeping.

PAVLO: Don't he just go on?

SGT. BRISBEY: Young Hummel here, tell him who you love. Dean Martin. Looks at ole Dino every chance he gets. And "Combat." Vic Morrow, man. Keeps thinkin' he's gonna see himself. Dino's cool, huh. Drunk all the time.

PAVLO: That's right.

SGT. BRISBEY: You fuckin' asshole. Henry. Listen. You ever think to yourself, "Oh, if only it wasn't Brisbey. I'd give anything. My own legs. Or one, anyway. Arms. Balls. Prick." Ever . . . Henry?

(*Silence.*)

SGT. WALL: No.

SGT. BRISBEY: Good. Don't. Because I have powers I never dreamed of and I'll hear you if you do, Henry, and I'll take them. I'll rip them off you.

(*Silence.*)

SGT. WALL: You'll be goin' home soon. I thought . . . we could plan to get together. . . .

SGT. BRISBEY: Right. Start a softball team.

SGT. WALL: Jesus Christ, Brisbey, ain't you ever gonna change? Ain't you ever gonna be serious about no—

SGT. BRISBEY: I have changed, Motherfucker. You blind or somethin' askin' me if I changed. You get the fuck outa here, hear me?

(WALL *is leaving, having left a pint of whiskey*.)

You take a tree, you cut off its limbs, whatta you got? You got a stump. A living feeling thinking stump.

PAVLO: You're not a tree, Brisbey.

SGT. BRISBEY: And what terrible cruelty is that? Do you know? There is responsibility. I want you to get me that rifle. To save you from the sin of cruelty, Pavlo.

(As PAVLO *is moving with alcohol, cotton, to prepare the shot*.)

You are cruel, Pavlo . . . you and God. The both of you.

PAVLO: Lemme do this, man.

SGT. BRISBEY: (As PAVLO *gives the shot*.) Do you know . . . if you were to get the rifle, Pavlo, I'd shoot you first. It's how you end up anyway. I'd save you time. Get you home quicker. I know you, boy.

PAVLO: Shut up, man. Relax . . .

SGT. BRISBEY: You've made me hate you.

PAVLO: I'm sorry. I didn't mean that to happen.

SGT. BRISBEY: No, no, you're not sorry. You're not. You're glad it's me, you're glad it's not you. God's always glad that way because it's never him, it's always somebody else. Except that once. The only time we was ever gonna get him, he tried to con us into thinkin' we oughta let him go. Make it somebody else again. But we got through all that shit he was talkin' and hung on and got him good—fucked him up good—nailed him up good . . . just once . . . for all the billion times he got us.

PAVLO: Brisbey, sometimes I don't think you know what you're sayin'.

(A CAPTAIN *enters upstage left, carrying clipboard*.)

CAPTAIN: Grennel.

GRENNEL: (*Appearing from the back, far upstage*.) Yes, Sir.

CAPTAIN: Go get me Hummel. He's down with Brisbey.

SGT. BRISBEY: I keep thinkin', Pavlo, 'bout this kid got his hand blown off and he kept crawlin' round lookin' for his fingers. Couldn't go home without 'em, he said, he'd catch hell. No fingers.

(PAVLO *shakes his head.*)

I keep thinkin' about ole Magellan, sailin' round the world. Ever hear of him, Pavlo? So one day he wants to know how far under him to the bottom of the ocean. So he drops over all the rope he's got. Two hundred feet. It hangs down into the sea that must go down and down beyond its end for miles and tons of water. He's up there in the sun. He's got this little piece of rope danglin' from his fingers. He thinks because all the rope he's got can't touch bottom, he's over the deepest part of the ocean. He doesn't know the real question. How far beyond all the rope you got is the bottom?

PAVLO: Brisbey, I'm gonna tell you somethin'. I tried to kill myself once. Honest to God. And it's no good. You understand me. I don't know what I was thinkin' about. I mean, you understand it was a long time ago and I'd never been laid yet or done hardly anything, but I have since and it's fantastic. I just about blew this girl's head off, it was fantastic, but if I'd killed myself, it'd never a happened. You see what I'm sayin', Brisbey? Somethin' fantastic might be comin' to you.

GRENNEL: (*Entering.*) Hummel. Man, the Captain wants to see you.

PAVLO: Captain Miller? Captain Miller!

(*He leaves.*)

SGT. BRISBEY: Pavlo!

GRENNEL: (*As he wheels* BRISBEY *off.*) How you doin', Brisbey?

PAVLO: (*Rushing up to the* CAPTAIN, *who stands with his clipboard.*) Sir, PFC Hummel reporting as ordered.

CAPTAIN: Good afternoon, Hummel.

PAVLO: Good afternoon, Sir.

CAPTAIN: Are you smiling, Hummel?

PAVLO: Excuse me, Sir.

CAPTAIN: Your ten-forty-nine says you're not happy at all;

it says you want a transfer out of this unit because you're ashamed to serve with us. I was wondering how could you be ashamed and smiling simultaneously, Hummel.

PAVLO: I don't know, Sir.

CAPTAIN: That's not a very good answer.

PAVLO: No, Sir.

CAPTAIN: Don't you think what you're doing here is important? You helped out with poor Brisbey, didn't you?

PAVLO: Yes, Sir.

CAPTAIN: That's my point, Hummel. There are people alive who would be dead if you hadn't done your job. Those invalids you care for, you feed them when they can't, you help them urinate, defecate, simple personal things they can't do for themselves but would die without. Have you asked any one of them if they think what you are doing is important or not, or if you should be ashamed?

PAVLO: Yes, Sir . . . more or less. But . . . I . . . just think I'd be better off in squad duty.

(*Distant firing and yelling are heard to which neither the* CAPTAIN *nor* PAVLO *respond. There is a quality of echo to the gunfire; then there is a clattering and* PAR-HAM, *a young Negro PFC, appears at the opposite side of the stage in full combat gear except for his helmet, which is missing. He has come a few steps onto the stage. He crouches.*)

PARHAM: Damn, baby, why that ole sarge gotta pick on me?

PAVLO: I'm Regular Army, Sir; I'm going to extend my tour.

CAPTAIN: You like it here, Hummel?

PARHAM: Damn that ole sarge. I run across that field I get shot sure as hell. (*He breathes.*) Lemme count to five. Lemme do it on five.

CAPTAIN: How many days left in your tour, Hummel?

PARHAM: Lemme do it like track and field.

PAVLO: I enlisted because I wanted to be a soldier, Sir, and I'm not a soldier here. Four nights ago on perimeter guard, I tried to set up fields of fire with the other men in the bunker—do you know what I mean, Sir? Designating who would be responsible for what sector of terrain in case of an attack? And they laughed at me; they just sat on the bunker and talked all night and they didn't stay low and they didn't hide their cigarettes when they smoked or anything.

PARHAM: FIVE!

(*And he runs no more than two steps before a loud explosion hits. He goes down, bounces, and rolls onto his back, slamming his fist into the ground in outrage.*)

DAMNIT! I KNEW IT! I KNEW IT! I KNEW IT!

CAPTAIN: You want the VC to come here?

PAVLO: I want to feel, Sir, that I'm with a unit Victor Charlie considers valuable enough to want to get it. And I hope I don't have to kill anyone; and I hope I don't get killed.

PARHAM: (*Still trying but unable to rise.*) Medic? Medic? Man, where you at? C'mon out here to me! Crawl on out here to me.

PAVLO: But maybe you can't understand what I'm saying, Sir, because you're an ROTC officer and not OCS, Sir.

CAPTAIN: You mean I'm not Regular Army, Hummel.

PAVLO: An ROTC officer and an OCS officer are not the same thing.

CAPTAIN: Is that so, Hummel?

PAVLO: I think so, Sir.

CAPTAIN: You want to get killed, don't you, Hummel?

PAVLO: No, Sir. No.

CAPTAIN: And they will kill you, Hummel, if they get the chance. Do you believe that? That you will die if shot, or hit with shrapnel, that your arm can disappear into shreds, or your leg vanish—do you believe that, Hummel? That you can and will, if hit hard enough, gag and vomit and die . . . be buried and rot—do you believe yourself capable of that? . . .

PAVLO: Yes . . . Sir. I . . . do . . .

PARHAM: Nooooooo! (*Quick pause. He looks about.*) Ohhh, shit, somebody don't help me, Charlie gonna come in here, cut me up, man. He gonna do me.

CAPTAIN: All right, Hummel.

PARHAM: Oh, Lord, you get me outa here, I be good, man. I be good, no shit, Lord, I'm tellin' it.

CAPTAIN: All right . . . you're transferred. I'll fix it.

(PAVLO *salutes. The captain salutes, pivots, exits.* PAVLO *moves to change into combat gear, which he finds in a footlocker. He exists.*)

PARHAM: What's happenin'? I don't know what's happenin'!

(*And the light goes, and he is alone in the jungle, in a center of flickering silver. It is night, there are sounds.*)

Hummel, c'mon. It's me, man, Parham; and I ain't jivin', mister. I been shot. I been truly shot.

(*He pauses, breathing, raises his head to look down at himself.*)

Ohhhh, look at me; ohhh, look at my poor stomach. Ohhhh, look at me, look at me. Oh, baby, stop it, stop bleedin', stop it, stop it; you my stomach, I'm talkin' to you, I'm tellin' you what to do, YOU STOP IT!

(*His hands are pressing furiously on his stomach. And he lies for a moment in silence before shuddering and beginning again.*)

SOMEBODY GET ME A DUSTOFF! Dustoff control, do you hear me? This here PFC Jay Charles Johnson Parham. I am coordinates X-ray Tango Foxtrot . . . Lima. . . . Do you hear me? I hurtin', baby . . . hear me. Don't know what to do for myself . . . can't remember . . . don't know what it is gone wrong. . . . Requesting one med-evac chopper. . . . I am one litter patient, gunshot wounds, stomach. Area secure. C'mon hear me . . . this ole nigger . . . he gonna die.

(*Two* VIETCONG, *appearing soundlessly, are suddenly upon him. One carries a rifle.*)

1ST VC: Hello, GI.

PARHAM: Oh, no. Oh, no. No.

1ST VC: (*Very singsong.*) Okay. Okay.

2ND VC: You numba one.

PARHAM: Get away from me! I talkin' to you, Charlie, you get away from me! You guys get away from me! MEDIC! ME—

(*They say, "Okay, okay," "You numba one."* At a
nod from the VIETCONG with the weapon, his partner
has jumped forward into a sitting position at PAR-
HAM's *head, one leg pinning down each shoulder, the
hands grasping under his chin, stuffing a rag into his
mouth. There are only the sounds of the struggle. The
other* VIETCONG *approaches and crouches over* PAR-
HAM, *holding a knife over him.* PARHAM *stares, and
his feet move slowly back and forth.*)

1ST VC: Numba one, you can see, GI? Airplane me . . .
Vietnam. Have many bomb. Can do boom-boom, you
stand! (*He moves the knife up and down.*) Same-same
you, many friends me, fini. Where airplane now, GI?
Where Very gun?

(*And he places the blade against* PARHAM's *chest, and*
PARHAM *behind his gag begins to howl, begins to flail
his pinioned arms and beat his heels furiously upon
the ground.*)

Okay, okay . . . ! Óng di dâu?

(*Then the knife goes in and the* VIETCONG *get up to
stand over* PARHAM, *as he turns onto his side and pulls
himself into a knot as if to protect himself, knees tight
to his chest, arms over his head. They unbuckle his
pistol belt, take his flak vest and billfold from his
pocket, and are working at removing his shirt when
they both straighten at a sound. They seize his fallen
rifle and run to disappear.* PAVLO *appears, moving
low, accompanied by* RYAN.)

RYAN: Man, I'm tellin' you let's get outa here.

PAVLO: (*Pointing.*) No, no. There. (*He has a circular belt
hooked over his shoulder, and he moves toward the
body.*) Just look.

(RYAN *is following.*)

Hey, man . . . hey . . . (*He rolls* PARHAM *over.*)
Ohhhhh . . . look at him.

RYAN: It's Parham.

PAVLO: Man, he's all cut. . . .

RYAN: Pavlo, let's get outa here! (*And he starts to move
off.*) What the hell's it matter?

PAVLO: I'll carry him.

RYAN: (*As* PAVLO *hands him his rifle.*) I ain't worried about who has to carry him, for chrissake, I wanna get outa here. (*On the move.*) I'm gonna hustle over there to the side there.

PAVLO: Nooooooo . . .

RYAN: Give you some cover.

(*And* RYAN *is gone, leaving* PAVLO *with the body. The carrier's procedure, which* PAVLO *undertakes through the following speeches, is this: He places the circular belt under the dead man's buttocks, one length along his back, the other below and across his legs, so that two loops are formed, one on either side of the man. He then lies down with his back to the dead man and fits his arms through the two loops. He grasps the man's left arm with his own right hand and rolls to his right so that the man rolls with him and is on his back. He then rises to one knee, keeping the body pressed tightly to his own. As* PAVLO *begins this task,* ARDELL *is there, appearing as* RYAN *departs.*)

ARDELL: How many that make?

PAVLO: What's that?

ARDELL: Whatta you think, man? Dead bodies!

PAVLO: Who the hell's countin?'

ARDELL: Looookeeeee. Gettin' ta *beeeee bad!*

PAVLO: This one's nothin'. When they been out here a couple a days, man, that's when it's interesting—you go to pick 'em up, they fall apart in you hands, man. They're mud—pink mud—like turnin' over a log, all maggots and ants. You see Ryan over there hidin' in the bushes. I ain't hidin' in no bushes. And Parham's glad about that. They're all glad. Nobody wants to think he's gonna be let lay out here.

ARDELL: Ain't you somethin'.

PAVLO: I'm diggin' it, man. Blowin' people away. Cuttin' 'em down. Got two this afternoon I saw and one I didn't even see—just heard him out there jabberin' away— (*And he makes a sound mimicking a Vietnamese speaking.*) And I walked a good goddamn twenty rounds right over where it sounded like he was: he shut up his fuckin' face. It ain't no big thing.

ARDELL: Like bringin' down a deer . . . or dog.

PAVLO: Man, people's all I ever killed. Ohhhh, I feel you
thinkin', "This poor boy don't know what he's doin';
don't know what he got into." But I do. I got a dead boy
in my hands. In a jungle . . . the middle a the night. I
got people maybe ten feet away, hidin'—they gonna
maybe cut me down the minute I move. And I'm
gonna . . . (*During all this he has struggled to load the
body like a pack on his back. Now he is rising. Is on his
knee.*) . . . take this dead thing back and people are
gonna look at me when I do it. They're gonna think I'm
crazy and be glad I'm with 'em. I'm diggin'—
   (*And the* FIRST VIETCONG *comes streaking out from a
   hiding place.*)
Ryan, Ryan, Ryan!
   (*And the* VIETCONG, *without stopping, plunges the
   knife into* PAVLO's *side and flees off.* PAVLO *falls, unable, because of the body on his back, to protect himself.*)
What happened?

ARDELL: The blood goin' out a hole in your guts, man;
turn you into water.

PAVLO: He hit me. . . .

ARDELL: *Turn you into water!* Blood goin' in the brain
make you think; in your heart make you move; in your
prick makes you hard, makes you come. *You lettin' it
drop all over the ground!*

PAVLO: I won't . . . I'll . . . noooooo. . . . (*Trying to
free himself of the body.*) Ryan . . .

ARDELL: The knowledge comin', baby. I'm talkin' about
what your kidney know, not your fuckin' fool's head.
I'm talkin' about your skin and what it sayin', thin as
paper. We melt; we tear and rip apart. Membrane, baby.
Cellophane. Ain't that some shit.

PAVLO: I'll lift my arm. (*But he can't.*)

ARDELL: Ain't that some shit.

PAVLO: Noooooo . . .

ARDELL: A bullet like this finger bigger than all your
fuckin' life. Ain't this finger some shit.

PAVLO: RYAN.

ARDELL: I'm tellin' you.

PAVLO: Nooooo.

ARDELL: RYAN!

PAVLO: RYAN!

ARDELL: (*As* RYAN *comes running on with a second soldier.*) Get on in here.

> (*The two soldiers struggle to free* PAVLO *from the body, as* SGT. TOWER *comes striding on and mounts his platform.* PAVLO, *being dragged off by the soldiers, yells and yells.*)

PAVLO: Ryan, we tear. We rip apart. Ryan, we tear. (*He is gone.*)

SGT. TOWER: You gonna see some funny shit, Gen'lmen. You gonna see livin' breathin' people disappear. Walkin' talkin' buddies. And you gonna wanna kill and say their name. When you been in so many fights and you come out, you a survivor. It what you are and do. You survive.

> (*As a body detail removes* PARHAM.)

ARDELL: Thin and frail.

SGT. TOWER: Gen'lmen, can you hear me?

ARDELL: Yes, Sergeant.

SGT. TOWER: I saw this rifle one time get blown right outa this boy's hands and him start wailin' and carryin' on right there how he ain't ever goin' back on no line; he'll die for sure, he don't have that one rifle in all the world. You listenin' to me, Gen'lmen? I'm gonna tell you now what you do when you lost and it black, black night. The North Star show you true north accurate all year round. You gonna see the Big Dipper and two stars on the end called the pointer and they where the water would come on outa that dipper if it had water in it, and straight out from there is this big damn star, and that the North Star, and once you know north you ain't lost no more!

> (*And* PAVLO *has appeared, walking slowly as in a dream, looking at* SGT. TOWER.)

PAVLO: YES, SERGEANT!

> (*An explosion hits, and* PAVLO, *yelling, goes down.*)

ARDELL: What you sayin'? Yes, Sergeant.

PAVLO: (*Struggling to rise.*) YES, SERGEANT!

ARDELL: Ask him what about that grenade come flyin'? How come if you so cool, If you such a tox, you don't know nothin' to do with no grenade but stand there holdin' it—get your abdominal and groin area blown to shit.

PAVLO: I DON'T KNOW WHAT YOU'RE TALKING ABOUT!

ARDELL: You walkin' talkin' scar, what you think you made of?

PAVLO: I got my shit together.

ARDELL: HOW MANY TIMES YOU GONNA LET 'EM HIT YOU?

PAVLO: AS MANY AS THEY WANT.

ARDELL: That man up there a fool, Jim.

PAVLO: Shut up.

ARDELL: You ever seen any North Star in your life?

PAVLO: (*On the move toward* YEN, *who is kneeling in the distance.*) I seen a lot of people pointin'.

ARDELL: They a bunch a fools pointin' at the air. "Go this way, go that way."

PAVLO: I want her, man. I need her. (*He touches her.*)

ARDELL: Where you now? What you doin'?

PAVLO: I'm with her, man.

ARDELL: You . . . in . . . her . . .

PAVLO: (*Taking her blouse off.*) . . . soon . . .

ARDELL: Why you there? . . .

PAVLO: I dunno. . . . Jus' wanna . . .

ARDELL: You jus' gonna ride. . . .

PAVLO: I jus' wanna . . .

ARDELL: There was one boy walkin' . . .

PAVLO: (*Seizing her, embracing her.*) I know; don't talk no shit.

ARDELL: Walkin' . . . singin' . . . soft, some song to himself, thinkin' on mosquitos and Coke and bug spray, until these bushes in front of him burst and his fine young legs broke in half like sticks. . . .

PAVLO: (*Rising, trying to get his trousers off.*) Leave me alone!

ARDELL: At seven his tonsils been cut out; at twelve there's appendicitis. Now he's twenty and hurtin' and screamin' at his legs, and then the gun come back. It on a fixed traversing arc to tear his yellin' fuckin' head right off.

PAVLO: Good; it's Tanner; it's Weber. It's Smith and not Pavlo. Minneti, not Pavlo. Klaus and you. You mother-fucker. But not Pavlo. Not ever.

ARDELL: You get a knife wound in the ribs.

PAVLO: It misses my heart. I'm clean.

ARDELL: You get shrapnel all up and down your back.

PAVLO: It's like a dozen fifteen bee stings, all up and down my back.

ARDELL: And there's people tellin' you you can go home if you wanna. It's your second wound. They're sayin' you can go home when you been hit twice and you don't even check. You wanna go back out, you're thinkin', get you one more gook, get you one more slopehead, make him know the reason why.

PAVLO: (*Whirling, scooping up a rifle.*) That's right. They're killin' everybody. They're fuckin' killin' every-body! (*The rifle is aimed at* ARDELL.)

ARDELL: Like it's gonna make a difference in the world, man, what you do; and somethin' made bad's gonna be all right with this one more you're gonna kill. Poor ole Ryan gets dinged round about Tay Ninh, so two weeks later in Phu Loi you blow away this goddamn farmer. . . .

(*A* FARMER, *wearing Vietnamese work clothes and a conical hat, appears in the distance, waving.*)

FARMER: Okay, GI, okay.

ARDELL: And think you're addin' somethin' up.

PAVLO: I blew him to fuckin' smithereens. He's there at twenty yards, wavin'.

FARMER: Okay, GI, okay. (*He sways in the distance.*)

PAVLO: (*Yelling at the* FARMER.) DUNG LYE. DUNG LYE. (*This is "Stop" in Vietnamese.*)

ARDELL: You don't know he's got satchel charges.

PAVLO: I do.

ARDELL: You don't know what he's got under his clothes.

PAVLO: I do. He's got dynamite all under his clothes. And I shoot him.

(*Gunshot, as* PAVLO *fires.*)

I fuckin' shoot him. He's under me. I'm screamin' down at him. RYAN. RYAN. And he's lookin' up at me. His eyes squinted like he knows by my face what I'm sayin' matters to me so maybe it matters to him. And then, all of a sudden, see, he starts to holler and shout like he's crazy, and he's pointin' at his foot, so I shoot it. (*He fires again.*) I shoot his foot and then he's screamin' and tossin' all over the ground, so I shoot into his head. (*Fires.*) I shot his head. And I get hit again. I'm standin' there over him and I get fuckin' hit again. They keep fuckin' hittin' me.

(*Explosion and* PAVLO *goes flying forward.*)

I don't know where I'm at. In my head . . . it's like I'm twelve . . . a kid again. Ardell, it's going to happen to meeeeeee. (*He is crawling.*)

ARDELL: What do you want me to do?

PAVLO: I don't want to get hit anymore.

ARDELL: What do you want me to do?

PAVLO: Tell me.

ARDELL: He was shot . . . layin' down under you, what did you see?

PAVLO: What?

ARDELL: He was squirmin' down under you in that ditch, what did you see?

PAVLO: I saw the grass . . . his head . . .

ARDELL: Noooooooooo.

PAVLO: Help me, I saw the grass, his head . . .

ARDELL: Don't you ever hear?

PAVLO: I want out, Ardell. I want out.

ARDELL: When you gonna hear me?

PAVLO: What are you tryin' to tell me? I saw blood . . . bits of brain . . .

ARDELL: Noooooooooooo!

PAVLO: The grass, the grass . . .

ARDELL: When you shot into his head, you hit into your own head, fool!

PAVLO: What? NOOOOOOOOOOOOOOO!

ARDELL: IT WAS YOUR OWN.

PAVLO: NOOOOOOOOOOOO.

(*As* ARDELL *has turned to leave.*)
Don't leave me you sonofabitch, I don't know what you're saying!
(*And* ARDELL *has stopped, with his back turned, far upstage.*)
JIVE MOTHERFUCKING BULLSHIT!
(*And* ARDELL *is leaving and gone.*)
And I . . . stood . . . lookin' . . . down . . . at that black, black Hudson River. . . . There was stars in it. . . . I'm a twelve-year-old kid. . . . I remember. . . . (*He is turning toward* YEN, *who is kneeling, singing.*) I went out toward them . . . diving . . . down. . . . (*He is moving toward* YEN, *crawling.*) They'd said there was no current, but I was twisted in all that water, fighting to get up . . . all my air burning out, couldn't get no more . . . (*Still moving toward* YEN.) and I was going down, fighting to get down. I was all confused, you see, fighting to get down, thinking it was up. I hit sand. I pounded. I pounded the bottom. I thought the bottom was the top. Black. No air.
(*The* OFFICER *enters, striding swiftly.*)
OFFICER: Yes!
(*He carries a clipboard, on which he writes as* PAVLO *runs up to him.* YEN, *though she remains kneeling, stops singing.*)
PAVLO: SIR! I've just been released from Ward Seventeen, gunshot wound in my side, and I've been ordered back to my unit, Second of the Sixteenth, First Division, and I don't think I should have to go. This is the third time I been hit. I been hit in the ribs and leg and back. . . . I think there should be more trainin' in duckin' and dodgin', Sir. I been hit by a knife, shrapnel, and bullets.
OFFICER: Could you get to the point?
PAVLO: That is the point. I want to know about this regulation sayin' you can go home after your second wounding?
OFFICER: Pardon, Hummel?
PAVLO: I been told there's this regulation you can go home

after your second wound. When you been hit twice, you can go home.

OFFICER: Hummel, wouldn't you be home if you were eligible to be home?

PAVLO: I don't know, Sir; but I wanted to stay the first two times, so I don't know and I was told I had the option the second time to go home or not, but I never checked and if I passed it by, Sir, I'd like to go back and pick it up.

OFFICER: You didn't pass it by; there's no such regulation.

PAVLO: It was a sergeant who told me.

OFFICER: These orders are valid.

PAVLO: Could you check, Sir?

OFFICER: I'm an expert on regulations, Hummel. These orders are valid. You've earned the Purple Heart. Now, go on back and do your job.

(*Raising his hand to salute, he pivots, as* PAVLO *is about to salute.*)

ARDELL: No, no.

PAVLO: I do my job.

(SGT. WALL *enters the bar, calling to* YEN. *He wears civilian clothes—slacks and a flowered, short-sleeved shirt.* YEN *moves quickly to the bar area, where she pets him and then moves to prepare a drink for him.*)

SGT. WALL: Come here, Pretty Piggy, we talk boocoup love, okay? Make plans go my home America.

YEN: Sao. (*Vietnamese for "Liar."*)

SGT. WALL: No lie.

SGT. TOWER: (*Atop his platform.* [PAVLO *standing before him*].) Gen'lmen. (*In a mournful rage.*) Lemme tell you what you do, the enemy got you, he all around you. You the prisoner. You listenin', Gen'lmen?

ARDELL: (*All despairing sarcasm.*) Yes, Sergeant.

SGT. TOWER: You got to watch out for the enemy. He gonna try to make you feel alone and you got no friends but him. He gonna make you mean and afraid; then he gonna be nice. We had a case with them North Koreans, this group a American POWs, one of 'em was wounded so he cried all night. His buddies couldn't sleep. So one

night his buddies picked him up, I'm tellin' you, they
carried him out the door into that North Korean winter,
they set him down in the snow, they lef' him there, went
on back inside. They couldn't hear him screamin' the
wind was so loud. They got their sleep. You got to
watch out for the enemy.

(PAVLO *pivots, turning away from* SGT. TOWER *and
into the bar, where* MAMASAN *greets him.* YEN *is still
with* SGT. WALL, *who is taking a big drink.*)

MAMASAN: Paaablooooo . . . how you-you. I give you
beer, okay?

PAVLO: (*Unmoving, rigid.*) Mamasan, chow ba.

SGT. WALL: (*—Having finished his drink, takes up as if in
midsentence.*) ". . . so who," he says, "was the first
motherfucker to sail 'round the world? Not Vasco da
Gama." I don't know what he's sayin'. "Who was the
first motherfucker to measure the ocean?" (*He is loud
and waving his arms.*) I don't know! He wasn't even
asking. MAMASAN! MAMASAN! ONE BEER! ONE
BEER, ONE SAIGON TEA! (*And he reaches now to
take* YEN's *hand and tug her gently around to his side of
the table, drawing her near to sit on his lap.*) Come
here; sit down. No sao. Fini sao. Boocoup love, Co Yen.
Boocoup love. (*His hand is on her breast, as she nibbles
his ear.*)

YEN: I think you maybe papasan America. Have many
babysan.

SGT. WALL: No . . . no.

YEN: I think you sao.

SGT. WALL: No lie, Yen. No wife America, no have babysan. Take you, okay?

PAVLO: Sarge!

(SGT. WALL *looks up to* PAVLO.)

Listen, I don't have too much time; I got to go pretty
soon. How long you gonna be talkin' shit to that poor
girl? I mean, see, she's the whore I usually hit on. I'm a
little anxious, I'd like to interrupt you, you gonna be at
her all fuckin' night. I'll bring her back in half an hour.

SGT. WALL: Sorry about that. Sorry—

PAVLO: I didn't ask you was you sorry.

SGT. WALL: This little girl's my girl.

PAVLO: She's a whore, man—

SGT. WALL: We got a deal, see, see; and when I'm here, she stays with me.

PAVLO: You got a deal, huh?

SGT. WALL: You guessed it, PFC.

PAVLO: Well, maybe you shoulda checked with me, you shoulda conferred with me maybe before you figured that deal was sound.

SGT. WALL: You have been informed.

PAVLO: But you don't understand, Sarge. She's the only whore here who moves me.

SGT. WALL: My baby.

PAVLO: You rear-echelon asshole!

SGT. WALL: (*Beginning to rise.*) What's that?

PAVLO: Where you think you are, the goddamn PX? This the garbage dump, man, and you don't tell me nothin' down here, let alone who I can hit on, who I can't hit on, you see what I'm sayin' to you, Fuckface.

YEN: Paablo . . . no, no . . .

PAVLO: You like this ole man?

YEN: (*Moving to face* PAVLO *and explain.*) Can be nice, Paablo . . .

PAVLO: Old man. Papasan. Can do fuck-fuck maybe one time one week. Talk, talk. Talk. No can do boom-boom. PAPASAN. NUMBA FUCKIN' TEN!

YEN: (*Angry at his stupidity.*) Shut up, Paablo. I do him. Fini him. Do you. Okay.

PAVLO: Shut up?

SGT. WALL: You heard her.

PAVLO: Shut up? (*His hand twisting in her hair.*) I don't know who you think this bitch is, Sarge, but I'm gonna fuck her whoever you think she is. I'm gonna take her in behind those curtains and I'm gonna fuck her right side up and then maybe I'm gonna turn her over, get her in her asshole, you understand me? You don't like it you best come in pull me off.

SGT. WALL: (*Switchblade popping open in his hand.*) I ain't gonna have to, Punk.

(PAVLO *kicks him squarely in the groin. He yells,
falls.*)

PAVLO: The fuck you ain't. Hey . . . were you ready for
that? Were you ready for that, ole man? (*Dragging him
along the ground, shoving him.*) Called crawlin', you
gettin' the hang of it, you ole man. Get up, get up.

(*And* SGT. WALL *moans as* PAVLO *lifts him.*)

I want you gone, you mother, you understand? I don't
wanna see you no more. You gonna disappear. You are
gonna vanish.

(*And he flings* SGT. WALL *away.* WALL *staggers, falls
and* PAVLO *picks the knife off the floor, goes for a
beer, as* SGT. TOWER *begins to speak.*)

SGT. TOWER: This is a grenade, Gen'lmen. M-twenty-six-A-
two fragmentation, Five-point-five ounces, composition
B, time fuse, thirteen feet a coiled wire inside it, like the
inside a my fist a animal and I open it and that animal
leap out to kill you. Do you know a hunk of paper flyin'
fast enough cut you in half like a knife, and when this
baby hit, fifteen meters in all directions, ONE THOU-
SAND HUNKS A WIRE GOIN' FAST ENOUGH!

(ARDELL *enters, joining* PAVLO, *who celebrates*)

PAVLO: Did I do it to him, Ardell? The triple Hummel?
Got to be big and bad. A little shuffle. Did I ever tell
you? Thirteen months a my life ago.

YEN: Paaaabloooo, boocoup love!

PAVLO: Thirteen months a my life ago.

(*And* SGT. WALL, *there in the corner, beginning to
move, is pulling pin on a grenade.*)

What she did, my ole lady, she called Joanna a slut and
I threw kitty litter, screamin'—cat shit—"Happy Birthday!" She called that sweet church-goin' girl a whore.
To be seen by her now, up tight with this odd-lookin'
whore, feelin' good and tall, ready to bed down. Feelin'—

(*And the grenade, thrown by* SGT. WALL, *lands.* WALL
flees, as PAVLO *drops to his knees, seizing the grenade.
He looks up in awe at* ARDELL. *The grenade is in his
hands in his lap.*)

Oh Christ!

(*And the explosion comes, loud; it is a storm going into darkness and changing lights. Silence. Body detail enters, as* ARDELL, *looking at* PAVLO *lying there, begins to speak. The body detail will wrap* PAVLO *in a poncho, put him on a stretcher, carry him to* ARDELL.)

ARDELL: He don't die right off. Take him four days, thirty-eight minutes. And he don't say nothin' to nobody in all that time. No words; he just kinda lay up and look, and when he die, he bitin' on his lower lip, I don't know why. So they take him, they put him in a blue rubber bag, zip it up tight, and haul him off to the morgue in the back of a quarter-ton, where he get stuck naked into the refrigerator 'long with the other boys killed that day and the beer and cheese and tuna and stuff the guys who work at the morgue keep in the refrigerator except when it inspection time. The bag get washed, hung out to dry on a line out back a the morgue. (*Slight pause.*) Then . . . lemme see, well, finally he get shipped home, and his mother cry a lot, and his brother get so depressed he gotta go out and lay his chippie he so damn depressed about it all. And Joanna, she read his name in the paper, she let out this little gasp and say to her husband across the table, "Jesus, Jimmy, I used to go with that boy. Oh, damn that war, why can't we have peace? I think I'll call his mother." Ain't it some kinda world? (*And he is laughing.*) Soooooooo . . . that about it. That about all I got to say. Am I right, Pavlo? Did I tell you true? You got anything to say? Oh, man, I know you do, you say it out.

(*Slight pause as* ARDELL *moves to uncover* PAVLO)
Man, you don't say it out, I don't wanna know you. Be cool as you wanna be, Pavlo! Beee cool; lemme hear you. . . . You tell it to me: what you think of the cause? What you think a gettin' your ass blown clean off a freedom's frontier? What you think a bein' RA Regular Army lifer?

PAVLO: (*Softly, with nearly embarrassed laughter.* Sheeeeee . . . ittttt. . . . Oh, lord . . . oh . . .

ARDELL: Ain't it what happened to you? Lemme hear it.

PAVLO: . . . Shit!

ARDELL: And what you think a all the "folks back home," sayin' you a victim . . . you a animal . . . you a fool. . . .

PAVLO: They shit!

ARDELL: Yeh, Baby; now I know you. It all shit.

PAVLO: It all shit!

ARDELL: You my man again.

PAVLO: It shit.

ARDELL: Lemme hear it! My *main* man.

PAVLO: SHIT!

ARDELL: Main motherfuckin' man.

PAVLO: OH, SHIT!

ARDELL: GO!

PAVLO: SHIT!

ARDELL: GET IT! GET IT!

PAVLO: (*—A howl into silence.*) SHHHHHHHHHHIIIIIII-IITTTTTTTTTTTTTTTttttttttt!

> (*And four men enter, carrying the aluminum box of a coffin, while two other men go across the back of the stage doing the drill, the marching and twirling rifles that were done at the end of Act One. They go now, however, in the opposite direction. The coffin is placed beside* PAVLO.)

ARDELL: That right. How you feel? You feel all right? You gotta get that stuff outa you, man. You body know that and you body smart; you don't get that outa you, it back up on you, man, poison you.

> (*The four men are placing* PAVLO *in the coffin. There is no precision in anything they do. All is casual, daily work.*)

PAVLO: But . . . I . . . I'm dead!

> (*The men turn and leave.*)

ARDELL: Real soon; got wings as big as streets; got large, large wings. (*Slight pause.*) You want me to talk shit to you? Man, sure, we siftin' things over. We in a bar, man, back home, we got good soft chairs, beer in our hands, go-go girls all around; one of 'em got her eye on you, 'nother one thinkin' little bit on me. You believe what I'm sayin'. You *home*, Pavlo. (*Pause.*) Now . . . you c'mon and you be with me. . . . We gonna do a little

singin'. You be with me. (*Sings*) Saw some
stockin's . . . on the street . . .

PAVLO: (*Faltering.*) Saw some . . . stockin's . . . on the
street . . .

(*Slight pause.*)

ARDELL: . . . Wished I was . . . between those . . .
feet . . .

PAVLO: Wished I was between those feet!

(*Slight pause.*)

ARDELL and PAVLO, *together.* Once a week, I get to town.
They see me comin', they jus' lay down. . . .

ARDELL: Sergeant, Sergeant, can't you see . . .

PAVLO: Sergeant, Sergeant, can't you see . . .

ARDELL: All this misery's killin' . . . me . . .

PAVLO: All this misery's killin'—

(*And* ARDELL *lets the coffin lid slam shut, cutting*
PAVLO *off.*)

ARDELL: Ain't no matter what you do . . . Jody done it
. . . all to you. . . .

(*Slight pause.* ARDELL *is backing away.*)

Lift your heads and lift 'em high . . . Pavlo Hummel
. . . passin' by . . .

(ARDELL *disappears upstage. The coffin stands in real
light.*)

MOONCHILDREN

by Michael Weller

The text of *Moonchildren* evolved over several productions beginning in 1970 at the Royal Court Theatre in London and continuing through the Arena Stage in Washington, D.C. (1971), the Royale Theatre on Broadway (1972), and settling finally Off-Broadway at the Theatre De Lys (1973–74). During this time three different versions were published (Faber & Faber, Delacorte, and Samuel French), but it wasn't until after the De Lys production that I had a chance to sit down with the benefit of hindsight and consolidate all my final thoughts about the play in a version that was satisfactory to me. This final "draft" has never appeared in print, so I welcome the present Dell edition as a chance to make the play available as I should like to see it performed.

M. W.

MOONCHILDREN *received its first American production at* ARENA STAGE, *Washington, D.C., November 1971, prior to the Broadway opening in February 1972.*

ARENA STAGE
Zelda Fichandler, *Producing Director*
Thomas C. Fichandler, *Executive Director*

The Cast
(IN ORDER OF SPEAKING)

The Students

MIKE	*Kevin Conway*
RUTH	*Maureen Anderman*
COOTIE (MEL)	*Edward Herrmann*
NORMAN	*Christopher Guest*
DICK	*Stephen Collins*
KATHY	*Jill Eikenberry*
BOB RETTIE (JOB)	*James Woods*
SHELLY	*Cara Duff-Mac Cormick*

The Others

RALPH	*Donegan Smith*
MR. WILLIS	*Robert Prosky*
LUCKY	*Ronald Mc Larty*
BREAM	*Howard Witt*
EFFING	*Ted Hannan*
UNCLE MURRAY	*Ben Kaplan*
MILKMAN	*Mark Robinson*
PLUMBER	*Richard David*
FATHER	*Russell Carr*

Produced by Zelda Fichandler
Directed by Alan Schneider
Setting by William Ritman
Costumes by Marjorie Slaiman
Lighting by Vance Sorrells
Production Manager: Hugh Lester
Technical Director: Henry R. Gorfein

By arrangement with Martin Rosen, Nepenthe Productions, Ltd., and the Royal Court Theatre

Synopsis of Scenes

ACT ONE

Scene 1. An evening in early fall
Scene 2. A few weeks later. Morning.
Scene 3. That afternoon.
Scene 4. A November evening.

ACT TWO

Scene 5. Morning, just before Christmas vacation.
Scene 6. Late spring, before graduation.
Scene 7. The following afternoon.

The place is a student apartment in an American university town.
The time is around 1965–66.

ACT ONE

Scene 1

(*The stage is dark. You can't see anything.*)

MIKE: I heard something. She definitely made a noise.

RUTH: Shut up.

MIKE: I'm telling you, I know the noise they make. That was it.

RUTH: For chrissakes, be quiet. You keep talking and she'll know we're here.

COOTIE: I was just thinking. I read somewhere about how they can see in the dark.

RUTH: I never read that.

COOTIE: No shit, I read they got these hundreds of thousands of millions of tiny, submicroscopic, photosensitive cells in each eyeball, so when it gets dark they can just turn on these cells and see like it was daytime.

MIKE: He's right, Ruth. Hey, Cootie, you're right. I remember reading that in a back issue of the *Vertebrate Review*.

COOTIE: That's it, that's the one. Special eyeball issue.

MIKE: Yeah, yeah. July.

RUTH: You guys must be pretty stupid if you believe that. What do you think they have whiskers for? The whole point of whiskers in the first place is so you can get around in the dark. That's why they stick out so far, so you don't bump into things. Chairs and refrigerators and that.

MIKE: Hey, shhhh. I think she's starting.

RUTH: Well, you're the one that got me going about whiskers in the first place, so don't tell me shhhhh.

MIKE: Okay, okay, I'm sorry, okay?

RUTH: So shut up if she's starting.

COOTIE: (*Pause*) How many kittens can they have at any one session?

MIKE: There's a recorded case of thirty-eight.

RUTH: Shhhh, for chrissakes.

COOTIE: What I want to know is how are we gonna see her when she starts giving birth?

RUTH: Jesus, how stupid can you get? We'll turn on the light.

COOTIE: Yeah, but the whole thing is how do we know when to turn on the light? Like, what if we're too early?

MIKE: Or too late?

COOTIE: Yeah, what if we're too late?

MIKE: Or right in the middle . . .

COOTIE: Holy shit, yeah, what if we flip on the old lights when she's halfway through a severe uterine contraction? She'll go apeshit and clamp up and kill the kitten. And if the kitty gets really lucky and wiggles free, it'll grow up into a pretty fucked-up animal.

MIKE: We're sowing the seeds of a neurotic adult cathood. . . .

COOTIE: . . . doo-wah, doo-wah . . .

RUTH: Hey, shut up, you guys, willya? Willya shut up?

COOTIE: We're just pointing out that's a shitty way to start life.

RUTH: I know the noise, all right?

MIKE: I think there's probably a more scientific way to watch a cat give birth.

RUTH: Everybody shut the fuck up.

(*A long pause.*)

NORMAN: How much longer are you guys gonna have the lights out?

COOTIE: Jesus Christ, Norman, why do you have to go creeping up like that? We forgot you were even in here.

NORMAN: I'm not creeping up. I'm just sitting here. Maybe you didn't notice when you came in, but I was reading this book. I mean, I thought you were only gonna have the lights out for maybe a few minutes or something, but you've already been in here for about an hour and . . . and I really can't read very well with the lights off. I mean . . . you know . . .

COOTIE: Norman, you can't rush a cat when it's giving birth. You try to rush a cat in those circumstances and you come smack up against nature.

MIKE: Norman . . .

NORMAN: What?

MIKE: Don't fight nature, Norman.

NORMAN: I'm not. I'm just trying to read this book.

COOTIE: (*Pause*) Is it a good book?

RUTH: For chrissakes, what's the matter with everyone?

NORMAN: I don't know. It's a pretty good book. I don't follow all of it. It's written in a funny kind of way so you forget a lot of it right after you've read it. A lot of guys in the mathematics department say it's pretty good. I don't know though.

RUTH: Hey, Norman, can't you go to your room if you want to read?

NORMAN: I don't want to.

COOTIE: Why not, Norman?

MIKE: Yeah, why do you want to creep around in here being all spooky and everything when you could just go to your room and read, huh?

NORMAN: I don't know.

COOTIE: We may be in here for hours and hours, Norman. Maybe even all night. The whole operation from initial labor to the biting off of the umbilical cord could very easily take an entire night. (*Pause.*) Norman?

NORMAN: All night, huh?

COOTIE: You never know.

RUTH: Brother, you try to get a few guys to shut up for a little while . . .

MIKE: (*Loud.*) C'mon, c'mon, hey everybody, let's have a little quiet around here. I don't want to see anyone panic and lose their heads and start running in all different directions knocking down passersby and trampling on innocent women and children.

RUTH: I swear to Christ, Mike, if you don't shut up, I'll kill you.

MIKE: Okay.

(*At this point, the hall door opens and the kitchen is lit up a little.* DICK *is standing in the doorway trying to see into the dark, where* NORMAN *is sitting at a round kitchen table with a book by him and* RUTH, MIKE, *and* COOTIE *are crouched around a cardboard carton with a hole in it.* NORMAN *grabs up his book to take advantage of the crack of light.* DICK *just stands there.* RUTH *and* COOTIE *speak on top of each other.*)

RUTH: Hey, c'mon, shut the door, Dick.

COOTIE: Shut the fucking door.

MIKE: (*After a pause.*) We'd really like you to shut the door, Richard.

(DICK *shuts the door and everything goes black again. A moment later it all lights up again because* DICK *has just opened the icebox and it's the kind that has an automatic light inside. So now we see* DICK *squatting in front of the icebox while the others watch him, except for* NORMAN *who's really trying like mad to read. You can see the kitchen pretty clearly now. The icebox is very old, dating from the time when electricity was replacing the iceman. It's just a box on legs with one of those barrel-shaped coolers with vents on top. You maybe can't see it yet, but on the door of the icebox there's a large inscription that reads "GOD IS COOL." Stacked neatly against one wall are eight hundred sixteen empty two-quart milk bottles, layer upon layer with planks between each level. It's a deliberate construction. There's a huge copper stack heater in one corner by the sink, and it has a safety valve at the top with a copper tube coming out of it and snaking into the sink. The floor is vinyl, in imitation cork, alternating light and dark, but the conspicuous thing about this floor is that it's only half-finished. Where the cork tiles end there is a border of black tar, by now hard, and then wooden floor in broad plank.*)

Around the kitchen table are six chairs, all from different sets. Various posters on the wall, but none as conspicuous as a map of Europe on the wall where the telephone hangs. The sink is full of dirty dishes. There is a pad hanging by the icebox, and a pencil. Everyone uses the kitchen in a special way. So DICK *is squatting in front of the open icebox.)*

RUTH: That's very cute, Richard.

MIKE: C'mon, shut the fucking icebox. We were in here first.

NORMAN: I was reading when you guys came in.

(DICK *turns to them, looks, then turns back to the icebox.)*

COOTIE: Dick, in my humble opinion you're a miserable cunt and a party pooper.

DICK: *(Standing.)* All right, now listen. This afternoon I went down to the Star Supermarket and got myself four dozen frozen hamburgers. Now that's forty-eight hamburgers, and I only had two of them for dinner tonight.

RUTH: And you never washed up.

MIKE: Hey, Dick, are those Star hamburgers any good?

DICK: Listen, I should have forty-six hamburgers, and when I counted just now there was only forty-three. Three hamburgers in one night. And for your information I've been keeping track of my hamburgers since the beginning of the semester. There's almost fifty hamburgers I can't account for.

COOTIE: Jesus, Dick, you should have said something before this.

MIKE: Yeah, Dick, you had all them hamburger thefts on your mind, you should have let it out. It's no good keeping quiet about something like that.

DICK: Look, I'm not about to make a stink about a couple of hamburgers here and there, but Jesus Christ, almost sixty of them. I'm putting it down on common stock and we're gonna all pay for it.

(DICK *turns on the light.)*

RUTH: Dick, willya turn out the light, please.

DICK: I'm sorry, but I've lost too many hamburgers. I'm putting down for four dozen.

(DICK *goes to the pad on the wall and makes an entry.*)

RUTH: Now willya turn the light out?

DICK: (*Examining list.*) Shit, who put peanut butter down on common stock?

MIKE: I did. I got a jar of chunky last Thursday and when I opened it on Saturday somebody'd already been in there. I didn't eat all that chunky myself.

DICK: Well I never had your peanut butter. I'm not paying for it.

MIKE: Well I never had any of your goddamn sixty hamburgers either.

COOTIE: I think I may have had some of that chunky peanut butter. Could you describe your jar of chunky in detail?

MIKE: Elegant little glass jar, beige interior . . .

(*Kathy enters through the front door, as opposed to the hall door. The hall door leads to everyone's rooms.*)

KATHY: Oh boy, look out for Bob.

(KATHY *starts across the kitchen to the hall door. She carries lots of books in a green canvas waterproof book bag slung over her shoulder.*)

RUTH: What's wrong with Bob?

KATHY: He's in a really shitty mood. I've seen the guy act weird before. This is, I don't know, pretty bad, I guess.

MIKE: Where is he?

COOTIE: Yeah, where's Bob?

MIKE: Good old Bob.

COOTIE: Where's good old Bob?

KATHY: And fuck you too. I'm serious.

NORMAN: (*Looking up from his book.*) Boy, I really can't absorb very much with everyone talking.

KATHY: We were just sitting there, you know, in Hum 105, and that prick Johnson started in about the old cosmic equation again.

NORMAN: What's the cosmic equation?

RUTH: So why'd that upset Bob?

KATHY: I don't know. That's the thing . . .

DICK: I bet Bob's responsible for some of my hamburgers.

I notice you and him never go shopping for dinner.

KATHY: It's really weird the way he sort of . . . well, like today, you know . . . I'm not kidding, he might be cracking up or something.

(BOB *enters through the front door, carrying his books. He looks all right. Everyone stares at him.*)

RUTH: Hi, Bob.

MIKE: Hi, Bob.

COOTIE: Hi, Bob.

NORMAN: Hello, Bob.

BOB: (*Pause.*) Hi, Mike, Hi, Ruth, Hi, Cootie, hello, Norman. (*Pause.*) Hi, Dick.

DICK: Listen, do you know anything about . . .

BOB: No, I haven't touched your fucking hamburgers.

DICK: Well someone has.

MIKE: How you been, good old Bob?

COOTIE: How's the old liver and the old pancreas and the old pituitary and the . . .

BOB: Is there any mail?

COOTIE: There's this really big package from Beirut. It took four guys to get it up the stairs.

MIKE: We think it's a harp.

RUTH: There's a letter in your room.

(BOB *looks at them quizzically, then goes down the hall.* KATHY *follows him.*)

RUTH: I think Kathy's right. There's definitely something wrong with Bob.

DICK: Yeah, he's out of his fucking mind, that's what's wrong with him.

RUTH: You can talk.

MIKE: Hey, c'mon, c'mon, let's have a little order around here. . . .

RUTH: Stop fucking around. You heard what Kathy said. Something's troubling Bob.

MIKE: So what?

COOTIE: Yeah, fuck Bob.

MIKE: Fuck good old Bob.

NORMAN: Maybe he's worried about the future. (*All look at him.*) I mean, you know, maybe he's worried about it. I mean, I don't know him all that well. Just, you know, maybe he's worried about what he's gonna do when, you know, after he graduates and everything.

DICK: He ought to be worried.

MIKE: You bet your ass he oughta be. Same goes for all of you guys. You oughta be worried, Dick. Cootie, you oughta be worried. I oughta be worried. I am. I'm fucking pertrified. You watch what happens at the graduation ceremony. There's gonna be this line of green military buses two miles long parked on the road outside and they're gonna pick us up and take us to Vietnam and we'll be walking around one day in the depths of the rain forest looking out for wily enemy snipers and carnivorous insects and tropical snakes that can eat a whole moose in one gulp and earthworms sixteen feet long and then one day when we least expect it this wily sniper'll leap out from behind a blade of grass and powie. Right in the head. (*Serious.*) I'm worried.

DICK: Anyone that can spell can get out of Vietnam.

NORMAN: I'm in graduate school. They can't get me.

DICK: Norman, you couldn't buy your way into the army.

NORMAN: I wouldn't go.

MIKE: Why wouldn't you go, Norman?

NORMAN: Huh?

COOTIE: Yeah, think of the army. What about them? They need good graduate students out there in the marshes of Quac Thop Chew Hoy Ben Van Pho Quay Gup Trin.

NORMAN: I don't agree with the war.

MIKE: Well, for God sakes then, let's stop it.

NORMAN: I had my medical and everything. I passed. I could've pretended I was insane or something.

DICK: Pretended?

RUTH: Hey, doesn't anyone here give a shit about Bob.

MIKE: Hey, c'mon, everyone that gives a shit raise your hand.

    (COOTIE, MIKE, DICK, *and* NORMAN *raise their hands.*) See, we all give a shit. So what should we do?

RUTH: Well, I don't know. Maybe we ought to try and find out what's troubling him.

DICK: Maybe he doesn't want us to know. Just maybe.

COOTIE: Yeah, what if he's teetering on the brink of a complete schizophrenic withdrawal and the only thing keeping him sane is knowing we don't know what's troubling him.

MIKE: It's our duty as classmates and favorite turds to leave him alone.

RUTH: Maybe something's wrong between him and Kathy.

DICK: Like what?

RUTH: I don't know. That's what I'm asking.

DICK: He doesn't give a shit about her. Not really. She's just a good lay, that's all.

RUTH: How would you know, Dick?

NORMAN: I thought they were in love.

DICK: Jesus, Norman, where the hell is your head at?

NORMAN: Huh?

MIKE: Define the problem, then solve it.

COOTIE: Yeah, what's troubling good old Bob?

MIKE: I think we oughta all go to bed tonight with notebooks under our pillows, and when we get a well-focused and comprehensive idea about the central dilemma of Bob's existence we oughta write it down in clear, concise sentences, with particular attention to grammar and punctuation.

COOTIE: Yeah, then we can meet in here tomorrow and pool our insights.

MIKE: That's a really great plan.

RUTH: I'd really like to know what's troubling him.

DICK: I'd really like to know who the fuck is eating my hamburgers.

NORMAN: Why don't you talk to him?

RUTH: What?

NORMAN: I mean, you know——Bob. If you want to find out what's troubling him, probably the best thing to do is talk to him and say what's troubling you or something like that, and then if he wants to tell you he can and if he doesn't feel like talking about it . . . then . . . well, you know . . .

RUTH: Yeah, maybe I'll do that.

NORMAN: (*Pause.*) Yeah, that's what I'd do if I wanted to know. I mean, I'm not saying I wouldn't like to know

what's troubling him. I'd really like to know if you find
out, but I . . .

(MIKE *has been kneeling by the cat box and peering
into it.*)

MIKE: Jesus Christ. Jesus H. fucking Christ.

NORMAN: What's wrong?

MIKE: She wasn't even in there.

COOTIE: What! All that time we were looking at an empty
box and she wasn't even in there?

MIKE: She must've slipped out while we had our backs
turned.

COOTIE: Sneaky little beastie.

MIKE: Cootie, you don't understand. She might be out
there in the road right now.

COOTIE: Right now.

MIKE: With all the traffic.

COOTIE: Oh, Christ, and all those architects driving home
drunk from seeing their mistresses . . .

MIKE: And trying to figure out what to tell the little
woman. I mean, she's been waiting up all night in a
chartreuse quilted sleeping gown with curlers in her
hair.

COOTIE: Worrying about the kiddies. Three boys twenty-
seven girls. They got appendicitis.

MIKE: Simultaneously. And when she called the kindly
family doctor he was away in Cuba . . .

COOTIE: Doing research for his forthcoming book . . .

MIKE: "Chapter Eight: Peritonitis and Social Democracy."

COOTIE: Jesus, I hope we're not too late.

(COOTIE *and* MIKE *rush off down the hall.*)

DICK: Hey, Norman, are these your bananas?

NORMAN: You can have one. I don't mind.

(DICK *takes one and puts the others back in the icebox.* COOTIE *sticks his head in around the hall door.*)

COOTIE: You coming, Ruth?

RUTH: No.

COOTIE: Your heart is full of bitterness and hate, Ruth.

(COOTIE'*s head disappears again.*)

DICK: You done the essay for Phil 720?

RUTH: No.

DICK: It's due tomorrow.

RUTH: Yeah?

DICK: Yeah.

NORMAN: Is that a good course, Philosophy 720?

RUTH: Nope. Professor Quinn is an albino dwarf queer with halitosis and he smokes too much.

DICK: He does not.

RUTH: Three packs of Pall Mall a day is too much. He's gonna die of cancer.

DICK: He's a genius.

RUTH: You have a thing about queers.

DICK: Fuck off, Ruth.

RUTH: You started it.

>   (RUTH *goes into hall.* DICK *stands and eats his banana, chewing slowly.* NORMAN *tries to read but* DICK's *presence distracts him.*)

DICK: How come you're reading that book?

NORMAN: I don't know. It's supposed to be pretty good.

DICK: What are you gonna do when you finish it?

NORMAN: (*Thinks.*) I'll start another one.

DICK: Yeah, but what happens when you forget this one. I mean, it'll be as if you hadn't even read it, so what's the point?

NORMAN: Oh, I don't know. I happen to believe you learn things even when you don't know it. Like, if you're reading something right now . . . I mean, I am reading something right now and maybe I'll forget it in a while . . . I mean, I'm forgetting a lot of it already, but I happen to believe I'm being altered in lots of ways I may not be aware of because of . . . well, you know, books and experiences. (*Pause.*) Life.

DICK: That's what you believe, huh?

NORMAN: Um, yes, I believe that.

>   (MIKE *and* COOTIE *enter, wearing heavy winter parkas and boots. They look like trappers.*)

COOTIE: Boy, if we're too late I hate to think of all the dead cats we'll have on our conscience.

MIKE: You gonna help, Dick.

DICK: Fuck off.

MIKE: How about you, Norman, aren't you gonna do your bit for the world of cats?

NORMAN: I'm just in the middle of this chapter.

(MIKE *and* COOTIE *shake their heads in disapproval and rush out.* NORMAN *tries to read again as* DICK *eats the banana, watching him.*)

Hey, it's really hard to read, you know, when someone's watching you and everything.

DICK: Don't you ever get the feeling you're really irrelevant?

NORMAN: I don't think so.

DICK: (*In one breath.*) I mean, you go into the Mathematics department every day and sit there looking out the window and thinking about cars and women and every now and then a couple of numbers come into your head and there's all these Chinese guys running around solving all the problems worth solving while you sit there wondering what the hell you're doing.

NORMAN: No, it's not like that. Well, you know, it's not that simple. I mean . . . (*Pause.*) I guess it's a lot like that. Are you doing anything relevant?

DICK: You can't get more relevant than Far Eastern studies. Ask me anything about the Far East and I'll tell you the answer. That's where everything's happening. China, Vietnam, Japan, Korea. You name it.

NORMAN: I guess I ought to know more about those things. I don't know, I keep thinking there's a lot of things I should know about.

DICK: The thing is, Norman, the way I see it, you're already deeply committed to the system. You take away black ghettos, stop the war in Vietnam, distribute the wealth equally throughout the country and you wouldn't be in graduate school.

NORMAN: How come?

DICK: You see, you don't know anything about what makes it all work, do you?

(DICK *throws the banana peel into the cat box.*)

NORMAN: Hey, you shouldn't throw that in there.

DICK: Why not?

NORMAN: Well, I mean, that's the box for the cat. Maybe she won't want to have kittens on a banana peel.

DICK: Norman, how long have you been living here?

NORMAN: Well, you know, about three months. A little longer maybe. About three months and two weeks altogether.

DICK: Have you ever seen a cat around here?

NORMAN: Well, I don't know. I'm out a lot of the time.

DICK: Norman, there is no fucking cat. We haven't got a cat. Boy, for a graduate student you got a lot to learn.
> (DICK *starts out but turns to look* NORMAN *over a last time and say* . . .)

Jesus.
> (*Then he's gone down the hall.* NORMAN *kneels by the cat box and examines it as some muffled piano chords fill the silence. It's* BOB *playing a lazy, rich, drifting progression, moody-Bill-Evans-style.* KATHY *walks through the kitchen in a man's robe carrying a towel. She lights the stack heater. From inside the hall we hear* DICK's *voice yelling.*)

DICK: STOP PLAYING THAT FUCKING NOISE. I'M TRYING TO READ. HEY, BOB.
> (KATHY *goes to the hall door and yells down.*)

KATHY: Mind your own goddamn business, Richard.
> (*A door slams, and the music, which had stopped momentarily, starts again, but louder.*)

> (*Turning.*) Hey listen, Norman. If you're gonna be in here for a while could you do me a favor and make sure no one turns off the water heater, 'cause I'm just taking a shower. And if you get a chance could you put on some coffee, 'cause I'll be coming out in about ten minutes and I'd like a cup when I come out. Okay?

NORMAN: Do you have any books on Vietnam?

KATHY: (*Pause.*) Yeah. A few.

NORMAN: Are they good books?

KATHY: Well, you know, some are, some aren't. Why?

NORMAN: I just, you know, wondered, that's all.
> (KATHY *watches* NORMAN *go to the stove and fumble around with the coffee percolator. She shrugs and*

goes out. We hear the bathroom door close and, moments later, the sound of a shower running.)

Actually, I've been thinking I'd like to read some books about Vietnam. I mean it's been going on all this time. I don't know, though. I've never read any books about it. Maybe if I could read one book, then I'd know a little more about it and I could decide if I wanted to read another. Would it be okay if I borrowed one of your books to start with? I'd give it back as soon as I finished it.

(*He looks around and sees he's alone. He goes out the door. We hear the bathroom door opening and a yell.*)

KATHY: Goddamnit, Norman, what are you doing in here?

NORMAN: I was wondering if you'd lend me . . .

KATHY: Hey, get the hell out of here, I'm taking a shower. (*A door slams.*)

NORMAN: I just wanted to know if it was okay for me to borrow one of those books about Vietnam.

KATHY: Well, Jesus Christ, can't you wait till I'm done?

NORMAN: Oh . . . yeah, I'm sorry. (*Pause.*) Is that all right with you?

KATHY: Hey, don't stand around out there. You can borrow as many goddamn books as you want, only get away from the door, 'cause it just so happens I don't like a lot of people standing around outside the bathroom door while I'm washing.

(NORMAN *comes back into the kitchen. He fixes a little more of the coffee, then goes to the hall door and yells down the hallway.*)

NORMAN: I'll just make the coffee first, and when you're finished in there, I'll come down to your room with you and get the book. Hey, listen, if you decide to have your coffee in here, could you go down to your room first and bring the book in with you? Yes, that's probably better. Hey, is that okay? (*Pause.*) Hey, is that okay?

(*No answer.* NORMAN *is left baffled, as the lights dim and* BOB's *piano chords keep going and going.*)

(*End of Scene 1.*)

Scene 2

(*It's a few days later.* NORMAN *is reading.* RUTH *is making sandwiches, and* COOTIE *and* MIKE *are rolling up a banner.*)

COOTIE: I don't know about the wording.

MIKE: I think it's pretty good wording.

COOTIE: I'm not too happy about it.

MIKE: You're unhappy about the wording.

COOTIE: Well, I'm not, you know, cut up about it or anything, but I'm definitely not as happy as I could be about it.

MIKE: Ruthie, we need an impartial third voice over here.

RUTH: Who wants orange marmalade?

MIKE: I'd like an orange marmalade.

COOTIE: I want two orange marmalade and one chunky peanut butter, please.

RUTH: How 'bout you, Norman?

COOTIE: And I wouldn't mind a chunky peanut butter and orange marmalade mixed.

RUTH: Hey, Norman, do you want sandwiches or not?

COOTIE: You gotta have sandwiches handy if you're coming, Norman. On your average march you'll find you get through a good two peanut butter and jellies before you even get to where you're supposed to demonstrate, and then after circling round and yelling militant slogans at the monument or park or poison gas plant or nuclear missile establishment for a couple hours, you're just about ready for another peanut butter and jelly.

MIKE: Or cream cheese and olives.

COOTIE: Bacon, lettuce, and tomato. I mean, I know you meet a lotta pretty groovy people at these marches, but you can't count on them having extra sandwiches for a new acquaintance.

RUTH: Hey, Norman, willya please tell me if you're coming with us or not?

NORMAN: (*Unfriendly.*) I'm going with Dick.

COOTIE: You're lucky there. You'll get hamburger on toasted roll if you go with Dick. He takes Sterno and cooks right out there in the middle of lines of chargin' cops and tear gas and mace and everything.

(DICK *enters*.)

MIKE: Hey, Dick, you better hurry up and get dressed for the march.

COOTIE: Yeah, Dick, you don't want to be late or all the best ass'll be grabbed up.

DICK: (*Indicating banner*.) What's it say?

COOTIE: "Buy Government bonds."

RUTH: You want some of our peanut butter and marmalade?

MIKE: What's this about giving away all our peanut butter and marmalade all of a sudden? He wouldn't give us any of his lousy hamburgers. We had to pay for those hamburgers on common stock.

DICK: Where's Kathy and Bob?

MIKE: Yeah, where's good old Bob? (*Yells*.) HEY, YOU GUYS, ARE YOU COMING?

KATHY: (*Inside*.) Yeah, hold on a minute, willya?

MIKE: They're coming.

COOTIE: Hey, Norman, I been watching you pretty closely for the last few days and I have this definite impression you've been displaying hostility toward me, Mike, and Ruth, in that order.

NORMAN: I'm just reading this book . . .

COOTIE: Don't be negative, Norman. You're trying to pretend I hadn't noticed your emotions. You happen to be up against a disciple of Freud, Jung, Adler, Pavlov, Skinner, and the honorable L. Ron Hubbard, to mention but a few. It just so happens I can detect subatomic trace particles of hostility within a six-mile radius of anywhere I am.

MIKE: It's no use contradicting him, Norman. If he says he can feel hostility, that's it. I mean, even I can feel it and I'm only moderately sensitive to hostility up to about a hundred eighty yards.

NORMAN: I'm not feeling hostile . . .

COOTIE: You're not only feeling it, you're dying to tell us about it. That's a basic axiom of hostility.

NORMAN: Oh, boy, you guys.

DICK: Leave him alone.

COOTIE: Dick, that's the worst thing you can do. I know you think you're being a good shit and everything, but if the guy is riddled with hostility and he doesn't get it out of his system it's gonna go haywire and zing all around inside his body till he's twenty-eight years old and then he'll get cancer.

RUTH: You know, we're gonna be really late if those guys don't hurry up . . . .

MIKE: That reminds me of a guy I was reading about. He got so pent up with hostility his head fell right down inside his body, no shit, that's what I was reading, right down between his shoulders.

COOTIE: Fell?

MIKE: Yeah, straight down till all you could see was these two little eyeballs peering out over his collarbone.

COOTIE: Mike.

MIKE: What, Mel?

COOTIE: (*Pause.*) Fell?

MIKE: (*Pause.*) Sank?

COOTIE: Subsided.

MIKE: Right.

COOTIE: In fact, as I remember it, his head eventually disappeared completely.

MIKE: Don't rush me, I'm coming to that. Now, Norman, I want you to pay very close attention because this case is a lesson in itself. You see, everybody used to warn this particular guy to loosen up and maybe see an analyst, but the guy refused on the grounds that it would cost too much, and that turned out to be really stupid economy, because with his head inside him like that he couldn't see anything and he had to hire a guy, full time, seven days a week, to lead him around. The guy was so tight with his money he tried to solve the problem by rigging up this ingenious system of mirrors, like a periscope, but the natural movements of his body kept knocking the mirrors out of alignment, so in addition to the guy that led him around, he had to hire another guy, full time, seven days a week, to keep readjusting the mirrors. You can imagine the expense involved.

COOTIE: There was a very fine article about that guy in the *Hostility Journal*, spring number. Did you happen to catch that article, Norman?

MIKE: Did it tell about what happened to him?

COOTIE: Well, it was one of those stories in two parts, and wouldn't you know it, that's just when my subscription ran out.

MIKE: Oh well, you missed the best part. You see, when his head got down as f . . . subsided as far as his stomach . . .

COOTIE . . . thank you . . .

MIKE: . . . He went and hired a top-notch transplant surgeon to replace his belly button with a flexible, clear plastic window so he could see where he was going.

COOTIE: Jumpin' Jehoshaphat!

MIKE: And I'm happy to announce, the operation was a complete success.

COOTIE: Fantastic! No problems with rejection or anything?

MIKE: Nope. The Dow Chemical Company set up a ten-man, two-woman research team and they developed a type of clear plastic window that matched the guy's antibodies perfectly. In a matter of weeks, the guy was able to live a completely normal life again, skin diving, stamp collecting, a lot of political work. He could even go to the movies when he felt like it, but he had to sit up on the back of the seat and it caused a lot of hard feelings with the people sitting directly behind him. But that's the great thing about the average movie-going audience; they respected his infirmity.

COOTIE: Fuck a duck!

MIKE: Shut up, sonny boy, I ain't finished yet.

COOTIE: There's more?

MIKE: Yeah, you see, the really incredible thing was when the guy woke up one morning and realized his head was still sinking . . .

COOTIE: . . . subsiding . . .

MIKE: . . . and he went to this doctor to check it out. He was just walking along, you know, and when he got to this corner to stop for a red light a dog peed on his leg, and when he bent forward to see what was making his pants wet a guy up on some scaffolding right behind dropped a pipe wrench on his back, and the impact of this wrench, plus the slightly inclined position of the guy's upper body, knocked his head back into place.

COOTIE: Hot diggity!

MIKE: Well, the guy went apeshit, jumping all over the place, singing songs right out there on the streets . . . and that's just when it all had to happen. This poor guy, after all his suffering, was finally looking forward to a happy and productive life . . .

COOTIE: Oh, shit, yeah, I remember now. The poor son of a bitch.

MIKE: Yeah, you 'member, he was just standing out there in the street stopping traffic in both directions, tears of humble gratitude streaming down his cheeks and some stupid . . .

(*He sees* KATHY *and* BOB *standing in the hallway door ready for the march.*)

. . . oh, hi, Bob, hi, Kathy.

RUTH: Hey, do you guys want some of our peanut butter and marmalade?

BOB: I've got an announcement.

COOTIE: We used to have a nearsighted canary . . .

RUTH: Listen, I gotta make these sandwiches and we're gonna end up short if I don't get some cooperation around here.

COOTIE: Hey, Norman hasn't even got a banner. Norman, aren't you gonna bring a banner?

BOB: Mel, willya please shut up. I'm trying to tell you guys something?

COOTIE: Well, fuck you, I'm talking to Norman. You want him to get all the way down to the demonstration and they disqualify him 'cause he doesn't have a banner.

RUTH: Everyone is gonna fucking well eat whatever I make.

DICK: You want some help.

RUTH: Look, it's not like I don't know how to make sandwiches . . .

MIKE: Hey, everyone, c'mon, c'mon, let's have a little order around here. Everybody stay where you are and don't panic. Okay, Bob, I think we got everything under control now.

BOB: Thank you.

MIKE: That's okay, Bob.

BOB: I've just got this . . .

MIKE: Bob?

BOB: What?

MIKE: Anytime.

BOB: What?

MIKE: Anytime you want a little peace and quiet so you can make an announcement without a lot of people talking over you, just ask me and I'll do what I can for you.

BOB: Thank you, Mike.

MIKE: That's okay, Bob, you're a good shit.

    (BOB *hesitates, trying to find words to frame his vague thoughts. When he speaks, it is halting. . . .*)

BOB: Look . . . I just thought maybe it was about time somebody around here . . .

MIKE: Do you want some water or anything?

RUTH: Oh for chrissake, shut up, Mike.

COOTIE: (*Cooling things.*) Yeah, shut yer mouth, sonny boy, yer creatin' a public nuisance.

RUTH: Go on, Bob.

BOB: No, no, look, all I want to say is . . . Norman, if there is one way to remain irrelevant and ineffective it's to sit with your nose buried in a book while life is raging all around you.

    (NORMAN *looks up and closes his book.*)

Thank you. Okay. Announcement . . .

    (BOB *walks around the room, again trying to think of how to put it. As he starts to speak . . .*)

MIKE: Earthquakes in Singapore . . . ?

RUTH: (*Incredible rage.*) SHUT UP!

BOB: Never mind.

MIKE: Sorry. I'm sorry.

KATHY: What's wrong, Bob?

BOB: Really, nothing, nothing at all. I just had this stupid thought the other day in humanities. Johnson was saying something idiotic, as usual, and I just started to watch him carefully for the first time talking to us, you know, thirty kids who think he's a prick, and I realized that he probably thinks all of us are pricks . . . and I just started to wonder what the fuck we're all doing. You know what I mean? What the fuck are we all doing, seriously, tell me, I'd really like to know . . . in twenty-five words or less. . . . No, no, sorry, come on, carnival time. Let's go marching.

KATHY: I found the letter, Bob.

BOB: What letter?

(KATHY *takes an official letter out of her bag.*)

Kathy, where the hell did you get that? Come on, give it here.

KATHY: We're supposed to be like all together in here. If you can't say it yourself, I'll say it for you.

(BOB *is momentarily confused, then realizes that* KATHY *thinks he was trying to tell everyone about the letter. He finds the situation absurd, annoying, and funny.*)

BOB: Kathy, that letter has nothing to do with anything and it's none of your business and would you please give it back.

(KATHY *hands the letter to* RUTH. RUTH *reads.*)

RUTH: Oh, fuck.

(RUTH *hands the letter on. Each reads in turn. It ends in* MIKE's *hands.* BOB *waits impatiently as the letter makes its round. He's embarrassed and then begins to find it funny that everyone, especially* KATHY, *has construed the letter as his problem.* MIKE *is by now looking quite seriously at him.*)

BOB: (*Laughing it off.*) It's just for the physical. I mean, I'm not dead yet.

(*As* BOB *says this, something amusing passes through his mind and he stops talking. He turns the thought over in his mind.* MIKE *is looking at the letter again. The others watch* BOB.)

MIKE: They misspelled your name?

(BOB *comes out of his brief daydream.*)

BOB: Huh?

MIKE: Jobert.

BOB: (*Amused.*) Oh, yeah.

MIKE: Jobert Rettie. Dear Jobert Rettie. Hi, Jobert.

BOB: Hi, Jike.

MIKE: Good old Jobert.

COOTIE: How ya feelin', good old Jobert?

BOB: Dead, how 'bout you?

> (MIKE *sees what's happening and comes to the rescue.*)

MIKE: (*Pause.*) Hi, Jel.

COOTIE: Hi, Jike.

MIKE: Hi, Jorman.

NORMAN: Huh?

MIKE: Hi, Jorman.

NORMAN: Oh, hi.

MIKE: Hi, Jathy, hi, Jick.

DICK: Fuck off.

MIKE: Juck off? Why should I juck off, Jick?

> (*The doorbell rings.* COOTIE *rushes over and answers it. At the door, a young man in a suit and tie and horn-rimmed glasses, with an attaché case which he has concealed just out of sight behind the doorframe.*)

COOTIE: Hi, Jister.

MIKE: Ask him his name, Jel.

COOTIE: What's your name?

RALPH: Ralph.

COOTIE: Hi, Jalph, I'm Jel and that's Jathy, Jorman, Jike, Jick, and Job, and we're just on our way down to city hall to beat the shit out of some cops. Wanna come?

> (RALPH *pauses momentarily, then launches his pitch.*)

RALPH: I'm from the University of Buffalo and I'm in the neighborhood doing market research. You don't mind my asking you a few questions, do you?

> (*As he says this last, he reaches down, takes up his concealed attaché case, bends his head down, like making ready for a dive, and advances swiftly but deliberately into the middle of the room. This swift movement, plus the running patter, is designed to force the average housewife to back away and give*

ground, but since COOTIE *merely steps aside when* RALPH *bends down for his attaché case, we are treated to the entire technique out of context.* RALPH *ends up in the middle of the room still bent over, motionless. He looks up and around and straightens himself, laughing nervously at everyone watching him.*)

Do all you people live here?

MIKE: No, we're just using the place for a few days. This is a fantastic coincidence because the guy that lives here just went away for a few days to do a series of special guest lectures at the University of Buffalo.

RALPH: Really? No kidding? That's some coincidence, huh? That's really a fantastic coincidence. Well, ahhh, here's what I'd like to do. I'd like to interview one of you people. I'll choose one of you at random and everybody else can listen and if the guy I choose has a particular opinion that differs significantly from what the rest of you believe, we'll just stop and take a consensus, okay? Hey, you guys all work, don't you? I mean, you're not students or anything?

COOTIE: We mostly hold various government jobs.

RALPH: I see. Are any of you married?

RUTH: I'm married to him (MIKE) and she's married to him (BOB *and* KATHY).

BOB: Actually, we're getting a divorce.

RALPH: Oh, I'm very sorry.

BOB: (*Very sincerely to* RALPH.) No, please. It's just, I've been dying for a while, nothing serious, you know, but now I've decided I'm definitely dead, you see, so I'll have to change my name. It's a legal technicality. We'll marry again under my new name. Jobert. (*Pause.*) Job.

RALPH: Oh . . . well . . . that's certainly very unusual. Now this is going to get a little difficult, really. I've got to improvise some of these questions because the standard form is pretty rigid, like, you know, it asks things about your children's opinions, and that would hardly apply in a case like . . .

MIKE: I have several kids by a former marriage.

RUTH: Hey, how come you never told me about that?

MIKE: If you remember, dear, we did discuss it.

RALPH: Can I just edge in here, I mean, ha-ha, I don't want to interrupt a little marital tiff or anything, but, ha-ha, you know. (*To* NORMAN.) And how about you sir, do you have any children?

NORMAN: I don't have any children. I'm not married.

RALPH: Well, sir, I would guess, am I right, I would guess that you are the oldest person staying here. I only mean that in the sense of responsibility. Am I right?

MIKE: The guy that actually lives here is older, but he's not here right now.

RALPH: No, he's lecturing, right? I remember, ha-ha. Now I'd just like to ask you the following question. Have you ever heard of a teaching program called the World Volumes Encyclopedia?

DICK: Hey, are you selling encyclopedias?

RUTH: Hey, yeah, are you trying to sell us a set of encyclopedias?

RALPH: I'd like to make it very clear that I am not authorized to sell any product, I'm merely doing market research.

MIKE: Jesus Christ, he's not even selling the fucking things. You go and write to the central offices and you wait for a whole year to hear from them and when they finally decide to send a guy around he's not even authorized to sell you a set. I'm not hanging around here listening to a guy that isn't even authorized to sell the World Volumes Encyclopedia while millions of women and children are dying out there in Vietnam.

(MIKE *grabs the banner and starts huzzahing as everyone follows him out of the door.* DICK *and* NORMAN *stay behind with* RALPH, *who is yelling after them.*)

RALPH: Hey, hey, listen, I can sell you a set if you want one.

(RALPH *turns to* DICK *and* NORMAN.)

Hey, do you guys really want to buy a set of encyclopedias? I can sell you a set. I got a number of deals and there's a special discount for government employees.

DICK: (*To* NORMAN.) You going?

NORMAN: Yes, I've been reading a lot about it lately.

DICK: You want to come with me?

NORMAN: Well, yeah, if you don't have any other plans.

DICK: Okay, hold on a minute.

> (DICK *goes out the hall door.*)

RALPH: Hey, who are all you people?

NORMAN: We just live here.

RALPH: I go to college. I don't really come from Buffalo. I live in town. I'm trying to earn some money in my spare time. Are you guys really government employees?

NORMAN: I'm a graduate student.

RALPH: Yeah, well, I didn't want to say anything, but I didn't really think you guys were government employees. What are you studying?

NORMAN: Mathematics.

RALPH: I wanted to study mathematics. My father said he wouldn't pay so I'm studying law. Boy, do I hate law. I'm living at home. Do you guys all live here together?

NORMAN: Yes.

RALPH: And . . . and the girls too?

NORMAN: Yes.

RALPH: Oh boy, what a life, huh? I'm gonna get me a car pretty soon. I'm saving up. The thing is, I'm not really doing too well selling encyclopedias. I can't pull it off. I wish I could figure out why. I've been thinking about it and I think maybe it's because I can't give the sales pitch credibility. That's pretty bad if I'm gonna be a lawyer because a lot of the time you have to defend people you know are guilty. The thing is, these encyclopedias are really shitty. (*He blushes.*) Sorry. I mean, you know, they're not very good.

> (DICK *reenters. He is carefully groomed and well-dressed in a pea jacket and well-laundered jeans. He wears a large, orange Day-Glo peace button.*)

DICK: You ready?

RALPH: You going out?

DICK: Listen, if you're gonna eat anything, lay off the hamburgers, okay?

> (DICK *and* NORMAN *start out.*)

NORMAN: I don't see why he has to go saying he's dead. I mean, that's only for him to have a physical. It's pretty easy to fail a physical. I've heard of guys that pretend . . .

(*They are gone.* RALPH, *alone, looks at the open door.*)

RALPH: Hey!

(*Blackout.*)

(*End of Scene 2.*)

Scene 3

(*A few hours later.* KATHY *is sitting in the kitchen, crying.* RUTH *comes in the front door. She has just returned from the march.*)

RUTH: Bob here?

KATHY: No.

RUTH: Hey, what's wrong. You want some coffee?

KATHY: Please.

(RUTH *takes off her coat and starts making coffee.*)

How was it?

RUTH: Weren't you there?

KATHY: No.

RUTH: I thought you and Bob were coming. You were on the bus and everything. I got lost when the cops charged. Boy, they really got some of those guys. Fucking pigs.

KATHY: When we got there he said he didn't feel like marching.

RUTH: Why not?

KATHY: Oh, Ruthie, I don't know. I don't know anything anymore. You devote two years to a guy and what does he give you? He never even told me about that letter. Drafted, and he didn't even tell me.

RUTH: He's not drafted. That letter's for the physical. All he has to do is act queer. They're not gonna take a queer musician.

KATHY: That's what I told him on the bus. He wouldn't even listen until I called him Job.

RUTH: What?

KATHY: He said he was dead. "Bob is dead."

RUTH: Bullshit, he's putting you on.

KATHY: That's what I mean. Me. He's even putting me on. Ungrateful bastard. The things I've done for him, Ruthie. Shit, I sound just like my mother. You know what I mean. I'm not complaining, but you know, you get tired of giving all the time and nothing's coming back. You know what I told him? I said he was the first guy I ever had an orgasm with. I mean, it really made him feel good. Now I gotta live with it. How can you explain something like that?

RUTH: Hey, no shitting around, did he really say he was gonna join?

KATHY: Ruthie, I'm telling you, he's serious. You know what he told me? He thinks the whole antiwar movement is a goddamn farce. I mean, Jesus, I really thought we were relating on that one. It's not like I'm asking the guy to go burn himself or anything but, I mean, he knows how I feel about the war and he's just doing it to be shitty. There's something behind it, I know that. He's like reaching out, trying to relate to me on the personal level by rejecting me but, like, I don't know how to break through. He says he's gonna study engineering in the army and then when he gets out he's gonna get some kind of plastic job and marry a plastic wife and live in a plastic house in some fucking plastic suburb and have two point seven children. Oh shit, Ruth, it's all too much. He went to a cowboy film.

RUTH: Well, you know, that's how it is.

KATHY: But Ruth, it's not like a fantasy scene. I know the guy. He'll go through with it. I mean, he really thinks he's serious. He doesn't see it's all part of a communication thing between him and me.

RUTH: I don't know. Like, maybe he's really serious. Mike's got this thing about physics. His tutor says he's a genius. Okay, maybe he is, like what do I know about physics? The thing is, he's gonna end up working for his old man in the lumber business. It's all laid out from the start. You have to fit in.

KATHY: You don't want him to do that, do you? If the guy

is into physics you've gotta really stand behind him and make it all happen for him.

RUTH: I don't know. You have some kids and everything. I mean it's not like you can't have a meaningful life if you get married and have kids.

KATHY: Wow, I don't believe you really mean that.

RUTH: Look, Kathy, I don't want Mike to saw wood for the rest of his life, but what can I do about it? Why shouldn't he get into wood? Like, what if he does physics for the rest of his life and he's a genius and ends up head of the department at some asshole university; you find out one day he's being financed by the CIA.

KATHY: These guys. They think they don't need you, so you go away and they freak out. Mike is a really brilliant guy. I mean, we all know that. You could really do things for him if you tried. You should've seen Bob when I first met him.

RUTH: I did.

KATHY: He used to compose all this really shitty music and like when he did something good he didn't even know it. You had to keep telling him yes, it's good, it's really great. A whole year it took for him to believe it. He's writing some fantastic stuff now, ever since, you know, I told him he was the first guy.

RUTH: Yeah, and look at him now.

KATHY: (*Crying again.*) You think you're really relating like crazy and then, I don't know, it's a whole new scene. It's like you don't even know him anymore.

RUTH: Maybe you ought to stop relating so hard.

KATHY: You don't know him, Ruth. I really know the guy and he needs me.

RUTH: Yeah, but maybe you ought to lay off for a while.
   (MIKE *bursts in through the front door.*)

MIKE: Holy shit, where were you?

RUTH: I got lost and came home.

MIKE: Christ, it was horrible. We got stopped by this line of cops. Me and Cootie were right up front so I told him we should get everyone to join hands and stand still. We're standing there and this one pig starts running toward Cootie and you know how he gets when he sees pigs and he always gets diarrhea. I don't know, he should have said something, but he got the urge so bad he started to run, you know, trying to find a toilet, and this dumb pig thought he was trying to resist arrest.

KATHY: Is he all right?

MIKE: They took him to the hospital. He's, I don't know, they said he'll be all right. He got it in the back.

(COOTIE *walks in.*)

COOTIE: Boy, what a shitty march. You had to go and get separated with all the eats. I could've really used a marmalade and chunky peanut butter.

RUTH: Hey, did you know, Bob really wants to join the army. He's not even gonna try and get out. He didn't even go to the march.

COOTIE: He didn't miss much.

KATHY: He went to a goddamn cowboy film.

COOTIE: Hey, is that the one with Kirk Douglas and Gina Lollobrigida and Curt Jurgens and Orson Welles and Tom Courtenay and . . .

KATHY: You guys are really something. You don't give a shit what happens to him. I thought we were, like, all together here. Smug bastards. I'll tell you something.

COOTIE: What's that, Kathy.

KATHY: You're no better than the people fighting this war.

(KATHY *storms out of the room down the hall.*)

MIKE: She's pretty cut up, huh?

RUTH: She thinks he's serious.

MIKE: Isn't he?

(COOTIE *starts jumping and singing, punctuating each note with a leap. He snarls the song.*)

COOTIE: We shall over cu—u—um,

We shall over cu—u—um,

We shall overcome some day—ay—ay—ay—ay

Oh, oh, oh, deep in my heart

I do believe.

We shall over . . .

MIKE: Shut up, Mel.

COOTIE: If Bob's really serious, we gotta stop the war quick so he doesn't get sent over there to get killed by an antipersonnel bullet.

(DICK *comes in, livid.*)

DICK: Fucking Norman is fucking out of his fucking mind. That's the last time I ever take him with me.

   (DICK *takes a bottle of milk from the icebox, kills it, and places it on the stack.*)

MIKE: Hey, what's the matter, Dick, didn't you get yourself some left-wing ass?

COOTIE: Don't be ashamed, sonny. If she's waiting out there in the hallway, bring her in and show us the goods.

DICK: Norman had a fucking gun with him. He took a fucking revolver to the march.

MIKE: Is he a good shot?

DICK: I'm not shitting around. We're sitting on the bus and he's telling me he's reading Ho Chi Minh on guerrilla war and he doesn't think marches are effective. So he says he's gonna use the marchers like an indigenous population and start a guerrilla war against the cops. I mean, I thought he was just fucking around. You know Norman. Then he pulls out this fucking revolver right there on the bus, people looking and everything, and he says he's gonna get a few cops and would I help him create a diversion. He's out of his fucking mind.

MIKE: How many'd he get?

DICK: Fuck you.

COOTIE: He got the girl, huh?

DICK: Where's Kathy and Bob?

RUTH: Bob's not here.

DICK: Kathy here?

RUTH: Leave her alone. She's upset.

COOTIE: Yeah, I wouldn't try to lay her just yet, 'cause she's still going with Bob.

   (DICK *walks out down the hall.*)

MIKE: That was a pretty stupid thing to say.

COOTIE: Just came out.

RUTH: Who cares? Everyone knows what dirty Dicky's up to. Except maybe Bob.

MIKE: And maybe Kathy.

RUTH: Kathy knows.

COOTIE: Do you think a guy could become a homosexual just by willpower? Could someone learn to like guys?

(*A knock on the front door.*)

RUTH: It's open.

(*In walks* LUCKY, *the downstairs neighbor, led by* MR. WILLIS, *the landlord.*)

WILLIS: Lucky tells me there's been a lotta noise up here. Is that right?

MIKE: Sorry, Mr. Willis, we had a little outburst up here. It's my fault. I just got a letter my sister had a baby.

COOTIE: We were celebrating.

WILLIS: That's all right, but keep it down. Lucky here was saying how you woke his wife up. She's a very ill person. I don't want any more complaints.

MIKE: Don't you worry about that, Mr. Willis, I'll take it on myself to keep this place really quiet.

LUCKY: Listen, I told you kids once before, and I'm not telling you again. You gotta get rid of those galvanized aluminum garbage cans in the yard and get plastic ones like everyone else.

RUTH: Listen, I don't see why we can't keep the ones . . .

MIKE: Ruth, now calm down, Ruth. I'm sorry, Lucky, but Ruth's pretty upset. Her father's fallen ill and they don't know for sure if it's . . . you know.

LUCKY: You got the galvanized aluminum ones out there. You'll have to get rid of the galvanized aluminum ones and get plastic.

WILLIS: I'll take care of the rest, Lucky. Thank you for bringing this particular grievance to my attention.

LUCKY: I'll give you till Monday, then I want to see plastic out there.

(LUCKY *leaves through front door.*)

WILLIS: Whew, I hope I seen the last of that loony today. Nothin' but complaints day and night. The guy was born with a hair across his ass. So who's gonna give the landlord a little coffee?

(RUTH *makes a move to get it.*)

WILLIS: Thanks, sweetheart. Brother, what a day, what a stinker of a day. Where's Bobby?

MIKE: He's dead.

WILLIS: Dead? He's dead? You guys really kill me, you guys. You got a whole sense of humor like nothin' else.

Dead, huh? Smart kid, Bobby. Hey, you been to the march?

COOTIE: Yep.

WILLIS: Great march. I watched it on Channel 8 in color. Brother, clothes you guys wear come out really good on color TV. You know, that guy Lucky can be a lotta trouble. He got a mind, like, you know, the size of a pinhead, you know what I mean? Just one sugar, sweetheart.

MIKE: You want the rent?

WILLIS: Rent, schment. I come to see how you guys are getting along and you talk to me about rent. How many landlords care, tell me that? One in a million, I can tellya. Hey, you decided whatya gonna do when you get out of college?

COOTIE: I'm gonna be a homosexual.

WILLIS: A homo. . . . You guys really slay me, you guys. What a sense of humor. You know, I'd give ten'a my other tenants for any one of you guys. You kids are the future of America. I mean that deeply, not too much milk, beautiful. Yeah, you kids live a great life up here. I got tenants complaining all the time about the way you kids carry on, and I'll tell ya something, you wanna know why they complain? 'Cause they'd give the last piece of hair on their heads to live like you kids are living.

RUTH: How's Mrs. Willis?

WILLIS: Huh? Oh, yeah, great, just great. Well, just between you and me and the wall she's gettin' to be a pain in the ass. She wants me to get rid of you, too. Why? I ask her. She don't like the way you live. Okay, I say, if you know so much, how do they live? She don't know and she don't wanna know. I try to tell her, you know, about the wild parties and stuff and taking drugs to have all new sensations in the body and the orgies with six or seven of you all at once. You should see her eyes light up. Same thing with all the tenants. When they hear what it's really like up here they go all funny. They'd pay me a hunnerd dollars to hear more, but they ain't got the nerve to ask. Get rid of them. That's all I hear.

Wamme to tell you something?

MIKE: If you got something to say you didn't ought to hold back.

WILLIS: Tremendous. You kids are tremendous. Listen. When the neighbors try to tellya about when they was young, don't believe it. It's a lotta bull, and I should know. When we was young it was so boring you fell asleep when you was twenty and you never woke up again. You hear them stories Lucky tells about the war. Crap. He's sittin' down there holdin' his dick and watchin' Doris Day on television. He'd give his left nut to know what's happenin' up here. This is the best cup of coffee I've had all day. I got a theory about it. It's when the head and the stomach don't talk to each other no more. That's when everything goes to hell. I'm gettin' so I don't know what I want half the time. I got these dreams, really crazy dreams. I got this one where I'm in a clearing, you know, it's right in the middle of the jungle and there's this tribe of Africans, I mean, like I don't know if they're Africans but they're livin' in the jungle and they're black so I figure they must be Africans. They got this skin. It's, you know, black, but really black. This maybe sounds kinda screwy, but it's really beautiful, this skin. It's a dream, remember. I'm not sayin' black skin is beautiful, if you see what I mean. I'm in charge of the whole works in this jungle and I got it all organized so the men live in one hut and the women live in another hut and there's a big sort of square in between where nobody's allowed after lights-out. They live like this all their life. There's no marryin' or anything. I'm a kind of witch doctor and I got this tribe believing . . . well, you know, they're just, like, Africans, and they don't know you gotta have a man and a woman to make babies, and I got 'em thinkin' you get babies when the moon shines down a girl's cunt and hits the inside of her womb. And I got this whole ceremony where a girl comes to me when she wants a baby and I tell her she gotta wait until it gets dark and the moon comes up. Then I tie her to a plank, face up, and tilt the plank so her thing is facing the moon and then I go to

the hut with the guys inside and get one of them to jerk
off on a leaf, you know, one of them tropical leafs that's
really big. Then I roll this leaf up like it's a tube and I
sneak across the square holding this leaf in my hand all
rolled up, until I get to the girl. She's lying there in the
moonlight all black and shiny and her thing is opened
right up 'cause she thinks . . . and I got this tube full
of jis in my hand, and I'm coming closer so I can smell
everything and . . . (*Comes out of it.*) Jesus, what am
I saying? I'm going crazy. It's just a dream, what I'm
telling you.

RUTH: That's the most beautiful thing I ever heard.

WILLIS: Listen, I got carried away. I didn't mean none of
that.

MIKE: Mr. Willis, if you'd've had the opportunities we've
had you'd've probably ended up one of the great poets of
the century, and I mean that includes Rimbaud, Rilke,
Williams, Pasternak, and Ginsberg.

COOTIE: And Whitman.

MIKE: Yes, Whitman included.

WILLIS: Oh Jesus, you kids, you kids. I feel like I can tell
you anything. Somebody could've thought I was pretty
screwy if I told them some of them things.

RUTH: How many landlords have poetry in their soul?

WILLIS: Yeah, yeah. Hey, I gotta run now. Listen, it's
really great having you guys around. If I could get some
of them other tenants to come up here and listen to you
the world would be a better place to live in, you know
what I mean?

MIKE: It would be a much better place.

COOTIE: A hundred percent better, at least.

RUTH: You're a beautiful person, Mr. Willis. Never be
ashamed of it.

WILLIS: No, I ain't. I ain't ashamed of myself. Hey, you
know what I was sayin' before about all them complaints. I lost a lotta tenants on account of you. I can't
afford anymore, so keep it quiet or I'll have to get rid of
you. Wonderful coffee, sweetheart. Seeya.

(WILLIS *leaves through front door.*)

RUTH: I wonder how long before they put him away?

(KATHY, *clothes a bit messed up, flounces into the kitchen and gets a glass of water.* DICK *follows her as far as the kitchen, as if he was trying to stop her, but when he gets to the doorframe he stops, feeling the tension in the room. He tries to button his shirt casually, not sure whether he wants the others to know what just happened between him and* KATHY.)

COOTIE: Hi, Dick, how's it hanging?

(KATHY *stiffens at the sink.* DICK *turns and goes down the hall out of sight.*)

MIKE: I still can't figure out what to get good old Bob for Christmas.

(*Before* KATHY *can reply, the doorbell rings. No one moves.*)

COOTIE: Whose turn is it?

KATHY: You're a miserable bastard.

COOTIE: What'd I say? We're just playing a chess tournament.

KATHY: Listen, this is my scene, mine. You guys stay out of it, okay, Ruth!

RUTH: It's her scene, guys, you stay out of it.

COOTIE: Roger.

MIKE: Sam.

COOTIE: Larry.

MIKE: Richard.

COOTIE: What's Richard getting Bob for Christmas?

(*The doorbell rings again, and* MIKE *jumps up to get it.* SHELLY's *standing there.*)

MIKE: Hello there, I don't know you.

SHELLY: Hi. Does Norman live here?

MIKE: Does anyone here know a Norman?

SHELLY: He said he lived here. I met him at the march today. He said to come here and wait for him. I been standing out in the hall 'cause, like, I heard someone talking and I didn't want to disturb anyone and then this guy just came out so I figured, well, it's now or never kind of thing. I'm Shelly.

RUTH: Come on in. I'm Ruth.

SHELLY: Oh, good, then Norman does live here because I wasn't sure when he gave me the address. Sometimes you meet a guy at a march and he'll like give you an address and you end up waiting for a few days and he never shows. Did that ever happen to you? It's happened to me a lot of times.

KATHY: Listen, everyone, I'm serious, I don't want him to know. I'll tell him when the time's right.

RUTH: It's your scene.

(KATHY *exits down hall.* SHELLY, *meanwhile, goes under the table and sits down on the floor.*)

SHELLY: I'm sorry about this. If you want to laugh go ahead. I'm used to it. It's just I've got this thing at the moment where I keep sitting under tables and I figured I'd better do it right away instead of pretending for a while I didn't sit under tables. I mean, sitting under the table is "me" at the moment, so why hide it? Have you ever done it?

RUTH: Want some coffee, Shelly?

SHELLY: I'm a vegetarian.

MIKE: Coffee's made from vegetables.

SHELLY: I don't drink coffee, thanks. I'll just wait for Norman.

COOTIE: Where's Norman?

SHELLY: Well, he was arrested for carrying a concealed weapon, but he said it's okay because he has a permit. He's really a total-action freak, and he's very committed to the whole peace thing.

COOTIE: Oh.

MIKE: Well now . . .

COOTIE: How about that.

(*Fade out.*)

(*End of Scene 3.*)

(*End of Act One.*)

ACT TWO

Scene 4

(NORMAN *is trying to read.* SHELLY *is under the table blowing bubbles.* MIKE *and* COOTIE *are playing chess.*)

MIKE: I still think you should've said something, Norman. I mean it's got nothing to do with putting you on. If Dick said we didn't have a cat, all right, I mean he's got a right to think that but, I mean, it's really irresponsible of him to go running all over the place saying we don't.

NORMAN: Well, you turned off the lights that time when you came in. I was trying to read.

MIKE: Yeah, but that was the nitty-gritty, no-nonsense, down-to-earth needs of the moment because a cat just won't give birth with the lights on.

NORMAN: Dick says you don't have a cat.

MIKE: Will you listen to what I'm trying to tell you?

COOTIE: You can't move there.

MIKE: Why not?

COOTIE: Mate in thirty-four.

MIKE: Shit, I didn't see that. Okay, your game.

(MIKE *and* COOTIE *start rearranging the pieces.*)

COOTIE: Yeah, you see, Dick gets these things and he'll tell you, like, we don't have a cat or something like that. We would've explained if you'd just come out and asked instead of getting all hostile and paranoid and thinking we were putting you on.

SHELLY: Wow, bubbles are really something else. I think they're maybe divine.

MIKE: Bubbles are divine, Shelly.

COOTIE: So's Bogart.

SHELLY: Oh, Bogart, wow.

COOTIE: You're pretty happy, aren't you, Shelly?

SHELLY: Oh . . . yeah. Like, it's the right foods. And being under the table.

MIKE: You gotta watch the paranoid thing, Norman.

NORMAN: You were putting me on about the cat.

MIKE: See, you got this very paranoid thing about the cat.

NORMAN: I have not . . .

COOTIE: And the worst thing is how you get all defensive about it every time we bring it up. We're not denying your validity to doubt, Norman. We're not rejecting you as a human being. It's just you have a very paranoid personality because you father's a cop and that means you grew up in a very paranoid atmosphere.

SHELLY: Wow, your father's a cop?

NORMAN: Well, you know . . .

SHELLY: You never told me that. I think that's really great. My brother always wanted to be a cop.

COOTIE: My uncle's a cop.

MIKE: Yeah, that's right, our uncle's a cop.

NORMAN: That's what I mean, you see . . .

MIKE: What do you mean?

NORMAN: Well, I mean, you've got to go making fun of my father being a cop.

MIKE: Look, Norman, it just so happens our uncle is a cop and why the hell should you be the only one around here with a cop in the family. You see, you got paranoid again, thinking we're putting you on. I mean, we could do the same thing. How do we know your father's a cop? We don't. We trust you.

COOTIE: Yeah, and if you'd've been outer-directed maybe you'd've seen you got a lot in common with us. A lot more than you ever expected.

MIKE: Then maybe we could've prevented that whole tragic episode with the gun.

NORMAN: Yeah, well, I don't know about you guys.

MIKE: You're not trying to say it wasn't a tragic episode.

COOTIE: It was an abortion of academic freedom, pure and simple.

MIKE: Here! Here!

COOTIE: I mean, when they can kick mathematics graduate students out of school just for trying to murder a few cops . . . And, by the way, Norman, I've heard that your being kicked out of school was the doing of the Dean of Admissions, a man who is known far and wide to be cornholing his widowed sister in the eye-sockets regularly . . .

MIKE: And without love.

COOTIE: And when the moon comes up he ties her to this plank . . .

MIKE: Mel . . .

COOTIE: So put that in yer pipe and smoke it. And don't try to tell us you enjoy having to schlepp down to the Hays Bick every night to wash dishes for a dollar ten an hour.

NORMAN: Oh, I don't know.

SHELLY: Hey, are you guys brothers?

MIKE: Now there. Look at that, Norman. Shelly's wondering about the relationship between Mel and me, and instead of being all paranoid about it and going crazy wondering she comes right out and asks.

SHELLY: Hey, are you?

COOTIE: Yeah, we're brothers.

SHELLY: Wow, I didn't know that either. I keep learning all these things about you guys.

MIKE: See, everything's cool now. Everybody trusts each other. That's what it's all about.

NORMAN: Well, I mean, with washing dishes I get more time to read. I've been thinking a lot and I guess it's like Dick said. I was pretty irrelevant before. Mathematics is pretty irrelevant no matter how you look at it, and bad mathematics is about as irrelevant as you can get.

SHELLY: I left school after the first month. I'm not saying I'm really relevant, yet, but like, some of my friends in school are really into bad scenes. School is evil. You can't find out where it's at when you're studying all the time to fit your head into exams. I'm getting to where I can read recipes all day and really get something out of it.

NORMAN: Yeah. I'm learning all this stuff about Vietnam. It's really something. I mean, I'm getting to the point where maybe I can do something really relevant about it.

MIKE: I wouldn't call that gun business relevant.

NORMAN: I was still in school when I thought of that.

SHELLY: Norman's got this fantastic idea.

NORMAN: Well, I haven't thought it all out yet . . .

SHELLY: No, Norman-baby, don't like close all up. It's the most relevant thing I ever heard of.

COOTIE: Jesus, Norman, how long have you been walking around with this idea all locked up inside you?

NORMAN: I didn't get it all at once. It sort of came in stages, but I think it's about right.

COOTIE: Man, you're gonna go crazy if you keep everything inside like that.

SHELLY: Tell them the idea, Norman.

NORMAN: Well, you see . . . (*Pause.*) I'm gonna set myself on fire as a protest against the war.

(COOTIE *and* MIKE *look at him and exchange brief glances.*)

I've thought about it a lot. I mean, I've read I guess about a hundred books about the war and the more you read the more you see it's no one thing you can put your finger on. It's right in the middle of the whole system, like Dick said. I shouldn't've tried to kill those policemen, but I didn't know then they were part of the system like everything else. No one's got the right to take anyone else's life, that's what I've decided. But I've still got the right to take my own life for something I believe in.

SHELLY: I'm gonna burn with Norman. We're gonna burn together. We've thought it all through and, like, if he burns himself alone that's just one person. Everyone'll say he's insane, but if two of us do it . . . wow. Two people. What are they gonna say if two of us do it?

MIKE: (*Pause.*) Three of us.

COOTIE: Four of us.

MIKE: You, too, huh?

COOTIE: It's the only way.

NORMAN: Hey, wait a minute. I've read a lot about the whole subject and I really know just why I'm gonna do it. I'm not just doing it for fun or anything. You can't just jump into it.

MIKE: Listen, Norman, you don't have to believe this if you don't want to but it's the truth, on my honor. Me and Cootie talked about the exact same thing a year ago. We were all ready to burn ourselves . . . .

COOTIE: It was more than a year ago.

MIKE: More than a year?

COOTIE: Almost a year and a half.

MIKE: That's right, a year and a half, boy, time really goes quick.

COOTIE: It sure does.

MIKE: The thing is, we decided against it because we figured two isn't enough.

COOTIE: You know how the papers can lie. "Brothers Burn!"

MIKE: Yeah, "Hippie Brothers in Suicide Pact." That kind of shit.

COOTIE: But think of it. With four of us!

NORMAN: You really want to do it?

MIKE: It's the only way.

NORMAN: I mean, I wasn't sure yet. I hadn't made up my mind definitely. I was still looking for another way.

SHELLY: No, Norman-baby, it's the only relevant gesture. Like you said.

(*A long pause while* NORMAN *thinks.*)

NORMAN: Okay.

MIKE: After the Christmas vacation.

COOTIE: No, no, after graduation. We'll study like mad and get fantastic grades and graduate with honors so they can't say we were cracking up or anything.

MIKE: Yeah, we'll get Phi Beta Kappa. I'd like to see them say we're insane when two Phi Beta Kappas go up in flames with the son of a policeman and the daughter of a . . . Hey, what does your father do?

SHELLY: Well, it's kind of funny. I mean, he's a pretty weird head in his way. He's got, like, six or seven jobs at any one time.

MIKE: That's okay, Daughter of a weird head with six or seven jobs at any given time. That covers the whole spectrum.

NORMAN: What does your father do? I mean, I know your uncle's a policeman because I trust you, but you never said what your father did. I was curious. Like, if they bring our fathers into it what'll they say about you?

COOTIE: He's a trapper.

SHELLY: Wow, that's really something else. Like, a fur trapper?

COOTIE: Furs and hides, you know. Rabbit and mink and muskrat and beaver and elk and reindeer and seal. Some otter. Penguin.

SHELLY: Wow, penguin.

COOTIE: Well, you know, he works the Great Northwest Territory up to the mouth of the St. Lawrence Seaway, and over to the Aleutians.

SHELLY: Boy, this'll really blow everyone's mind.

MIKE: Yeah, this'll make everyone think twice, all right.

COOTIE: You know, we can't tell anyone about this. If word gets out they'll send squads of police around here and we'll get arrested and put under psychiatric observation and we'll get subjected to a battery of tests that make you look nuts no matter how you answer.

NORMAN: I won't say anything.

SHELLY: Oh, wow, like you don't even have to worry about me.

NORMAN: I didn't even know there were any trappers left.
(*A knock on the door.*)

MIKE: Come in.

VOICE: C'mon, c'mon, open up in there.
(MIKE *opens the door and finds two cops standing there.* BREAM *is elderly and* EFFING *is young.*)

BREAM: You live here?

MIKE: Yes, sir.

BREAM: Look, you know what I mean, you and who else.

MIKE: Well, there's me and my brother Cootie . . . um, Mel, and there's Norman, Dick, Bob, Kathy, and Ruth.

BREAM: Kathy and Ruth, huh? Those are girl's names.

MIKE: Kathy and Ruth are both girls, sir.

BREAM: Don't block the doorway.

(MIKE *stands aside as* BREAM *and* EFFING *enter.* EFFING *wanders around the room, inspecting.*)

(*Indicating Shelly.*) Which one's she? You Kathy or Ruth?

SHELLY: I'm Shelly.

BREAM: Shelly, huh? You didn't say nothin' about no Shelly.

MIKE: She doesn't live here, sir.

BREAM: Visiting?

SHELLY: I'm with Norman.

BREAM: You're Norman, huh?

NORMAN: She's my girl friend.

BREAM: Good, we got that straight.

EFFING: Hey, Bream, this here's a map of Europe.

BREAM: Yeah. Now listen. There's been a complaint from the people across there. I know you kids are students and you probably think you own the goddamn country, but I got some news for you. There's laws around here and you gotta obey them just like everyone else.

MIKE: We appreciate that, sir.

EFFING: Hey, Bream, look at all them milk bottles.

BREAM: Yeah. Now listen. I don't want to hear any more complaints about you guys. I'm a reasonable man, which is something you can get verified by askin' anyone on the force, but when I gotta put up with a lotta stupid complaints I can cause trouble, and I mean real trouble, with a capital T.

EFFING: Hey, look at all them dishes in the sink, Bream.

BREAM: Yeah.

NORMAN: What was the complaint?

BREAM: What do you mean, what was the complaint? The complaint was guys and girls parading around in here bare-ass. Now look, I'm not the kind of dumb cop that goes around throwing his weight everywhere to prove he's some kind of big shot. I don't need to, you follow me. I know what I know and I know what I don't know, and one of the things I know I don't know is what the hell the kids are up to nowadays, but okay. That's my problem. If you wanna run around naked that's okay by me, and I hope you kids take note of the fact that I'm winking one eye when it comes to the law about cohabitation.

MIKE: We appreciate that fact, sir. It was the first thing we noticed.

COOTIE: I sure appreciate it. I think I can speak for Norman and Shelly, and if any of the other guys were here they'd appreciate it a lot.

MIKE: I mean it's not as if we underestimate the life of a cop. For chrissakes, I mean, our uncle's a cop. His father's a cop. A lot of us around here are pretty close to the world of cops.

BREAM: You got cops in the family?

EFFING: Hey, Bream, look at this heater.

BREAM: Yeah.

MIKE: It's not like we don't know what you guys have to put up with. It can be a pretty crappy job.

BREAM: I don't know . . .

MIKE: I'm not saying it doesn't have its rewards. My uncle's life is full of rewards. His father's life is very meaningful.

BREAM: Yeah, that's what I mean.

(COOTIE *gets up and starts to leave the room.*)

EFFING: Hey, Bream, the kid's leaving the room.

COOTIE: I got a call from nature.

BREAM: That's legit. You go ahead, kid.

(COOTIE *goes out the front door.*)

EFFING: Hey, Bream, the kid says he's going to the euphemism and what if he's got some stuff on him or something. He can flush it down and come back clean.

BREAM: He's okay.

EFFING: Jesus, Bream. Sir.

BREAM: The guy's new on the job. He don't know the score yet.

MIKE: You know how some people exaggerate. I mean, look what they say in the papers about you guys.

Maybe, like after a shower we'll come in here to get an anchovy snack or chocolate milk or something, and we forget to put something on . . .

EFFING: Look at that, Bream, the girl keeps sitting under there . . .

BREAM: Goddamnit, Effing, who's in charge around here?

EFFING: But she's sitting under there . . .

BREAM: Did we come here to investigate a complaint about a girl sitting under the table?

EFFING: No, sir, but . . .

BREAM: The girl happens to be well within her rights as a taxpaying citizen of the community to sit under any table she wants, and until we get complaints about her sitting under there we leave her alone. Understand?

EFFING: Yeah, yeah, yeah . . .

SHELLY: Thanks.

BREAM: That's okay, lady. The kid's a rookie. They give us pros a bad name. Now let me tell you something about the people complaining about you. They look in here and see you guys bare-assed and they're complaining because they're so sick of looking at each other they gotta go spying on you. We know about them people. They're strict Roman Catholics. Twelve kids in four rooms. The old man can't keep it in his pants for ten minutes running. So they got troubles, right, and everyone that's got troubles wants to give troubles to someone else. So they make a complaint, and that's well within their rights as law-abiding citizens of this community. I got enough troubles without their goddamn complaints. I got enough to do watching the Vietnam freaks and the niggers and the loonies going up on buildings with high-power rifles picking off everyone down below. Let me give you some good advice. Get curtains. They got some fiber glass curtains at Woolworth's, you can't tell them from real cotton. Twelve dollars and fifty cents a pair and they come in eight colors, plain and patterned. You get some curtain rods for a dollar sixty-nine apiece and for a total of twenty-eight dollars and thirty-eight cents you save yourself from a lot of crazy neighbors. If you can't afford twenty-eight dollars and thirty-eight cents, get some gingham, thirty-nine cents a yard at Penney's. Measure your windows and allow a foot extra at each end. All you gotta do is take up a three-inch hem at each end, fold it over once, and hand stitch. A couple of curtain rings and you're in business. Can you remember that, or d'you want me to write it down?

SHELLY: Hey, yeah, would you do that?

(BREAM *takes out a notebook and starts to write.* EFFING *is nervous.*)

EFFING: The kid's been gone a long time.

BREAM: I got eyes, Effing.

EFFING: Yeah, yeah, yeah, okay.

BREAM: (*Writing.*) So, what are you kids gonna do with yourselves? (*Pause.*) Am I being nosy or something?

MIKE: No, I mean, there's a lot of opportunities all over the place. We're not jumping into anything without we've looked the whole thing over.

BREAM: Smart kids. Boy, that's really something. Cop sending his kid to college. They must pay him pretty good, huh?

NORMAN: I guess so.

BREAM: Yeah, what's he a sergeant . . . lieutenant or something?

NORMAN: He's Chief of Police for Erie County.

BREAM: (*Whistles.*) Whew! Pretty good. That shut me up okay. Chief of Police. Oh boy, that's really something.

NORMAN: It's just his job, you know.

BREAM: Look, ah, here's your instructions. I want them up by Wednesday. Any complaints after that and all of you guys'll be in court, father or no father, you understand me? This ain't Erie County.

MIKE: Yes, sir.

NORMAN: Okay.

(COOTIE *returns and stands in the door. There's a pause.*)

COOTIE: That's better.

(*End of Scene 4.*)

Scene 5

(RUTH *is scraping some cat food into a bowl. A cat comes in and eats.* RUTH *keeps glancing at her watch.*)

RUTH: Kitty-kitty-kitty-kitty-kitty. Chomp, chomp. Good girl. Make a lot of milk for the kitties.

(*Kathy comes in from the hall and throws herself down on a chair.*)

KATHY: Oh, Jesus, Ruth, how am I ever gonna tell him?

RUTH: Who?

KATHY: Bob, for chrissakes. Who else?

RUTH: Well, how should I know?

KATHY: I never slept with Dick. I know you got the idea I did, but it's not true. He never got all the way. . .

RUTH: . . . Okay. . .

KATHY: . . . yet. (*Pause.*) I'm not saying I wouldn't like to.

RUTH: So go ahead.

KATHY: Well don't try to pretend it doesn't mean anything to you. You know as well as I do it'll kill Bob if he ever finds out I'm even thinking of sleeping with Dick.

RUTH: That's how it goes.

KATHY: Ruthie, look, we've known each other since freshman year. I can tell when you're thinking something. This is really a big decision I've gotta make. What am I gonna do about Bob? I mean, it feels like maybe we're you know, finished, but I like the guy. I really like him a lot and I respect his music. But I know he could never relate to me as a friend. It's gotta be tied up with sex. I mean, Richard really seems to dig me, but I don't know. He's pretty together. He's not the kind of guy you could really do something big for. Not like Bob.

RUTH: Oh, for shit's sake, Kathy, Dick is a fucking parasite.

KATHY: That's not fair, Ruth.

RUTH: Fair, shit. Do you know what that guy's doing to get into graduate school? You ever heard of Professor Roper in the Eastern studies department?

KATHY: He's Dick's tutor.

RUTH: Yeah, and he also happens to be queer as a three-dollar bill, and Dick is fucking his wife to keep her quiet so good old Roper can suck cock with all those graduate students from Thailand or Malaya, or whatever the hell they are.

KATHY: Who said?

RUTH: Who said? For chrissakes, Kathy, the whole goddamn school knows about it. Dirty Dicky.

KATHY: That's why?

RUTH: Yeah, what else? I mean, the guy washes eight times a day.

KATHY: Oh, man, how long have you guys known about this? I mean, like why didn't anyone ever tell me? You can't just let him screw up his future like that. Hasn't anyone tried to do anything about it?

RUTH: Like tell him Mrs. Roper's got clap?

KATHY: Ruthie, the guy must be really suffering.

RUTH: Oh shit, Kathy, let's not have the big savior thing.

KATHY: That's not very funny.

RUTH: Look, we're all gonna graduate pretty soon, and we're all gonna go away, and probably we'll never see each other again except maybe like at Christmas or something. So why don't you worry about yourself and never mind about Dick and Bob. They'll be okay.

KATHY: Boy, you sure have changed, Ruth. I don't know. You sure have changed.

(BOB *comes through front door carrying books*.)

BOB: I don't believe it. It's incredible. You know what happened today in counterpoint class? Remember I was telling you about Eric Shatz?

RUTH: . . . three armpits . . . ?

BOB: The very one.

KATHY: (*Nicely*.) Bob . . .

(BOB, *who has gone to the icebox to steal some of* DICK's *hamburgers, stops short in whatever gesture he is holding, only for a moment though, just long enough to cut* KATHY. *When he resumes his story, he is talking only to* RUTH, *who is wrapping a Christmas present*.)

BOB: Today Shatz turned in this perfect, spotless, clean counterpoint exercise. I mean, for someone as filthy as

Shatz, that's a miracle. They say his high-school year-book voted him "The Most Likely to Attract Infectious Disease."

(BOB *has the hamburgers out by now.* KATHY, *being all nice, takes the hamburgers from him, indicating that she'll cook.* BOB *goes away from her and sits with* RUTH.)

He picks his nose and squeezes his pimples right there in class, and his counterpoint exercises have to be seen to be believed. He writes them in pencil, and if he makes a mistake or something, he spits on his eraser and rubs the paper about a hundred times . . . per note, so by the time he hands it to Professor Bolin, it's just this gray sludge with lots of little black things swimming around on it. Anyway, about a week ago, when Shatz handed over his work, Professor Bolin put on a pair of gloves before he'd take it, so Shatz must've got the message and this week when Bolin called for homework, Shatz set this beautiful, clean exercise down on the piano. We couldn't believe it. Bolin just sat there staring at it, and we all sat staring at Bolin, and after about ten minutes, no shit, it took that long, Bolin turned to us and said, "Free will is an illusion." Isn't that too much?

KATHY: Bob, can I talk to you . . . ?

(BOB *ignores her.*)

BOB: The thing is, Bolin's got a Ph.D. He's also written two books and a couple of hundred symphonies and string quartets and they say he taught himself twenty-two languages in four hours or something . . .

KATHY: Please, Bob, I want to talk to you . . .

BOB: And another thing, Bolin's wife got drunk at a faculty party for the music department last year and she yelled, "Fuck Shönberg, I wanna dance," and then she went and laid the only black professor in the school, which all goes to show that when Bolin tells you free will is an illusion . . . you better believe it.

KATHY: (*Pointed.*) Bob, I would like to talk to you . . .

BOB: Hey, Ruth, did I ever tell you the one about the guy that died and came back to life as Job?

KATHY: Oh don't start that shit again.

BOB: Again? It started over a month ago. I mean, even Bolin caught on after two lessons. Of course he still makes me walk around the music building every time I put down parallel fifths, but that's how it goes, life is trying at the best of times, every cloud has a silver lining, a stitch in time saves nine . . .

(RUTH *looks at her watch.*)

RUTH: I've gotta go.

BOB: Did I say something?

RUTH: No. Kathy wants to talk to you about sleeping with Dick.

KATHY: Ruth . . . bitch!

(RUTH *goes out the front door, grabbing her coat on the way.*)

BOB: (*Pause.*) Meanwhile, back at the ranch . . . You'll never believe this, but when I came in just now, I didn't expect that. Bedbugs, maybe. Thermonuclear war . . .

KATHY: She had no right.

BOB: I'm trying to think of something appropriate to say, like "Name the first one after me." That's Job. J-O-B. Job.

KATHY: Please, Bob, can I say something . . .

BOB: Do you have trouble pronouncing the name Job?

KATHY: Jesus Christ, you're impossible.

BOB: Ah, yes, but I exist, nonetheless.

KATHY: You've just cut me right out. You're not even trying to relate to me anymore. (*Pause.*) Well, you're not.

BOB: No, Kathy. The fact is, I like you a lot. I, um, sort of love you, if you know what I mean.

KATHY: I don't really want to sleep with Dick.

BOB: Then don't.

KATHY: It's just, he tried to get me that night after the demonstration.

BOB: I know. He told me.

KATHY: That shit.

BOB: I thought it was pretty good of him.

KATHY: He never got into me, you know.

BOB: That's nice.

KATHY: Oh, Bob, I'm sorry.

DOD: If Bob were around I'm sure he'd forgive you.

KATHY: What'll we do?

BOB: What do you mean? Like study or something?

KATHY: Bob, how does it stand? Is it . . . it's over, isn't it?

BOB: Between us, you mean?

KATHY: Yes.

BOB: If that's what you want.

KATHY: Of course I don't want it. I love you a lot.

BOB: Okay, so let's study for Phil 720.

KATHY: Oh, for chrissakes, show some emotion. I don't know where I'm at with you half the time.

BOB: Look, what's the big hang-up? If you want to stay with me, okay. If you want to move into Dick's room, go ahead. If you don't know for sure stay one night with me and one night with him till you start feeling a definite preference for one of us . . .

KATHY: Jesus Christ, Bob, what's the matter with you?

BOB: I'm Job. Bob's dead.

KATHY: (*Is in a furious slow burn. She stands and goes toward the hall door.*) All right . . . all right . . . (*Before she can exit a knock on the door stops her. A game. Who's going to open the door.* BOB *picks up a book and starts reading. Another knock.* KATHY *sighs. She's above these silly games. She opens the door on a middle-aged man in well-cut coat. A businessman from head to foot. This is* MURRAY, BOB's *uncle.*)

MURRAY: Hi. Does Bob Rettie live here?

(BOB *looks up from his book.*)

BOB: Murray!!

MURRAY: Can I come in?

BOB: What the hell are you doing here?

MURRAY: Guy flies a couple thousand miles to see his nephew, maybe he can come in, huh?

BOB: Yeah, yeah. Come in, come in . . . sit down. . . .

MURRAY: Hey, I bet you're surprised to see me, huh? Maybe a little happy.

BOB: Yeah, I mean I haven't seen you for a couple thousand years or something.

MURRAY: (*to* KATHY.) It's longer than that since he wrote.

BOB: Oh, ah, that's Kathy. My uncle.

MURRAY: How do you do.

KATHY: Hi.

MURRAY: You drink a lot of milk, huh?

BOB: Yeah.

(*They laugh.*)

MURRAY: Where'd you get that goddamn icebox?

BOB: Oh, you know. . .

MURRAY: Is this the way you been living? Bobby boy, why didn't you tell me. Write a letter, say Murray, I need a little cash, I'd've sent you some money for a decent refrigerator.

BOB: Murray, we're living okay.

MURRAY: So I'm sorry for breathing. Did I interrupt something?

BOB: No. Nothing at all.

MURRAY: Are you two . . . ah. . .

BOB: Yeah—Murray, look, sit down, take your coat off . . .

MURRAY: Hey, Bobby, Bobby-boy. You got long hair . . .

BOB: Yeah, it keeps growing.

MURRAY: Still proud, huh? (*to* KATHY.) Just like his mother . . . (MURRAY *looks at the two of them and shrugs . . .*) Well what can I say . . .

KATHY: Look, I think I'll . . .

BOB: How long you in town for?

MURRAY: Oh, you know. Business.

KATHY: Excuse me, I'm gonna . . .

BOB: How's the kids?

MURRAY: Oh, fine, fine, keep asking about you.

BOB: Auntie Stella?

MURRAY: Oh. You know. We got a new house . . .

BOB: Great. Where you going, Kathy . . . ?

KATHY: (*Has been edging toward the door. Quietly.*) I'll be in Dick's room if you want me.

(KATHY *exits.*)

MURRAY: Is she okay?

BOB: (*Flat.*) Yeah. It's her time of the month, you know.

MURRAY: Say no more. You don't have to tell me about that. Nice girl. Very nice (*laughs*). So . . .

BOB: Come through New York?

MURRAY: Yeah, you know, passed through.

BOB: You passed through New York, huh?

MURRAY: (*Uneasy.*) Yeah, sure, you know . . .

BOB: D'you see Mom?

MURRAY: Yeah, yeah, sure. She'd maybe like a letter every now and then. Your own mother.

BOB: It's not like that, Murray. When I see her I see her.

MURRAY: (*Shivers.*) Jesus Christ.

BOB: You okay?

MURRAY: Sit down, Bobby-boy.

BOB: I'm okay like this.

MURRAY: I got something to tell you, you should maybe be sitting down when I tell you.

> (BOB *sits.* MURRAY *pulls his chair close and takes* BOB'*s head in his hands.* BOB *is stiff.*)

MURRAY: Bobby-boy, oh Bobby. I'd like to see more of you, kid. Me and the family. You maybe come out and visit, huh?

BOB: (*Flat.*) What's happened, Murray?

MURRAY: How am I supposed to tell you?

> (*Pause.*)

BOB: (*Long pause.*) Cancer.

> (MURRAY *nods.* BOB *doesn't see him.*)

How long's she got?

MURRAY: A week, two weeks. I don't know. Any time now.

BOB: Those operations . . . kidney trouble. Oh, shit, why didn't someone tell me?

MURRAY: You got your studies, we should worry you to death?

BOB: (*Flat.*) Fuck you all.

MURRAY: I thought . . . I thought maybe you and me fly to New York tonight.

BOB: Yeah, get in there quick for the payoff. That'll be just great.

MURRAY: She don't know yet.

BOB: Yeah. "Hi, Mom, I just came flying in with Murray a couple of weeks before Christmas vacation to see you for no good reason." You think she won't guess?

MURRAY: She doesn't have to. We can always tell her something.

BOB: You planning to keep it from her, too? I bct it's the first thing she thought of. Two years. She had that first operation two years ago. She's been dying for two years and I didn't even fucking know it.

MURRAY: I don't want to hurt anybody.

BOB: (*Pause.*) I'll pack some stuff. No, you stay here. I want to be alone.

> (BOB *goes down the hall.* MURRAY *sits. Very short pause, then* MIKE *and* COOTIE *burst in through the front door, laden with Christmas presents. They see* MURRAY, *cross the kitchen to the hall door, exit, and start arguing loudly just outside in the hallway. After a moment they reenter,* MIKE *leading. Deferential.*)

MIKE: Me and my friend were wondering if you could settle a little argument for us.

MURRAY: What?

MIKE: Were you or weren't you the guy behind the bar in *Key Largo*, starring Humphrey Bogart and Edward G. Robinson?

MURRAY: I'm Bob's uncle.

MIKE: (*To* COOTIE.) He's Bob's uncle.

COOTIE: Are you a for-real uncle?

MURRAY: (*Confused.*) Yeah, yeah, I'm his uncle.

COOTIE: Maternal or paternal?

MURRAY: I'm related to Bob through his mother. She was . . . she's my sister.

MIKE: That means you and him have different names.

MURRAY: Yeah, he's a Rettie, I'm a Golden.

MIKE: That's a pretty convincing story, mister.

COOTIE: Most of the pieces fit pretty good.

> (MIKE *and* COOTIE *start toward the hall.* SHELLY *comes in the front door.*)

SHELLY: Hi, everyone.

MIKE: Hiya, Shelly.

COOTIE: Good old Shelly, hiya.

(MIKE *and* COOTIE *are gone down the hall.*)

SHELLY: Hey . . . Excuse me, do you know if Norman's here?

MURRAY: I don't know who Norman is.

SHELLY: One of the guys here. I mean, like he lives here. You someone's father?

MURRAY: I'm Bob's uncle.

SHELLY: Bob? Oh, yeah, Job.

(SHELLY *sits under the table.*)

I'm waiting for Norman. Hey, are you, like, a for-real uncle?

MURRAY: You kids keep asking that.

SHELLY: You don't think of him with an uncle.

MURRAY: Look, if you don't want me to stay in here, I'll go and help Bob.

SHELLY: No, you stay here. Like, I enjoy company. Hey, is he here?

MURRAY: I'm afraid I don't know your friend Norman.

SHELLY: I mean Job. Your nephew.

MURRAY: Yes, he's here. I'm waiting for him.

SHELLY: He's, like, in here somewhere? Inside the apartment?

MURRAY: Yes. Look, you want to go down and ask him about Norman, go ahead.

SHELLY: Is he in the toilet?

MURRAY: He's in his room.

SHELLY: Wow, that's like, really weird.

MURRAY: He's just packing, that's all.

SHELLY: Yeah, but I mean, if you're his for-real uncle how come you're like sitting in here when he's down there?

MURRAY: Look, he . . . (*Weeping softly.*) . . . I don't know.

SHELLY: Hey, you're really crying like crazy. What's the matter? I thought you were, like, waiting for him to come back here, you know, like, to the apartment or something. I just wanted to know because I'm waiting for Norman to come back so I thought we could maybe sit here together waiting and that would be something we had in common, then you told me he was in his room packing and everything and I thought that was sorta weird 'cause if you're like his for-real uncle you could just go down there and be with him. Why's he packing?

BOB: (*Entering with bag.*) Okay. I'm ready.

SHELLY: Hey, Job, you going away?

BOB: I'll be back in a few days.

SHELLY: Like, you mean, you're not just going home early for Christmas vacation.

BOB: No.

SHELLY: Oh. Okay. Hey, Merry Christmas, you guys.

BOB: Merry Christmas.

MURRAY: Merry Christmas.

(DICK *comes in through the front door.* BOB *and* MURRAY *start out.* DICK *is baffled.*)

DICK: Hey, you going?

BOB: Yeah. Kathy's in your room. (*Pause.*) She doesn't like it from behind.

(BOB *and* MURRAY *are gone.*)

DICK: Where's he going?

SHELLY: I don't know, but the guy with him is his for-real uncle and he's a weird head.

(KATHY *comes into the kitchen.*)

KATHY: Hey, did Bob just go out?

SHELLY: Wow, he didn't even tell you?

DICK: He left with his uncle.

KATHY: Uncle?

SHELLY: Yeah, like it's his for-real uncle, I'm pretty sure.

KATHY: Jesus, why didn't he say something. I mean, I been waiting for him down there . . .

SHELLY: Well the uncle said Job went down to his room to pack, and I mean, like if you were in there with him and he started putting a lot of socks and underwear and toilet stuff in a suitcase you should've got suspicious and asked him something, like where's he going.

KATHY: Look, I went to the bathroom, okay?

SHELLY: Ya didn't flush.

KATHY: Mind your own fucking business, Shelly. What does he expect me to do? How can I make plans for the Christmas vacation if he just . . . shit, he could've said something.

(DICK, *in a feeble attempt to avoid* KATHY's *rage, tries to sneak out down the hallway.*)

And listen, you, you have a lot of nerve telling him about that night.

DICK: I didn't say anything.

KATHY: He said you told him.

DICK: Honest, Kathy, I never did.

KATHY: (*Vague.*) I'm really getting to hate this place.

(KATHY *starts down the hall.* DICK *starts after her.*)

DICK: Kathy!

(*Before* DICK *can get down the hall,* RUTH *rushes in through the front door, breathless.*)

RUTH: Oh, wow, have I ever had the most fantastic experience!

(DICK *goes down the hall, slamming the door.*)

(*Yelling.*) You're a shit, Dick.

SHELLY: You seen Norman?

RUTH: Oh, hi, Shelly. Hey, let me tell you about what just happened to me. It really blew my mind.

(*From down the hall, we hear voices singing.*)

MIKE & COOTIE: (*Singing, offstage.*)
WE WISH YOU A MERRY CHRISTMAS
WE WISH YOU A MERRY CHRISTMAS
WE WISH YOU A MERRY CHRISTMAS
WE WISH YOU A MERRY CHRISTMAS
WE WISH YOU A MERRY CHRISTMAS
WE WISH YOU A MERRY CHRISTMAS
WE WISH YOU A MERRY CHRISTMAS
WE WISH YOU A MERRY CHRISTMAS
AND . . .

(MIKE *and* COOTIE *rush in from the hall dressed in Santa Claus costumes and end the song.*)

A HAPPY NEW YEAR.

MIKE: We got a present for you, Ruth.

SHELLY: Hey, where'd you get those?

COOTIE: We're doing collections this year. Yep.

MIKE: You want to see the great old present we got ya?

RUTH: I was just gonna tell Shelly what happened when I went to see Quinn. You know Quinn, the albino dwarf . . .

MIKE: Oh, yeah, old Quinn.

COOTIE: Good old Quinn.

RUTH: Yeah, right. Well I had to see him about homework for the Christmas vacation and, I mean, like, he was the last person I wanted to see. I always thought he was a vicious little bastard. I mean, he can be pretty shitty.

MIKE: They say he shot a man in Abilene.

COOTIE: In the back.

RUTH: Listen, willya. I went into his office and he's standing by the window, you know, three-feet high and everything. I thought he was probably gonna ask why I wasn't doing any homework, and I had this whole speech worked out about how I thought he was a pretentious little snot and how I frankly didn't give a shit about philosophy and even less of a shit about him, if that's possible and . . . oh, you know, I was really going to kill him. Anyway, he told me to come over to the window, so I came over and we both stood there looking out. Snow everywhere, like, white wherever you looked and a lot of snow coming down like in those paperweights you shake up, and there's all these kids down below coming out of the building, all little lumps moving across the white in slow motion, and we're looking at them, just the two of us for, I don't know, about a minute or two, and then he just turns to me, like without any warning, and says this incredibly beautiful thing . . .

MIKE: Hey, don't you want to see the nifty present we got ya?

RUTH: Let me tell you what the guy said, willya?

MIKE: Right, you tell us what Quinn said, then we'll show you the present.

RUTH: Yeah.

MIKE: Will you look at the present first then tell us what Quinn said?

RUTH: For Christ's sake stop fucking around and listen.

MIKE: All right, what did Quinn say?

COOTIE: I'd like to hear what Quinn said.

(*As* RUTH *is about to speak,* KATHY *runs through from the hall and out the front door with a valise in hand.*

DICK *shouts from offstage down the hall.*)

DICK: (*Offstage.*) Kathy. (DICK *enters and on his way across the room and out the front door, buttons his overcoat.*) Kathy!

(RUTH'*s face shows worry as she watches this. Seconds after* DICK *exits, she takes her coat and follows, leaving* MIKE, COOTIE, *and* SHELLY *alone. There is a pause.*)

MIKE: Things around here are getting a little out of control, Cootie.

COOTIE: You feel that way, huh?

MIKE: I do.

COOTIE: Well, what are we gonna do about it, movies or rollerskating?

MIKE: Cootie, sometimes you're really a dumb asshole.

COOTIE: But then sometimes, I'm not. (*Gets up and walks down the hall slowly.*)

SHELLY: Hey!

(MIKE *exits after* COOTIE, *leaving* SHELLY *alone.*)
(*Slow fade.*)
(*End of Scene 5.*)
(*End of Act Two.*)

ACT THREE

Scene 6

*(Most of the posters are down. A bare feeling.
Around graduation. There are some letters on the
table. RUTH, alone, is reading her letter. DICK comes in
from outside, dressed for warm weather, perhaps carrying a box. He opens the icebox.)*

DICK: Shit, nothing left.

RUTH: We cleaned it.

DICK: Anyone gone yet?

RUTH: No. Why don't you look at your grades?

DICK: *(Opens letter.)* Jesus.

RUTH: Bad?

DICK: Fucking awful.

RUTH: Do you graduate?

DICK: Yeah, just.

RUTH: They sent Kathy's grades here.

DICK: That was tactful.

RUTH: Maybe she'll be around to pick them up. I got into
graduate school.

DICK: Great.

RUTH: Philosophy.

DICK: Philosophy?

RUTH: Yeah! *(pause)* I mean, you know, why not?
(DICK starts toward the hall.)
Hey, Dick, I don't get it. You know that day she left,
just before Chirstmas . . . did you get into her?

DICK: How fucking low can you stoop, Ruth?

RUTH: No, I mean, you know, just, she must've done something to fuck you up this bad.

DICK: Kathy did not fuck me up.

RUTH: Yeah, well, ever since she left you've been looking like really terrible. You never even studied for finals. I mean, you were the academic head around here. Hey, you did get her, didn't you, and I bet she told you you were the first guy that ever turned her on.

(DICK *starts out again.*)

Did she? Oh, come off it, Dick, I just . . . I thought we were friends.

DICK: You know what that goddamn fucking little cunt told me? Just before she left? She told me I was screwing Roper's wife. Me, screwing Roper's wife.

RUTH: Well, you know Kathy.

DICK: She said everybody in the whole fucking school knew about it. It got back to Roper.

RUTH: Wow, I bet he was pretty pissed off, huh?

DICK: He was pretty good about it, considering. He pulled me in after a tutorial and gave me the old "Richard, my boy" speech. He thought I started the rumor. Me. Shit. "Richard, my boy, it's said you're doing unenviable things to my wife. My boy, that particular assignment has already been well seen to. It's not like you to claim credit for someone else's work." You ever tried to do a paper for someone who thinks you've been saying you're screwing his wife? Shit. Poor old fairy. Boy, what a fucking mess.

(BOB *comes in the front door.*)

RUTH: Hey, Bob, you got your grades.

BOB: Oh, yeah. (*He looks.*)

RUTH: How'd you do?

BOB: Okay. This for Kathy?

RUTH: Yeah.

(BOB *starts to open* KATHY's *letter.*)

Hey, that's private property.

BOB: What the fuck's gotten into you all of a sudden. (*Reads.*) A, A, A, A . . . B minus. B minus in Poetry 210. Man, she really went to pieces without us. I hope

she hasn't had a nervous breakfown or anything. Whew,
B minus.

(*A knock on the door.* DICK *opens it. It's* LUCKY.)

LUCKY: Listen. I just seen Mr. Willis. He wants you out by
tomorrow night.

BOB: How ya been, Lucky?

LUCKY: What? Oh, yeah. Well, if you want a hand, you
know where to find me.

RUTH: Thanks a lot, buddy.

LUCKY: Don't get fresh, girlie. Don't give me lip. You can
talk how you want when you're with your own kind, but
you show some respect when you're with Lucky. Smart
alecks. Think you know everything. You don't, you
know . . . you don't know what it's like living downstairs. I live downstairs. You seen me . . . you seen
me out there, sitting out there. Well, you seen me . . .

BOB: Yeah, yeah, lots of times.

LUCKY: All right. That's what I mean. I sit out there. I'm
out there. I got my Budweiser. I got my pretzels. Oh
yeah . . . I'm not just sitting out there, you know. I'm
watching. I'm keeping my eyes open. (*He's slowly going
into a trance.*) I see them cars go by, all them cars.
Fords. I see Fords out there. Chevies. Lincolns. Olds-
mobiles. Plymouths. I see the odd Cadillac, oh yeah,
don't worry about that. It's all up here. You think I'm
just sitting there with my Budweiser and pretzels. Think
you know it all, oh yeah.

DICK: Don't worry, we took care of it.

LUCKY: Huh?

DICK: We did like you said. Got rid of those plastic garbage cans and got some galvanized aluminum.

LUCKY: All right, that's what I mean. Now, if you want
any help, I'll tell you what you do. You come downstairs. Okay?

(*As* LUCKY *goes, we see him look around and call
"Kitty-Kitty."*)

RUTH: Guess I'll pack.

(*Gets up to leave.* DICK *starts taking down one of his
posters.*)

BOB: Where's everyone?

RUTH: Mike and Mel went out with Norman. They're meeting Shelly at the flicks. *Casablanca.* You should see the marks they got. They're both magna cum.

DICK: Magna cum. Sneaky bastards.

RUTH: Yep.

(RUTH *goes out down hall.*)

DICK: You staying for graduation?

BOB: No, you?

DICK: (*Shakes head no.*) Hey, you really going into the army?

BOB: Yeah, as a hostage. I don't know. What are you doing?

DICK: Shit, I don't know.

BOB: Anything lined up for the summer?

DICK: Yeah, delivering milk. It's your friendly college graduate, Mrs. Miller. "Such a shame, the boy went to college." Maybe I'll get sterilized, save any kids having to go through all this. She really was a bitch, you know.

BOB: I guess so.

DICK: Guess so, shit, I hope she gets cancer of the tits and suffers like crazy while she's dying. Honest to Christ, she's the first person I ever met I could really kill.

BOB: Yeah.

DICK: Oh, great humility scene.

BOB: No, it's just, you know, that's how it goes.

DICK: You know something, Bob? You know what's wrong with you?

BOB: I been waiting all this time for someone to tell me. What's wrong with me, Dick?

DICK: You let her get your balls, Bob.

BOB: That was pretty careless, wasn't it?

DICK: No shit, Bob. I remember when you got stung by that bee in the humanities quadrangle. I always wondered about that. I mean, you're supposed to yell when something like that happens. You don't stand there wondering if you should say something. You're really dead, you know.

BOB: Yeah, well, that's what I was trying to tell everyone right before Christmas. I thought I might just try it out, you know, being dead. Didn't feel any different.

DICK: I don't get it.

BOB: No, it's a pretty weird thing.

DICK: I gotta pack.

BOB: Yeah.

    (DICK *leaves the room.* MIKE *and* COOTIE *burst in through the front door, panting heavily.*)

MIKE: Oh shit, man, we've really had it. Christ, how could the guy do it? I thought he was kidding.

    (RUTH *comes in with a small suitcase.*)

RUTH: Hey, you guys better hurry up and pack. We gotta be out of here tomorrow.

COOTIE: Ruth, sit down, huh. Something pretty bad just happened. Seriously, no shitting around.

RUTH: Where's Norman?

COOTIE: Norman's . . . he just . . . oh shit.

MIKE: He set himself on fire.

BOB: He what?

MIKE: All that stuff he was reading. He just . . . I don't know. He got this idea. Oh, fuck, how could the stupid bastard ever . . . shit.

RUTH: I thought you guys were going to see *Casablanca*.

MIKE: No, we had to tell you that. He had this plan. Honest to shit, we didn't know he was serious. Him and Shelly. We thought he's just . . . we went to the common and he took all his clothes off and poured gasoline all over himself.

COOTIE: We were just shitting around, Ruth. Honest. If we thought he was serious, we'd've stopped him, you know.

MIKE: It was that fucking Shelly.

RUTH: You fucking stupid . . .

MIKE: I'm telling you, it wasn't our fault. He wouldn't have lit the match. I know he poured the gasoline, but he'd never've lit the match.

BOB: He's . . .

MIKE: Oh shit, it was awful. He just sat there turning black. I didn't want to look, but I couldn't turn away. His skin just, Christ, it just fell away from his face and his blood . . . (*Puts head in hand.*)

RUTH: Stupid fucking guys. You should've known. Where's Shelly?

COOTIE: She went crazy, Ruth. She just cracked up. We had to practically knock her out. She's okay now.

(SHELLY *comes in the front door. Her eyes are closed and her fists clenched.* RUTH *runs to her, doesn't know what to do.*)

RUTH: Shelly, oh, Shelly, Jesus . . .

SHELLY: (*Teeth clenched.*) Fucking guys.

(NORMAN *comes in. He's soaking wet and carries a gasoline can.* MIKE *and* COOTIE *rise.*)

MIKE: See, everything's cool now. Everybody trusts each other. That's what it's all about.

(MIKE *smiles oddly at the others.*)

COOTIE: (*Registering it all.*) Holy shit!

(MIKE *and* COOTIE *leave the room.*)

SHELLY: (*Yells.*) Creeps (*To* RUTH.) You got any first-aid stuff?

RUTH: Yeah.

(RUTH *gets a box from the pantry. It's a huge white box with a red cross on it, obviously stolen.*)

BOB: Hey, what happened?

NORMAN: (*Sits.*) I'm all right.

SHELLY: Don't talk, Norman. Would you make him some coffee?

RUTH: Yeah. Those guys said you burned yourself.

NORMAN: No, I'm okay.

(RUTH *makes coffee while* SHELLY *ties a bandage around* NORMAN's *wrist.*)

SHELLY: Sorry if this hurts. Hey, Ruth, those guys are really bastards. They gotta learn you don't joke around sometimes.

BOB: Hey, were you really gonna burn yourself?

NORMAN: Well, you know . . .

SHELLY: We were all supposed to do it. All four of us. We waited all this time for them to graduate with good grades and everything. Six months almost. I mean, like, the war could've ended. Fucking creeps. They went and put water in the gasoline can.

NORMAN: I think I might be getting a cold.

SHELLY: We're making coffee, Norman. Keep cool.

BOB: Hey, were you really serious?

NORMAN: Well, I thought, you know, with the war and everything.

SHELLY: Water, shit.

NORMAN: Well, there was some gas in that can.

SHELLY: Fucking creeps.

NORMAN: I definitely smelled some gas when I poured it over me.

SHELLY: Hold still, Norman.

NORMAN: I mean, I knew there was something wrong when I kept holding the match to my wrist and nothing happened.

SHELLY: What do you mean, nothing happened. What's wrong with you, Norman. You call that burn on your wrist nothing? It's the worst burn I ever saw. We're lucky we didn't get arrested.

NORMAN: I've seen movies of the Buddhist monks setting themselves on fire. They usually go up pretty quick in the movies. I bet it hurts a lot. My wrist really hurts.

(RUTH *brings* NORMAN *some coffee.*)

RUTH: Listen, we have to be out of here by tomorrow.

NORMAN: All right.

RUTH: Well, what are you gonna do?

NORMAN: I haven't thought about it too much. I thought I was going to be dead by now. I hadn't planned beyond that.

RUTH: You got a place to stay?

SHELLY: He'll stay with me.

NORMAN: Yeah, okay.

RUTH: We'll have to have a big cleanup in case Willis comes around.

NORMAN: I was thinking maybe I'll try to get back into graduate school. I'm getting sick of washing dishes.

(BOB *has been taking down his map of Europe from the wall.*)

BOB: I think I'll go to Europe.

NORMAN: I'm not really angry at Mel and Mike. In a way I'm kind of glad I'm not dead.

SHELLY: I think those two guys are really evil.

(RUTH *goes down the hall.*)

BOB: You ever been to France?

SHELLY: I went last summer.

BOB: What's it like?

SHELLY: Shitty. They're really uptight in France. I got busted in Calais. Two weeks in prison with the runs. That's no joke.

BOB: Maybe England.

NORMAN: I was in England once.

BOB: What's it like?

NORMAN: I went on a bicycle trip with the Youth Hostel Organization. My father sent me.

BOB: How was it?

NORMAN: It was okay.

SHELLY: England's a lousy place.

NORMAN: I don't know. I met some nice people. I saw Buckingham Palace. The food's not very good, but it didn't rain much. I guess it was a pretty valuable experience. I remember thinking at the time my horizons were a lot wider after that trip. I don't remember why I thought that. Maybe I'll go back there one day.

BOB: Oh well, there's always Italy or Greece.

SHELLY: If you go over there, check out Algeria. Algeria's really something else.

   (MR. WILLIS *opens the door.*)

WILLIS: Okay if I step in? Hey, what have you done to your hand?

NORMAN: It's just a burn.

WILLIS: Too bad, huh? Look, how's about if I see everyone for a minute? Everybody here?

BOB: (*Yelling.*) DICK, RUTH, MIKE, COOTIE, C'MERE A MINUTE. MR. WILLIS WANTS US.

WILLIS: Hey, hey, hey, you don't have to do that. You don't have to yell on account of me.

   (*All come in.*)

Hi, how's everybody? Gettin' ready for the big day? You gonna wear them long robes and everything, hey? All that fancy ceremony. Pretty good, huh? Listen, I just wanna give the place a quick once-over because I'll tell you why. I got this tenant moving in pretty soon so I gotta be sure everything's okay. Get rid of them milk bottles, that's the first thing, and I'll pick up the rent for this month, okay? How 'bout this floor, huh? You gonna finish it? Hey, I asked a question, who's supposed to be doing this floor?

BOB: I am, Mr. Willis.

WILLIS: So how come you leave it half-finished?

BOB: Sorry, I never got the time.

WILLIS: Well, you get it. I give you good money for them tiles, put me back a hunnered bucks. How many land-lords you find'll do that?

BOB: Yeah, okay.

WILLIS: By tomorrow night, understand? Now, let's have a little look round the place.

(WILLIS *goes down the hall followed by* BOB, RUTH, COOTIE, *and* MIKE.)

NORMAN: Mike.

(MIKE *turns.*)

Listen, I just want to tell you, I'm not angry about what happened.

MIKE: What do you mean?

SHELLY: You're a real creep pulling a trick like that.

MIKE: That's what I get for saving his life?

SHELLY: It's none of your business. It's the existential right of every living person to take his own life.

MIKE: No one's stopping you now.

NORMAN: What I wanted to say is, if you and Mel are coming back next year to go to graduate school, maybe we can share a place. I mean, you know, I could come down here early and look around.

MIKE: You going home for the summer?

SHELLY: He's staying with me.

NORMAN: Yeah, well I might go home for a few weeks. Visit my folks. The best way is you write to my father, care of the Police Department, Erie County, and if I'm not at home he'll know where to forward it.

MIKE: Right. Me and Cootie'll be up in the great North-west Territory helping Dad with the furs. If you don't hear from us, just go ahead and find a place for all of us, 'cause sometimes the mail gets delayed.

NORMAN: Don't worry, I'll get a place.

MIKE: Commissioner of Police, Erie County.

NORMAN: That's right.

(MIKE *smiles at him, not without warmth. In come*
COOTIE, RUTH, BOB, DICK, *and* MR. WILLIS.

WILLIS: Not bad. I'll tellya what I'll do. I'll keep the fifty-
dollar deposit for holes in the plaster and the broken
window.

COOTIE: Hey, we didn't break that window. That was broken when we moved in.

WILLIS: That's not my problem, Cootie. I keep the fifty
and if any of you guys got an objection, you want to
take it up with me, let's have it. Look, I got a living to
make like everybody else in town. Maybe you think I'm
being a rotten guy, but you wait. You go out there in the
world and you're gonna see things, you'll think old Willis was Snow White and the Seven Dwarfs all rolled into
one. You're gonna see dishonesty, you're gonna see
mean people, you see swindlers, killers, queers, you see
guys trying to double-park on Saturday morning, you
take my word. The thing I love about you kids is you're
honest, you're direct. There's no shitting around with
you. Yeah, I know it sounds corny, but I'm gonna miss
having you guys around. You gotta save this poor
fuckin' country, and excuse my language. There was a
time, I can remember, when you paid your taxes and
you knew your money was goin' into the right things.
Good, wholesome things. Look at it nowadays. Two
blocks away there's a house full of guys known all over
the neighborhood to practice open homosexuality. Open
homosexuality two blocks away, and there's kids playing
right outside that house every day. I don't know. I'd go
jump in the lake if it wasn't for you kids. I never knew
anyone like you, and I been around, let me tellya. You
know where you are, you know where you're going, and
you know how to get there. That's never happened before in the history of this whole fucking country. God
bless you kids, and good luck. I'll take a check for the
rent.

COOTIE: (*Sings.*) For he's a jolly good fellow . . .

OTHERS: (*Joining in.*) For he's a jolly good fellow,
For he's a jolly good fellow,

That nobody can deny.
That nobody can deny.
That nobody can deny.
> (*Etc., all the way through.* WILLIS *beams, entirely un-
> aware of the spoof.*)
> (*End of Scene 6.*)

Scene 7

> (*The next afternoon. The kitchen is bare of furniture.
> The icebox is gone, only a few milk bottles left. Only
> one chair left.* BOB *is laying the vinyl tiles.* COOTIE
> *comes into the room with his* FATHER. *He grabs the
> last valise by the front door.*)

COOTIE: Hey, Bob, I'm going.

BOB: Yeah, we'll see you.

COOTIE: Yeah.

> (MIKE *comes into the kitchen from the hall door.*)

MIKE: You going?

COOTIE: Yeah. Oh, this is my father. That's Mike, that's
Bob.

BOB: Hi.

MIKE: Hi.

FATHER: A pleasure.

MIKE: What?

FATHER: It's a pleasure meeting you.

MIKE: Oh, yeah, right.

COOTIE: Well, see you guys. Hey, what you doing next
year?

BOB: Oh, I got a job in a department store.

COOTIE: Playing piano?

BOB: Harp.

COOTIE: Great. Well, see ya.

BOB: See ya.

MIKE: Yeah, see ya, Cootie.

FATHER: Nice meeting you boys.

> (COOTIE *leaves with his* FATHER.)

MIKE: They don't look like each other. Good old Cootie. Where's Norman?

BOB: He left about an hour ago.

MIKE: Never said good-bye or anything.

BOB: You should've seen it, putting all his stuff in the back of a police car.

MIKE: What?

BOB: Yeah, his old man's Commissioner of Police, or something.

MIKE: I'll be fucked.

(RUTH *comes in from the hall with two suitcases and sets them down by some other suitcases near the door.*)

RUTH: I guess that's it. Where's Cootie?

MIKE: He just left with his dad.

RUTH: Some friend. No good-bye or anything.

MIKE: We'll see him next year.

RUTH: No we won't.

(MIKE *and* RUTH *go down the hall for their last luggage.* DICK *and the* MILKMAN *enter through the front door with empty cartons. They load the remaining bottles.*)

DICK: Hey, I wouldn't mind a little help here. I gotta catch a train.

MILKMAN: I don't understand you guys. You're supposed to be college graduates. Eight hundred and fifty-seven two-quart milk bottles. That's not the kind of thing a grown-up person does. You're supposed to be grown-ups. I don't get it.

(*The phone is ringing.*)

DICK: That's the last one.

MILKMAN: Okay. I just hope you guys don't think you can go through life hoarding milk bottles like this. I got enough to do without this. I got a regular route. (*To* DICK.) Look, if you want to pick up a lot of bottles, put your fingers right down inside, you get more that way.

DICK: Okay. Hey, you guys, you're a lot of help.

(MILKMAN *and* DICK *go out with their cartons.*)

BOB: (*Answering phone.*) Hello, oh yes, how are you? No,

this is Bob. Bob Rettie. No, music. Yes, of course I remember you. No, he's not in right now.

(MIKE *and* RUTH *have reentered, motioning* BOB *that
they have to go. He motions back that it's okay. He
waves good-bye as they pick up their suitcases and
begin to leave.*)

RUTH: Hey, good luck.

BOB: Yeah, yeah, you too. See ya, Mike.

MIKE: See ya.

(RUTH *and* MIKE *exit through the front door.*)

BOB: (*Back on phone.*) Sorry, Mrs. Roper, I was just saying good-bye to some people I . . . some friends of
mine. I don't know if he'll be back or not. Can I leave a
message? (*Pause.*) Look, Mrs. Roper, I'm very sorry
about that but there's nothing I can do if he's gone. I
can tell him to call you if he comes back. Mrs. Roper,
look, calm down. Listen, I'm hanging up now, all right?
I gotta hang up now. Good-bye, Mrs. Roper.

(BOB *hangs up and returns to the floor tiles.* DICK
comes in alone through front door.)

DICK: Boy, that guy was sure pissed off about the bottles.
You should've seen the look on his face.

BOB: Hey, you know that guy you studied with, Professor
Roper?

DICK: (*Pause.*) Yes.

BOB: His wife just called.

DICK: What'd she want?

BOB: She just . . . I don't know. Nothing, I guess. Pretty
weird.

DICK: Yeah, pretty weird.

(DICK *puts on his coat and takes up his bags.*)

BOB: Hey, Dick.

DICK: What?

(*They look at each other.*)

BOB: I don't know. See ya.

DICK: Yeah.

(*As* DICK *is leaving, he sees* KATHY, *who is standing
in the doorway.*)

KATHY: Hi. Can I come in? (DICK *moves aside. He and*

BOB *stare at* KATHY. *This makes her a little nervous.*)
Everyone gone?

DICK &
BOB: (*Together.*) Yeah . . .
    (*They exchange a nervous glance.*)

BOB: Except for me and Dick. We're still here. We're right in front of you, as a matter of fact . . .

DICK: That's a nice coat she's wearing. That's a very nice coat, Kathy.

KATHY: (*Knows something is going on but doesn't know what.*) Thanks.

BOB: Hey, Dick. (DICK *leaves.*) See ya. (*To himself.*)

KATHY: Finishing the floor?

BOB: Evidently.

KATHY: Kind of late, isn't it? (*Pause.*) Did they send my grades here?

BOB: Right there. You did really shitty.

KATHY: (*Gets the letter.*) Bob, listen . . . I'm sorry about . . . sounds pretty silly.

BOB: No, I accept your apology for whatever you think you did.

KATHY: I saw Ruth the other day. She said you've been . . . well, pretty bad this semester.

BOB: Did she say that?

KATHY: I wish I'd known . . . couldn't you have . . . you should have told me to stay.

BOB: Well, it slipped my mind. Sorry.

KATHY: You shouldn't be so ashamed of your feelings.

BOB: Okay.

KATHY: I'm serious. You've gotta learn to let go. Like your music. It's all squinched and tidy.

BOB: Okay. I'll work on that.

KATHY: Oh, Bob.

BOB: What?

KATHY: I really wish you'd've told me. I'd've come back. I never really related to Richard.

BOB: I'll tell him when I see him.

KATHY: Yeah, you're right. Why the hell should you be nice? Oh well, good luck . . . and, you know, when you see your mother say hello for me.

BOB: Okay.

KATHY: How is she?

BOB: She's okay. Sort of dead.

KATHY: I like her, Bob. You're lucky. She's, you know, she's a real person.

BOB: No, she's you know, a real corpse.

KATHY: All right, have it your way.

BOB: No, it's not what I wanted particularly. No, taken all in all, from various different angles, I'd've preferred she lived. I'm pretty sure of that.

KATHY: (*Pause.*) She's not really.

BOB: School's over.

KATHY: Bob, do you know what you're saying?

BOB: Kathy, please get the fuck out of here.

KATHY: But, I mean, Ruth never told me . . . Didn't you tell anyone?

BOB: Yeah, I just told you.

KATHY: But, I mean . . . when . . . when did . . .

BOB: Christmas. No, no, it was the day after.

KATHY: (*Sits.*) Jesus, Bob, why didn't you tell anyone? I mean, how could you live for six months without telling someone?

BOB: (*No emotion.*) Oh I don't know. A little cunning. A little fortitude. A little perseverance. (*Pause.*) I couldn't believe it. Not the last time anyway. They put her in this room. I don't know what they call it. They bring everybody there just before they kick the bucket. They just sort of lie there looking at each other, wondering what the hell they got in common to talk about. I couldn't believe that anyone could look like she looked and still be alive. (*Pause.*) She knew. I'm sure of that. (*Pause.*) Once, I remember, she tried to tell me something. I mean this noise came out of somewhere around her mouth, like somebody running a stick over a fence or something, and I thought maybe she's trying to tell me something. So I leaned over to hear better and I caught a whiff of that breath. Like fried puke. And I was sick all over her. (*Pause. Brighter.*) But you want to know something funny, and I mean this really is funny, so you can laugh if you like. There was this lady dying next to my mother and she kept talking about her daughter Susan. Well, Susan came to visit the day I puked on Mom. And you know what? It was only Susan Weinfeld which doesn't mean anything to you but she happens to have been the girl I spent a good many of my best months as a sophomore in high school trying to lay. In fact her virginity almost cost me a B+ in history and here we were, six years later, staring at each other across two dying mothers. I want to tell you something, Kathy. She looked fantastic. And I could tell she was thinking the same thing about me. I mean that kind of scene doesn't happen every day. It was like . . . (*thinks*) . . . it was like how we were the first time. Maybe, just possibly, a little better. So we went out and had a coffee in Mr. Doughnut and started groping each other like crazy under the counter and I mean we just couldn't keep our hands off each other so I suggested we get a cab down to my mother's place since, you know, there happened to be no one there at the moment. But the funniest thing was when we get down to Mom's place and you know all those stairs you have to go up and there's Susan all over me practically screaming for it and I start fumbling around with the keys in the lock and none of them would fit. I must've tried every key about fifty fucking times and none of them would fit. Boy, what a drag. (*Pause.*) Oh, we got in all right. Finally. I had to go downstairs, through the Salvatore's apartment, out the window, up the fire escape and through Mom's place but when I opened the front door, guess what? There's poor old Susan asleep on the landing. She really looked cute. I hated to wake her up. Anyway, by the time we'd made coffee and talked and smoked about a million cigarettes each we didn't feel like it anymore. Not really. We did it anyway but, you know, just to be polite, just to make some sense out of the evening. It was, taken all in all, a pretty ordinary fuck. The next morning we made plans to meet again that night. We even joked about it, you know, about what a super-fucking good time we'd have, and if you ask me, we could've probably really gotten into something incredible if we'd tried again, but when I went to the hospital I found out good old Mom had croaked sometime during the night and somehow I still don't know why to this day . . . I never got in touch with Susan again. And vice versa. It's a funny thing, you know. At the funeral there were all these people. Friends of Mom's—I didn't know any of them. They were all crying like crazy and I . . . well . . . (*Pause.*) I never even got to the burial. The car I was in broke down on the Merritt Parkway. Just as well. I didn't feel like seeing all those people. I'd sure love to have fucked Susan again, though.

KATHY: Bob . . . I . . .

BOB: (*Abstract.*) Anyway . . . I just didn't feel like telling anyone. I mean, I wasn't all that upset. I was a little upset, mostly because I thought I ought to be more upset, but as for your actual grief, well. Anything interesting happen to you this semester . . . Kathy? (KATHY *has risen.*) Going? (KATHY *is going out the door.*) Give my regards to that guy you're rescuing at the moment, what's-his-name. (KATHY *is gone.* BOB *shrugs. The cat wanders in from the hallway.*) Hey, cat, what are you doing hanging around here? All the humans gone west. (*Puts the cat outside and shuts the door. He nudges the tiles with his toe and looks around at the empty room.*) Hey, guys, guess what happened to me. I want to tell you about this really incredible thing that happened to me . . . (*He is faltering now, choking slightly, but he doesn't know he's about to crack. His body is doing something strange, unfamiliar.*) Hey, what's happening . . . (*He's crying now.*) Oh fuck, come on, come on. Shit, no, no . . .

(*Fade.*)
(*End of Play.*)

THE TAKING OF MISS JANIE

by Ed Bullins

THE TAKING OF MISS JANIE *was presented at the New Federal Theatre, in New York City, during the 1974–75 theatre season, and later was moved to the Mitzi Newhouse Theater, at Lincoln Center. The production was directed by Gilbert Moses. The stage manager was Oz Scott; sets and lighting were by Kurt Lundel and Charles Cosler. Costumes were by Judy Dearing. The cast was as follows:*

MONTY	*Adeyemi Lythcott*
JANIE	*Hilary Jean Beane*
RICK	*Kirk Kirksey*
LEN	*Darryl Croxton*
SHARON	*Lin Shaye*
PEGGY	*Robbie McCauley*
FLOSSIE	*Dianne Oyama Dixon*
LONNIE	*Sam McMurray*
MORT SILBERSTEIN	*Robert B. Silver*

The producers were Woodie King, Jr., and Joseph Papp.

The People

MONTY
Black. Midtwenties. A student type but with a street background.

JANIE
White. Early twenties. Blond. Brown eyes. Fairly good figure. A California beach girl turned perennial student. An air of innocence. Moody. Reflective. Too all-American looking and well-scrubbed to be overtly sexy, but very attractive to men.

PEGGY
Black. Early twenties. Intelligent. Not pretty. Strong features. Excellent body, though large-proportioned. Speaks in an affected manner to conceal her Southern background. Tender. Sensitive.

LONNIE
White. Late twenties. Hides an uneasiness behind a super cool pose.

LEN
Black. Light-skinned. Bush hair. Intellectual-artistic-political-aware. Early twenties.

SHARON
White. Brunette. Pretty. A California lotus-eater. Early twenties.

FLOSSY
Black. Sensual. Soul Sister. A woman of the streets, but not a whore. Early twenties.

RICK
Black. Light brown-skinned. Intellectually aggressive. An early revolutionary, cultural nationalist. Early twenties.

MORT SILBERSTEIN
White. A post-beatnik mythic figure.

TIME: *The sixties.*
PLACE: *California and Elsewhere.*

An abstract depiction of a decade of cheap living spaces—for students, artists, musicians, poets, and other transients—studio apartments with pull-down wall-beds, sofas, couches and cots in dingy rooms, single beds in motel rooms, etc. But the stage is uncluttered.

The locales could be Los Angeles, San Francisco, Manhattan, Boston, etc.

AT RISE: JANIE *sits on the edge of a roll-out bed, almost tearful, but attempting to communicate with* MONTY, *who lounges beside her, half-covered by a sheet, sexually spent for the moment.*

JANIE: (*Not looking at him at first.*) It's sad . . . so sad . . . I don't even understand it. . . . Once you said . . . no . . . no . . . many times you've told me . . . that anything's possible. . . . But I wouldn't believe you. I *couldn't* believe you. . . . You made the world, life, people . . . *everything* . . . seem so grim . . . And I knew it couldn't be that way . . . It couldn't. . . . Even while I felt sad most of the time. Even while I suffered and had what you called "The Blues." . . . Even though I didn't understand why you refused to give into sadness . . . to feeling down and beat . . . I . . . I still didn't believe, Monty. I didn't. I still didn't believe that I have so little understanding of the world. . . . Oh, Monty, I have so little understanding of people and life . . . and I don't know *you*, who I thought was my friend, at all. . . . And now . . . and now I don't know what's going to happen to me. . . . For such a do next. We've been friends for such a long time. Such a long time. . . . Ten years . . . ? God, it's been that long. . . . I don't know what I'll do now. . . . I don't know what's going to happen to me. . . . For such a long time I thought of you as one of my few friends. A special friend, really. Do you understand that, Monty? . . . My special friend . . . And now you rape me . . . you rape me!

(*She begins to cry softly.* MONTY *raises his head from the pillow, then reaches over and pulls her to him and kisses her until she quiets. She doesn't resist.*)

(*Janie catches her breath.*) Oh, Monty . . . Monty . . . why . . . why?

MONTY: (*Annoyed.*) Why, what?

JANIE: (*Surprised.*) What did you say? . . . What did you mean by that?

(*Silence except for a tinny sounding radio playing the Beatles, off somewhere.*)

Monty . . . please . . . what did you mean? I don't understand . . .

MONTY: (*Accusing.*) You understand, Janie . . . You've always understood, Miss Janie.

JANIE: "Miss Janie" . . . you haven't called me that in years. Why do you call me that now?

MONTY: (*Rolls over; caresses her.*) It's just something that I keep for you, Janie. You remember . . . one of the few things that's especially ours.

JANIE: (*She moves away from him and stands.*) Stop! . . . Why are you forcing your will on me? Why are you taking me like this?

MONTY: Because I want you, that's why.

JANIE: (*Moves toward door.*) Well you can't have me. You can't just take what you want and use me like this.

(*He rises and stalks her.*)

MONTY: Shut up, bitch! . . . You phony, whining white bitch!

JANIE: (*Hurt and tearful.*) Don't call me that. . . . Please don't say that, Monty.

MONTY: Shut up, I said! . . . I've wasted too much love and caring on you already. From the first moment you met me you knew it would come to this . . . And you've got the nerve to cry and act like this.

(*He pulls her to him and kisses her and "dry fucks" her until he begins arousing some response against her will.*)

JANIE: No . . . ! No, I didn't. I wanted to be friends with you, Monty. Friends, that's all. Oh, please . . . not again. . . . Not that, please . . .

(*As he corners her the lights change and slides appear showing a college campus and college scenes. The* MUSIC *fades out. Campus sounds are heard.*

MONTY *and* JANIE *momentarily disappear in the darkness upon stage, and a slide comes on with their images. They are meeting, looking somewhat younger and are dressed in the southern California collegiate styles of the late 1950s.*

The slide holds for a moment, then the light comes up on MONTY *and* JANIE *as they play out the scene.*)

JANIE: Hello. You're in my creative writing class, aren't you?

MONTY: Yeah . . . I think so.

JANIE: I loved the poetry you read today.

MONTY: Thanks.

JANIE: But it was so bitter.

MONTY: Oh.

JANIE: Do you call that Black Poetry?

MONTY: Hey . . . my name's Monty.

JANIE: Mine's Janie.

MONTY: Pleased to meet cha, Miss Janie.

JANIE: (*Surprised.*) What did you say?

MONTY: What did ya think I said?

JANIE: (*Curious.*) Why did you say that?

MONTY: Oh, just a little joke of mine, I guess.

JANIE: (*Confused.*) You guess? . . . But I don't think I . . .

MONTY: Let's just keep it between ourselves, huh?

JANIE: (*Thoughtful.*) If you say so. . . . But I don't think I understand you very well.

MONTY: Hey . . . you want to go to a party tonight, Miss Janie?

JANIE: Oh, don't call me that.

MONTY: Why? It fits you like a pair of panty hose.

JANIE: (*Blushes.*) Do you have to say that?

MONTY: Nawh . . . I don't have to say nothin' if I don't wanna. . . . Hey . . . what about the party?

JANIE: (*Doubtful.*) Where?

MONTY: At my place.

JANIE: I don't know . . . but I might be able to come.

MONTY: Well . . . I'll be expecting you.

JANIE: Will you be reading any of your poetry that you were reading in class?

MONTY: I don't know . . . but if you come, I'll read something for you, Miss Janie.

JANIE: I don't know if I like you calling me that.

MONTY: Just let it be our little secret.

JANIE: (*Puzzled.*) You mean we've got secrets already?

MONTY: (*Winks.*) Sho nuf, Miss Janie. . . . Here, let me give you my address. It's not so far from here.

JANIE: If you read tonight, please don't sound so despairing. . . . Tee hee . . . you're almost scary, ya know?

> (*Party* MUSIC *rises. The lights come up as voices are heard.*
>
> *It is* MONTY's *apartment. The party preparations are nearly complete.* MONTY *is off in the kitchen doing the last chores.*
>
> *Out front* LEN *and* RICK, MONTY's *roommates, are in their daily ritual of debate.* LEN *wears Levi's and sandals; he has a large, uncombed "natural."* RICK *wears a black suit, white shirt, white bow tie, and white bucks upon his feet. His head is shaven and glistens. He wears eyeglasses that glisten also.*)

RICK: But Brother Len, these devils are jivin'. . . . They ain't nothin' but stone paper tigers.

LEN: I agree with you, my brother . . . at least on some of your points of argument.

RICK: What points? What points, Brother Len? That he, the devil, is going to give the Blackman ten percent of this land? Five of these states of the so-called great United States of America? Can you believe the devil's gonna do that, brother?

LEN: Well, Brother Rick, I must confess that I find that a bit farfetched.

RICK: (*Excited.*) Farfetched? Farfetched, he says.

LEN: Yes. I said "farfetched"!

RICK: (*Calls to* MONTY.) Did you hear that, Brother Monty? Did you hear what this deaf, dumb, and blind *negro* said?

LEN: Deaf, dumb and blind? Negro! Now, listen, Rick
. . . just because I don't . . .

(MONTY *sticks his head from the kitchen.*)

MONTY: Hey . . . what did you say, Rick?

RICK: (*Makes the most of the moment.*) I said that the
Blackman has slaved in this devil's land for four
hundred years. I said that the Blackman must have freedom, justice and equality . . . plus self-determinism
. . . to . . .

LEN: You didn't say that just now, man! You've been
mouthing those clichés before memory!

RICK: Clichés! Clichés!

MONTY: Len! Rick! Say . . . cool it!

(RICK *is on his feet, strutting back and forth like an
immaculate bantam rooster.*)

RICK: The Blackman has slaved in this devil's land for four
hundred years, Brother Len. And you call that a cliché!
I know what I am saying, from hearing the righteous
black word, and you call it farfetched? A cliché?
Brother . . . listen to me . . . this white man is a paper tiger!

(*The doorbell rings.* RICK *moves toward it.*)

RICK: I'll get it. Your . . . ahhh . . . guests . . . must
be arriving, Monty.

(*He opens the door;* JANIE *stands on the other side,
wearing dark glasses.*)

JANIE: (*Shyly.*) Hello . . . I . . .

RICK: I'm sorry. You must have the wrong address.

(*He slams the door in* JANIE'S *face.*)

MONTY: (*Comes out of the kitchen.*) Hey . . . man . . .
what's goin' on?

LEN: Is that somebody you know, Monty?

(MONTY *opens the door;* JANIE *still stands there, a
bewildered expression on her face beneath her
shades.*)

MONTY: Janie . . . c'mon in.

JANIE: (*Nervous.*) Hi, Monty. . . . Is there something
wrong?

MONTY: C'mon in, Janie. C'mon. You're here now.

(*He reaches out and pulls her inside. She looks around apprehensively.* LEN *gets to his feet;* RICK *has stopped his pacing and stands in the center of the floor.*)

RICK: (*With arms folded.*) Well, well, well, well . . .

LEN: (*Smiling, going over to* JANIE.) Hello. . . . My name's Len.

JANIE: Hi. I hope I'm not too early.

MONTY: This is Janie, Len.

LEN: Pleased to meet cha. Can I get you anything?

JANIE: Oh . . . I don't know.

RICK: Well . . . isn't anyone going to introduce me? I live here too, you know?

LEN: We thought that you had met her out in the hall, Rick.

MONTY: Hey, Janie . . . that's Rick over there. These two clowns are my roommates.

LEN: Welcome . . . welcome, Janie.

JANIE: Thank you . . . but it looks like I'm really early.

MONTY: Don't let it bother you, kid. Why don't you come in the kitchen with me while I finish up. Do you know how to make avocado dip?

JANIE: (*Following.*) You mean Mexican style?

(MONTY *and* JANIE *enter the kitchen.* RICK *looks at* LEN *incredulously.*)

RICK: Did you see how he brought that devil lady right in here on us?

LEN: Shhh . . . man . . . she'll hear you.

RICK: (*Raising his voice.*) I hope she does. I hope her ole red ears burn off from hearin' my words.

LEN: Hey, Rick, man . . . you knew this was gonna be a mixed party. Both Monty and myself told you that we were goin'a invite people from school. And you know that's a mixed scene, man.

RICK: Yes, I knew, Brother Len . . . But I don't have to accept it.

LEN: Well, what you gonna do, man? Leave?

RICK: Leave? Brother Len, I have no intention of going anywhere tonight, except to bed, later on.

LEN: But you not gonna be draggin' the party, are ya, man?

RICK: Me a drag? On the contrary, my brother. There would be little or no party if it wasn't for me. Have the times of your young lives. I just simply don't have to accept the validity of this scene, that's all.

LEN: And why not, man?

RICK: Because it's phony, irrelevant and it comes straight out of some of you so-called negroes' fantasy bags.

LEN: Awww, Rick, man. Just listen to that. . . . You are goin'a be a big drag tonight.

RICK: Relax, Brother Len. I'm here . . . naturally. I'm in the room. You'all got your scene goin'. Swell. I just ain't gonna deal with it like I'm a part of it. I'm checkin' yawhl out . . . dig?

LEN: Awww, you jive turkey. Monty and I are just lookin' for some good times. We don't want to get into all that Black crap tonight. . . .

(JANIE *enters, wearing an apron and carrying a tray. Glad for the interruptions*:)

Well . . . what do we have here?

JANIE: (*Smiling.*) Who wants to try my guacamole?

(RICK *sits down, crosses his legs and folds his arms.*)

LEN: Guacamole? How wonderful.

RICK: No thanks . . . I don't want any.

JANIE: Oh, no? But it's so good.

(*She places the tray down and licks the tips of her fingers.*)

RICK: I wouldn't eat anything that was touched by you, Miss Ann.

JANIE: (*Brightly.*) My name's Janie, Rick.

LEN: Now we're not going to have any of that, Rick.

JANIE: (*Smiling.*) Is there anything wrong? Have I done anything that I shouldn't?

RICK: Yes . . . you were born.

LEN: Now that's the last straw, Rick.

(JANIE *moves between* LEN *and* RICK. *She looks down at* RICK.)

JANIE: Len, don't take everything so personal. Rick is just doing his thing, aren't you, Rick?

RICK: You have no idea of what my thing is, devil lady.

LEN: (*Horrified.*) Rick!

JANIE: (*Sits next to* RICK *on couch.*) You're a Black Nationalist, aren't you, Rick?

    (RICK *stands and steps to the middle of the room.*

      MONTY *enters from the kitchen. He carries bottles of beer.*)

RICK: (*With back to* JANIE.) Those who know don't say, and those who don't know don't ask.

MONTY: (*Hands out beer.*) Hey . . . that's heavy, Rick. That sounds like that other one you always sayin'. How does it go?

RICK: (*Refuses beer.*) It's unimportant . . . in this context, my brother.

LEN: The first last and the last first!

MONTY: (*Not quite serious.*) Yeah. What goes around comes around . . . Or somethin' like dat.

    (*He and* LEN *slap five.*)

JANIE: Rick . . . please tell me about Black Nationalism. (*The doorbell rings.*)

RICK: (*Turns and faces* JANIE.) You personify that line of poetry which says: ". . . each year they send a thousand of their best into the ghetto."

JANIE: I do?

RICK: Yes, you do. You come in here with your dirty blond hair and evil blue eyes and act the presumptuous beast that you are!

    (*The doorbell rings again.*)

LEN: Do you want me to get that, Monty?

MONTY: Nawh, man . . . I got it.

JANIE: (*Smiling.*) Rick. You haven't even seen me since I've been here. My eyes aren't blue . . . they're brown. And I don't know what you mean that I'm one of the thousand that . . .

RICK: It doesn't matter what color your eyes are. You're still one of those sent in by the Zionist Youth Conspiracy.

JANIE: Zionist? Oh, how funny, Rick . . . Tee hee . . . I'm of German and English extraction . . . both sides. I'm not a Jewish anything.

(MONTY *opens the door.* PEGGY *stands there. She wears a sweater and Levi's. Her hair is cut short in a boyish Afro; she wears glasses.*)

MONTY: Hey, stuff. How're doin'?

PEGGY: Okay, Monty. I'm not too early, am I?

MONTY: Nawh. Come on in. Have a beer.

(*He shuts the door after* PEGGY *enters.*)

PEGGY: Hey, Monty . . . you gonna read tonight? I brought some of my latest work over.

JANIE: Oh, good, you are going to have some Black poetry read tonight. I knew I should have come. I think that's wonderful!

PEGGY: Say wha . . . ?

MONTY: Hey, Peg . . . this is Janie. Janie's in a class of mine at City College.

PEGGY: Oh?

JANIE: Hello, Peggy. Monty and I have Creative Writing together.

PEGGY: (*Sarcastic.*) Well, bully for yawhl.

MONTY: (*To* PEGGY.) You know these two clowns.

RICK: As-salaam alaikum, Sister Peggy.

PEGGY: Salaam, Brother Rick.

JANIE: (*Alert.*) What did you say?

MONTY: I gotta check out the stove, folks. . . . Be right back.

(*He exits to the kitchen.*)

LEN: Want somethin' to drink, Peg?

PEGGY: I'll take some wine, if you have any, Len.

LEN: No sooner said than done.

(LEN *goes into the kitchen.*)

JANIE: What did you two say just now? . . . Rick . . . Peggy . . .

(RICK *and* PEGGY *ignore* JANIE.)

PEGGY: Haven't seen you in a month of gospel bird days, brother.

RICK: Just tryin' to be Black here in the white wilderness of North America, sister.

(RICK *and* PEGGY *embrace and give an approximation of a traditional African greeting.*)

It's sure good to see your Black self here, sister.

PEGGY: It's good to have my Black self here, brother. But who's this pale thing on the couch belong to?

JANIE: (*On couch; apprehensive.*) Did you two say something? Are you speaking about me?

RICK: You'll have to get Monty to explain this beast to you, Sister Peg. If I had my way, I'd po' gasoline on the blond, *brown*-eyed devil and watch it burn.

JANIE: (*Stands.*) Oh, I wish you all wouldn't talk like that. You have such a strange sense of humor. I guess I just have to learn to become hep.

PEGGY: (*With raised eyebrows.*) Hep?

(PEGGY *and* RICK "crack-up.")

(JANIE *takes off the apron and goes behind* PEGGY *and tries to tie it on her.*)

JANIE: Here . . . Peggy . . . maybe you'd like to help out Monty some. I'm not very good in a kitchen.

PEGGY: (*Pushes* JANIE *away.*) Hey, woman . . . Why don't you be cool?

(MONTY *and* LEN *come out of the kitchen. The door-bell rings.*)

LEN: I'll get it.

MONTY: The gumbo's almost ready.

JANIE: Monty . . . What should I do with this apron?

RICK: What is that gumbo made from, Brother Monty?

(LEN *opens the door.* LONNIE *and* SHARON *stand in the hall.*)

PEGGY: Hey . . . what kind of party you got goin' here, Monty?

MONTY: Relax, Peggy. Everything's cool.

RICK: I asked you what did you put in the gumbo, brother?

MONTY: Ground beef! I put ground beef in it, man. You know I wouldn't try to get you to eat pork.

JANIE: Oh, I just love ham. . . . Do you have any ham, Monty?

PEGGY: No. He doesn't have any ham.

JANIE: Are you sure?

RICK: The pig . . . pork . . . swine is the foulest diseased poison that man can consume.

(LEN *has invited the couple in.* LEN *takes the girl's hand and leads her.*)

LEN: Hey, folks . . . This is Sharon. . . . She's a friend of mine.

SHARON: Pleased to meet cha.

PEGGY: I can believe that.

MONTY: (*To male stranger.*) What's your name, buddy?

JANIE: Hi, Lonnie.

LONNIE: It's Lonnie, man. Janie asked me to come by and check her out. I'm her ole man, kinda.

RICK: (*Making a speech.*) The pig is part rodent. You can recognize its rat genes by its rodent-like tail.

JANIE: Lonnie. You're just in time.

LONNIE: (*Cool.*) Yeah . . . baby.

PEGGY: In time for what?

JANIE: I'm having such a marvelous time. Monty . . . your friends are so interesting and colorful.

MONTY: (*Annoyed.*) Say . . . there's drinks in the kitchen.

RICK: The swine is part snake. . . . It can even eat other snakes without getting sick. Cause it's a cannibal as well.

JANIE: Who's the girl you came in with, Lonnie?

LONNIE: She's somebody who rode up in the elevator with me, dig? You can see where she's comin' from, can't ya?
    (LEN *and* SHARON *are embracing, kissing and are in private conversation.*)

RICK: The pig is part dog. It has a dog-like nature, and you become part dog when you consume the beast.

MONTY: You are what you eat, right man?

PEGGY: Exactly.
    (*Intermittently some go into the kitchen briefly and return with drinks. The improvisational quality of the party remains.*
    The doorbell rings again.)

MONTY: Hey . . . I'm tired of goin' to the door. COME IN!
    (FLOSSY *sticks her head in the door.*)

FLOSSY: Hey . . . is this where it's happenin'?

MONTY: Hey, Flossy . . . come on in, baby.

JANIE: Monty . . . you have so many friends.

LONNIE: (*Talking to* LEN.) Yeah, man . . . I just got off a gig.

LEN: You did, huh?

PEGGY: Can you dig it? Gig.

JANIE: Lonnie blows a horn in a jazz combo.

LONNIE: (*Super cool.*) It's my ax, baby. My ax.

FLOSSY: (*Kissing* MONTY.) This is for you, daddy.

MONTY: Thank you, little mamma.

PEGGY: (*To* FLOSSY.) I don't think we've met. My name's Peggy.

FLOSSY: Nawh, I don't guess we have. I'm Flossy.

RICK: We are in the time of the Fall of America. We are witnesses to the end.

> (MUSIC *plays and some of the couples are in a semi-dance movement.*
>
> *The lights change in color and depth, and the shadows deepen as the room takes on a surreal quality.*)

LONNIE: I always did say spades really knew how to party.

MONTY: Hey, man. Check yourself with that spade crap.

JANIE: Oh, Monty . . . he didn't mean nothin'.

RICK: (*To* LONNIE.) Say devil . . . how did you ever learn how to play black music?

LONNIE: You mean jazz, man.

LEN: That's what the brother said, man.

SHARON: Len, you're not going to start anything, are ya?

LONNIE: I just went to school . . . and learned a little and started playin', man.

RICK: He went to school to learn how to play our music. Check that out, brothers.

FLOSSY: I'm scarfish as a bear. Where's the grease, Honey?

MONTY: In the kitchen, baby. It should be ready by now. Hey, everybody . . . food's on.

RICK: I never knew Germans could play jazz.

LONNIE: Maybe Germans can't, man. But I'm Jewish.

PEGGY: Jewish.

SHARON: That's what he said. So am I. There's nothin' wrong with being Jewish, is there?

RICK: A German . . . and a Jew . . . going together. That's heavy. That's very heavy.

LONNIE: Well, man, I don't feel responsible for what some foreigners did.

JANIE: Let's not talk about that. It's too horrible.

RICK: Your daddy murders six million people and it's too horrible for you to listen to, huh?

SHARON: It wasn't her father. She couldn't help what was goin' on.

FLOSSY: (*Off.*) Hey, Monty, baby! . . . This sangria is boss!

LEN: They've got you brainwashed, I see.

RICK: It's sad but true, brothers. The so-called negroes in America is in love with his slave master. . . . Jews are fraternizing and lying down with their executioners and exterminators. Woe woe woe . . . the last days of civilization are at hand.

(*The lights deepen more. And* MORT SILBERSTEIN *comes through the door singing and dancing a stylized rock horah.*

The room divides into two camps: one black, the other white.

MORT SILBERSTEIN *wears a greasy vest, a black bowler hat, baggy gray tweed pants, red suspenders, white sneakers, and a short-sleeved denim shirt beneath his dark brown vest. He has on dark glasses and affects an unkempt beard.*

He sings and dances about the room like a shadow as the characters make their speeches. And he passes out marijuana cigarettes to everyone, while the other characters pass in turn through a colored spotlight and give their raps.)

MONTY: (*Steps into spotlight; smokes a joint.*) This white chick, Janie, thinks she's got my nose open. Thinks she's stringin' me along. But I got news for her. She treats me like this cause I'm black. Who does she think she is? I'm as good, nawh, better than any white dude she could have. Really, I'm doin' this girl a favor by payin' some attention to her. Look at all the broads around me. Peggy . . . Flossy . . . I bet I could even have Sharon if Len didn't go for her. But I don't cut into my buddies' chicks. All I got to do is snap my fingers and I could have almost any woman I wanted. So why should I get my guts tied up in knots about this blond fake. She's nothin' but a tease. Says she likes my poetry. Tell me now, how could a white broad love "Down with Whit-ey" poetry? Tells me she loves my mind. Haaa . . . I wouldn't have much of a mind if I believed her. She came to my party, the one where I invited her, and told her corny little boyfriend where she'd be. Who does she think she is? She can't make a fool out of me. She's mine even if she doesn't know it yet. And I'm gonna take her when I'm ready. And the time's right. That's right, get her. Take her, get her, have her . . . whatever I gotta do. I dig her blond lookin' self. And I don't care how long it takes to get her. I got all the time in the world. 'Cause the world is what you make it.

(MORT SILBERSTEIN *steps into the light with* MONTY.)

MORT SILBERSTEIN: What's happenin', brother?

MONTY: Mort Silberstein . . . I see you made it down, man.

(*They slap five.*)

MORT SILBERSTEIN: Yeah, man, I brought you a lid. You know the price has gone up, don't cha, man? That bread you laid on me evaporated, man.

MONTY: Hey . . . man . . . we agreed on what it was to be, right?

MORT SILBERSTEIN: Yeah, man, but the price done gone up.

MONTY: How much, man?

MORT SILBERSTEIN: Say, look, man . . . I need me ten more dollars. Can you let me hold ten bucks, man?

MONTY: Nawh, man. . . . My pockets are on empty.

MORT SILBERSTEIN: But, man, I need the bread to get my-self together, man. I gotta make this rally, man. It's about your Civil Rights, ya know, man. And I ain't got no carfare or wine money.

MONTY: I'm sorry, Mort.

MORT SILBERSTEIN: But Martin Luther King's gonna be preachin' peace, man . . . And Malcolm X is gonna be rappin' some righteous revolutionary truth, man.

MONTY: I'm sorry, Mort.

MORT SILBERSTEIN: But I need it, Monty, man. Let me hold another ten. The shit's good, ain't it? We always been straight with each other, ain't we, man? But I gotta get myself together. It takes a lot of energy fightin' for the rights of you people. I'm a poet, man. Not no Freedom Rider . . . so you got to give me some consideration. . . . Well, how 'bout five dollars then, man?

(*The lights go down on them. It comes up on* JANIE.)

JANIE: (*Smokes a joint, ladylike.*) I'm not really lonely. At least so I would know it. But there's not many people I can relate to . . . or even talk to. That's why I like Monty as a friend. He's nice. Sensitive. Serious. And with so much talent. That's why I can't allow him to get too close to me. I want him as a friend. That's all. It's not because of Lonnie. I'm tired of Lonnie. But he's like a bad habit I can't shake. I once thought he was the one for me. But I was younger and more innocent and didn't realize the vast differences and problems that lay between us. Lonnie will never be anything more than Lonnie, I guess, he'll never have a big name in jazz. Never really do more than be a second-rate sideman at the Whiskey A-Go-Go. So it isn't Lonnie that keeps me from letting Monty have his way with me. Nor is it because Monty's black and I'm white. Gee . . . I think colored people are neat. And I've made it with black guys before. And I guess I'll do it some more. But not with Monty. He's a friend. A lifelong friend, I hope. And I know that men and women more often than not sacrifice their friendships when they become lovers. So I'll be true to Monty. To keep our friendship alive. And perhaps our relationship will mature into the purest of loves one day. An ideal black/white love. Like sweet grapes change with age and care into a distinctive bouquet upon choice, rare wines.

(*The lights change subtly.* MONTY *steps into the light with* JANIE.)

MONTY: You called, Janie? . . . I came as soon as I got the message that you wanted to see me.

JANIE: Oh, Monty, I didn't know who else to turn to. I need your help.

MONTY: You know I'll do anything I can for you. Just ask.

JANIE: There's nobody else I could have turned to, Monty. It's so personal and private I couldn't tell my other friends. They all know one another and word would have gotten out. You are my last resort, Monty.

MONTY: What is it, Janie? What can I do? Who do you want killed, Miss Janie?

JANIE: Please don't treat this as a joke. . . . Monty . . . I have to have an abortion.

MONTY: You do?

JANIE: Yes . . . Lonnie and I have broken up. I don't want to see him any more. And I can't have a baby now anyhow. I'm at UCLA . . . and Daddy would never understand or forgive me. And I'd die if anybody knew. Will you help me? Will you? Please, Monty.

MONTY: Sure . . . sure . . . I'll drive you down to Tijuana . . . or even El Paso, if necessary. When we get back you can stay at my place. I've got my own pad now. And nobody will have to know where you are or how you're doin' until you're ready. You can even pretend that you're my woman.

JANIE: You're such a good friend, Monty.

MONTY: (*Serious.*) You know I've always loved you, Janie.

(*She places her fingers across his lips.*)

JANIE: Shhssss . . . Monty . . . please . . . don't say things that we'll both regret later.

MONTY: Why does it have to be this way between us, Janie?

JANIE: I don't know. It's just that I think of you as somebody special for me. And I refuse to spoil that secret, special feeling.

MONTY: You're wrong, you know, Miss Janie.

JANIE: That's impossible. . . . You know that, Monty.

MONTY: Well, we better start making our plans for the trip. It'll all be over in a day or so.

JANIE: Monty . . . I won't have any money until my dad sends me my monthly allowance.

MONTY: That's okay. I've got enough in my checking account. I can stop at the bank on our way out of town.

JANIE: What would I do without you, Monty? You know, in my own way, I love you very much. Please . . . let's neither of us ever do anything to destroy what we have together.

MONTY: I'll try and do my part, Miss Janie. C'mon . . . it's time to split.

JANIE: You know . . . I don't even resent that silly name you call me too much anymore, Monty. It's grown on me like you have.

(*He lifts her and cradles her in his arms. Then he carries her away as the lights go down.*)

(*Lights up on* PEGGY.)

PEGGY: Now that was a romantic scene . . . huh? Yeah . . Monty can really act romantic when he tries. Even with me. You know he married me finally. Yeah. One day he up and proposed. And we got married soon afterward at the county courthouse with Len acting as best man. And then he got me to drop out of school and go to work for a bank to support him and send him to school. It was half-way slick on his part. He shoulda been a con man. He had me goin' for a good while. I was strung out. See, I loved him. Really loved him. And still do. As only a black woman can love a black man. But he never loved me. Damn, I don't believe Monty ever loved anybody except Monty. He's selfish, ya know. And kinda cruel. But I dig him. Still do. And I had some good moments with him. All those other girls he had didn't matter. I knew he never really cared about them. Not even Janie. But she's conceited enough to think they had something going. White girls are some dizzy critters. I know. Cause I know about Blackmen better than they know about themselves. My father was black. And my husband, Monty, was too. So I know. Even though I was innocent and wouldn't believe the truth for a long time. But Monty never treated me right. He always would be sayin' that he had to have time to do his thing. That's why I was workin' and gettin' my mind messed up 'cause he was doin' his thing. Wow! . . . sure was a heavy trip. The scenes we went through for the time we were together. We broke up about a dozen times. I even had a baby one of the times while we was broke up . . . and I put it up for adoption be-

fore we went back together again. But I learned a lot
from Monty. A whole lot. And I wouldn't trade those
happy moments with him for nothin'. Cause loneliness is
a fatal disease . . . and I've got a terminal case. . . .
But that moment of love with him was delicious. And
you know . . . even the pain was sweet though bitter.
(PEGGY *lingers in the light.* FLOSSY *joins her.*)

FLOSSY: Don't feel blue, girl. None of them are worth it.
Men are no good, that's all. They either be tricks or they
be out to put you in one, so forget 'em. We women gotta
do our own thing.

PEGGY: But why we got to get our lives cluttered up with
these white things? First these white heifers that be after
our men . . . then white studs who think they be after you.

FLOSSY: Well, you should know, girl.

PEGGY: Yeah, I should know somethin', Flossy Mae . . .
'cause after I finally broke from Monty for good I married me a white boy. Yeah, a white boy. 'Cause he
wasn't no man yet. I guess that was the one way to finally get completely away from Monty. Marry a devil.
His pride was hurt so bad he didn't even see me for
years afterward. Almost finally became a real Black Nationalist and revolutionary. But the years without him
have been very very lonely, girl. And no little white boy
or booze, scag, or LSD or nothin' could fill them.

FLOSSY: It's the fault of those funky white bitches who
think they can lick and suck the world up like a bowl of
buttermilk. Our men especially.

PEGGY: Don't blame them, Flossy. Don't blame anybody.
Now I don't blame you, do I? And you and Monty had
your thing goin' under my nose, you bitch. I got out
my front door to work. And you'd be in the back door
with my man.

FLOSSY: Well, you know that my thing is making it with
my friendgirl's ole men, honey.

(*A light comes up on another part of the stage. It
shows* MONTY *and* JANIE.)

JANIE: (*Calls.*) Hello, Hello, Monty . . . Monty,
hello . . .

MONTY: Hi, Janie . . . how you doin'?

JANIE: I came up to Frisco to visit you, Monty. Since you've moved up here I've missed you a lot. You don't think Peggy will mind, do you?

MONTY: Nawh . . . nawh . . . you know Peggy always liked you.

JANIE: Good. . . . Then I'll stay the week with you. You can take me all around beautiful San Francisco and show me everything.

FLOSSY: (*Moves toward* MONTY; *calls out.*) Hey . . . Monty . . . Monty, my man. I'm here.

JANIE: Who's that, Monty?

MONTY: It's Flossy . . . a friend of mine. She comes over and keeps me company while Peggy's at work.

　　(FLOSSY *enters and she and* MONTY *kiss passionately and begin lovemaking.*)

JANIE: Oh, excuse me. I didn't know you would have company, Monty. I thought we would be alone until Peggy came. I thought we'd be able to watch the city lights from high atop here on Potrero Hill and talk of our old school days. I didn't know you had someone besides me . . . somebody real . . . somebody black and sensual as the night who would blot out my pale image like a cloud covering a dim, far constellation.

　　(*Lights down on* JANIE *and* MONTY. FLOSSY *returns to* PEGGY'*s area.*)

FLOSSY: That Monty was a no-good nigger. He'd sit that ole white girl in one room and have her read his poetry and stuff while he screwed me until my tongue hung out in the next room. Chile . . . it was a scream. With those thin walls you could hear a roach pee on a soda cracker . . . and the stains on the couch. What did you have in your head when you saw that, girl?

PEGGY: Ha ha . . . I was ignorant; I thought that the cats kept gettin' up there and were messin' around.

FLOSSY: Ooeeee . . . and the way Monty would sock it to me, girl, that lil white broad musta thought we were tearin' down the house with all that humpin'. I knew she'd be gettin' hot as a ten cent pistol cause when we'd come out, she'd turn all red lookin', and her eyes would be waterin'.

PEGGY: Yeah . . . and when I got home from work at midnight everybody would still be lookin' funny. Smiling secretly to yourselves. Damn, I was dumb. I thought it was because of the wine and pot.

FLOSSY: Nigger men ain't no good, Peggy. We sisters should start takin' those niggers' heads off behind the stuff they be pullin' on us.

PEGGY: Maybe so . . . maybe so . . . at least I could agree with you at one time. When I cared about men. But I'm a liberated lesbian now. See, I had to learn to cope with the world the best way I could. Sister Power is where it's at!

FLOSSY: Right on!

PEGGY: (*Tender.*) You're still my friend, ain't you, Flossy? (*The two women embrace and kiss passionately, then walk off into the shadows, hand-in-hand.*
Lights change. Up on LONNIE.*)

LONNIE: (*Hands in pockets, casual.*) Yeah, man, it wasn't the times that betrayed us . . . it was ourselves. We each fed on the other's weaknesses instead of gettin' it together like the rhetoric says and giving some support to each other to make it through. Yeah, I went with Janie. Was really heavy into it with her for a while. But there were too many things keeping us apart. Her fear of what her parents would say, for one. And her always lookin' to be liberated . . . or somethin'. She was a school chick. All the time in college and never knowing what she was there for or what she wanted out of it. Her mother and father went to college, ya know. So she's got to make a career of it. . . . And her having her own friends, and trying to have her own scene. That cat Monty's okay, but anybody can see what he's after. But Janie won't admit it. I'm a jazz musician, see. Play electric guitar. Not a big timer. But I make it in L.A. okay, with a few gigs in Vegas, up in Tahoe and around Palm Springs to make ends meet. And being around spades all the time in the music business I gets to know them, you see. They okay, if they keep their distance and know their place. Some of my best friends . . . you know? But you got to give them dudes credit. They got lots of the broads psyched out. They got a whole super stud/super spade thing goin' for them. I had to finally cut Janie loose because of our different points-of-view. She and her hang-ups got to be a drag. And that was a good little while ago that we broke it off. Yeah . . . she had three abortions while we were together. She would tell me after she got them, after it was all over. I hated seeing that happen without being able to say anything about it; ya know, being a part of that made me feel guilty. I once told her that she was murdering our spirit and soul when she did that. She told me that she didn't believe in spirit and that everyone knew that the spades had all the soul. Guess she was high on somethin'. I told her that she was killing our future. She said she was afraid of the future. And she was never happy with me after that. I guess she thought I threatened her liberation. . . . And she and I have been through and done ever since. Now I'm into a new thing. I'm into the true spirit now, ya know, religion. I belong to the Baha'i World Faith. All mankind are my family

> (LONNIE *takes a pair of dark glasses from his shirt pocket and puts them on.*
> RICK *joins him.*)

RICK: (*Disdain.*) Well . . . if it isn't one of the Chosen People.

LONNIE: You talkin' to me, man?

RICK: Is there somethin' wrong with your eyes, devil? There's nobody here but us.

LONNIE: Hey . . . stop tryin' to intimidate me. You tryin' to start a fight, ain't cha?

RICK: (*Ridicule.*) How could even I start a fight with a nonviolent devil?

LONNIE: Why you gotta cast me as the devil, man?

RICK: (*Self-righteous.*) Because you are the son of Yacub . . . the original devil!

LONNIE: Look, man, everyone makes their own devil. Dig it? I'm really a child of God like you are and all mankind. So I don't see why you got to be comin' down on me for something I ain't had no part in?

RICK: You are equally as guilty as your brothers and your father.

LONNIE: Listen, man, you got a rap for everybody ain't ya? You got one for your black brothers, for chicks and you got another rap . . . yeah, man . . . I remember when you were quotin' Shakespeare and Omar Khayyam at the Young Socialist parties to all the little white broads you say you hate now. That was only last semester, man, and now your rap for me is that I'm the devil. Your game is weak, Rick, man.

RICK: Your reign on earth is nearly up, devil. You have ruled your allotted six thousand years and now it is time for the Blackman to rise.

LONNIE: Shut up! Shut up, will ya? You're worse than those fanatic Zionists I grew up with.

RICK: First Israel will fall!

LONNIE: Hey . . . that's got nothin' to do with me. I ain't a Jew no more. Hey! I don't want to hear that crazy crap you're talkin'!

RICK: Allah will sweep you white European devils into the sea.

LONNIE: Can't you just treat me like a human being?

RICK: Your time is nearly at hand, devil.

LONNIE: You know what, man? . . . I liked you better when you had a sense of humor.

RICK: Death to devils! Destroy the enemies of the Black people!

LONNIE: I'll see you later, man. You've lost your cool. And I never did think you'd start believing your own bullshit.

   (LONNIE *exits.*

   RICK *stands for a moment, relishing his victory. He puffs out his chest and walks into the shadows.*

   The light changes. LEN *appears.*)

LEN: By my appearance you wouldn't take me to be a great teacher, would you? But I am. A great teacher and influencer of men . . . and lover of the finer things of life, such as art, literature, theater, fast cars, good food, and women, especially. In fact I nourished those tastes in my friend Monty. And some of it has been taken and cultivated by him, especially the finer ones like drama.

Yes . . . yes, indeed . . . and it was I who first taught
Rick about nationalism . . . *Black* Nationalism. He
read Garvey in the books I loaned him and encountered
the righteous brothers of the Nation of Islam at my Sunday Black cultural discussions and teas. And I was the
first to explain to him who was the most Honorable Eli-
juh Muhammad . . . and cite The Messenger's importance to contemporary Black America. Now you might
ask what's so great about pullin' his coat to things he
would find out sooner or later, but you're now seeing
Rick in his neophyte state. Before this decade is out, the
sixties, he becomes a large national figure on the Black
revolutionary scene and falls after his rise like so many
of his brothers in the struggle. . . . But it was nationalism that lit the fires in his ambitious heart. So don't put
down nationalism. It is the stuff that fuels revolutions.
Agreed? . . . One can even say that the Zionists are the
nationalists of Israel, couldn't one? And that Al-Fatah
and other Arab terrorist organizations are the nationalists of Occupied Palestine. Nationalism translated means
National Liberation, wherever that nation stands. But
these are arguments that will take too long to deal with.
Tonight you are looking into some of the makings of the
sixties . . . which, of course, went to make the seventies. Just think . . . at this moment in our story the
Kennedys have still to be disposed of, Malcolm X hasn't
passed from the scene, Watts has to happen, Martin Luther King, Jr., must go to the mountain . . . never to
return. Ah . . . many things are spoken of here. And
the writer of this integrated social epic hints at only
some surface manifestations of the times, for he did not
know the impact of these accidental associations. He did
not know that through me he would discover the kernel
of political truth of the era, the seminal social vision of
the sweep of so much history. . . . But I have gotten
long-winded. There's so much to say and so little time.
But remember, more political and cultural phenomena
came out of southern California in the midcentury than
Richard Nixon and Walt Disney.

(*Lights change slightly, and* SHARON *joins* LEN.)

SHARON: Len . . . you're not a Black Nationalist, are you?

LEN: Why, of course not, Sharon, dear. I just know all about it. In fact, I know about almost everything.

SHARON: Yes, you know so much about all the Black stuff . . . but those fanatics and radicals that collect around you . . .

LEN: Sharon . . . I am an intellectual. I can intellectually examine any human proposition but I don't allow my feelings to become involved.

SHARON: Oh . . . how do you do that?

LEN: I can find rationalizations for everything, my dear.

SHARON: How clever. So you don't think I'm a devil after all?

LEN: Well at least not a big one . . . ha ha . . .

SHARON: You're cute too, Len. . . . Ah . . . you're not going to think I'm a tramp when I give you some of my body, are you?

LEN: A tramp? How could I? You're from a nice middle-class Jewish background. How could I think that?

SHARON: I was pretty wild during my last year of high school and my one year of junior college.

LEN: That was mere teenybopper rebellion, Sharon. Adolescent adjustment to approaching maturity.

SHARON: I made it with over seventy fellahs before I lost count.

LEN: There's nothing to feel guilty about. It was done in the innocence of youth. You were a child of the times, my dear.

SHARON: Guys would say that I looked like Liz Taylor and they'd all want to make it with me. And what was a girl to say?

LEN: It must have been pretty harrowing to have come through that stage.

SHARON: At drive-ins, in the back seats of convertibles, at their pads while their mothers were sunning themselves at the beach.

LEN: Come here, Sharon. Let me hold you and make you forget those terrible times.

SHARON: Actually, it was a lot of fun for a while. But I'm

glad you're so understanding, Len. That's what I need
. . . a man who is willing to try and understand me.

(*Lights change.* LEN *moves away. And* SHARON
speaks:)

SHARON: And we were married . . . Len and I. At the
First Unitarian Church. It was a dull wedding. But my
mother was happy and cried. And my sister didn't act
too snobbish. Even lots of my old beaus came. And it all
turned out lots better than I thought it would. I was
glad, in fact. And Len and I settled down in an apartment close to City College where Len was in his fifth
year, even though it's a two-year school. And we started
getting used to each other. Which was easier said than
done. In fact, it was hell. You know, it took us over five
years before we really sorta ironed out our difficulties.
But the times we had, my God! We gave a million parties. And I momentarily fell back into my bad habits
with men. But it wasn't serious, so Len and I discussed it
and decided it was merely an aspect of my neurosis. And
we moved at least a dozen times. Sometimes trying to
get away from each other. And I tried to break away
from Len when he wasn't trying to put me down or in
my place or in the kitchen and it was pretty terrible for
a while. We even broke up a number of times. But that's
history now. We're back together and are making it. We
have a pretty large son now who is spoiled bad as hell
and looks just like Len. Len's got his own business now.
I kid him about his Marxist days now that he's a working capitalist, but he reminds me that he's really an intellectual. We're one of the lucky couples. We made it.
But it took a lot of doing. And let me tell you, it's not
easy being married to a Blackman . . . even if he's an
intellectual or not. But we're making it.

(SHARON *hesitates, and is joined by* MORT SILBER-
STEIN.)

MORT SILBERSTEIN: Well, well . . . if it isn't the poor little bourgeoise nice non-Kosher girl.

SHARON: You talkin' to me fellah?

MORT SILBERSTEIN: Nawh . . . I'm not talkin' to you,
honey. I'm talkin' to the girl who lays all the spades in

town then adds racial suicide to cultural injury by marrying one.

SHARON: You're very insulting. You have no business talking to me that way.

MORT SILBERSTEIN: I have every right in the world. Every right in the world. It's because of women like you from good Jewish homes that go out and betray their heritage and upbringing that we Jews are being threatened with extinction in the world. Why do you have to go out and disgrace us by making a display of yourself?

SHARON: You've got your nerve to talk to me, Mort Silberstein. You live with a German girl. From Germany!

MORT SILBERSTEIN: Who told you that? Has Monty been talking about me behind my back?

SHARON: Who would bother to talk about a nothing like you?

MORT SILBERSTEIN: You can't trust anybody these days . . . especially spades. That's really rank . . . runnin' me down behind my back.

SHARON: Well I'm glad you didn't try and deny it.

MORT SILBERSTEIN: Yeah, it's true. But I just live with her. I'm not marrying her.

SHARON: You have your nerve to talk like that to me. Why aren't you with a Jewish girl?

MORT SILBERSTEIN: A Jewish girl? Are you kiddin'? I had a mother who tried to drown me in chicken soup and bury me beneath lox and bagels.

SHARON: Well don't you ever want to start a family and settle down?

MORT SILBERSTEIN: Are you serious? If I got married I'd probably end up with someone exactly like you. You'd probably have me out selling insurance or real estate to keep you.

SHARON: What's so wrong about that? Len works. I wouldn't have a man unless he took care of me the best way he knew how.

MORT SILBERSTEIN: Haven't you girls heard of women's liberation? What are you talking about down at B'nai B'rith these days . . . the miracle of Israel? How a bunch of European imperialists made the desert green and fertile? You'd have to go get a job drivin' a cab or somethin' before I'd look at you. I'd never take care of a lazy bitch like you.

SHARON: It's a wonder you're not sniffin' around that little Janie character. Everyone else is. She could take care of you with the allowance she gets from her folks.

MORT SILBERSTEIN: I'm not much of a herd animal. Let the bucks have their dough. Besides, she's a middle-class goy. Don't you realize that I'm a radical poet? I wouldn't be caught dead near her . . . The proto-all-American plastic facist cunt! That would be like makin' it with Tricia Nixon. Bad news. I'll leave her for the black studs.

SHARON: What's so different about the girl you're stayin' with?

MORT SILBERSTEIN: Nina? Well, Nina's a Marxist. And a revoluntionary Leninist-Trotskyite. To Marxists race and cultural group take second and third place to the international world struggle for national liberation.

SHARON: Ahhh . . . you ex-Hasidic Jews are all nuts. Leave me alone, will ya? I have a baby who is half-black. That's the only reality I can deal with now. I don't care who killed Jesus.

(*Lights change.* SHARON *and* MORT SILBERSTEIN *disappear.*

FLOSSY *appears.*)

FLOSSY: Some party, hey? I come to all of Monty's parties. Some are better than this one . . . and some are worse. I don't live around here. Hardly no black people do except the ones you see here tonight. That's why it's such an integrated scene. Mostly college dudes and broads. Sure is phony, huh? But I like Monty. We buddies . . . fuckin' buddies. We make it every once in a while. I like it with him. He makes me feel like a real woman and a lady at the same time. He's . . . well, you know, intelligent and nice. And he don't put me down when I act crazy or wild. Or when I can't pronounce those big words some of them be usin' around here or know what they mean. These other brothers here are messed up, but Monty's gettin' it together. If he could ever get his nose

out of these white bitches behinds, he'd be better off. But
he and Peggy might do a thing. But I don't see no future
in it. They both got a lot of hang-ups, if you know what
I mean. He don't even like her as much as he like me,
but I'm too much out runnin' the street to have a guy
like Monty depend on me. So Peggy can have him. I'll
still see him when I want. And things will be okay. As
long as he don't get too strung-out behind these white
bitches.

(JANIE *joins her.*)

JANIE: Hello Flossy, how are you doing?

FLOSSY: Okay, I guess, until now.

JANIE: Oh, why did you say that?

FLOSSY: 'Cause I fixed my mouth to say that and that's
what I said.

JANIE: Oh . . . don't you like me, Flossy?

FLOSSY: You're okay, I guess.

JANIE: But there's somethin' wrong. Have I done anything?

FLOSSY: Nawh, you ain't done nothin' wrong. Just be
white, that's all.

JANIE: Flossy, I didn't know you were a Black Nationalist.

FLOSSY: I was in the temple for a minute . . . but aside
from that . . . I just don't like the way you carry yourself.

JANIE: I don't understand. Are you talking about Monty
and I? We're only friends, that's all.

FLOSSY: We only friends too . . . but he don't look at me
the way he looks at you.

JANIE: Maybe he's got what he wants from you . . . and
he wants what he thinks he can get from me.

FLOSSY: Maybe. Say . . . you're pretty hip in your own
way. I'm gonna tell ya somethin'.

JANIE: You are? What's that?

FLOSSY: The Game. I'm gonna tell ya what it is and then
show you how to play it.

JANIE: You are? It's not going to hurt or anything, is it?

FLOSSY: Nawh. It all happens in the mind. You won't feel
a thing except understanding.

(FLOSSY *pulls her into a corner and begins talking in whispers.*

FLOSSY *slaps five with her;* JANIE *clumsily and timidly slaps palms.*

FLOSSY *cracks-up;* JANIE *giggles.*

RICK *appears as the girls fade out.*)

RICK: Ain't this some jive! Ain't it? Here I am with my Black self in some jive-time stuff as this. Here I am with my roommates . . . stone integrationists . . . and vanilla fever freaks. Wow! It's sad. These so-called negroes ain't never gonna get themselves out of slavery. Len, my old friend and once intellectual peer, is on the eve of marrying one of these devil ladies. And Brother Monty, the poor poet brother, is waitin' for Miss Ann . . . Oh, excuse me . . .waitin' for *Miss Janie* to give him some lovin'. Been waitin' for a good time and will wait for years, I'm told. In fact, this whole thing is about the negro gettin' ready to get himself some of blond Miss Janie. What a drag. I've been to better parties, I'll tell ya. My Black brothers . . . two white-women lovers. Now ain't that a blip? How sad. No wonder so many of we black people were so confused all of the sixties and now into the seventies . . . we were in a war . . . and was lovin' the enemy. With all the sisters out here in the world these deaf, dumb, and blind negroes are waitin' for the devil's women to give them some of their stale, ole cold, funky butts and make them feel like men. But the sisters in this scene are comin' out of some strange bags, I'll kid you not. This neighborhood is too close to Hollywood. This is Babylon! The beginning of the end. The folks here are just jiving their lives away. I just see that I have to get myself out of here. That's right. I gotta split. I can't do nothin' round here. I'm just about on my way too . . . soon as this party's over and I can catch me a ride downtown.

(*A car horn is heard.*) (PEGGY *walks up to* RICK.)

PEGGY: Hey, Rick. I can give you a ride. I drive a little no-top sports car now since I divorced Monty and temporarily married my new husband. That's before I cut men loose completely . . . dig?

RICK: It won't take you out of your way, will it, sister?

PEGGY: Nawh. Just let me know when you're ready to motor.

RICK: Thank you, sister. For someone who has so many problems you're really a real woman. . . . In some ways, at least . . . ha ha . . .

PEGGY: Well what do you think I'd be?

RICK: (*Self-righteous and pompous.*) Sister . . . you must admit . . . you live a very unnatural way of life. . . . I know it developed over a time of suffering . . . Your disillusionment with your unfulfilled life . . . your loss through resignation of your baby . . . your exploitation by your blackman . . . your search for love and emotional and physical security . . . your penis envy . . . and, ah . . . other masculine/feminine conflicts and encounters. . . . Now take this scene. This is where your relationship with Brother Monty nurtured. That's heavy. At wine and pot parties to impress white girls!

PEGGY: Hey, listen, Rick . . .

RICK: (*Speech-making.*) The devil has mastered his tricknology to such a state as to turn you, sister, into a freak and to convert your man into an animal without culture or history, hungering after pale flesh.

PEGGY: No, Rick. Don't distort things so much. We didn't party to impress white girls. Or anybody. They were just there, that's all. And we wanted them there. The girls . . . and the boys. Our heads were into that then. It was the thing to do. We believed in America. The whole trip. And America was boring and we were young. We were just thinking that that was the best way to have a good time. We had to socialize in some way, didn't we?

RICK: But nevertheless, you went from this room into an unfortunate marriage to a confused negro which you keep mentioning, and the subsequent divorce, and then marriage to a white boy . . .

PEGGY: He wasn't a boy! He wasn't . . . Man . . . stop being so goddamn condescending . . . and . . . and . . .

RICK: Historical!

PEGGY: Awww . . . fuck you!

RICK: Yes . . . ha ha ha . . . sister . . . or should I say *mister* . . . to you?

PEGGY: Say "Ms.," Rick. I'm not ashamed now for anything I've done or anything that I am or do now.

RICK: But to have this Western madhouse of North America drive you into becoming a freak, sister.

PEGGY: Freak! You call me a freak? Well look what happened to you, Rick. You became something called a Cultural Nationalist. Hahh! In fact, you thought you invented it. And when the media pumped your head full of your own bull, you wigged out on a Section Eight trip. What was it now? . . . Torturing young Black women? Freaking out? Oh, I know . . . or at least what I heard . . . you were under stress and had been keeping your thing together with speed cause those other comic opera political clowns . . . The Big Black Cats . . . were on your case after the big-shoot-out and assassination at UCLA. . . .

RICK: Hey! Hey! . . . you got it all wrong and backward. You don't know what you're talkin' about, sister. In fact, you are incorrect! So why don't you just keep quiet about all that? It ain't even happened yet. So be cool.

PEGGY: But you haven't let me tell all of your future yet, Brother Rick.

RICK: I already know my future. It is going to be glorious!

PEGGY: If you think so, Rick. If you think so. But do you know what?

RICK: What's that, sister?

PEGGY: We all failed. Failed ourselves in that serious time known as the sixties. And by failing ourselves we failed in the test of the times. We had so much going for us . . . so much potential. . . . Do you realize it, man? We were the youth of our times . . . And we blew it. Blew it completely. Look where it all ended. Look what happened?

(*They are looking out front at the audience.*)

We just turned out lookin' like a bunch of punks and freaks and fuck-offs.

RICK: It has been said: "That if one doesn't deal with reality, then reality will certainly deal with them."

PEGGY: Amen.

RICK: But I am not allowing myself to be held to blame. I am not allowing myself to be other than glorious. History will vindicate me.

PEGGY: Hey, man . . . you know, you never left yesterday. You're confused like all of us. Hey . . . do you still want that ride out of here?

RICK: Nawh, sister. Not really, anymore. I'll make it the best way I can. Are you going now?

PEGGY: Nawh, brother. Not now. I'm going to stay over and sleep with Monty. Give him a little action, ya know? If I don't I'll never get him and have him all to myself for the few years we were together. I have to try and save him from himself, don't I? I can't just let the Miss Janie's dance off with the world, can I?

RICK: Go get 'em, tiger. Ya know, it be about what you make it anyway.

(*Lights fade on them. It comes up on* MORT SILBERSTEIN.)

MORT SILBERSTEIN: (*Smokes a joint.*) This is a crazy scene, ain't it? An honest-to-God creepy insane looney bin. A picture of the times, I say. And you can't forgive the creator of this mess for the confusion. That's what happens when you mix things up like this. It throws everything out of kilter. Jews, niggers, politics, Germans, time, philosophy, memory, theme, sociology, past, drugs, history, sex, present, women, faggots, men, dikes, phonys, assholes . . . everything bunched up together. Looks like the worst party of the decade, right? Probably the worse goddamn party in memory. Huh . . . ? Hey, you got any money? Have ya, huh . . . ? How about lendin' me ten bucks? Ten bucks, okay? How about it? Okay . . . ? no? Well, then, five. C'mon. Five fucken' bucks for Christ sakes! Look . . . I ain't no crummy wino. I got some kinda class. It takes at least five bucks to cop some scag. Now ain't that right? So be a good guy and let me have ten. You won't even miss it. Take it off your taxes as a donation to art. . . . I'm a Beat Poet from the fifties, see. Put it on your expense account . . . or somethin'. I can get a nickel bag

of smoke and get fixed up for a ten. What? You say
I've lost my bearings and am quoting East Coast seventies prices? Wow! Dig him. A drug culture freak.
Hey, man, I'm only tryin' to get a fucken high on, not
earn a fucken degree.

(MONTY *enters.*)

Hey, Monty. Tell these folks how bad I need ten bucks.

MONTY: Hey, man, I ain't in it.

MORT SILBERSTEIN: You ain't in it? If you ain't in it, then
who is?

MONTY: You ain't serious about nothin', Mort. I gotta cut
you loose.

MORT SILBERSTEIN: Well, will ya dig that? He says I ain't
serious. Man if I ain't fucken serious about gettin' fixed
up then you don't know what serious is.

MONTY: Listen, I gotta cut you loose, white boy. You ain't
nothin' but a hang-up. Messin' around with you will get
somebody killed. In fact it already has and will.

MORT SILBERSTEIN: (*Turns away.*) Awww . . . you
spades.

(MONTY *grabs* MORT SILBERSTEIN *by the collar.*)

MONTY: If you say that again, I'll crush your filthy nose.

MORT SILBERSTEIN: See what I mean? See what I mean? It
always comes to this with you guys. Shit, man! We lost
people in Mississippi too, hero. Where were you at Kent
State, huh, Freedom Rider? I been with you for a long
time and on a long long trip . . . from Scottsboro and
back . . . and now you coppin' out with mashin' my
nose and talkin' that Third World Black People's crap.
The Arabs ain't black, man? You ain't got no place in
Palestine! You can't even go to Algiers no more! . . .
And the Egyptians sold your mammy!

(MONTY *punches him.* MORT SILBERSTEIN *begins to
cry.*)

The whole goddamn world has gone and went fuckeroo
. . . and I don't care. I'm sick and need a fix and I
don't give a fuck no more about nothin'. Kiss my Lower
Eastside ass, blackie.

MONTY: (*Shouting.*) I don't want to be a whiteman, do
you hear me, Mort Silberstein? I don't want to be a to-

ken Jew even. I'm me. You understand? It's taken a long time but I know that now.

MORT SILBERSTEIN: (*Screaming.*) All I know is that I am a Zionist junkie . . . and I don't give a shit for fertilizer . . . but what are you still gettin' your rocks off a blond meat for and still talkin' that Black shit!

MONTY: Shut up! Shut up your goddamn mouth before I kill ya.

MORT SILBERSTEIN: (*Quieter, serious.*) You can't kill me anymore than you can kill the last century. I'm in your head nigger like your nightmares.

MONTY: (*Scared.*) No! Nothin's in my head except Congo drums and Freeway sounds and the "A" train bearing down on 125th Street.

(*They wrestle about the stage.*
The other party members move about as if sleep-walking.)

MORT SILBERSTEIN: You're in love with my father . . . and his father's father . . . not the wet slime presence of Miss Janie.

MONTY: Shut up! You don't know what you're talking about!

MORT SILBERSTEIN: You're in love with MARX!

(MONTY *hits him and screams:*)

MONTY: MAO!!!

MORT SILBERSTEIN: You're thrilled by FREUD!

(MONTY *hits him and screams:*)

MONTY: FANON!!!

MORT SILBERSTEIN: You suck EINSTEIN!

(MONTY *hits him again and screams:*)

MONTY: VOODOO!!!

MORT SILBERSTEIN: You're freaky for JESUS!

(MONTY *beats* MORT SILBERSTEIN *unconscious, then rests.*
The others in the room wake and stir.)

PEGGY: Wow, honey . . . that was some bad grass. Hey . . . you and Mort Silberstein have a disagreement or somethin'?

LONNIE: Say, I'm splittin'. . . . This looks like a bust to me. Hey, Janie, you ready to make it, baby?

JANIE: Nawh. I think I'm gonna stick around awhile. Monty's going to tell me the story of his life.

(*She exits into the kitchen.*)

PEGGY: (*Shrugs.*) In that case I guess I better get my hat too. You need a ride, Lonnie?

LONNIE: Why not, doll?

(LONNIE *and* PEGGY *exit.*)

LEN: I'm going to bed, Monty. See you in the morning. We can clean up this mess then, brother.

SHARON: Wait for me, Len. You know . . . you're kinda frantic for me. And besides, we're getting married soon.

(LEN *and* SHARON *exit through the back door.*)

FLOSSY: (*Kisses* MONTY.) It was a boss party, baby. I'll see you next week, huh? Come on by my place and lay up some. Oweee . . . I'll be as hot as snot for you by then, sugar.

RICK: Wait up, sister. You're on your way back to the ghetto, ain't cha? I need some company back to civilization. Well, Brother Monty, it ends the way it ends, doesn't it?

MONTY: Yeah, man . . . this is the beginning of the sixties . . . but it seems like forever. And I'm so goddamn tired already. We got a long way to go, ain't we?

RICK: You said it, not me, brother. Not me. Hey . . . anything I can do for you before I disappear?

MONTY: (*Points to the body.*) Yeah, man . . . throw this thing out in the trash on your way out.

RICK: Okay, brother. For you it'll be no problem. Cause I know you'd do the same for me.

(RICK *and* FLOSSY *grab* MORT SILBERSTEIN *and drag him out.*

JANIE *comes out of the kitchen. She wears her dark glasses and has her hair combed out.*)

MONTY: I never knew it would come to this.

JANIE: Neither did I. If anyone told me that after knowing you all these years you'd turn on me and rape me, I'd tell them that they don't know you at all. Or what makes up our wonderful relationship.

MONTY: I'm sorry I disappointed you. But I never had a chance to cop before. Funny. For twelve . . . thirteen years . . . I've never really been close enough to you to use an opportunity to take you like I wanted.

JANIE: Oh, yes you have. . . . You just never knew it, that's all. Some people have thought that all you ever had to do was push me and I'd fall over backward and my legs would fly open for you. But they never really knew us. . . . Never knew what we had and now have lost.

MONTY: Probably. We have been good friends, you know. Really, actually, true friends.

JANIE: Should I take a bath first?

(*He begins undoing her clothes.*)

MONTY: So many things kept us apart. So many things. . . . You know . . . if our signs were compatible, I'd probably have tried to marry you.

JANIE: Oh, no, you've always been too color conscious.

MONTY: Yeah . . . you're right.

JANIE: Remember the friend we had who hanged herself?

MONTY: Sure. How can I forget? We were a couple of her closest friends, or so we thought.

JANIE: She just went up on Mount Tamapais and tied a rope to a tree branch and swung off.

MONTY: Are you going to scream and fight me, Miss Janie?

JANIE: I know you too well, don't I, Monty? I'd feel so icky doing something like that.

(*The lights dim. He fully undresses her.*)

MONTY: I've never wanted anyone as much as I have wanted you.

JANIE: Don't tell me what you tell all the others.

MONTY: You . . . I'm going to enjoy this very very much.

JANIE: She just put the noose over her head and felt her spirit dance away.

(MONTY *pushes her back on the couch as he tears the last of her clothes away and the lights go down to blackness.*)

SAME TIME, NEXT YEAR

by Bernard Slade

Characters

GEORGE   A man
DORIS   A woman

Setting

The entire action of the play takes place in a room in a traditional country-style inn, two hundred miles north of San Francisco.

Act I

Act II

ACT ONE

Scene 1

THE TIME: *A day in February, 1951.*

THE PLACE: *A bed-sitting room in the cottage of a country-style inn near Mendocino, north of San Francisco. The beamed ceilings, wood-burning fireplace, wallpaper, durable antique furniture, and burnished brass lamps and fittings give the setting a feeling of comfortable warmth and respectable tradition. The room is large enough to contain a sturdy double bed, chintz-covered sofa and armchairs, and a baby grand piano. There are two leaded pane glass windows, a closet door, a door leading to a bathroom and another door that opens to an outside patio. The room's aura of permanence is not an illusion. The decor has been the same for the past twenty-five years and will not change for the next twenty-five.*

AT RISE: GEORGE *and* DORIS *are asleep in bed. He is twenty-seven with a likable average face and an intense nervous energy that gives everything he does a slightly frenetic quality but doesn't always cover his deep-seated insecurity. Something wakes him and as he groggily turns over his eyes fall upon the sleeping form of* DORIS *beside him. He sits bolt upright in bed, instantly wide awake.*

GEORGE: (*Fervently.*) Oh Jesus.

(*He slips out of bed and we see he is wearing only*

boxer shorts. He grabs his sports coat from the floor, puts it on and surveys the clothes strewn about the room. They include the rest of his clothes and her blouse, skirt, stockings, bra, girdle, and shoes.)
Jesus H. Christ.

(He looks back at DORIS *and then quickly moves to the dresser where he grabs a bottle of Wildroot Cream Oil, massages it into his scalp and starts to comb his short, tousled hair.*

While he is doing this DORIS *wakes up, sits up in bed, watches him. At this point in time she is slightly overweight with ordinary pretty looks and a friendly, unself-conscious, ingenuous manner that makes her immediately appealing despite the fact that at twenty-four she hasn't had the time or the education to find out who or what she is yet. When she speaks there is a forced gaiety to her voice.)*

DORIS: Hey, that's a real sharp-looking outfit.

(At the sound of her voice he turns around to look at her.)

GEORGE: Uh—hi.

(They eye one another for a moment.)

DORIS: What time is it?

GEORGE: Uh—my watch is on the bedside table.

(As she leans over to look at his watch, he makes a distracted attempt to clean up the room. This consists of picking up his trousers and his right shoe. He puts on his trousers during the following.)

DORIS: *(Puzzled.)* It says ten to eleven.

GEORGE: No, it's twenty-five after seven. It's always three hours and twenty-five minutes fast.

DORIS: Why?

GEORGE: When I got it back from being fixed at the watch-maker's it was set three hours and twenty-five minutes fast. I decided to keep it that way.

DORIS: *(Bewildered.)* Doesn't that mix you up?

GEORGE: No, I'm very quick with figures.

DORIS: But what about other people?

GEORGE: *(Agitated.)* Look, it's *my* watch!

DORIS: What are so sore about?

(*He takes a deep breath.*)

GEORGE: (*Grimly.*) Because we're in a lot of trouble.

DORIS: Yeah?

GEORGE: God, why do you have to look so—so luminous!

DORIS: Luminous?

GEORGE: I mean it would make everything so much easier if you woke up with puffy eyes and blotchy skin like most women.

DORIS: I guess God figured chubby thighs was enough.

GEORGE: Look, this thing is not just going to go away. We've got to talk about it.

DORIS: Okay.

(*She gets out of bed, pulls the sheet out, puts it around her over her slip and heads across the room.*)

GEORGE: What are you doing?

DORIS: I thought I'd clean my teeth first.

GEORGE: Dorothy, sit down.

(*She opens her mouth to speak.*)

Please—sit.

(*She moves to a chair, sits with the sheet wrapped around her.*

He places for a moment, gathering his thoughts before he turns to face her. When he speaks it is with great sincerity.)

Dorothy, first of all, I want you to know last night was the most beautiful, fantastic, wonderful crazy thing that's ever happened to me and I'll never forget it—or you.

DORIS: Doris.

GEORGE: What?

DORIS: My name's Doris.

GEORGE: (*Thrown.*) Why didn't you say so earlier? All last night I called you Dorothy and you never said anything.

DORIS: I didn't expect us to end up this—you know— (*She trails off.*) Then when I did try to tell you—you weren't listening.

GEORGE: When?

DORIS: (*Embarrassed.*) It was—you know—in the middle of—things.

(*He fixes her with a look of smoldering intensity.*)

GEORGE: It was incredible, wasn't it?

DORIS: It was—nice. (*Sensing he expects something more.*) Especially the last time.

GEORGE: (*Anguished.*) I know—I'm an animal!

(*He throws the shoe he is holding into the sofa, moves away to look out of the window.*

She takes this opportunity to kneel down to gather up some of her clothes.)

I don't know what got into me. I just—what was the matter with the other two times?

DORIS: What? Oh—well, the first time was so fast and the second—look, I feel funny talking about this.

GEORGE: (*Earnestly.*) It was a very beautiful thing, Doris. There was nothing disgusting or dirty in what we did.

DORIS: Then how come you're looking so down in the dumps?

GEORGE: Because my wife is going to *kill* me!

DORIS: Why should she find out?

GEORGE: She knows already.

DORIS: You said she was in New Jersey!

GEORGE: (*Gloomily.*) It doesn't matter. She *knows*.

DORIS: How come?

GEORGE: Look, I don't want to talk about it! (*He stares at her.*) Doris, was it as incredible for you as it was for me?

DORIS: (*Curiously.*) Do all men like to talk about it a lot afterward?

GEORGE: (*Defensively.*) Why? You think I'm some sort of—of eccentric or something?

DORIS: No, I just wondered. See, I was a virgin when I got married. At least technically.

GEORGE: Technically?

DORIS: Well, I was pregnant. I don't count that.

GEORGE: (*Doubtfully.*) Doris, that counts.

DORIS: I mean it was by the man I married.

GEORGE: Oh, I'm sorry.

(*She sits, puts on stocking during following.*)

DORIS: That's okay. Harry and me would've got married anyway. It just hurried things up a bit. (*Brightly.*) Turns out I get pregnant if we drink from the same cup.

(*He looks at her, pales a little, and gulps.*)
What's the matter?

GEORGE: (*Quickly.*) It's okay. Trojans are very reliable.

DORIS: Who are?

GEORGE: Never mind. (*He stares at her.*) We're in a lot of trouble, Doris.

DORIS: Why?

GEORGE: I think I love you.

DORIS: Better not start up something we can't finish, George.

GEORGE: Maybe it's too late for that. (*Suddenly.*) It's crazy! It's really crazy! I mean I don't even know if you like *Catcher in the Rye*!

DORIS: What?

GEORGE: I have this test for people. If they don't like *Catcher in the Rye* or *Death of a Salesman* I won't even date them!

DORIS: I never even finished high school.

GEORGE: (*Wildly.*) You see? I don't even *care*! And I'm really a *snob* about education!

(*He moves and bleakly stares out of window.* DORIS *puts on her skirt and blouse during the following.*)
Of course I should've known this would happen. You see there's something I didn't tell you about me, Doris.

DORIS: What?

GEORGE: When it comes to life I have a brown thumb. I mean nothing goes right. Ever.

DORIS: How do you mean?

GEORGE: Well, let me think of something that will give you the picture. (*He thinks.*) Okay. I was eighteen when I first had sex. It was in the back seat of a parked 1938 Dodge sedan. Right in the middle of it—we were rear ended.

DORIS: Gee, that's terrible. Did you have insurance?

GEORGE: And take last night. You know what they were playing on the juke box when we met?

(*She shakes her head.*)
"If I Knew You Were Coming I'd've Baked a Cake"!

DORIS: (*Puzzled.*) So?

GEORGE: So that's going to be "our song"!

(*He moves to angrily throw a log on the smoldering fire.*)

Other people would get "Be My Love" or "Hello, Young Lovers." Me—I get "If I Knew You Were Coming I'd've Baked a Cake"!

DORIS: (*Sentimentally.*) You're very romantic. I like that.

(*He looks at her.*)

GEORGE: And what about you? I think I've fallen in love with you, Doris. Now you want to know the luck I have? I'm happily married!

DORIS: (*Curiously.*) Are you Jewish?

GEORGE: (*Thrown.*) No, I'm not Jewish.

(*He takes off coat, puts on shirt.*)

As a matter of fact, I'm the result of a very strict Methodist upbringing.

DORIS: Is that why you feel so guilty?

GEORGE: Don't *you* feel guilty?

DORIS: Are you kidding? Half my high school graduating class became nuns.

GEORGE: Yeah, I guess Catholics have rules about this sort of thing.

DORIS: They have rules about everything. That's what's so great about being Catholic. You know where you stand and all.

(*He looks at her for a moment, shakes his head, starts to pace.*)

GEORGE: I tell you, Doris, I feel like slitting my wrists.

DORIS: Are you Italian?

GEORGE: What's with you and nationalities?

DORIS: You're so emotional.

GEORGE: I happen to be a CPA I mean I can be as logical as the next person.

DORIS: You don't strike me as an accountant type.

GEORGE: It's very simple. (*He shrugs.*) My whole life has always been a mess. Figures always come out right. Black and white, nice and tidy. I like that. What are you?

DORIS: Italian.

GEORGE: (*Thrown.*) Then why aren't you more emotional?

(*She moves to fire and warms her hands.*)

DORIS: If you're brought up in a large Italian family it's enough to turn you off emotion for life, you know?

GEORGE: I wondered why you weren't crying or yelling or anything.

DORIS: I got up this morning and did all that in the john.

GEORGE: Crying?

DORIS: Yelling.

GEORGE: I didn't hear you.

DORIS: I put a towel in my mouth.

GEORGE: Oh, I'm sorry.

DORIS: That's okay. There's no use crying over spilt milk.

GEORGE: You're right.

DORIS: Then why are we feeling so lousy?

GEORGE: (*Soberly.*) Because we're both decent, honest people and this thing is tearing us apart. I mean I know it wasn't our fault but I keep seeing the faces of my children and the look of betrayal in their eyes. I keep thinking of the trust my wife has placed in me. The times we've shared together. Our wedding vows. And you know the worst part of it all? Right at this moment, while I'm thinking all these things I have this fantastic hard on!

(*She looks at him for a moment, not moving.*)

DORIS: (*Finally.*) I wish you hadn't said that.

GEORGE: I'm sorry. I just feel we should be totally honest with each other.

DORIS: No, it's not that. I have to go to confession.

(*He looks at her for a second, breaks into rather a forced, incredulous laugh, moves away, turns to her, chuckles.*)

GEORGE: This is really very funny, you know that?

DORIS: Tell me—I could use a good laugh.

GEORGE: We're both crazy! I mean this sort of thing happens to millions of people every day. We're just normal, healthy human beings who did a perfectly healthy, normal thing. You don't use actual names in confession, do you?

DORIS: No.

GEORGE: Good. You want to know what I think about marriage and sex?

DORIS: I don't want to miss confession, George.

GEORGE: After you've heard what I have to say maybe you won't need to even go.

    (*He moves and sits cross-legged before her.*)

Look, suppose you compare a husband or a wife to a good book. So you got this great book and you read it—it's terrific; you love it. So you read the book again. Still good. So you read it again and again and again and even after maybe a hundred times you still enjoy it. Well, you know the book by heart now, so for a little variety you read it standing up, then lying down, then upside down, backwards, sideways, every way you can think of. You still like it, but Jesus, how many ways are there to read a book? Just once in a while you want to hear a new story, right? It doesn't mean you *hate* the old book. You'll read it again—later. Who knows? Maybe you'll appreciate it more. (*A beat.*) You understand what I'm saying?

DORIS: There's no use crying over spilt milk?

GEORGE: (*Getting to his feet.*) Doris, you've missed the whole point!

DORIS: What is the point?

GEORGE: (*Intensely.*) I've got to go to bed with you right now!

    (*He embraces her passionately and starts to smother her with kisses.*)

DORIS: George, we can't!

GEORGE: Why not?

DORIS: You'll feel even worse afterwards!

GEORGE: (*Still kissing her.*) I won't, I won't! I'm over that now!

DORIS: How come?

GEORGE: I just remembered something!

DORIS: What?

GEORGE: The Russians have the bomb! We could all die tomorrow!

DORIS: (*Somewhat out of breath.*) George—you're clutching at straws!

    (*He grabs her by the shoulders, looks deep into her eyes.*)

GEORGE: Don't you understand? We're both grown-up people who have absolutely nothing to be ashamed or afraid of!!!

(*There is a knock at the door. Both freeze, their eyes reflecting total panic. Then they go into frantic action as they both dive for the clothes on the floor. He gets her girdle but is not aware of what is in his hand. She, clutching the sheet and her shoes, bumps into him as she first tries to get under the bed and then heads for the bathroom door.*)

GEORGE: (*Panic-stricken—in a desperate hiss.*) Don't go into the bathroom!

(*She freezes.*)

DORIS: Why not?

GEORGE: It's the first place they'll look!

(*She heads for the window and climbs out onto the balcony as he frantically tries to make the room presentable.*

He looks around, sees she has disappeared but doesn't know where as he heads for the door.)

I'm coming!

(*He opens the door about six inches and squeezes outside, closing the door behind him.*

We hear a muffled exchange offstage before the door reopens and he reenters pushing a cart containing breakfast.)

Doris?

(*She doesn't appear and, puzzled, he looks under the bed, then in the closet, then moves to the window, pushes it open and leans outside.*)

Doris?

(*While he is doing this she comes back into the room through the other window, moves to behind him, claps a firm hand on his shoulder, speaks in a deep voice.*)

DORIS: You have a woman in here?

(*He leaps about a foot in the air with a yelp, turns to face her. She giggles and finally he gives a sheepish grin.*)

GEORGE: It's okay, it was old Mr. Chalmers with my breakfast. I was very calm. He didn't suspect a thing.

DORIS: He didn't ask about the girdle?

GEORGE: What girdle?

> (*He looks in his hand, sees he is still clutching her
> girdle. Anguished.*)

Oh—great! Now he probably thinks I'm a—a homo!

DORIS: What do you care?

GEORGE: I stay here every year.

> (*She moves to peek under platters on breakfast cart.*)

DORIS: How come?

GEORGE: There's this guy I went to school with who went
into the wine business near here. I fly out the same
weekend every year to do his books.

DORIS: From New Jersey?

GEORGE: He was my first client. It's kind of a sentimental
thing.

DORIS: Oh. (*She looks at him.*) Uh—can I have my girdle
back?

GEORGE: Oh, sorry—sure.

> (*He extends girdle, she reaches for it but he keeps
> hold of the other end, so they are both holding an
> end.*)

Doris, there's something I want to tell you.

DORIS: What?

GEORGE: You probably think I do this sort of thing all the
time. I mean I know I must appear smooth and glib—
sexually. Well, I want you to know that since I've been
married this is the very first time I've done this. (*A
beat.*) Do you believe me?

DORIS: Sure, I could tell. Hey, you mind if I have some of
your breakfast? I'm starved!

GEORGE: Oh sure—help yourself, I'm not hungry.

> (*She takes her girdle, pulls a chair up to the cart and
> starts to eat as he starts to pace.*)

It's funny, even when I was single I was no good at
quick, superficial affairs. I had to be able to really *like*
the person before— (*Turning to her suddenly.*) What
do you mean, you could tell?

DORIS: What? Oh—I don't know—the way you tried to get

your pants off over your shoes and then tripped and hit your head on the bedpost. (*Her eyes twinkling.*) Little things like that.

(*He smiles at her affectionately.*)

GEORGE: It's great to be able to be totally honest with another person, isn't it?

DORIS: It sure is.

(*His expression changes.*)

GEORGE: Doris, I haven't been totally honest with you.

DORIS: No?

GEORGE: No. (*He takes a deep breath.*) Okay—here it comes—the big one. (*She waits expectantly.*) I told you I was a married man with two children.

DORIS: You're not?

GEORGE: No. I'm a married man with *three* children.

DORIS: I don't get it.

GEORGE: I thought it would make me seem less married.

(*Under her gaze he becomes agitated and starts to pace.*)

Look, I just didn't think it through. Anyway, it's been like a lead weight inside me all morning. I mean denying little Debbie like that. I'm sorry, I was under a certain stress or I wouldn't have done it. You understand?

DORIS: Sure, we all do nutty things sometimes.

(*He smiles in relief.*)

So how come your wife doesn't travel with you?

GEORGE: Phyllis won't get on a plane.

DORIS: She's afraid of flying?

GEORGE: Crashing.

(*He watches her eat for a moment.
She looks up.*)

DORIS: What's the matter?

GEORGE: Nothing. I just love the way you eat.

(*She grins at him, holds up coffeepot.*)

DORIS: You wanta share a cup of coffee?

(*He nods, pulls up a chair opposite her, gazes at her as she pours coffee.*)

GEORGE: Doris, I've been thinking. Sometimes if you *know* why something happened it makes it easier to understand.

DORIS: You mean like us?

GEORGE: Right. Doris, do you believe that two total strang ers can look across a room and both have this sudden, overwhelming, totally irrational desire to possess one another in every possible way?

(*She considers for a moment.*)

DORIS: No.

GEORGE: (*Puzzled.*) Neither do I—so I guess that can't be it. Then how did this whole thing start?

DORIS: It started when you sent me over that steak in the restaurant.

GEORGE: They didn't serve drinks. Steak was all they had.

DORIS: What made you do it?

GEORGE: Impulse. Usually I never do that sort of thing. I have this—this friend who says that life is saying "yes." (*He shrugs.*) The most I can generally manage is "maybe."

DORIS: Your wife sounds like a nice person.

(*He reacts.*)

So why'd you do it?

GEORGE: I guess I was lonely and you looked so—so vulnerable and—well, you had a run in your stocking and your lipstick was smeared.

DORIS: You thought I looked cheap?

GEORGE: (*Quickly.*) No—beautiful. I'm attracted by flaws. I don't know—somehow they make people seem more human and—approachable.

(*She gazes at him affectionately.*)

That's why I like Pete Reiser better than say—Joe Di-Maggio.

DORIS: Pete Reiser's a baseball player?

GEORGE: He keeps running into walls. I like that.

DORIS: (*Gently.*) You know something, George? You're a real nice guy.

(*They smile tenderly at one another.*)

What made you think I was a medium rare?

GEORGE: I'm very intuitive.

DORIS: I'm well-done.

(*This jolts George out of his romantic mood.*)

GEORGE: Well-done? How can anyone like meat well-done?

DORIS: Harry always has his that way.

GEORGE: Oh. What were you doing in the restaurant anyway?

DORIS: I was on my way to a retreat. I go this same weekend every year.

GEORGE: (*Thrown.*) To—uh—meditate?

DORIS: Yeah, you might call it that. But not about God or anything. More about—well—myself.

(*He waits, awkwardly.*)

See, I got pregnant when I was just eighteen and so I never had a chance to—well—live it up. Oh, I don't know what I'm trying to say. (*She shakes her head, gives a little laugh.*) Sometimes I think I'm crazy.

GEORGE: Why?

DORIS: (*Awkwardly, thinking it out.*) Well, look at my life. I got three little kids underfoot all the time, so I'm never alone. I live in a two-bedroom duplex in downtown Oakland, we got a 1948 Kaiser that's almost half paid for, a blond, three-piece dinette set, a Motorola TV, and we go bowling at least once a week. (*A beat.*) I mean, what else could anyone ask for? But sometimes things get me down, you know? It's dumb!

GEORGE: I don't think it's dumb.

DORIS: I don't know. Sometimes I—I don't know what I *think* about anything, you know? I mean I'm almost twenty-five and I still feel—well—half-formed.

(*He doesn't say anything.*

A look of wonder comes to her face.)

Will you listen to me? Honest, you make me say things out loud I haven't even *thought* to myself. (*She smiles at him.*) I noticed that right after I met you last night.

GEORGE: (*Eagerly.*) We had instant rapport! Did you notice that too?

DORIS: No, but I know we really hit it off. (*A beat.*) You want some more coffee?

(*He shakes his head and watches her as she rises, moves to get sheet from where it was stuffed under the sofa, takes it to bed and starts to make bed.*)

GEORGE: What happens to your kids when you go on your retreat?

DORIS: Oh, Harry takes them to see his mother in Bakersfield. It's her birthday.

GEORGE: She doesn't mind you not going?

DORIS: No, she hates me.

GEORGE: Why?

DORIS: Because I got pregnant.

(*He moves to help her make up bed.*)

GEORGE: But her son had something to do with that too.

DORIS: She's blocked that out of her mind. Oh, I don't blame her. You see, Harry was in first year of dental college.

GEORGE: I don't get the connection.

DORIS: He had to drop out of school and take a job selling waterless cooking.

GEORGE: Oh.

(*He moves away, watches her make up bed for a moment.*)

Look, Doris, naturally we're both curious about each other's husband and wife. But rather than dwelling on it and letting it spoil everything, why don't we do this? I'll tell you two stories—one showing the best side of my wife and the other showing the worst. Then you do the same about your husband. Okay?

DORIS: Okay.

GEORGE: I think I should go first.

DORIS: Why?

GEORGE: Because I already have my stories prepared.

(*She nods, sits cross-legged on bed.*)

I'll start with the worst side of her.

DORIS: Go ahead.

GEORGE: (*Grimly.*) Phyllis knows about us.

DORIS: You said that before. How could she possibly know?

GEORGE: Because she has this—thing in her head.

DORIS: You mean like a plate?

GEORGE: (*Thrown.*) Plate?

DORIS: I got this uncle who was wounded in the war so

they put this steel plate in his head and he says he can tell when it's going to rain.

(*He looks at her for a moment.*)

GEORGE: Jesus, I'm in a lot of trouble.

DORIS: Why?

GEORGE: Because I find everything you say absolutely *fascinating!*

DORIS: Tell me about your wife's steel plate.

GEORGE: What? (*Brought back to earth, miserably.*) No, it's not a plate—it's more like a bell. (*Becoming agitated.*)

I could be a million miles away but whenever I even *look* at another woman it goes off like a fire alarm! Last night at 1:22. I just know she sat bolt upright in bed with her head going, ding, ding, ding, ding!

(*He nervously moves to breakfast cart and absently starts wiping off the lipstick marks on the coffee cup with his handkerchief.*)

DORIS: How'd you know it was 1:22?

GEORGE: I have peripheral vision and I noticed my watch said 4:47.

DORIS: That's crazy.

GEORGE: Okay, I happen to have personal idiosyncrasies and I happen to like my watch to be—

DORIS: No, I didn't mean that. I mean about your wife's bell and all.

GEORGE: Look, I know it's just an imaginary bell but it's very real to me!

(*He throws his lipstick-smeared handkerchief into the fire.*)

DORIS: (*Incredulous.*) You just threw your hankie into the fire.

GEORGE: We can't be too careful.

DORIS: Tell me something nice about her.

GEORGE: What? Oh—she made me believe in myself. (*He looks at her. Seriously.*) It's probably hard for you to imagine, but I used to be very insecure.

DORIS: How did she do that? Make you believe in yourself?

GEORGE: She married me.

DORIS: Yes, that was very nice of her.
  (*He looks at her.*)
I mean bolstering you up and all.
  (*He lies on the couch.*)
GEORGE: Okay, your turn. Tell me the worst story first.
DORIS: Well—it's hard—
GEORGE: (*Eagerly.*) To pick one?
DORIS: No, to think of one. Harry's the salt of the earth—
  everyone says so.
  (*He sits upright.*)
GEORGE: Look, you owe me one rotten story.
DORIS: Okay. This is not really rotten but—well—
  (*She gets off the bed, moves to fire, looks into it for a
  moment.*)
On our fourth anniversary we were having kind of a
rough time. The kids were getting us down and—well,
we'd gotten in over our heads financially but we decided
to have some friends over anyway.
  (*She moves to look out of window.*)
Now Harry doesn't drink much, but that night he had a
few beers and after the Gillette fights he and some of the
guys started to talk and I overheard him say his time in
the Army were the best years of his life.
GEORGE: (*Puzzled.*) What's wrong with that? A lot of guys
  feel that way about the service.
  (*She turns to face him.*)
DORIS: Harry was in the Army four years. Three of those
  years were spent in a Japanese prison camp! (*A beat.*)
  And he said this on our anniversary! Oh, I know he
  didn't mean to hurt me—Harry would never hurt any-
  one—but, well, it—hurt, you know? (*A beat.*) You're
  the only person I've ever told.
GEORGE: You want some more coffee?
DORIS: I'll get lipstick on the cup.
GEORGE: I don't care.
  (*He moves to pour her coffee.*)
DORIS: You wanta hear a story about the good side of him?
GEORGE: Not really.
DORIS: But you have to! I mean, I don't want you to get
  the wrong impression about Harry.

GEORGE: Okay, if you insist.

(*She moves to bed, plumps pillows.*)

DORIS: Well, Harry's a real big, kind of heavyset sort of guy, you know?

GEORGE: I wish you hadn't told me that.

DORIS: Oh, you don't have to worry. He's gentle as—as a puppy.

(*She sits on the downstage side of the bed, facing front and clasps a pillow to her chest.*)

Anyway, he tries to do different things with each of the kids, you know?

(*He sits beside her on the bed, hands her coffee.*)

Thanks. So, he was having a hard time finding something special to do with Tony, our four-year-old. Then he gets the idea to take him out to the park and fly this big kite. Well, he tells Tony about it—really builds it up—and Tony gets real excited. So this one Saturday last winter they go out together, but there's no wind and Harry has trouble getting the kite to take off. Well, it's kind of cold and Tony, who's pretty bored by now—he's only four years old—asks if he can sit in the car. Harry says, "Sure." (*She starts to smile.*) About an hour later I happen to come by on my way home from the laundro-mat and I see Tony fast asleep in the car and Harry, all red in the face and out of breath, pounding up and down, all alone in the park, with this kite dragging along behind him on the ground. (*Her smile fades.*) I don't know—somehow it really got to me.

(*He looks at her, touched more by her reaction than by the story itself.*)

GEORGE: Yeah, I know. Helen has some nice qualities too.

DORIS: Who's Helen?

GEORGE: (*Puzzled.*) My wife of course.

DORIS: You said her name was Phyllis.

(*Caught—a split moment of panic.*)

GEORGE: I know—I lied.

(*She stares at him bewildered. Agitated.*)

Helen—Phyllis—what's the difference? I'm married!

(*He gets up, paces.*)

Look, I was nervous and I didn't want to leave any

clues! I mean I was scared you'd try to look me up or something!

DORIS: Is your real name George?

GEORGE: Of course it is! You don't think I'd lie about my own name do you?

DORIS: (*Baffled.*) You're crazy.

GEORGE: Well, I never claimed to be consistent!

DORIS: (*Gently.*) Crazy.

> (*She holds out the coffee cup to him, their hands touch and they become aware of the contact.*
> *Their eyes meet. He sits beside her.*)

GEORGE: (*Tenderly.*) It's funny, isn't it? Here we are having breakfast in a hotel room, gazing into each other's eyes, and we're both married with six kids between us.

DORIS: You got pictures?

GEORGE: (*Thrown.*) What?

DORIS: Pictures of your kids.

GEORGE: (*Uncomfortably.*) *Well, sure,* but I don't think this is the time or place to—

> (*She moves for her purse.*)

DORIS: I'll show you mine if you show me yours.

> (*Getting snapshots from purse.*)

I keep them in a special folder we got free from Kodak.

> (*She returns to bed, hands him snaps.*)

Where are yours?

GEORGE: (*Still off-balanced.*) Uh—you have to take the whole wallet.

> (*He extracts wallet from his back pocket, hands it to her.*
> *They are now seated side by side on the bed, looking at each other's snapshots.*)

DORIS: Oh, they're cute! Is the one in the glasses and baggy tights the oldest?

GEORGE: (*Looking at snap.*) Yes, that's Michael. Funny-looking kid isn't he?

DORIS: He wants to be Superman?

GEORGE: Peter Pan. Sometimes it worries me. (*Looking at snaps in his hand.*) Why is this one's face all screwed up?

DORIS: Oh, that's Paul—it was taken on a roller coaster. Isn't it natural? He threw up right after that.

GEORGE: Yeah, he's really—something. I guess he looks like Harry, huh?

DORIS: Both of us really. (*Looking at snap.*) What's your little girl's name?

GEORGE: Debbie. That was taken on her second birthday. We were trying to get her to blow out the candles.

DORIS: She has her hand in the cake.

GEORGE: Yeah, neat is not her strong suit.
   (*They look at one another.*)

DORIS: You have great-looking kids, George.

GEORGE: You too.

DORIS: Thanks.
   (*There is a slight pause.*)

GEORGE: Doris?

DORIS: Yeah?

GEORGE: Let's dump the lot of them and run away together!
   (*She looks at him astonished, and the lights fade.*)

Scene 2

THE TIME: *A day in February, 1956.*

THE PLACE: *The same.*

AT RISE: GEORGE, *wearing a charcoal suit and pink shirt of the period, has just hung a home-made sign reading* "HAPPY FIFTH ANNIVERSARY, DARLING" *on the front door. He has put on a few pounds, his hair has just started to thin, and at thirty-two he gives the impression of more substance. It is just an impression. Although his manner is more subdued than five years ago and his insecurities flash through less frequently, it is only because he has learned a degree of control of his mercurial moods. He takes a small birthday cake from a box and places it beside two plates and forks on the coffee table.*

DORIS: (*Offstage.*) Damn!

GEORGE: What's the matter?

DORIS: (*Offstage.*) It's my merry widow.

GEORGE: Your what?

DORIS: (*Offstage.*) Merry widow. It mashes you in and pushes you out in all the right places. It also gives you this pale, wan look because it cuts off all circulation.

GEORGE: Be sure and let me know when you're coming out.

DORIS: (*Offstage.*) Right now.

GEORGE: Wait a minute!

> (*He quickly moves to the piano, sits.*)

Okay—now!

> (*As she enters he sings and plays "If I Knew You Were Coming I'd Have Baked a Cake."*
>
> *She is dressed in a strapless, black cocktail dress that was considered chic in the suburbs in the fifties; is slimmer than before and more carefully put together. The most striking physical change in her is her very blond hair, shaped in a Gina Lollobrigida cut. She has acquired some of the social graces of middle-class suburbia, is more articulate than before, and has developed a wry, deprecating wit that doesn't hide a certain terseness of manner.*
>
> *He stops playing, moves to her and embraces her.*)

GEORGE: Happy anniversary, darling.

> (*He hands her a glass of champagne, they toast, drink, and he indicates the cake.*)

Cut the cake and make a wish.

> (*They move to sit on the sofa and he watches her as she cuts the cake.*)

What did you wish?

DORIS: I only have one wish.

GEORGE: What?

DORIS: That you keep showing up every year.

> (*They kiss.*)

GEORGE: I'm always surprised that you do. I was really surprised the second year.

> (*He crosses to the piano and refills their glasses with champagne. He gives one to* DORIS.)

Of course I had less confidence in my personal magnetism then. You know that was one of the best ideas you ever had?

DORIS: Meeting here every year?

GEORGE: No, refusing to run off with me. Weren't you even tempted?

DORIS: Sure I was. I still am. But I had the feeling that if we had run off together we'd end up with—well—with pretty much the same sort of nice, comfortable marriage we both already had at home.

(*They sit and drink.*)

GEORGE: How are things at home?

DORIS: We moved to the suburbs. Right now everyone's very excited. Next week they're going to connect the sewers. Well it's not exactly the life of Scott and Zelda, but we'll survive.

GEORGE: (*Surprised.*) You started reading!

DORIS: Oh, you don't know the half of it. I joined the Book-of-the-Month Club.

GEORGE: Good for you.

DORIS: (*Kidding herself.*) Listen, sometimes I even take the *alternate* selections.

GEORGE: (*Sincerely.*) I'm really proud of you, honey.

DORIS: Well, it was either that or group mambo lessons. You still live in New Jersey?

GEORGE: No, we moved to Connecticut. We bought an old barn and converted it.

DORIS: What's it like?

GEORGE: Drafty. Helen's got the decorating bug. At my funeral just as they're closing the lid on my coffin I have this mental picture of Helen throwing in two fabric swatches and yelling, "Which one do you like?" That's the bad story about her.

DORIS: What else is new?

GEORGE: We had a baby girl.

DORIS: Oh, George, that's marvelous! You have pictures?

GEORGE: (*Grins.*) I knew you'd ask that.

(*He takes out pictures, hands them to her.*)

DORIS: (*Looking at snaps.*) Oh, she's adorable. It's funny. I still like to look at new babies but I don't want to *own* one anymore. You think that's a sign of maturity?

GEORGE: Could be.

> (*He takes out cigar.*)

Here, I even kept one of these for you to give to Harry. It's from Havana.

DORIS: Harry still thinks I go on retreat. What should I tell him? It came from a Cuban nun?

> (*She takes the cigar, moves to put it in her purse.*)

So how are the rest of the kids? How's Michael?

GEORGE: Oh, crazy as ever. He had this homework assignment, to write what he did on his summer vacation. Trouble is, he chose to write what he actually did.

DORIS: What was that?

GEORGE: Tried to get laid. He wrote in great comic detail about his unfortunate tendency to get an erection on all forms of public transportation. The school almost suspended him.

DORIS: You're crazy about him, aren't you?

GEORGE: He's a very weird kid, Doris.

DORIS: And he really gets to you. Come on—admit it.

GEORGE: Okay, I admit it. He's a nice kid.

DORIS: See? Was that so hard?

> (*He looks at her for a moment, crosses to her, impulsively kisses her.*)

DORIS: What was that for?

GEORGE: Everything. This. One beautiful weekend every year with no cares, no ties and no responsibilities. Thank you, Doris.

> (*He kisses her again. The embrace grows more passionate. They break.*)

DORIS: (*Breathlessly.*) Gee, I just got all dressed up.

> (*They sink onto the bed. He is lying half on top of her when the phone rings.*)

DORIS: Someone has a rotten sense of timing.

GEORGE: Let it ring. It's probably only Pete wanting to know how much he owes the IRS.

DORIS: Chalmers probably told him we're in.

GEORGE: Damn.

> (*Without changing his position he reaches out and takes the phone.*)

Hello.

(*His expression changes—slowly but drastically.*)
Is there anything wrong? Yes, this is Daddy—Funny?
(*He slowly rolls off* DORIS *to a tense position on the edge of the bed.*)
Well, that's probably because Daddy was just—uh—I had a frog in my throat, sweetheart. It came out huh? Which one was it?
(*He sits with the phone in his hand, bent over, almost as if he has a stomachache.*)
Of course, the tooth-fairy will come, sweetheart—Why tonight, of course—It doesn't matter if you can't find it, darling, the tooth-fairy will know—Well, I wish I could be there to find it for you too, honey, but Daddy's working—Oh, in my room.
(*At this point* DORIS *gets off the bed and unobtrusively starts to clean up the room.*)
Yes, it's a very nice room—Well, it has a fireplace and a sofa and a big comfortable b—
(*He can't bring himself to say "bed."*)
—bathroom. Well I'd like you to come with me too, sweetheart. Maybe next year—I'm afraid not, sweetheart. You see Daddy has to finish up his—business—well, I'll try—Yes, I love you too, honey—Yes, very much.
(*He hangs up and puts his head in his hands.*

   DORIS *crosses to him and wordlessly puts a comforting hand on his shoulder.*)
Oh, God, I feel so *guilty!*
(*He rises and moves away.*)

DORIS: Debbie?

GEORGE: Her tooth came out. She can't find it and she's worried the tooth-fairy won't know! Oh, God, that thin, reedy little voice. Do you know what that *does* to me!

DORIS: Sure, that calm exterior doesn't fool me for a minute.

GEORGE: You think this is *funny?*

DORIS: Honey, I understand how you feel but I really don't think it's going to help going on and on about it.

GEORGE: Doris, my little girl said, "I love you, Daddy,"

and I answered her with a voice still *hoarse with passion*!

DORIS: I think I've got the picture, George.

GEORGE: Don't you ever feel guilty?

DORIS: Sometimes.

GEORGE: You've never said anything.

DORIS: I just deal with it in a different way.

GEORGE: How?

DORIS: Privately.

(*Agitated,* GEORGE *starts pacing around the room.*)

GEORGE: I don't know, maybe men are more—sensitive than women.

DORIS: Have a drink, George.

GEORGE: Perhaps women are more pragmatic than men.

DORIS: What's that mean?

GEORGE: They adjust to rottenness quicker. I mean, they're more inclined to live for the moment. (*Offhandedly.*) Anyway, you have the church.

DORIS: The church?

GEORGE: Well, you're Catholic, aren't you? You can get rid of all your guilt at one sitting. I have to *live* with mine.

DORIS: I think *I'll* have a drink.

(*She moves to pour herself a drink.*)

GEORGE: Boy, something like that really brings you up short!

(*Holding out his trembling hands.*)

I mean *look* at me! I tell you, Doris—when she started talking about the tooth-fairy—well, it affected me in a very profound manner. (*A beat.*) On top of that I have indigestion you can't *believe*. It hit me that hard, you know?

DORIS: George, I have three children too.

GEORGE: Sure, sure—I know. I don't mean that you don't *understand*. It's just that we're different people and your guilt is less—acute.

DORIS: Honey, what do you want me to do? Have a guilt contest? Is that going to solve anything?

GEORGE: What do you want me to do, Doris?

DORIS: I think it might be a terrific idea if you stopped talking about it. It's only making you feel worse.

GEORGE: I can't feel worse. That pure little voice saying—
(*He stops, tries to shake it off with a jerk of his head.*)
No, you're right. Forget it. (*Shakes his head again.*)
Forget it. Talk about something else. Tell me about
Harry. Tell me the good story about Harry.

    (*During the following,* GEORGE *tries to concentrate
but is obviously distracted and nervous.*)

DORIS: Okay. He went bankrupt.

    (*This momentarily jolts him out of his problem.*)

GEORGE: How can anyone go bankrupt selling TV sets?

DORIS: Harry has this one weakness as a salesman. It's a
compulsion to talk people out of things they can't afford.
He lacks the killer instinct. (*Reflectively.*) It's one of the
things I like best about him. Anyway, he went into real
estate.

    (GEORGE *is staring out of the window.*)

Your turn.

GEORGE: What?

DORIS: Tell me your story about Helen.

GEORGE: I already did.

DORIS: You just told me the bad one. Why do you always
tell that one first?

GEORGE: It's the one I look forward to telling the most.

DORIS: Tell me the nice story about her.

GEORGE: Oh.

    (*Moving about the room.*)

Well—Chris—that's our middle one—ran into a lawn
sprinkler and gashed his knee really badly. Helen drove
both of us to the hospital.

DORIS: Both of you?

GEORGE: I fainted.

DORIS: Oh.

GEORGE: The nice part was she never told anybody.

DORIS: You faint often?

GEORGE: Only in emergencies.

DORIS: Is it the sight of blood that—

GEORGE: Please, Doris! My stomach's squeamish enough
already. Maybe I will have that drink.

    (*He moves to liquor, speaks overcasually.*)

Oh, listen, something just occurred to me. Instead of my

leaving at the usual time tomorrow night would you
mind if I left a little earlier?

DORIS: (*Puzzled.*) When did you have in mind?

GEORGE: Well, there's a plane in half an hour.

(*She stares at him astounded.*)

DORIS: You want to leave *twenty-three hours early?*

(*He moves to suitcase, starts to pack and continues
through the following as she watches with unbeliving
eyes.*)

GEORGE: Look, I know how you feel—I really do—and I
wouldn't even *suggest* it if you weren't a mother yourself
and didn't understand the situation. I mean I wouldn't
even *think* of it if this crisis hadn't come up. Oh, it's not
just the tooth-fairy—she could have *swallowed* the tooth.
I mean it could be lodged God knows where! Now I
know this leaves you a bit—uh—at loose ends but
there's no reason for you to leave too. The room's all
paid up. Anyway, I'm probably doing you a favor. If I
did stay I wouldn't be very good company. Uh—have
you seen my hairbrush?

(*He looks around, sees it is beside her.*)

Doris, would you hand me my hairbrush?

(*Without a word she picks it up and throws it at him
with much more force than necessary. It sails past his
head and crashes against the wall.*

There is a pause.)

I think I can explain that. You feel somewhat rejected
and, believe me, I can understand that but I want you to
know my leaving has nothing to do with *you and me!*

(*She just stares at him.*)

Doris, this is an *emergency!* I have a *sick child* at home!

DORIS: (*Exploding.*) Oh, will you *stop* it! It's got nothing
to do with the goddamn tooth-fairy! You're consumed
with guilt and the only way you can deal with it is by
getting as far away from me as possible!

GEORGE: Okay, I feel guilty. Is that so strange? (*Intensely.*)
Doris, don't you understand? We're *cheating!* Once a
year we lie to our families and sneak off to a hotel in
California and commit adultery! (*Holding up his hand.*)

Not that I want to stop doing it! But yes, I feel guilt. I admit it.

DORIS: (*Incredulous.*) You *admit* it! You take out ads! You probably stop strangers in the street! It's a wonder you haven't hired a *skywriter*! I'm amazed you haven't had your shorts monogrammed with a scarlet "A" as a conversation starter! You think that by *talking* about it, by wringing your hands and beating your breast it will somehow excuse what you're doing? So you wander around like—like an open nerve saying, "I'm cheating but look how *guilty* I feel so I must really be a nice guy!" And to top it all, you have the incredible arrogance to think you're the only one in the world with a conscience! Well, that doesn't make you a nice guy. You know what it makes you? A *horse's ass*!

(*There is a pause.*)

GEORGE: (*Finally.*) You know something! I liked you better *before* you started reading.

DORIS: That's not why you're leaving, George.

GEORGE: Doris, it's not the end of the world. I'm not leaving you permanently.

(*Turning to finish packing.*)

We'll see each other again next year.

(*He shuts suitcase, snaps locks.*)

DORIS: (*Quietly—with finality.*) There's not going to be a next year, George.

(*He turns to face her.*)

GEORGE: You don't mean that.

(*He suspects by her face that she does.*)

I can't believe that! Just because I have to leave early one year you're willing to throw away a lifetime of weekends? How can you be so—so *casual*?

DORIS: I don't see any point in going on.

(*He starts to shake his head.*)

GEORGE: Oh no. Don't do that to me, Doris.

(*He takes suitcase, moves to deposit it by the door during following.*)

Don't try to manipulate me. I get enough of that at home.

(*Getting raincoat, putting it on.*)

That's not what our relationship is about.

DORIS: (*Soberly.*) What is it about, George?

GEORGE: You don't *know*?

DORIS: Yes. But it seems to be completely different from how you think about us. That's why I think we should stop seeing each other.

GEORGE: (*Finally.*) My God, you really *are* serious.

DORIS: George, what's the point of going on if we're going to come to each other burdened down with guilt and remorse? What joy is there in that?

GEORGE: (*Frustrated—indicating door.*) Doris, I have a commitment there.

DORIS: (*Quietly.*) And you don't have a commitment here?

GEORGE: (*Bewildered.*) Here? I thought our only commitment was to show up every year.

DORIS: Nice and tidy, huh? Just two friendly sexual partners who meet once a year, touch and let go.

GEORGE: Okay—so maybe I was kidding myself. I'm human.

DORIS: Well, so am I.

GEORGE: (*Sincerely.*) But you're different. Stronger. you always seem able to—cope.

(*She moves away, looks into the fire. She speaks slowly, deliberately unemotional.*)

DORIS: George, during the past year I picked up the phone and started to call you five times. I couldn't seem to stop thinking about you. You kept slopping over into my real life and it scared hell out of me. More to the point I felt *guilty.* So I decided to stop seeing you.

(*He is shaken.*

She turns to face him.)

At first I wasn't going to show up at all but then I thought I at least owed you an explanation. So I came.

(*She turns away.*)

When you walked in the door I knew I couldn't do it. That despite the price it was all worth it.

(*A pause.*)

GEORGE: (*Finally—anguished.*) Oh God, I feel so *guilty!!*

DORIS: (*Quietly—flatly.*) I think you'd better leave, George.

(*There is a pause.*)

GEORGE: I love you, Doris. (*A beat.*) I'm an idiot. I suspect I'm deeply neurotic, and I'm no bargain—but I do love you.

(*He moves to her, gently turns her to face him.*)

Will you let me stay?

(*They embrace, break, and gaze at one another.*)

Doris, what are we going to do?

(*She reaches out and takes his hand.*)

DORIS: Touch and hold on very tight. Until tomorrow.

(*They embrace. The lights slowly fade and the curtain falls.*)

Scene 3

THE TIME: *A day in February, 1961.*

THE PLACE: *The same.*

AT RISE: GEORGE, *still wearing his raincoat and hat, is talking on the phone. His unpacked suitcase is in the middle of the floor and it is apparent that he has just arrived. As he talks he takes off his raincoat and throws it on the bed.*

GEORGE: (*Irritably—into phone.*) No of course I haven't left Helen. I'm on a business trip. I come out here every year—I am not running away from the problem! (*Becoming more angry.*) Of course I know it's serious. I still don't think it's any reason to phone me long distance and—Look, frankly, I don't think this is any of your business and to be totally honest I resent—(*He gives an exasperated sigh.*) Yes, I saw a doctor—He said it's no big deal, that every man has this problem at one time or another and—Look, if we *have* to discuss this you may as well learn to pronounce it correctly. It's impotence, not impotence— (*Incredulous.*) What do you mean, did I catch it in time? It's a slight reflex problem not a terminal illness! (*Frustrated.*) It's not something you have to "nip in the bud." Look, how did you find out about this anyway?—Dropped a few hints?

What *sort* of hints?—You asked her and she looked funny. Terrific. (*Exasperated again.*) Yes, of course I'm trying to do something about it—I don't have to tell you that—Look, will you let me deal with this in my own way I'm going to be okay—Soon—I just *know*, that's all. (*Flaring.*) I just *feel* it, okay?—I'm seeing someone out here who's an expert. (*His patience exhausted.*) Look, I don't think we should be even *discussing* this!—I'm sorry, I'm going to hang up now. (*Firmly.*) Goodbye, Mother!

(*He slams the receiver down, picks up his raincoat, looks at bed, throws raincoat over chair, turns blankets and sheets down, tosses hat into chair revealing that his hairline has receded noticeably. He then crosses to his suitcase, puts it on rack, opens it, extracts pajamas and robe and exits to bathroom. There is a slight pause before the front door opens and* DORIS *enters. She is obviously very, very pregnant. Her hair is back to her normal color and her face looks softer than before. Perspiring slightly, she puts her case down.*)

DORIS: (*Calling.*) George!

GEORGE: (*Offstage—from bathroom.*) Be right out, darling!

(DORIS, *holding her back, moves to look out of the window. When* GEORGE, *now dressed in robe and pajamas, enters from the bathroom her back is towards him. He stops, smiles at her tenderly.*)

How are you, lover?

(*She turns to face him, revealing her eight months pregnant stomach. His smile fades and his expression becomes frozen. He just stares, unable to speak.*)

DORIS: (*Finally.*) I know. I've heard of middle-aged spread but this is ridiculous.

GEORGE: (*In a strangled voice.*) My God, what have you done to yourself?

DORIS: Well, I can't take all the credit. It was a mutual effort.

(*He continues to stare at her.*)

Honey, when you haven't seen an old friend for a year isn't it customary to kiss them hello?

GEORGE: (*Still stunned.*) What? Oh, sure.

(*He moves to her, gives her a rather perfunctory kiss.*)

DORIS: Are you okay? You look funny.

GEORGE: (*Flaring—moving away.*) Funny? I'm hysterical!

DORIS: What's that mean?

(*He tries to regain control.*)

GEORGE: Well—naturally, I'm—surprised, okay?

DORIS: *You're* surprised. I insisted on visiting the dead rabbit's grave! (*Puzzled.*) Why are you wearing your pajamas and robe in the afternoon?

GEORGE: (*Irritably.*) I'm rehearsing for a Noël Coward play! Why the hell do you think?

DORIS: Oh, I'm sorry, darling. I'm afraid all that dirty stuff is out. That is, unless you have a ladder handy.

GEORGE: Doris, do you mind? I'm in no mood for bad taste jokes!

DORIS: Oh, come on, honey—where's your sense of humor? Look at it this way—maybe it's nature's way of telling us to slow down.

(*He watches her as she moves to a chair and awkwardly negotiates herself into the seat. She kicks off her shoes, massages her feet, looks up to find him staring at her with a baleful expression.*)

George, is there something on your mind?

(*He moves away to the window.*)

GEORGE: Not anymore.

DORIS: Then why are you so jumpy?

(*He wheels to face her.*)

GEORGE: You must be eight months pregnant!

DORIS: Why are you so shocked? I am married.

GEORGE: You think that excuses it?

DORIS: What exactly are you trying to say?

GEORGE: I just consider it damned—irresponsible!

DORIS: (*Amused.*) Well, I have to admit, it wasn't planned!

GEORGE: (*Frustrated.*) I mean coming here in—in that condition!

DORIS: Well, I'm sorry you're disappointed, darling, but we'll just have to find some other way to—communicate.

GEORGE: Great! You have any ideas?

DORIS: We could talk.

GEORGE: Talk? Talk I can get at home!

DORIS: (*Grinning.*) Well, sex *I* can get at home. And as you can see, that's not just talk.

GEORGE: What the hell is that supposed to mean?

DORIS: (*Shrugs.*) Well, I've never had any cause to complain about Harry in that department.

GEORGE: Oh really? And what does that make me? Chopped liver?

(*She has been watching him with a curious expression.*)

DORIS: George, what is the *matter* with you?

GEORGE: Matter? I'm the only man in America who just kept an illicit assignation with a woman who—who looks like a—frigate in full sail! And you ask what's the matter?

DORIS: (*Calmly.*) No, there's something else. You're not yourself.

GEORGE: Let me be the judge of who I am, okay?

DORIS: Why are you so *angry*?

GEORGE: What was that crack about Harry? Is that supposed to reflect on me? You don't think I have normal desires and sex drives?

DORIS: Of course not. You're very normal. I just meant I look forward to seeing you for a lot of reasons *beside* sex. Do you think we would have lasted this long if that's all we had in common?

GEORGE: (*Grudgingly.*) No, I guess not.

DORIS: We're friends as well as lovers, aren't we?

GEORGE: Yes. (*He sighs.*) I'm sorry, Doris. I've—I've had a lot on my mind lately and—well, seeing you like that took the wind out of my sails. You want a drink?

DORIS: No, you go ahead. Alcohol makes me go a funny shade of pink.

(*She watches him as he moves to extract a bottle from his suitcase.*)

You want to tell me about it?

GEORGE: No, it's not something I can really *talk* about.

(*He moves to get glass, pours drink, shrugs.*)

It's just I was looking forward to an—intimate weekend.

DORIS: You think we can only be intimate through sex?

GEORGE: I think it sure helps.

DORIS: Oh, maybe at the beginning.

GEORGE: The beginning?

DORIS: Well, every year we meet it's a bit strange and awkward at first but we usually solve that in between the sheets with a lot of heavy breathing.

GEORGE: Doris, if we're not going to do it, would you mind not talking about it?

DORIS: I just meant maybe we need something else to— break the ice.

GEORGE: (*Pouring himself another drink.*) I'm willing to try anything.

DORIS: How about this? Supposing I tell you something about myself I've never told anyone before in my life?

GEORGE: I think I've had enough surprises for one day.

DORIS: You'll like this one.

(*She gets out of the chair with some difficulty and moves to look out of window.*

He watches and waits.)

I've been having these sex dreams about you.

GEORGE: When?

DORIS: Just lately. Almost every night.

GEORGE: What sort of dreams?

(*She turns to face him.*)

DORIS: That's what's so strange. They're always the same. We're making love under water. In caves, grottos, swimming pools—but always under water. Isn't that weird? (*She shrugs.*) Probably something to do with me being pregnant.

GEORGE: Under water, huh?

(*She nods.*)

DORIS: Now you tell me some deep, dark secret about yourself.

GEORGE: I can't swim.

DORIS: (*Puzzled.*) Literally?

GEORGE: (*Irritably.*) Of course literally! When I tell you I can't swim I simply mean I can't swim!

DORIS: How come?

GEORGE: I just never learned when I was a kid. But I never told anybody—well, Helen found out when she pushed me off a dock and I almost drowned—but my kids don't even know. When we go to the beach I pretend I'm having trouble with my trick knee.

DORIS: You have a trick knee?

GEORGE: No. They don't know that either.

(*She moves to him, puts her hand on his cheek.*)

DORIS: You see, it worked.

(*He looks puzzled.*)

We're talking just like people who have been to bed and everything.

(*She moves to another chair, carefully lowers herself into it. The effort tires her.*)

Boy, I'll tell you—that Ethel Kennedy must really like kids.

GEORGE: Hey, I'm sorry about—earlier. I'm glad to see you anyway.

DORIS: You want to tell me what it was all about?

(*He looks at her for a moment.*)

GEORGE: Okay, I may as well get it out in the open. I mean it's nothing to be ashamed about.

(*He takes a turn around the room.*)

It's very simple really. It's my—sex life. Lately, Helen hasn't been able to satisfy me.

DORIS: (*Surprised.*) She's lost her interest in sex?

GEORGE: Oh, she tries—God knows. But I can tell she's just going through the motions.

DORIS: Do you have any idea why this is?

GEORGE: Well, Helen's always had a lot of hang-ups about sex. For one thing she's always thought of it as just a healthy, normal, pleasant function. Don't you think that's a bit twisted?

DORIS: Only if you're Catholic.

GEORGE: (*Earnestly.*) You're joking but there's a lot to be said for guilt. I mean if you don't feel guilty or ashamed about it I think you're missing half the fun. To Helen—

sex has always been good, clean—*entertainment*. No wonder she grew tired of it.

(*He finds* DORIS's *gaze somewhat disconcerting.*)

Look, I don't know, for some reason my sex drive has increased while hers has decreased.

DORIS: That's odd. Usually, it's the other way around.

GEORGE: (*Defensively.*) Are you accusing me of lying?

DORIS: Of course not. Why are you so edgy?

GEORGE: Because—well, I don't think it's fair to talk about this behind her back when she's not here to defend herself.

(*She watches him as he moves to pour another drink.*)

DORIS: Would you like to get to the more formal part of your presentation?

GEORGE: What? Oh—okay. I'll start with the nice story about her.

DORIS: You've never done that before. You must be mellowing.

GEORGE: Doris, do you mind? Where was I? Oh—yeah. We were checking into a hotel in London and there was a man in a morning coat and striped trousers standing at the front entrance. Helen handed him her suitcases and sailed on into the lobby. The man followed her in with her suitcases and very politely pointed out that not only didn't he work at the hotel but that he was the Danish Ambassador. Without batting an eye she said, "Well, that's marvelous. Maybe you can tell us the good places to eat in Copenhagen." And he did. The point is it doesn't bother her when she makes a total ass of herself. I really admire that.

DORIS: And what don't you admire?

GEORGE: It's that damned sense of humor of hers!

DORIS: Oh, those are the stories I like the best.

(*He looks at her for a moment, then launches headlong into the story.*)

GEORGE: We'd come home from a party and we'd had a few drinks and we went to bed and we started to make love. Well, nothing happened—for me—I couldn't—well, you get the picture. It was no big deal—and we laughed about it. Then about half an hour later, just as I was dropping off to sleep she said, "It's funny when I married a CPA, I always thought it would be his eyes that would go first."

DORIS: (*Finally.*) She was just trying to make you feel better, George.

GEORGE: Well, it didn't. Some things aren't funny.

(DORIS *doesn't say anything.*)

I suppose what I'm trying to say is that the thing that bugs me most about Helen is that she broke my pecker!

DORIS: (*Gently.*) You're impotent?

GEORGE: Slightly. (*He gives a shrug.*) Okay, now five people know. Me, you, Helen and her mother.

DORIS: Who's the fifth?

GEORGE: Chet Huntley. I'm sure her mother has given him the bulletin for the six o'clock news.

DORIS: I thought that might be it.

GEORGE: You mean you can tell just by *looking* at me?

DORIS: (*Sympathetically.*) When did it happen, honey?

GEORGE: Happen? Doris, we're not talking about a freeway accident! I mean you don't wake up one morning and say, "Oh shoot, the old family jewels have gone on the blink." It's a—a gradual thing.

DORIS: And you really blame Helen for this?

GEORGE: Of course not. I—I wanted to tell you but I just couldn't think of a graceful way of working it into the conversation. (*He gives a short, hard laugh.*) To tell you the truth I was just waiting for you to say "What's new?" And I was going to say "Nothing, but I can tell you what's old."

DORIS: How's Helen reacting?

GEORGE: Oh, we haven't talked about it much but I get the feeling she regards it as a lapse in one's social responsibility. You know, rather like letting your partner down in tennis by not holding your serve. (*He gives a little laugh.*) Look, it's not great tragedy. As they say in Brooklyn, "Just wait 'til next year."

(*She is not smiling.*)

Seriously, I'll be okay. Send no flowers. The patient's not dead yet—just resting.

(*She extends her hand.*)
Doris, that statement hardly calls for congratulations.

DORIS: I need help to get out of this chair.

(*He pulls her out of the chair.*
  Takes his face between her hands. Simply.)
I'm really sorry.

(*They look tenderly at one another for a moment
before he suddenly jerks away.*)

GEORGE: What the hell was that?

DORIS: The baby kicking.

GEORGE: (*Moving away.*) Well, everyone else has taken a
shot at me. Why not him?

DORIS: (*Puzzled.*) It's strange. He hasn't been kicking lately. Maybe he resents the bumpy ride up here.

(*Sees that* GEORGE *is not really listening.*)
Is there anything I can say that will help?

GEORGE: What? Honey, you can say anything you want except "It's all in your head." I mean I'm no doctor but
I have a great sense of direction.

(*As she starts to talk.*)
Look, to tell you the truth, I'm not too crazy about this
whole discussion. Let's forget it, huh?

DORIS: Okay. What do you want to talk about?

GEORGE: Anything but sex. How'd you feel about being
pregnant?

DORIS: Catatonic, incredulous, angry, pragmatic, and finally maternal. Pretty much in that order.

GEORGE: Your vocabulary's improving.

DORIS: Ah, you didn't know. You're talking to a high
school graduate.

GEORGE: (*Puzzled.*) How come?

DORIS: Well, I was confined to bed for the first three
months of my pregnancy, so rather than it being a total
loss I took a correspondence course.

GEORGE: (*Admiringly.*) You're really something, you
know that?

DORIS: There's kind of an ironic twist to all this.

GEORGE: Oh?

DORIS: Well, I didn't graduate the first time because I got

pregnant. And now I did graduate because— (*She grins, taps her stomach.*) Appeals to my sense of order.

GEORGE: (*Teasing.*) I didn't know you had a sense of order.

DORIS: That's unfair. I'm much better at housework lately. Now I'm only two years behind in my ironing. Must be the nesting instinct. Anyway, the day my diploma came in the mail Harry brought me a corsage and took me out dancing. Well, we didn't really dance—we lumbered. Afterwards we went to a malt shop and had a fudge sundae. That's the nice story about him.

GEORGE: He still selling real estate?

DORIS: Insurance. He likes it. Gives him an excuse to look up all his old Army buddies.

(*He regards her as she stands with her stomach thrust out and both hands pressed on either side of her back.*)

GEORGE: Doris, are you comfortable in that position?

DORIS: Honey, when you're in my condition you're not comfortable in any position.

(*He takes her arm, leads her to a chair.*)

GEORGE: Come on, sit over here.

(*He helps lower her into the chair. As he does a strange expression comes to his face.*)

DORIS: Thanks. How are the kids?

GEORGE: (*Vaguely.*) What? Oh, fine. Michael got a job with Associated Press.

DORIS: Oh, darling, that's marvelous. I'm so proud of him. (*She notices that he is staring at her with an odd, fixed expression.*) George, why are you looking at me like that?

GEORGE: (*Too quickly.*) No reason. It—it's nothing.

DORIS: Does my stomach offend you?

GEORGE: No, it's not that. Tell me your other story about Harry.

DORIS: I had trouble telling him I was pregnant. When I finally did he looked at me for a moment and then said "Is there a revolver in the house?" George, you're doing it again! What *is* it?

GEORGE: (*Exploding.*) It's obscene!

DORIS: (*Bewildered.*) What is?

GEORGE: When I touched you I started to get excited!!!!
(*He paces around.*)
What kind of pervert am I? (*He turns to look at her.*)
I'm staring at a two hundred pound woman and I'm getting hot! Just the *sight* of you is making me excited.
(*She looks at him for a moment.*)

DORIS: (*Finally.*) Let me tell you something. That's the nicest thing anyone's said to me in months.

GEORGE: (*Very agitated.*) It's not funny!

DORIS: Aren't you pleased?

GEORGE: Pleased? It reminds me of my seventh birthday!

DORIS: What?

GEORGE: My uncle gave me fifty cents. I ran two miles and when I got there the candy store was closed!

DORIS: (*Puzzled.*) But doesn't this solve your—problem?

GEORGE: (*Frustrated.*) The idea doesn't solve anything! It's the execution that counts!

DORIS: (*Pleased.*) I really got to you, huh?

GEORGE: (*Tightly.*) Excuse me.
(*Without another word, he marches to the piano, sits and aggressively launches into a Rachmaninoff concerto. Surprisingly, he plays extremely well. Not quite concert hall material but close enough to fool a lot of people. DORIS watches, absolutely astounded. She finally recovers enough to get out of her chair and move to the piano where she watches him with an incredulous expression.*)

DORIS: (*Finally.*) That's incredible! Are you as good as I think you are?
(*He continues to play until indicated.*)

GEORGE: How good do you think I am?

DORIS: Sensational.

GEORGE: I'm not as good as you think I am.

DORIS: You sound marvelous to me.

GEORGE: It's the story of my life, Doris. All the form and none of the ability.

DORIS: (*Puzzled.*) But for ten years that piano has been sitting there and you haven't touched it. Why tonight?

GEORGE: It beats a cold shower.

DORIS: You play to release sexual tension?

GEORGE: Any kind of tension. Any frustration in my life and I head right for the piano. (*A wry shrug.*) You don't even get this good without a lot of practice.

(DORIS *shakes her head in wonder.*)

DORIS: George, you're full of surprises.

GEORGE: Yeah, I know—you live with a man for ten days but you never really know him.

DORIS: Why didn't you tell me you played before?

GEORGE: I had other ways of entertaining you.

DORIS: Well, I always knew you had wonderful hands.

(*He stops playing, looks at her.*)

GEORGE: Look, lady, I only work here. I'm not allowed to date the customers.

(*She smiles, moves away. He starts playing again.*)

DORIS: George? You still feel—frustrated?

GEORGE: I have the feeling it's going to take all six Brandenburg concertos.

DORIS: You'll be exhausted.

GEORGE: That's the idea.

DORIS: But—

GEORGE: (*Irritably.*) Doris, I've been waiting three months for—for the balloon to go up! Well, it's up and it's not going to come down until something—

DORIS: Honey, come here.

(*He stops playing, looks at her.*)

Come on.

(*He gets up from the piano and moves to her. She starts to untie his robe.*)

GEORGE: Doris—

DORIS: It's okay. It'll be okay.

GEORGE: But you can't—

DORIS: I know that.

GEORGE: Then how—

DORIS: Don't worry, darling. We'll work something out.

(*She kisses him very tenderly. Gradually he becomes more involved in the kiss until they are in a passionate embrace. Suddenly she backs away, clutching her stomach, her face a mixture of surprise and alarm. Then she grimaces with pain.*)

GEORGE: (*Alarmed.*) What is it?

   (*She is too busy fighting off the pain to answer.*)
   Doris?

   (*The pain has knocked the breath out of her and she gasps to catch her breath.*)
   Doris, for God's sake, what is it?

   (*She looks at him unbelivingly, not saying anything.*)
   Doris, what *the hell is the matter?*

DORIS: (*Finally.*) If—if memory serves me correctly—I just had a labor pain.

   (*He stands stock still, trying to absorb this.*)

GEORGE: You—you can't have! (*Clutching at straws.*) Maybe it's indigestion.

DORIS: No, there's a difference.

GEORGE: How can you be *sure?*

DORIS: I've had both.

GEORGE: But you can't be in labor! When is the baby due!

DORIS: Not for another month.

   (*He stares at her for a moment and then puts his hands to his head.*)

GEORGE: My God, what have I *done?!*

DORIS: What have *you* done?

GEORGE: I brought it on. My—my selfishness.

DORIS: George, don't be ridiculous. You had nothing to do with it.

GEORGE: Don't treat me like a child, Doris!

DORIS: Will you stop getting so excited?

GEORGE: Excited? I thought I had troubles before. Can you imagine what *this* is going to do to my sex life?

DORIS: George, will you— (*She stops.*) I think I'd better—sit down.

   (*He quickly moves to her, leads her to a chair.*)

GEORGE: (*Anguished.*) Jesus, what kind of a man am I? What kind of man would do a thing like that?

DORIS: George, may I say something?

GEORGE: (*Very agitated—moving around.*) Look, I appreciate what you're trying to do, honey, but nothing you can say will make me feel any better.

DORIS: I'm not trying to make you feel any better.

   (*This stops him in his tracks.*)

GEORGE: What are you trying to say?

DORIS: We're in a lot of trouble. I'm going to have a baby.

GEORGE: I know that.

DORIS: I mean now. I have a history of short labor and—
(*She stops as another labor pain starts.*)

GEORGE: Oh, Jesus!
(*He quickly moves to her, kneels in front of her and she grabs his hand in a viselike grip as she fights off the pain.*)
Oh, Jesus!
(*The pain starts to subside.*)
How—how do you feel?

DORIS: Like—like I'm going to have a baby.

GEORGE: Maybe it's a false alarm. It has to be a false alarm!

DORIS: Honey, try and get a hold of yourself. Get on the phone and find out where the nearest hospital is.

GEORGE: Hospital? You want to go to a hospital?

DORIS: George, like it or not, I'm going to have a baby.

GEORGE: But we're not married!
(*She stares at him.*)
I mean it's going to look—odd!
(*She gets up.*)

DORIS: Get on the phone, George.
(*Moving towards the bathroom.*)
And make sure you get the directions.

GEORGE: Where are you going?

DORIS: The bathroom.

GEORGE: Why?

DORIS: I don't have time to answer questions!
(*She exits to bathroom.*
He quickly moves to telephone, frantically jiggles receiver bar.)

GEORGE: (*Into phone.*) Hello, Mr. Chalmers? George. Can you tell me where the nearest hospital is?—Well, it's my—my wife. Something—unexpected came up. She got pregnant and now she's going to have the baby—How far is that? (*With alarm.*) Oh, my God!—Get—get them on the phone for me, will you? (*He covers receiver with hand, calls out.*) Are you okay, Doris? (*There is no answer. Panicking.*) Doris! Doris, answer me!

DORIS: (*Offstage from bathroom—obviously in pain.*) In—a minute. I'm—busy.

GEORGE: Oh, Jesus. (*Into phone.*) Hello—Hello, I'm staying at the Sea Shadows Inn just outside Mendocino and—I—I heard this—this groaning from—the next room. Well, I knocked on the door and found this—this lady—who I'd never met before, in labor and—Do *you* have to know that?—I still don't see why—Okay, George Peterson!—Well, I didn't time it exactly but—About three or four minutes I think—Hold on. (*Calling out.*) Doris, who's your doctor?

DORIS: (*Offstage—with an effo*rt.) Doctor Joseph——Harrington. Oakland. 555–78–78.

GEORGE: (*Into phone.*) Doctor Joseph Harrington in Oakland. His number is 555–7878—Yes, I have a car and I'm certainly willing to help out if—I'll get her there—Right, right—Uh, could you answer one question?—Would—uh—erotic contact during pregnancy be the cause of premature—No reason, I just wondered and—Right, I'll do that!

(*He hangs up, calls out.*)

They're phoning your doctor. He'll meet us there at the hospital.

(DORIS *appears in the doorway of the bathroom, a strange look on her face. She doesn't say anything.*)

Doris, did you hear me?

DORIS: I don't think we're going to make it to the hospital.

(*The blood drains from his face.*)

GEORGE: What?

DORIS: My water just burst.

GEORGE: Oh, dear God.

DORIS: We're going to have to find a doctor in the area.

GEORGE: But supposing we *can't!*

DORIS: You look terrible. You're not going to faint, are you?

GEORGE: (*In total shock.*) Doris, I'm not a cabdriver! I don't know how to deliver babies!

DORIS: George, this is no time to start acting like Butterfly McQueen.
> (*She heads toward the bed.*)

Get the nearest doctor on the phone.
> (*He races back to phone as she half sits and half lies on the bed.*)

GEORGE: (*Into phone.*) Who's the nearest doctor?—Get him on the phone! Fast! This is an emergency!
> (DORIS *has gone into another labor spasm.*
>> GEORGE, *phone in hand, moves to her, puts his arm around her, grabs her hand.*)

It's okay—hold on. Hold on, Doris. Hold on. There—there—hold on. You okay?

DORIS: (*Weakly.*) This'll——teach you to fool around—with a married woman. (*Blurting.*) George. I'm scared!

GEORGE: You're going to be okay. Everything—(*Into phone.*) Yes? (*Standing up—yelling.*) His answering service! You don't understand. She's in the last stages of labor!—Well, get in your car and drive down to the goddamn course! Just *get* him!
> (*He hangs up.*)

It's okay—he's on the golf course but it's just down the road. Chalmers is getting him.
> (DORIS *is staring at him with a look of total panic.*)

Doris, what is it?

DORIS: I—I—can feel the baby!!
> (*He stares at her, absorbs the situation, and we see a definite transformation take place. He rolls up the sleeves of his robe.*)

GEORGE: (*Calmly.*) All right, lean back and try to relax. I'll be right back.
> (*He exits quickly to the bathroom.*)

DORIS: (*Screaming.*) George, don't leave me!

GEORGE: (*Offstage.*) Hold on, baby.

DORIS: George!
> (*He reappears with a pile of towels.*)

GEORGE: It's okay, I'm here. It'll be all right.

DORIS: What—are those—for?

GEORGE: Honey, we're going to have a baby.

DORIS: We?

GEORGE: Right. But I'm going to need your help.

(She goes into a spasm of labor and he sits on the bed beside her.)

Okay—bear down—bear down. Come on, baby.

(The lights start to fade.)

You're going to be fine. Just fine. You think I play the piano well? Wait until you get a load of how I deliver babies.

(The lights have faded and the stage is dark.)

ACT II

Scene 1

THE TIME: *A day in February, 1965.*
THE PLACE: *The same.*
AT RISE: GEORGE *is unpacking his suitcase. Thinner than the last time we saw him, he is wearing an expensive conservative suit, his hair is gray and is worn unfashionably short. His manner is more subdued than before and he looks and acts older than his years. The door opens and* DORIS *bursts into the room. She is wearing a brightly colored granny gown, beads, sandals, and her hair is long and flowing. She is carrying a decal-decorated duffel bag.*

DORIS: Hey, baby! What do ya say?
(*She throws her duffel bag into a chair and herself into the arms of a very surprised* GEORGE. *She kisses him passionately, backs off and looks at him.*)
So—you wanta fuck?
(*He takes an astonished moment to absorb this.*)
GEORGE: (*Finally.*) What?
DORIS: (*Grins.*) You didn't understand the question?
GEORGE: Of course I did. I just think it's a damned odd way to start a conversation.
DORIS: Yeah? I've always found it to be a great little icebreaker. Besides, I thought you might be feeling horny after your flight.

(GEORGE *continues to eye* DORIS *with a mild conster- nation.*)

GEORGE: I didn't fly, I drove.

DORIS: From Connecticut?

GEORGE: From Los Angeles. We moved to Beverly Hills about ten months ago.

(He manages to yank his eyes away from [to him] DORIS*'s bizarre appearance and resumes hanging up his clothes.)*

DORIS: How come?

GEORGE: Oh, a number of reasons. *(Shrugs.)* I got fed up standing knee-deep in snow trying to scrape the ice off my windshield with a credit card. Besides, there are a lot of people out here with a lot of money who don't know what to do with it.

DORIS: And you tell them?

GEORGE: I'm what they call a Business Manager.

DORIS: Things going okay?

GEORGE: I can't complain. Why?

DORIS: Because you look shitty.

(He turns to look at her.)

Are you all right, honey?

GEORGE: I'm fine.

DORIS: You sure there's not something bothering you?

GEORGE: Yes—you. Do you always go around dressed like a bad finger painting?

DORIS: *(Grinning.)* No. I have to admit that today I am a little—well—visually overstated.

GEORGE: Why?

DORIS: I guess I wanted to make sure you knew you were dealing with the "new me." Sort of "show and tell."

GEORGE: You look like a refugee from Sunset Strip.

DORIS: Berkeley. I went back to school.

GEORGE: *(Bewildered.)* What for?

DORIS: *(Grins.)* You mean what do I want to be when I grow up?

GEORGE: Well, you have to admit it's a bit strange becom- ing a schoolgirl at your age.

DORIS: Are you kidding? Listen, it's not easy being the only one in the class with clear skin.

(*She moves to get her duffel bag, unpacks it through the following.*)

GEORGE: (*Sitting.*) What made you do it?

DORIS: It was a dinner party that finally pushed me into it. Harry's boss invited us for dinner and I panicked.

GEORGE: Why?

DORIS: I'd spent so much time with kids I didn't know if I was capable of carrying on an intelligent conversation with anyone over five who wasn't a supermarket checkout clerk. Anyway, I went and was seated next to *the* boss. Well, I surprised myself. He talked—then I talked—you know, just a real conversation. I was feeling real cool until I noticed him looking at me in a weird way. I looked down and realized that all the time we'd been talking I'd been cutting up the meat on his plate. At that moment I *knew* I had to get out of the house.

GEORGE: But why school?

(*She stretches out on the bed.*)

DORIS: It's hard to explain. I felt restless and—undirected and I thought an education might give me some answers.

GEORGE: What sort of answers?

DORIS: (*Shrugs.*) To find out where it's really at.

GEORGE: (*Gets up.*) Jesus.

DORIS: What's the matter?

GEORGE: That expression.

DORIS: Okay. To find out who the hell I was.

GEORGE: You don't get those sort of answers from a classroom.

DORIS: I'm not in the classroom all the time. The demonstrations are a learning experience in themselves.

GEORGE: Demonstrations against what?

DORIS: The war of course. Didn't you hear about it? It was in all the papers.

GEORGE: (*Curtly.*) Demonstrations aren't going to stop the war.

DORIS: You have a better idea?

GEORGE: Look, I didn't come up here to discuss politics.

DORIS: Well, so far you've turned down sex and politics. You want to try religion?

GEORGE: I think I'll try a Librium.

> (*She watches him as he takes pill out and moves to take it with a glass of water from the drink tray.*)

DORIS: George, why are you so uptight?

GEORGE: That's another expression I hate.

DORIS: Uptight?

GEORGE: There's no such word.

DORIS: You remind me of when I was nine years old and I asked my mother what "fuck" meant. Know what she said? "There's no such word."

GEORGE: And now you've found out there is you feel you have to use it in every other sentence?

DORIS: George, what's bugging you?

GEORGE: Bugging me? I'll tell you what's "bugging" me. The blacks are burning down the cities, there's a Harvard professor telling my children the only way to happiness is to become a doped-up zombie, and have a teen-age son with hair so long that from the back he looks exactly like Yvonne de Carlo.

DORIS: (*Grins.*) That's right, baby—let it all hang out.

GEORGE: I wish people would *stop* letting it "all hang out." Especially my daughter. It's a wonder she hasn't been arrested for indecent exposure.

DORIS: That's a sign of age, honey.

GEORGE: What is?

DORIS: Being worried about the declining morality of the young. Besides, there's nothing you can do about it.

GEORGE: We could start by setting some examples.

DORIS: What are you going to do, George? Bring back public flogging?

GEORGE: It might not be a bad idea. We could start with the movie producers. My God, have you seen the films they're making today? Half the time the audience achieves a climax before the movie does!

DORIS: It's natural for people to be interested in sex. You can't kid the body, George.

GEORGE: Maybe not but you can damn well be *firm* with it.

> (*She giggles, gets off the bed, moves toward him.*)

DORIS: When you were younger I don't remember you as being exactly a monk about that sort of thing.

GEORGE: That was different! Our relationship was not based upon a casual one night stand!

(*She affectionately rumples his hair.*)

DORIS: No, it's been *fifteen* one night stands.

GEORGE: It's not the same. We've *shared* things. My God, I helped deliver your child, remember?

DORIS: Remember? I think of it as our finest hour.

(*She kisses him lightly, moves away to pour herself a drink.*)

GEORGE: How is she?

DORIS: Very healthy, very noisy, and very spoiled.

GEORGE: You don't feel guilty about leaving her alone while you're at school?

DORIS: Harry's home a lot. The insurance business has been kind of slow lately.

GEORGE: How does he feel about all this?

DORIS: When I told him I wanted to go back to school because I wanted some identity he lost his temper and said, "You want identity? Go build a bridge! Invent penicillin but get off my back!"

GEORGE: I always said Harry had a good head on his shoulders.

DORIS: George, that was the *bad* story about him. How's Helen?

GEORGE: Helen's fine. Just fine.

DORIS: Tell me a story that shows how really lousy she can be.

GEORGE: (*Surprised.*) That's not like you.

DORIS: We seem to need something to bring us closer together.

GEORGE: I don't understand.

DORIS: I thought a really bad story about Helen might make you appreciate me more.

(*This finally gets a small smile from* GEORGE.)

GEORGE: Okay.

(*She sits with her drink and listens.*)

As you know, she has this funny sense of humor.

DORIS: By funny I take it you mean peculiar?

GEORGE: Right. And it comes out at the most inappropriate times. I had signed this client—very proper, very old money. Helen and I were invited out to his house for cocktails to get acquainted with him and his wife. Well, it was all pretty awkward but we managed to get through the drinks all right. Then as we went to leave, instead of walking out the front door I walked into the hall closet. Now that wasn't so bad—I mean anybody can do that. The mistake I made was that I *stayed* in there.

DORIS: You stayed in the closet?

GEORGE: Yes. I don't know—I guess I figured they hadn't noticed and I'd stay there until they'd gone away—okay, I admit I didn't think things through. I was in there for about a minute before I realized I'd—well—misjudged the situation. When I came out the three of them were staring at me. All right, it was an embarrassing situation but I probably could have carried it off. Except for Helen. You know what she did?

DORIS: What?

GEORGE: She peed on the carpet.

DORIS: (*Incredulous.*) She did *what?*

GEORGE: Oh, not right away. First of all, she started to laugh. Her face was all screwed up and the laughter was sort of—squeaky. Then she held her stomach and tears started to roll down her face. Then she peed on their Persian rug.

(DORIS *is having trouble keeping a straight face.*)

DORIS: What did you say?

GEORGE: I said, "You'll have to excuse my wife. Ever since her last pregnancy she's had a problem." Then I offered to have the rug cleaned.

DORIS: Did that help?

GEORGE: They said it wasn't necessary. They had a maid.

(DORIS *finally explodes into peals of laughter.*)

You think that's funny?

DORIS: I've been meaning to tell you this for years, but I think I'd like Helen.

GEORGE: (*Irritated.*) Would she come off any worse if I told you I lost the account?

DORIS: George, when did you get so *stuffy?*

GEORGE: Stuffy? Just because I don't like my wife urinating on my clients' carpets does not mean I'm stuffy!

DORIS: Okay, maybe not just that but—well—look at you. (*She gets up, gestures at him.*) I mean—Jesus—you scream Establishment.

GEORGE: I am not a faddist!

DORIS: What's that mean?

GEORGE: I have no desire to be like those middle-aged idiots with bell bottom trousers and Prince Valiant haircuts who go around saying "Ciao."

DORIS: I wasn't talking about *fashion*. I was talking about your attitudes.

GEORGE: My attitudes are the same as they always were. I haven't changed at all.

DORIS: Yes, you have. You used to be crazy—and insecure and dumb and a terrible liar and—*human*. Now you seem so *sure* of yourself.

GEORGE: That's the last thing I am.
(*She is surprised by his admission.*)

DORIS: Oh?
(*He looks at her for a moment, frowns, moves to look into the fire.*)

GEORGE: I picked up one of Helen's magazines the other day and there was this article telling women what quality of *orgasms* they should have. It was called "The Big O." (*He turns to face her.*) You know what really got to me? This was a magazine my mother used to buy for its *fruitcake* recipes.

DORIS: The times they are a changing, darling.

GEORGE: (*Troubled.*) Too fast. I don't know, twenty, thirty years ago we were brought up with standards—all right, they *were* blacks and whites but they were standards. Today—it's so confusing.

DORIS: Well, that's at least a step in the right direction.
(*She moves to him and kisses him.*)

GEORGE: When did I suddenly become so appealing?

DORIS: When you went from pompous to confused.
(*They kiss again.*)
So what's your pleasure? A walk by the ocean, dinner, or me?

GEORGE: You.

DORIS: Gee, I thought you'd never ask.

> (*She steps back a pace and whips her dress off over her head revealing that she is just wearing a pair of bikini panties.*)

GEORGE: My God.

DORIS: What is it?

GEORGE: Doris—you're not wearing a *bra*!

> (*She giggles, embraces him.*)

DORIS: Oh, George, you're so *forties*.

> (*She starts to nibble on his ear.*)

GEORGE: (*Becoming passionate.*) I happen to be an old-fashioned—man.

DORIS: The next thing you'll be telling me you voted for Goldwater.

GEORGE: I did.

> (*She takes a step back from him.*)

DORIS: Are you putting me on?

GEORGE: Of course not.

> (*Without another word she picks up her dress and puts it on.*)

What—what are you doing?

DORIS: (*Furious.*) If you think I'm going to bed with any son of a bitch who voted for Goldwater, you've got another think coming!

GEORGE: Doris, you can't do this to me! Not *now*!

DORIS: Oh, can't I? I'll tell you something—not only will I not go to bed with you—I want fifteen years of fucks back!

GEORGE: Doris, this is a very *delicate mechanism*!!

> (*She stares at him unbelievingly.*)

DORIS: My God, how could you vote for a man like that?

GEORGE: (*Moving toward her.*) Could we talk about this later.

DORIS: (*Pushing him away.*) No, we'll talk about it *now*! Why?

GEORGE: (*Frustrated—yelling.*) Because I have a son who wants to be a rock musician!!

DORIS: What kind of reason is *that*?

GEORGE: (*Sitting.*) The best reason I can come up with right now in my condition!

DORIS: Well, you're going to have to do a lot better!

GEORGE: Okay, he was going to end the war!

DORIS: By bombing the hell out of innocent people!

GEORGE: What innocent people? They're *Reds*!

DORIS: They just wanted their country back!

GEORGE: Oh, I'm sick of hearing all that liberal crap! We've got the H bomb. Why don't we use it!

DORIS: *Are you serious?*

GEORGE: Yes, I'm serious. Wipe the sons of bitches off the face of the earth!

(*She stares at him for a moment.*)

DORIS: (*Quietly, incredulous.*) My God, I don't know anything about you. What sort of a man are you?

GEORGE: Right now—very frustrated.

DORIS: All this time I thought you were a liberal Democrat. You told me you worked for Stevenson.

GEORGE: (*In a tired voice.*) That was years ago.

DORIS: What changed you? What happened to you?

GEORGE: (*Bitterly.*) I grew up.

DORIS: Yeah, well in my opinion you didn't turn out too well.

GEORGE: Let's forget it, huh?

DORIS: Forget it? How can I forget it? I mean being stuffy and—and old-fashioned is one thing but being a Fascist is another!

GEORGE((*Flaring.*) I am not a Fascist!

DORIS: You're advocating mass murder!

GEORGE: Doris—drop it, okay! Just—drop it!

DORIS: How could you *do* this to me? Why, you stand for everything I'm against!

GEORGE: Then maybe you're against the wrong things!

DORIS: You used to think the same way I did.

GEORGE: I changed!

DORIS: *Why?*

GEORGE: Because Michael was killed! How the hell else did you expect me to feel!!

(*There is a long pause as she stands transfixed, trying to absorb this.*)

DORIS: (*Finally.*) Oh—dear—God. How?

GEORGE: He was trying to get a wounded man onto a Red Cross helicopter and a sniper killed him.

(*Without a word she moves to him, starts to put her arms around him.*

He brushes her away, rises and moves to window and stares out.)

DORIS: (*Finally—almost in a whisper.*) When?

(*There is a pause.*)

GEORGE: (*Dispassionately.*) We heard in the middle of a big July 4th party. Helen went completely to pieces—I'll never forget it. I didn't feel a thing. I thought I was in shock and it would hit me later. (*He turns to face her.*) But you know something? It never did. The only emotion I can feel is blind anger. I didn't shed a tear.

(*She doesn't say anything.*)

Isn't that the darnedest thing? I can't cry over my own son's death. I loved him but—for the life of me—I can't seem to cry over him.

(*She doesn't move as he crosses to shakily pour himself a drink.*)

Doris, I'm sorry about—everything. Lately I've been a bit on edge and—

(*The glass slips out of his hand, he tries to save it but it hits the dresser and smashes.*)

Oh, great! Will you look at that—I've gone and cut myself. If it isn't—one—damn thing—after—

(*He starts to sob.* DORIS *moves to him and puts her arms around him. He sinks into a chair, and buries his head into her chest as the curtain falls.*)

Scene 2

THE TIME: *A day in February, 1970.*

THE PLACE: *The same.*

AT RISE: DORIS *and* GEORGE *are lying on top of the rumpled bed lazily enjoying the afterglow of lovemaking.* GEORGE *is wearing jeans with a butterfly on the seat and longish hair. His manner reflects a slightly self-*

conscious inner serenity. DORIS *is wearing an attractive kimono but during the scene will don clothes and makeup that will project an image of chic, expensive, good taste.*

DORIS: It's amazing how good it can be after all these years, isn't it?

GEORGE: All these years? Honey, if you add up all the times we've actually made it together we're still on our honeymoon.

(*A slight pause.*)

DORIS: George, did you know I'm a grandmother?

GEORGE: No, but I think you picked a weird time to announce it.

DORIS: You think it's decadent having sex with a grandmother?

GEORGE: Only if it's done well.

(*He pats her hand.*)

Anyway, you're the youngest looking grandmother I've ever had a peak experience with.

DORIS: (*Getting off bed.*) My mother thanks you, my father thanks you, my hairdresser thanks you and my plastic surgeon thanks you.

(*He watches her as she lights a cigarette, sits at dresser, peers into mirror, starts to brush hair and apply makeup.*)

When Harry says, "You're not the girl I married," he doesn't know how right he is.

GEORGE: Didn't Harry like your old nose?

DORIS: He thinks this *is* my old nose.

GEORGE: He never noticed?

DORIS: (*Flippantly.*) Pathetic, isn't it? A new dress I could understand—but a whole nose?

GEORGE: Well, to be totally honest I really can't see much of a difference either.

DORIS: Who cares? It looks different from *my* side. Makes me *act* more attractive.

GEORGE: Why do you feel you need a validation of your attractiveness?

DORIS: (*A slight shrug.*) A woman starts feeling a little insecure when she gets to be forty-four.

GEORGE: Forty-five.

DORIS: See what I mean? Anyway, that's this year's rotten story about Harry. Got one about Helen?

(*He grins, gets off bed, dons shirt, denim jacket and sandals during the following.*)

GEORGE: There was a loud party next door. Helen couldn't sleep and she didn't want to take a sleeping pill because she had to get up at six the next morning. So she stuffed two pills in her ears. During the night they melted. The next morning as the doctor was digging the stuff out of her ears he said, "You know these *can* be taken orally." Helen just laughed.

DORIS: If that's the worst story you can tell about her you must be a very happy man.

(*He sits on the piano bench.*)

GEORGE: Well, let's say I've discovered I have the *potential* for happiness.

(*The phone rings.* DORIS *immediately moves to answer it.*)

DORIS: (*Into phone.*) Hello. (*Just a hint of disappointment.*) Oh, hi, Liz. No, it's sixty—not sixteen guests—That's right—a brunch—We've catered a couple of parties for her before—No problem. She sets up tables around the pool and there's room for the buffet on the patio—Right. Anyone else call?—Okay, I'll be at this number.

(*She hangs up, turns to* GEORGE, *who has been watching her.*)

Sorry, busy weekend. I had to leave the number.

GEORGE: Does Harry know you're here?

DORIS: No, he still thinks I go on the retreat. Don't worry.

(*She moves and proceeds to get dressed during the following.*)

GEORGE: I'm not worried.

DORIS: Then why are you frowning?

GEORGE: I'm getting some bad vibes again.

DORIS: Again?

GEORGE: When you first walked into the room I picked up

on your high tension level. Then after we made love I sensed a certain anxiety reduction but now I'm getting a definite negative feedback.

DORIS: How long you been in analysis?

GEORGE: How did you know I was in analysis?

DORIS: (*Drily.*) Just a wild guess. What made you go into therapy?

GEORGE: (*With a shrug.*) My value system changed.

  (*He casually plays some soft, pleasant chords at the piano as he talks.*)

One day I took a look at my $150,000 house, the three cars in the garage, the swimming pool, and the gardeners and I thought—"*Why?*" I mean did I really want the whole status trip? So—I decided to try and find out what I did want and who I was.

DORIS: And you went from analysis to Esalen to Gestalt to Transactional to encounter groups to Nirvana.

  (*He stops playing, swivels to face her, speaks in a calm, reasonable voice.*)

GEORGE: Doris, just because many people are trying to expand their emotional horizons doesn't make the experience any less valid. I've learned a lot.

DORIS: I've noticed. For one thing you learned to talk as if you're reasoning with someone about to jump off a skyscraper ledge.

GEORGE: (*Grins.*) Okay—okay. I know I tend to overcompensate for my emotionalism and sometimes there's a certain loss of spontaneity. I'm working on that.

DORIS: I'm glad to hear it. What else did you find out?

GEORGE: (*Simply.*) That behind the walls I've built around myself I'm a warm, caring, loving human being.

  (*She looks at him for a moment.*)

DORIS: I could have told you that twenty years ago. How does Helen feel about this "voyage of self discovery"?

GEORGE: At first she tended to overact.

DORIS: In what way?

GEORGE: She threw a grapefruit at me in the Thriftimart. It was natural that we'd have some interpersonal conflicts to work through but now it's cool. She's into pottery.

DORIS: But how do you make a living?

GEORGE: We live very simply, Doris—we don't need much. What bread we do need I can provide by simple, honest labor.

DORIS: Like what?

GEORGE: I play cocktail piano in a singles bar in the Valley.

(*The phone rings again.* DORIS *quickly moves to answer it.*)

DORIS: (*Into phone.*) Hello—Oh, hi, Liz—No way. Tell him that's our final offer—I don't care how good a location it is—That's bull, Liz, he needs us more than we need him. If he doesn't like it he can shove it but don't worry—he won't. Anything else?—Okay, you know the number.

(*She hangs up.*)

I'm buying another store.

GEORGE: Why?

DORIS: Money.

(*She continues to dress.*)

GEORGE: Is that why you went into business? Just to make money?

DORIS: Of course not. I wanted money *and* power. And it finally penetrated my thick little head that attending C.R. groups with ten other frustrated housewives wasn't going to change anything.

GEORGE: C.R. groups?

DORIS: Consciousness raising.

(*He nods.*)

I take it you *are* for Women's Liberation?

GEORGE: Listen, I'm for any kind of liberation.

DORIS: That's a cop-out. Women have always been exploited by men and you know it.

GEORGE: We've *all* been shafted, Doris, and by the same things.

(*He gets up.*)

Look, let me lay this on you. I go to a woman doctor. The first time she gave me a rectal examination she said, "Am I hurting you or are you tense?" I said, "I'm tense." Then she said, "Are you tense because I'm a woman?" and I said, "No, I get tense when *anybody* does that to me." (*A beat.*) You see what I mean?

DORIS: I don't know but I *do* know that the only time a woman is taken seriously in this country is when she has the money to back up her mouth. The business has given me that.

GEORGE: (*Mildly.*) Well, I guess it's nice to have a hobby.

DORIS: Hobby? We grossed over half a million dollars the first year.

GEORGE: Honey, if that's what you want I'm very happy for you. (*A slight shrug.*) It's just that I'm not into the money thing anymore.

(*She looks at him for a moment.*)

DORIS: (*Lightly.*) George, you ever get the feeling we're drifting apart?

GEORGE: No. In many ways I've never felt closer to you.

DORIS: Really? I don't know, sometimes I think our lives are always—out of sync.

GEORGE: We all realize our potential in different ways at different times. All I ask is that you don't lay *your* trip on me, that's all.

(*She moves to purse, extracts check.*)

DORIS: Then let me lay this on you. (*She hands him check.*) Here—it's the money you loaned me to start the store.

GEORGE: (*Looking at check.*) It's three times the amount I gave you.

DORIS: Return on your investment.

GEORGE: I can't accept this, Doris.

DORIS: (*Firmly.*) You can and you will. I'm not going to have any lover of mine playing piano in a singles bar. Sounds tacky.

(*They smile at one another.*)

GEORGE: You never used to order me around.

DORIS: I've come a long way, baby.

GEORGE: The important thing is does it give you a sense of fulfillment?

DORIS: Fulfillment? Let me tell you about fulfillment.

(*She moves to finish dressing.*)

I went into Gucci's the other day and I noticed a suede

suit I liked and asked one of their snotty salesgirls the price. She said, "Seven hundred dollars," and started to walk away. I said, "I'll take five." She turned and said, "Five? Why on earth would you want five?" and I said, "I want them for my bowling team." *That's* fulfillment.

GEORGE: So you have everything you want?

DORIS: (*Lighting cigarette—flippantly.*) With one minor exception. Somewhere along the way I seem to have lost my husband.

GEORGE: Lost him?

DORIS: Well, I don't know if I've lost him or simply misplaced him. He walked out of the house four days ago and I haven't heard from him since.

GEORGE: How do you feel about that?

DORIS: George, do me a favor—stop acting as if you're leading a human potential group. It really pisses me off.

GEORGE: That's cool.

DORIS: *What's* cool?

GEORGE: For you to transfer your hostility and feelings of aggression from Harry to me. As long as you *know* that's what you're doing.

DORIS: You mind if I tell you something, George? You're beginning to get on my nerves.

GEORGE: That's cool too.

DORIS: Jesus.

GEORGE: I mean it. At least it's *honest*. That's the key to everything—total honesty.

DORIS: Oh really? And are you totally honest with Helen?

GEORGE: I'm trying.

DORIS: Have you told her about us?

GEORGE: No—but I could.
  (*She grimaces.*)
Really, I think that today she's matured enough to handle it.

DORIS: George, you're full of shit.

GEORGE: I can buy that—if you're really being *honest*.

DORIS: Believe me, I'm being honest.

GEORGE: Well, at least it's a start. But what about that other garbage?
  (*She starts to speak.*)

Oh come on, Doris! (*Imitating her.*) "I don't know if I lost him or simply misplaced him." I mean what sort of crap is that?

(*She looks at him for a moment.*)

DORIS: Okay, you have a point.

GEORGE: Is there someone else?

DORIS: I don't think so. I *know* there isn't with me. (*Getting agitated.*) That's what really gets to me. Did you know I've been married for over twenty-five years and I've never cheated on him *once!*

(*He doesn't say anything.*)

Well, you know what I mean.

GEORGE: What is it then? Boredom?

DORIS: No. Oh, Harry's not exactly Cary Grant anymore but then neither is Cary Grant.

GEORGE: So how do you feel about all this?

DORIS: You're doing it again, George.

(*He doesn't say anything.*)

Okay, I think—

GEORGE: No, don't tell me what you think. Tell me what you *feel.*

DORIS: Like I've been kicked in the stomach.

GEORGE: That's good.

(*She looks at him.*)

What else?

DORIS: Angry, hurt, betrayed and—okay, a little guilty. But you know something? I *resent* the fact that he's made me feel guilty.

GEORGE: Why do you feel resentment?

DORIS: (*Angrily.*) Look, I didn't marry Harry because he had a head for business! Okay, it so happens that I discovered *I* did. Or maybe I was just lucky—I don't know. The point is, I don't love Harry any less because he's a failure as a provider. Why should he love me any less because I'm a success?

(*He doesn't say anything, she sighs.*)

I don't know—one of these days I'm going to know exactly how I *do* feel.

GEORGE: You don't know?

DORIS: It varies between Joan of Arc, Rosalind Russell and Betty Crocker.

GEORGE: Well, I suppose most women are going through a transitional period.

DORIS: (*With a wry grimace.*) Yeah, but what am I going to do tonight?

GEORGE: Have you told him you still love him?

DORIS: Love him? Why does he think I've been hanging around with him for twenty-seven years?

GEORGE: (*In his calm, reasonable voice.*) I just mean that right now his masculinity is being threatened and he probably needs some validation of his worth as a man.

DORIS: And how the hell do I do all that? I mean that's *some* trick.

GEORGE: Total honesty, Doris. Is it so hard for you to tell him that you understand how he feels?

DORIS: Right now—it is, yes.

GEORGE: Oh?

DORIS: I mean why the hell should I apologize for doing something well? It's *his* ego that's screwed us up. I mean I really *resent* that!

GEORGE: You want him back?

DORIS: Right at this moment I'm not sure I do. Ask me tomorrow and I'll probably give you a different answer.

GEORGE: Why?

DORIS: (*Simply.*) Tomorrow I won't have you.

GEORGE: I'm always with you in spirit.

DORIS: It's not easy to spiritually put your cold feet on someone's back.

GEORGE: Is that a proposal, Doris?

DORIS: You interested?

GEORGE: Are you?

DORIS: For two cents.

GEORGE: Leave Helen and Harry?

DORIS: Sure. Present a united back.

(*He is looking at her, trying to determine whether she's serious.*)

Don't look so panicky, George. I'm only three quarters serious.

(*There is a pause.*)

GEORGE: Well, when you have your head together and are completely serious why don't you ask me again.

DORIS: I bet you say that to all the girls.

GEORGE: No.

(*She cups his face in her hands and kisses him.*)

DORIS: Thanks.

GEORGE: And stop feeling so insecure.

DORIS: About what?

GEORGE: You're as feminine as you always were.

(*She looks at him for a moment.*)

DORIS: I know Gloria Steinem would hate me, but I'm glad you said that. (*She gives a little shrug.*) I guess I'm not as emancipated as I thought I was.

GEORGE: None of us are.

(*She grins at him.*)

DORIS: You hungry?

GEORGE: Yes.

DORIS: Well, you're a lucky man because tonight our dinner is being catered by the chicest, most expensive French delicatessen in San Francisco.

GEORGE: How'd we swing that?

DORIS: The owner has a thing about you.

(*As she moves toward the door.*)

It's all in the trunk of my car.

GEORGE: You need any help?

DORIS: Yes. Set the table, light the candles, and when I come back make me laugh.

GEORGE: I'll try.

DORIS: That's okay. If you can't make me laugh just hold my hand.

(*She exits.*

He moves to prepare the table for the food. The phone rings. He hesitates for a moment before picking up the receiver.)

GEORGE: (*Into the phone.*) Hello—No, she's not here right now. Who is this? (*His face freezes.*) Harry!—Uh, hold—hold on a moment.

(*He places the phone on the floor, stares at it for a moment. Then he paces in a circle around it, his mind wrestling with the alternatives. He stops, stares at it, takes a deep breath, picks up the receiver.*)

Hello—Harry, we're two adult, mature human beings and I've decided to be totally honest with you—No, Doris is not here right now but *I'd* like to talk to you—Because I know you and Doris have been having a rough time lately and—We're very close friends. I've known Doris for twenty years and through her I feel as if I know you—Well, we've been meeting this same weekend for twenty years—The Retreat? Well, we can get into that later but first I want you to know something. She loves you, Harry—she really loves you—I just know, Harry—Look, maybe if I told you a story she just told me this morning it would help you understand. A few months ago Doris was supposed to act as a den mother for your ten-year-old daughter Georgina and her Indian guide group. Well, she got hung up at the store and was two hours late getting home. When she walked into the house she looked into the living room and do you know what she saw? A rather overweight, balding, middle-aged man with a feather on his head sitting cross-legged on the floor very gravely and gently telling a circle of totally absorbed little girls what it was like to be in a World War II Japanese prison camp. She turned around, walked out of the house, sat in her car and thanked God for being married to a man like you—Are you still there, Harry?—Well, sometimes married people get into an emotional straitjacket and find it difficult to communicate how they truly feel about each other. Honesty is the key to everything—Yes, we've had a very close, very intimate relationship for twenty years and I'm not ashamed to admit that it's been one of the most satisfying experiences of my life—My name? My name is Father Michael O'Herlihy.

(*The lights start to dim as he keeps talking.*)

No, she's out saying a novena right now—Yes, my son, I'll tell her to call you.

(*The curtain has fallen.*)

Scene 3

THE TIME: *A day in February, 1975.*
THE PLACE: *The same.*
AT RISE: DORIS *is alone on the stage silently mouthing "twenty-one, twenty-two, twenty-three" as she finishes transferring some red roses from a box into a silver vase. She is well dressed but her clothes are softer, more feminine and less fashionable than the last time we saw her. She turns as* GEORGE *enters. His hair has been trimmed to a "conservatively long" length and his raincoat covers his comfortably rumpled sports coat, pants, and turtleneck sweater. They drink one another in for a moment before they embrace affectionately.*

GEORGE: You feel *good.*
DORIS: So do you. (*She looks at him.*) But you *look* tired.
GEORGE: (*Grins.*) I've looked this way for years. You just haven't noticed.
   (*She doesn't say anything but we see the concern in her eyes. He turns away, takes off his raincoat and throws it over a chair during the following.*)
Anyway, I feel better now I'm here. This room's always had that effect on me.
DORIS: I know what you mean. I guess it proves that maybe you can't buy happiness but you can certainly *rent* it. (*She gazes around the room affectionately.*) It never changes, does it?
GEORGE: About the only thing that doesn't.
DORIS: I find that comforting.
GEORGE: Even old Chalmers is the same. He must be seventy-five by now. (*He smiles at her.*) Remember when we first met how even then we called him Old Chalmers?
   (*She nods.*)
He must have been about the same age we are now.

DORIS: *That* I don't find comforting.

GEORGE: We were very young.

(*They gaze at one another for a moment.*)

DORIS: Have we changed, George?

GEORGE: Of course. I grew up with you. Remember the dumb lies I used to tell?

DORIS: (*Nods.*) I miss them.

GEORGE: I don't. It was no fun being that insecure.

DORIS: And what about me? Have I grown up too?

GEORGE: Oh, I have the feeling you were already grown up when I met you.

(*They smile at one another.*)

Tell me something.

DORIS: Anything.

GEORGE: Why is it that every time I look at you I want to put my hands all over you?

(*She moves to embrace him.*)

DORIS: That's another thing that hasn't changed. You always were a sex maniac.

GEORGE: (*Nuzzling her.*) Softest thing I've touched in months is Rusty, my cocker spaniel.

(*She looks at him in surprise.*)

DORIS: Oh?

(*He avoids the unspoken query by moving away to the fireplace.*)

GEORGE: Let's see if I can get this fire going.

(*She watches him as he throws another log on.*)

You know I figured out with the cost of firewood today it's cheaper to buy Akron furniture, break it up, and burn *it.*

DORIS: Things that tight?

GEORGE: No, I'm okay. I've been doing some teaching at UCLA.

DORIS: Music?

GEORGE: Accounting. (*He shrugs, gestures at the window.*) It seems with everything that's happening out there figures are still the only things that don't lie.

(*She moves to pour two cups of coffee from a coffeepot that has been set up on a tray.*)

Doris, why'd you sell your business?

DORIS: (*Surprised.*) How did you know that?

GEORGE: I'll tell you later. What made you do it?

DORIS: I was bought out by a chain. (*A slight shrug.*) It was the right offer at the right time.

GEORGE: But I thought you loved working.

DORIS: Well, there was another factor. Harry had a heart attack.

> (*She hands him a cup of coffee.*)

It turned out to be a mild one but he needed me to look after him—so—

> (*She shrugs.*)

GEORGE: You don't miss the action?

DORIS: Not yet. I guess I'm still enjoying being one of the idle rich.

> (*He sits with his coffee as she moves to get a cup for herself.*)

GEORGE: But what do you do with yourself?

DORIS: Oh—read, watch TV, play a little golf, visit our grandchildren—you know, all the jet set stuff.

GEORGE: Harry's okay now?

> (*She sits opposite him.*)

DORIS: Runs four miles a day and has a body like Mark Spitz. (*Grins.*) Unfortunately, his face is still like Ernest Borgnine's. You want to hear a nice story about him?

GEORGE: (*Unenthusiastically.*) Sure.

DORIS: Right after the heart attack when he came out of intensive care he looked up at the doctor and said, "Doc, give it to me straight. After I get out of the hospital will I be able to play the piano?" The doctor said, "Of course" and Harry said, "Funny, I couldn't play it *before.*"

> (GEORGE *gives a polite smile, gets up, moves to look out of the window.*)

You don't understand—it wasn't that it was that funny. It's just that Harry *never* makes jokes but he saw how panicky I was and wanted to make me feel better.

GEORGE: Doris, how are you and Harry? You know—emotionally.

DORIS: Comfortable.

GEORGE: You're willing to settle for that?
  (*She moves to pick up his raincoat.*)
DORIS: Oh, it's not such a bad state. The word's been given
  a bad reputation by the young. (*She looks around for
  his luggage.*) Where's your luggage? Still in the car?
GEORGE: I didn't bring any.
  (*She looks at him.*)
  I—I can't stay, Doris.
DORIS: (*Puzzled.*) Why?
GEORGE: Look, I have a lot to say and a short time to say
  it so I'd better start now.
  (*She waits.*
  He takes a breath.)
First of all, Helen's known about us for over ten years.
DORIS: (*Finally.*) When did you find out?
GEORGE: Two months ago.
DORIS: She never confronted you with it before?
GEORGE: No.
  (*She slowly sits.*)
DORIS: I always wondered how we managed to pull it off. I
  guess we didn't. What made her finally tell you?
GEORGE: She didn't. She has this—this old friend—
  Connie—maybe I've mentioned her before. She told me.
  (*He shakes his head unbelievingly.*) All those years and
  Helen never even hinted that she knew. (*A beat.*) I
  guess that's the nicest story I've ever told about her.
DORIS: Your wife's an amazing woman, George.
GEORGE: She's dead.
  (*She just looks at him.*)
She died six months ago. Cancer. It was all—very fast.
  (*She slowly gets up, moves to look into the fire.*)
I'm sorry to blurt it out like that. I just couldn't think of
a—a graceful way to tell you.
  (*She nods, her back still to him.*)
You okay, honey?
DORIS: It's so strange. I never met Helen. But—but I feel
  as if I've just lost my best friend. It's—crazy.
  (*He doesn't say anything. She turns to face him.*)
It must have been awful for you.

GEORGE: You cope. You don't think you can but—you cope.

(*She moves to him, touches his cheek with her hand.*)

DORIS: The kids okay?

GEORGE: They'll survive. I don't think I could have got through the whole thing without them.

(*He moves away.*)

Then of course there was—Connie.

DORIS: Connie?

GEORGE: She'd lost her husband a few years ago so there was a certain—empathy.

DORIS: Oh?

GEORGE: She's a friend, Doris. A very good friend. We've always felt very—comfortable—together. I suppose it's because she's a lot like Helen.

(*She reacts with a slight frown.*)

Is there something the matter?

DORIS: I just wish you'd tried to reach me.

GEORGE: I did. That's when I found out you'd sold the stores. I called and they gave me your home number. I let the phone ring four times, then I hung up. But it made me feel better knowing you were there if I needed you.

DORIS: I wish you'd spoken to me.

GEORGE: I didn't want to intrude. I didn't feel I had the right.

DORIS: My God, that's terrible. We should have been together.

GEORGE: I've been thinking about us a lot lately. Everything we've been through together. The things we shared. The times we've helped each other. Did you know we've made love a hundred and thirteen times? I figured it out on my Bomar calculator.

(*He is fixing fresh cups of coffee.*)

It's a wonderful thing to know someone that well. You know, there is nothing about you I don't know. It's two sugars, right?

DORIS: No, one.

GEORGE: Cream?

(*She shakes her head.*)

So, I don't know everything about you. I don't know who your favorite movie stars are and I couldn't remember the name of your favorite perfume. I racked my brain but I couldn't remember.

DORIS: (*Smiles.*) That's funny. It's My Sin.

GEORGE: But I do know that in twenty-four years I've never been out of love with you. I find that incredible. So what do you say, Doris, you want to get married?

DORIS: (*Lightly.*) Married? We shouldn't even be doing this.

GEORGE: I'm serious.

DORIS: (*Looking at him.*) You really are, aren't you?

GEORGE: What did you think I was—just another summer romance? A simple "yes" will do.

DORIS: There's no such thing, George.

GEORGE: What is it?

DORIS: I was just thinking of how many times I've dreamed of you asking me this. It's pulled me through a lot of bad times. I want to thank you for that.

GEORGE: What did you say to me all those times?

DORIS: I always said "yes."

GEORGE: Then why are you hesitating now?

(*Pause.*)

Do you realize I'm giving you the opportunity to marry a man who has known you for twenty-four years and every time you walk by still wants to grab your ass?

DORIS: You always were a sweet talker.

GEORGE: That's because if I told you how I really felt about you it would probably sound like a medley of clichés from popular songs. Will you marry me?

DORIS: (*Pause.*) I can't.

GEORGE: Why not?

DORIS: I'm already married.

GEORGE: You feel you have to stay because he needs you?

DORIS: No, it's more than that. George, try and understand.

(*She moves away and turns to him.*)

When I look at Harry I don't only see the way he is now. I see all the other Harrys I've known. I'm sure he feels the same way about me. When we look at our children—our grandchildren—old movies on TV—anything—we share the same memories. (*A beat.*) It's—comfortable. Maybe that's what marriage is all about in the end—I don't know. (*A slight pause.*) Didn't you feel that way with Helen?

(*There is a short pause.*)

GEORGE: (*Exploding.*) Goddamit!

(*He smashes his coffee cup into the fireplace.*)

I was the one who got you back together three years ago! Why did I *do* a stupid thing like that! I mean why the hell was I so goddamn generous!?

DORIS: Because you felt the same way about Helen then as I do about Harry now.

GEORGE: What's that got to do with anything?!

DORIS: If I hadn't gone back to Harry you might have been stuck with me permanently and you were terrified.

(*He looks at her, manages a sheepish grin.*)

GEORGE: You could always see through me, couldn't you?

DORIS: That's okay. I always liked what I saw.

GEORGE: Well, I want you now.

DORIS: I'm still available once a year.

(*He doesn't say anything.*)

Same time, same place?

(*She catches a certain look in his eyes.*)

What is it?

(*He looks at her for a moment, paces, turns to face her.*)

GEORGE: (*Awkwardly.*) Doris—I—I need a wife. I'm just not the kind of man who can live alone. I want you to marry me but when I came here I—I knew there was an outside chance you'd say "no." What I'm trying to say is—if you don't marry me I'll probably end up marrying Connie. No—that's a lie—I will marry her. She knows why I came here today. She knows—all about you. The point is, she's not the sort of woman who would go along with our—relationship. (*A beat.*) You understand?

(DORIS *manages a nod.*)

I suppose what I'm saying is that if you don't marry me we won't ever see each other again.

(DORIS *is frozen, he moves to take her hand.*)

You're trembling.

DORIS: The thought of never seeing you again terrifies me.

GEORGE: Doris, for God's sake—marry me!

DORIS: (*Finally—torn.*) I'm sorry—I can't.

(*He looks at her for a long moment.*)

Don't hate me, George.

GEORGE: I could never hate you. I was just trying to think of something that would break your heart, make you burst into tears and come with me.

DORIS: You know us Italians. We never cry.

(*He makes a gesture of helplessness, stands.*)

GEORGE: What time is it?

(*She holds out her wrist, he looks at her watch, reacts.*)

Five-fifty-five.

DORIS: No, it's only two-thirty. I always keep my watch three hours and twenty-five minutes fast.

GEORGE: (*Puzzled.*) How long you been doing that?

DORIS: About twenty odd years.

GEORGE: Why would anyone want to do that?

DORIS: Personal idiosyncrasy.

(*There is an awkward pause.*)

GEORGE: Well—I—I have a plane to catch.

(*She nods, stands. They look at one another.*)

You know, I can't believe this is happening to us.

(*She doesn't say anything.*)

Yeah. Well—

(*They embrace and kiss, clumsily and awkwardly, almost like two strangers. They break, he picks up his raincoat, moves to door, turns to look at her.*)

GEORGE: Who were your favorite movie stars?

DORIS: Lon McAllister, Howard Keel, Cary Grant, Marlon Brando, and Laurence Olivier.

GEORGE: You've come a long way.

DORIS: We both have.

(*He opens door, looks at her.*)

GEORGE: Always keep your watch three hours and twenty-five minutes fast, huh?

(*He exits quickly, shutting the door behind him.*

DORIS stands for a moment trying to absorb the shock of his departure. Then, trancelike, she moves to the closet where she gets her suitcase, puts it on the sofa, and starts to pack but stops to look lovingly around the room, drinking in the memories before her eyes come to rest upon the vase of roses. She slowly moves to the roses, takes one out, closes her eyes and rests it gently against her cheek. She holds this pose for a long moment before her eyes jolt open as the door crashes open and GEORGE, perspiring and very agitated, bursts into the room, holding his suitcases. He drops his cases with a thump, fixes her with an angry, frustrated look.)

Okay, you win goddamit! You can't look a gift horse in the mouth!

DORIS: (*Astounded.*) But—but what about Connie?

GEORGE: (*Yelling.*) There is no Connie! I made her up!

(*She just stares at him, dumbfounded.*)

No, that's a lie too. There is a Connie but she's sixty-nine years old!

(*DORIS is still speechless.*)

Doris, I wanted you to *marry* me and I figured if you thought there was someone else you'd—okay, maybe I didn't think it through. I was desperate, okay? (*Getting even more agitated.*) Look, for once in my life I wanted a happy ending, can't you understand that?! Listen, I don't want to talk about it anymore!

(*Still speechless she watches him march to the bed and start to furiously undress. He turns to look at her.*)

Okay! You're right about that too! If you had married me we might have just ended up with a "comfortable" ending!

(*She opens her mouth to speak.*)

Look, I'm in no mood to figure it out right now. All I know is I'm back and I'm going to keep coming back every year until our bones are too brittle to risk contact.

(She starts to laugh, her laughter builds and then almost imperceptibly changes to something else and we realize that she is crying. She moves blindly into his arms, still sobbing. He gently tips her face up so that he can look at her and speaks very softly.)

After twenty-four years? Why now?

DORIS: *(Through her tears.)* Because I love—happy—endings!

(He picks her up, places her on the bed and as she lies beside her the lights slowly dim until there is just a pin spot on the vase of roses. Finally, this too fades, the stage is dark, and the play is over.)

GEMINI

by Albert Innaurato

Act One

Scene 1: June 1, 1973. Early Morning.
Scene 2: That Evening.

Act Two

Scene 1: June 2, 1973. Morning.
Scene 2: That Evening.

The setting shows the backyards of two adjoining row houses in the Italian section of South Philadelphia. They are small, two-story, brick houses typical of the poorer sections of most big cities. In one house live the Geminianis, Fran and Francis, and in the other the Weinbergers, Bunny and Herschel. In the Geminiani yard is a fig tree, and along one side a high alley fence with a gate. The Weinberger yard contains an old ladder, a rusty, old tricycle, garbage cans, and a certain amount of general debris, and is also bounded by an alley wall, behind which is a high utility or telephone pole.
Gemini was first performed in a workshop production at Playwrights Horizons, and was later presented at the PAF Playhouse, Huntington, N.Y., before being produced by the Circle Repertory Company in New York City. On May 21, 1977, it opened at the Little Theatre, New York City, produced by Jerry Arrow and Jay Broad representing the Circle Repertory Company and the PAF Playhouse. It was directed by Peter Mark Schifter and had a setting by

Christopher Nowak, costumes by Ernest Allen Smith, and lighting by Larry Crimmins, with the Broadway production being supervised by Marshall W. Mason. The cast, in order of appearance, was:

FRANCIS GEMINIANI	*Robert Picardo*
BUNNY WEINBERGER	*Jessica James*
RANDY HASTINGS	*Reed Birney*
JUDITH HASTINGS	*Carol Potter*
HERSCHEL WEINBERGER	*Jonathan Hadary*
FRAN GEMINIANI	*Danny Aiello*
LUCILLE POMPI	*Anne DeSalvo*

Characters

FRAN GEMINIANI is forty-five, working class, boisterous, and friendly. He is slightly overweight, coughs a lot from mild emphysema.

FRANCIS GEMINIANI, his son, is about to celebrate his twenty-first birthday. He is also plump, a little clumsy, is entering his senior year at Harvard.

LUCILLE POMPI is Fran's lady friend, very thin, early forties, working class, but strives hard to act in accordance with her ideas of ladylike behavior and elegance.

BUNNY WEINBERGER, the Geminiani's next-door neighbor, is a heavy-set, blowsy woman, about forty, once very beautiful and voluptuous, now rough talking and inclined to drink too much.

HERSCHEL WEINBERGER, her son, is sixteen, very heavy, asthmatic, very bright, but eccentric. He is obsessed with Public Transportation in all its manifestations, and is shy and a little backward socially.

JUDITH HASTINGS, Francis's classmate at Harvard, is a month or two younger than Francis. She is an exceedingly, perhaps even intimidatingly, beautiful Wasp. She is extremely intelligent, perhaps slightly more aggressive than she should be, but is basically well meaning.

RANDY HASTINGS, her brother, has just finished his freshman year at Harvard. Like Judith, he is a quintessential, very handsome Wasp.

The play takes place on June 1 and 2, 1973. The latter marks Francis's twenty-first birthday.

ACT ONE

Scene 1

(The sound of garbage men emptying the garbage in the alley. They are making an immense noise. It is just past dawn and they are banging lids, overturning cans, and yelling to one another.

FRANCIS GEMINIANI *appears at his bedroom window. He is dressed in a T-shirt, his hair is wild, his glasses are awry. He has just been awakened and is in a rage.)*

FRANCIS: Shut! Will you please shut up! Why aren't you men more civilized? Oh Jesus Christ!

(He sets a speaker on the windowsill, and turns on the final portion full blast of Isolde's narrative and curse from Act I of Tristan und Isolde. BUNNY WEINBERGER *appears at the second floor window of her house. She is in a torn nightgown and faded robe, and is also in a rage.)*

BUNNY: Francis! Francis! Why are you playing that music at six o'clock in the mornin'? You got somethin' against my gettin' a good night's sleep?

FRANCIS: *(Leaning out his window.)* Do you hear the garbage men?

BUNNY: Sure. They're just doing their job. That's the trouble wit you college kids—got no respect for the working man. Besides, I got an uncle out there. (*Shouts out to alley behind fence.*) Hi ya, Uncle Jerry!

VOICE: (*From behind the fence.*) Hi ya, Bun!

BUNNY: How's your hammer hanging? (*Then to* FRANCIS.) See, I got connections. You stick wit me kid, I'll get you a job.

(*A knocking is heard at the front door of the* GEMINI-ANI *house.*)

And now you got them knockin' at your door. You woke everybody up. Ain't you gonna answer it?

FRANCIS: I'm going back to bed.

(*He takes the speaker off the sill.*)

BUNNY: Good. Maybe we'll have some quiet.

(*She disappears inside her bedroom. The knocking continues. The garbage men fade away.* FRANCIS *has now put on a very quiet passage from Act IV of Verdi's* I Vespri Siciliani. *After a moment a knocking is heard at the gate in the fence, the entrance to the* GEMINIANI *yard.* FRANCIS *does not come to his window. More knocking. A pause. Then a rolled up sleeping bag comes sailing over the fence, followed by a small knapsack.* RANDY HASTINGS *appears at the top of the fence. He climbs over and jumps into the yard. He looks around. Suddenly a large knapsack, the kind that has an aluminium frame, appears at the top of the fence.* RANDY *takes it, and puts it down on the ground. Next we see a rolled up tent, a second sleeping bag on the fence, then a tennis racquet, and then* JUDITH HASTINGS. *She perches on top of the fence, looks around, and then jumps into the yard.* RANDY *has piled everything neatly together in the middle of the yard. They are both in worn jeans and sneakers. They circle about the yard, peeking into* BUNNY'S *part curiously.* JUDITH *notices the fig tree and smiles. She knocks at the back door. No answer.* RANDY *tries to open it, but it is latched from the inside. He then peeks into the window to the left of the door and sees* FRANCIS *sleeping in his room. He smiles at* JUDITH, *and they climb into* FRANCIS's *room.*)

JUDITH AND RANDY: Surprise! Surprise!

> (*The music stops.* FRANCIS *leaps out of bed.*)

JUDITH: (*Inside the room.*) Put your glasses on, it's Judith . . . .

RANDY: . . . and Randy. What's the matter?

FRANCIS: What are you doing here?

JUDITH: Come to see you, of course—

FRANCIS: Why?

JUDITH: It's your birthday tomorrow, your twenty-first.

> (*At this moment* HERSCHEL *dashes out of the back door of his house and into the yard. He hurls himself onto the rusty tricycle and, making subway engine noises, careens about the yard.*)

RANDY: (*Looking through screen door.*) Francis, who's that?

FRANCIS: (*With* JUDITH *in kitchen window.*) Herschel next door.

RANDY: What's he doing?

FRANCIS: Hey Herschel, what are you doing?

HERSCHEL: I'm pretending I'm a subway engine.

FRANCIS: Which one?

HERSCHEL: Three nineteen AA four six five AA BZ substratum two. Built in 1945, in April, first run on Memorial Day.

FRANCIS: Herschel is into Public Transportation.

> (BUNNY *comes out of her house, still in the same torn and smudged nightgown and housecoat. She has a quart beer bottle in one hand, and a cigarette in the other.*)

BUNNY: What the fuck's goin' on out here, hanh? Why you up so early?

> (HERSCHEL, *making engine noises, heads right for her. She sidesteps the tricycle easily.*)

Jesus Christ, it's that engine you're goin' a see.

FRANCIS: (*From window, still with* JUDITH. RANDY *has come out to get a better view.*) Bunny, these are friends of mine from school. Judith Hastings and her brother, Randy. (*Indicates* BUNNY.) This is my neighbor, Bunny Weinberger.

BUNNY: I didn't know they had girls at Harvard.

FRANCIS: Judith is at Radcliffe.

BUNNY: This is my son, Herschel. He's a genius. He's gotta IQ of 187 or 172, depending on which test you use.

(*To* HERSCHEL, *who is still careening about.*)

Stop that fuckin' noise! He's also got asthma, and he tends to break out.

HERSCHEL: (*To* RANDY.) You want to see my collection of transfers?

RANDY: (*With a shrug.*) Sure.

(HERSCHEL *dashes into his house.*)

BUNNY: (*Looking after him.*) Well, all geniuses is a little crazy. You kids look hungry, so damn skinny.

(*She is poking* RANDY *in the stomach.*)

RANDY: Do you think so?

BUNNY: I guess you're scholarship students at Harvard, hanh? Although Francis is on scholarship you wouldn't know it to look at him. You wan' some breakfast?

JUDITH: That would be very nice.

(BUNNY *starts for her door.*)

FRANCIS: Get the roaches out of the oven first, Bunny.

BUNNY: (*Good-naturedly.*) Oh, go fuck yourself. I ain't had a live roach in here in a year, unless you count Herschel, I think he's part roach. Whatayas want? Fried eggs and bacon alright?

RANDY: Sure.

BUNNY: He's normal, at least.

(*She goes inside.*)

FRANCIS: So . . . you're just here for the day?

JUDITH: For the day? Some people go away to the beach from the city, we have come away to the city from the beach.

RANDY: Can you say that in French?

JUDITH: (*Coming out of the house.*) *Il y a des gens qui va . . .*

FRANCIS: (*Interrupting.*) How'd you get here?

JUDITH: We hitchhiked, of course.

FRANCIS: You rich people are all crazy. It would never occur to me to hitchhike.

JUDITH: That's because you couldn't get picked up.

RANDY: Come on, Judith, you can help me set up the tent.

FRANCIS: (*From his room, putting on his pants.*) Tent?

RANDY: Sure. We always sleep outside. We could put it up under this tree. What kind is it?

JUDITH: Fig, idiot.

RANDY: What's a fig tree doing in your yard?

FRANCIS: (*Coming out of house, pants on, but barefoot.*) You'll have to ask my father, he planted it. But look, I don't want . . . I mean . . . well, you see, it's my father. I mean you can't stay here. He doesn't like company.

RANDY: But I thought wops loved company.
   (JUDITH *hits him.*)

FRANCIS: Mafia.

JUDITH: The Mafia?

FRANCIS: You know, the Black Hand, Cosa Nostra, the Brotherhood . . .

RANDY: Your father's in the . . .

FRANCIS: Hit man.

JUDITH: Oh, come on!

FRANCIS: He offs Wasps. It was bred into him at an early age, this raving hatred of white Anglo-Saxon Protestants, they call them white people.

RANDY: (*Looks worried.*) White people?

FRANCIS: He collects their ears after he murders them, he has a collection in his room . . .
   (*Starts picking up their camping equipment and hands it to* JUDITH *and* RANDY.)
I'll tell you what, let's go to the bus terminal, I'll finish getting dressed, we'll put your stuff in a locker, I'll show you around, we'll take a few pictures, then you can go back later tonight. I'll get my camera.
   (*He runs inside.*)

RANDY: You mean we have to carry this junk around some more?

JUDITH: (*At* FRANCIS'*s window.*) Why don't you come back with us—we've got plenty of room—Mother will love you—you can cook for us.

FRANCIS: (*Appears at window.*) I can't. I have a job.

RANDY: You can watch me work out.

JUDITH: Oh, Randy, grow up! I wanted to see you . . .

FRAN: (*Offstage.*) Yo, Francis, you home!

FRANCIS: Oh, Jesus Christ!

(RANDY *is trying to escape for his life.* JUDITH *is holding him back.*)

FRAN: (*Offstage, yelling.*) Yo, Francis, we're back!

(FRAN *unlocks the gate, which had a chain and padlock. He appears with an empty trash can,* LUCILLE *right behind him, holding three freshly pressed shirts on hangers.* FRAN *sets the trash can under his kitchen window, and then notices the visitors in his yard. Yelling into window.*)

You got company?

JUDITH: (*Hastily.*) My name is Judith Hastings, and this is my brother Randy. We know Francis from Harvard.

FRAN: Oh yeah? I'm his dad. I didn't know Igor had friends. He just sits around all day, no job, nothin'. My name's Francis too. (*Turns to* RANDY.) But you can call me Franny, or Fran, or Frank. (*Turns to* JUDITH.) And you can call me honey, or sweetness and light, or darling, whatever you like.

(*Indicates* LUCILLE, *who is trying to blend into the fence, because she has been surprised in a housecoat.*)

This is Lucille.

LUCILLE: Oh, dear.

JUDITH: Well, we were just leaving.

FRAN: Leavin'? But you just got here, you can't leave.

LUCILLE: (*Attempting elegance.*) Well, Fran, thanks for comin' over . . .

(*She hands* FRAN *his shirts.*)

Of course, I was rather surprised, it's bein' so early, my dress.

BUNNY: (*Appears in her window.*) Hi ya, Fran.

FRAN: Yo, Bun.

BUNNY: (*Sees* LUCILLE.) I see you got The Holy Clam wit you. I'm cookin' breakfast.

LUCILLE: (*To* JUDITH *and* RANDY, *still explaining.*) And then I have to wash my hair . . .

BUNNY: Shut up, Lucille, you keep washin' it and it's gonna fall out, and not just your hair. Hey, you kids, you wan' some oregano in these eggs?

FRAN: Why? They're still gonna be Irish eggs.

BUNNY: I gotta Jew name, but I'm Irish. Real name's Murphy.

FRAN: You still got roaches in that oven?
(*Coughes from emphysema, then laughs.*)

BUNNY: You still got rats up your ass?

LUCILLE: Bunny! (*Then to* FRAN.) Stop smoking, hanh?

BUNNY: (*In her window, with a mixing bowl, singing.*)
"Oh I got plenty of nothin'
and nothing's got plenty of me
Got my butt
Got my boobs
Got my cup of tea
Ain't no use complainin'
Got my butt
Got my boobs
Got my boobs!"
(*Dialogue continues over* BUNNY's *song.*)

FRAN: (*To* RANDY *and* JUDITH.) You just get here?

JUDITH: You're sure you want us to stay?

FRAN: Whataya mean am I sure?

RANDY: We're Wasps . . .

FRAN: So? I'm broad-minded. Is that a tent?

RANDY: We like to sleep outside.

FRAN: You kids is all nuts, you know that? So put it up!
(*Scratches.*)

LUCILLE: (*Setting up a lawn chair.*) Stop scratching that rash.

FRAN: That's my fig tree, you know! I planted it.

LUCILLE: (*To* BUNNY, *who is singing* "Got My Boobs".)
Bunny!
(*She sits down.* BUNNY *is now screeching her final* "Got My Boobs." LUCILLE *jumps up.*)
Bunny!
(BUNNY *laughs, and goes back to cooking.* LUCILLE, *with the situation under control, sits down for a chat.*)
So how do you do? My name is Lucille Pompi. I have a son at Yale and my daughter is a dental technician, she works at The Graduate Hospital, special shift, and my late husband . . .

FRAN: *Sta'zit'*, Lucille, these kids look hungry. You must be on scholarship at Harvard, though Francis is on scholarship you'd never know it to look at him. We got lots of food in, only thing that keeps him from jumpin' out the window when he's home.

(*Indicating* FRANCIS's *room. Coughs.*)

LUCILLE: Turn away from people when you cough, hanh?

(RANDY *and* JUDITH *are pitching the tent under the tree.*)

FRAN: We got brebalone and pepperoni, how 'bout some while horseshit finishes up the eggs? We also got pizzel. Francis loves them but I got a whole box hid.

JUDITH: Oh, I'm sure breakfast will be more than enough.

FRAN: But you don't understand. That's gonna be a Irish breakfast—that's a half a egg, a quarter slice a bacon . . .

(*Scratches.*)

LUCILLE: (*Genteel.*) The Irish mean well, but they don't know how to eat. (*To* FRAN, *genteel manner gone.*) Don't scratch that rash!

FRAN: I'll get everything together.

JUDITH: I'll help you.

FRAN: Well, thank you, sweetheart. What's your name again?

JUDITH: Judith.

(*He lets her go in first and admires her figure. He shakes his head appreciatively and winks at* RANDY *who winks back laughing.* RANDY *continues pitching the tent.*)

LUCILLE: (*To* RANDY, *after* FRAN *and* JUDITH *have exited.*) My son, Donny Pompi, is at Yale, he's a sophomore on the basketball team and in pre-med. He's on a Branford Scholarship. Do you know him?

RANDY: I go to Harvard.

LUCILLE: But he's at Yale. Wouldn't you know him?

RANDY: No, I go to Harvard.

LUCILLE: Is there a difference?

FRAN: (*Coming out of the kitchen, yelling.*) Yo, Francis! Where's your manners? Was you raised in the jungle?

(FRAN *and* JUDITH *come into the yard, he is carrying*

a typing table with a tray of food on it, and she has a
cake and napkins.)

Sometimes I wonder about him, his mother used to say
when he was born he broke the mold, maybe she was
right.

(LUCILLE *starts serving, and repeating absentmindedly*
after FRAN.)

Now, we got here: Coffee cake . . .

LUCILLE: Coffee cake . . .

FRAN: Jelly doughnuts . . .

LUCILLE: Jelly doughnuts . . .

FRAN: Black olives, green olives, pitted black olives—
they're easier to digest, chocolate-covered donuts—

(*He holds one up.*)

—they're Francis' favorites so eat them first and save
him some pimples—

(LUCILLE *is embarrassed.*)

—brebalone, pepperoni, pizzel, biscuits, a fiadone Lucille baked last week and some hot peppers. Don't be
shy.

(*He gives* LUCILLE *a squeeze.*)

RANDY: Thanks

FRAN: Yo, Francis! Where the hell are you?

BUNNY: (*Enters carrying a huge tray of food.*) Here's
breakfast.

(*She is followed out by* HERSCHEL, *who is carrying a*
huge box. BUNNY *notices that the* GEMINIANI *tray is*
on a typing table, so she sets her tray on a trash can
that is under her kitchen window, and drags the
whole thing to the center of the yard. She hands
RANDY *a plate with a fried egg on it.*)

HERSCHEL: (*To* RANDY.) Here's my collection of transfers.

RANDY: Lot of them.

(*Sits down in front of tent to eat.*)

HERSCHEL: (*Following* RANDY.) Four thousand seven
hundred and twenty-two. They start at eighteen seventy-
three.

BUNNY: Biggest collection in the state outside of a museum. That's what my uncle works at the PTC told me.

HERSCHEL: (*Opening one of the albums.*) These are from the old trolleys; they're my favorites, they're buried, you see.

FRAN: Yo, Francis!

FRANCIS: (*Inside, yelling.*) Jesus Christ in Heaven, I'm coming.

FRAN: That's my Ivy League son.

FRANCIS: (*Entering the yard.*) Lot of food.

FRAN: These kids gotta eat. Looka how skinny they are. You don' gotta eat, but that's all you do.

BUNNY: (*About* HERSCHEL, *who is gulping large quantities of food.*) This is another one. Looka him put that food away. Slow down!

(HERSCHEL *chokes.*)

Oh, oh, he's gonna have a asthma attack. I think he does it to punish me. You ever try to sleep with someone havin' a asthma attack in the next room? Drives you bananas. (*To* HERSCHEL, *still gulping.*) Take human bites for Christ' sake! Jesus, it's like a threshing machine: Varroom! Varroom!

FRAN: (*To* JUDITH.) Don' be bashful we got plenty.

JUDITH: I'm not bashful.

FRAN: Eat then!

BUNNY: (*Lunges at* HERSCHEL *with the flyswatter.*) Slow down! The end of the world ain't for another twenty minutes.

(*He slows down.*)

That's right.

(*She looks at his neck.*)

Look at them mosquito bites. You been pickin' them? I says, you been pickin' them?

HERSCHEL: No.

BUNNY: (*Starts to beat him with the flyswatter.*) I told you and I told you not to pick at them, they'll get infected.

FRAN: (*To* RANDY.) You got a appetite, at least.

JUDITH: (*Stands up, to* FRAN.) *Egli è casa dapertutto.*

FRAN: (*Not having understood.*) Hanh?

FRANCIS: She's an Italian major at Radcliffe.

JUDITH: (*Very conversationally.*) *Questo giardin me piace molto. Il nostro camino non furo facile, ma siamo giovane e* . . .

    (*They all look at her, puzzled.*)

LUCILLE: You see dear, that's Harvard Italian. We don't speak that.

FRAN: What did you say?

JUDITH: (*Very embarrassed, sits down.*) Oh, nothing.

FRAN: You see, my people over there was the niggers. The farmhands, they worked the land. We're Abruzzese; so we speak a kinda nigger Italian.

LUCILLE: Oh, Fran! He means it's a dialect.

BUNNY: (*Looking* FRAN *over mock-critically.*) Niggers, hanh? Let me look, let me look. Yeah, I thought so. Suspicious complexion.

    (*She grabs his crotch.* LUCILLE *scowls.*)

FRAN: (*To* BUNNY.) You're not eatin' as much as usual, Bun.

BUNNY: I'm eatin' light, got stage fright. Gotta go a court today.

FRAN: Yeah, why?

LUCILLE: Oh, Bunny, please, not in front of the kids!

BUNNY: That bitch, Mary O'Donnel, attacked me. I was lyin' there, mindin' my own business, and she walks in, drops the groceries, screams, then throws herself on top of me.

FRAN: Where was you lyin'?

BUNNY: In bed.

FRAN: Who's bed?

BUNNY: Whataya mean: Who's bed? Don' matter who's bed. No matter where a person is, that person gotta right to be treated wit courtesy. And her fuckin' husband was no use; he just says: Oh, Mary! turns over and goes back to sleep. So's I hadda fend for myself. She threw herself on top a me, see, so I broke her fuckin' arm. Well, you woulda thought the whole world was fuckin' endin'. She sat there and screamed. I didn't know what to do. It was her house. I didn't know where nothin' was and she's a shitty housekeeper. So I shook her fuckin' husband's arm and said get the fuck up I just broke your fuckin' wife's arm. But he shook me off, you know how these men are, afta, so's I put on my slip, and I put on my dress and got the hell out of there. I'll tell you my ears was burnin'. That witch has gotta tongue like the murders in the Rue Morgue. Then, of all the face, she's got the guts to go to the cops and say I assaulted her. Well, I was real ashamed to have to admit I did go after Mary O'Donnel. She smells like old peanuts. Ever smell her, Lucille?

(LUCILLE *shudders and turns away.*)

So's I gotta go to court and stand trial. But I ain't worried. I gotta uncle on the force, he's a captain. Come on, Herschel. Sam the Jew wan's a see his kid today.

(*She picks up her tray.*)

LUCILLE: (*Not moving.*) I'll help clean up.

JUDITH: (*Jumping up.*) So will I.

BUNNY: Good, 'cause I gotta get ready to meet my judge. I'll show youse where everything is.

HERSCHEL: (*To* RANDY.) Do you want to see my collection of subway posters?

RANDY: (*After some hesitation.*) Well, alright.

HERSCHEL: (*Following* RANDY *into house, with his transfers.*) I have eight hundred . . .

BUNNY: (*Holding door for* LUCILLE.) Right this way, the palace is open.

(FRAN *and* FRANCIS *are left alone.*)

FRAN: I didn't know your friends was comin'.

FRANCIS: I didn't cither.

FRAN: They are your friends, ain't they?

FRANCIS: It isn't that simple.

FRAN: You kids is all nuts, you know that? It was that simple when I was growin' up. You hung out on the corner, see, and the guys you hung out wit was your friends, see? Never stopped to think about it.

FRANCIS: Those guys you hung out with were pretty quick to drop you when you had all the trouble with the bookies, and when mother left. You might say they deserted you.

FRAN: Yeah, yeah, you might say that.

FRANCIS: So then, they weren't friends.

FRAN: 'Course they was. People desert other people, don' make no difference if they're friends or not. I mean, if they wasn't friends to begin wit, you couldn't say they deserted me, could you?

FRANCIS: I guess not.

FRAN: Francis, this Judith, she's really somethin'. I didn't know you had the eye, you know?

FRANCIS: How was your trip to Wildwood?

FRAN: Well, Lucille had a fight wit Aunt Emma. That's why wc came back. It was over water bugs. I didn't see no water bugs. But Lucille said they was everywhere. Aunt Emma thought she was accusin' her of bein' dirty. So we came back.

FRANCIS: Lucille is quite a phenomenon.

FRAN: She's good people, she means well. There ain't nothin' like a woman's company, remember that, my son, there ain't nothin' like a woman. You can think there is. I thought the horses was just as good; hell, I thought the horses was better. But I was wrong. But you gotta be careful of white women. I guess us dagos go afta them; hell, I went afta you mother, and she was white as this Judith, though not near as pretty. But you gotta be careful of them kinda women. A white woman's like a big hole, you can never be sure what's in there. So you be careful, even if she is a Italian major. What do you want for your birthday tomorrow?

(*They start clearing the yard, folding the chairs, putting trash cans back in place, typing table back in the house.*)

FRANCIS: Not to be reminded of it.

FRAN: C'mon, we gotta do somethin'. That's a big occasion: Twenty-one! I know what! You and your guests can have a big dinner out wit Lucille and me to celebrate.

FRANCIS: Oh, I think they'll have left by then.

FRAN: They just got here!

FRANCIS: Well, you know how these kids are nowadays, all nuts. They can't stand to be in one place more than a few hours.

FRAN: But they just pitched their tent under the fig tree, even. No, no, I think you're wrong. I think we're in for a visit. And I hope so, they seem like nice kids.

FRANCIS: Well, they're a little crazy; you know, speed, it twists the mind.

FRAN: Speed?

FRANCIS: Yeah, they're both what we call speed freaks. That's why they're so skinny.

FRAN: You mean they ain't on scholarship?

FRANCIS: They're on speed.

FRAN: Oh my God, them poor kids. They need some help. I'm gonna call Doc Pollicarpo, maybe he could help them.

(RANDY *comes out of* BUNNY's *house, carrying heavy books.*)

RANDY: Herschel lent me his books on subways . . .

(*He sits them down in front of the tent.*)

FRAN: You poor kid.

RANDY: (*Misunderstanding.*) Well . . .

FRAN: No wonder you're so skinny.

RANDY: I'm not that skinny.

FRAN: Some other kid started you on it? Somebody tie you down and force it into your veins?

RANDY: What?

FRAN: Looka his eyes—that's a real strange color. I guess that proves it. You got holes in your arms too?

RANDY: What—why?

FRAN: Come here and sit down, you need rest, you need good food, have a black olive, that's good for speed.

RANDY: (*Shocked.*) Speed?

FRAN: And your sister too? That beautiful young girl on speed? It's a heartbreaker. That stuff it works fast, that's why they call it speed.

(FRANCIS *nods in agreement.*)

You can see it rot the brain.

RANDY: But I'm not on . . .

(*Looks at* FRANCIS, *understanding.* FRANCIS *shrugs.*)

FRANCIS: My father got it in his head you were on speed.

RANDY: I never touch it.

FRAN: (*Understanding.*) Oh, yeah, let's make a fool of the old man. (*Yelling.*) Yo, Lucille, get the hell out of here. (*To* RANDY.) I'm sorry, young man, my son is a little twisted. His mother used to say when he came along he . . .

FRANCIS: (*Has heard this many times.*) . . . when he came along he broke the mold.

FRAN: (*Yelling.*) Lucille! I'm not gonna call you again.

LUCILLE: (*Coming out.*) I'm here. And don't scratch that rash, makes it worse.

FRAN: (*Yelling.*) Yo, Bun, good luck wit the judge! (*To* LUCILLE.) Come on.

> (*Heads toward the kitchen, turns back.*)

Randy, if you're gonna smoke pot out here, do it quiet.

LUCILLE: Oh, I'm sure he's too nice a boy to . . .

FRAN: Lucille, get inna house!

> (FRAN, *with* LUCILLE, *enters house.*)

RANDY: What's all this about speed? That's what I call a sixties mentality.

FRANCIS: Where's Judith?

RANDY: Still cleaning up, I guess.

> (*Pulls out a box of joints.*)

Want some pot?

FRANCIS: Why'd you come? You could have given me some warning.

RANDY: We're not an atomic attack.

> (*He starts boxing with* FRANCIS.)

FRANCIS: You dropped in like one.

> (RANDY *starts doing push-ups.*)

What are you doing?

RANDY: I've been working out every day and taking tiger's milk and nutriment . . .

FRANCIS: What about "Wate-On"?

RANDY: Overrated.

> (*Rolls over on his back.*)

Hey, hold my legs.

FRANCIS: You want to play: "Sunrise at Campobello"?

RANDY: Smart ass, I want to do sit-ups.

> (FRANCIS *kneels and gets a hold of* RANDY's *feet.* RANDY *starts doing sit-ups.*)

FRANCIS: (*Grunts.*) One. . . . Three. . . . You weren't this bad last spring. Even though you did drag me to the gym once—I even had to take a shower—I stumbled around without my glasses, I couldn't see anything, my arms were out like Frankenstein's—they thought I was very strange.

(*He looks down at his arms.*)

My arms are getting tired—and what is this supposed to do?

RANDY: (*Still lying on the ground.*) I'm tired of being skinny.

FRANCIS: You aren't that skinny.

RANDY: I'm grotesque looking. Look at my chest. (*Lifts shirt.*) I look like a newborn duck. I want pectorals, I want biceps, I want shoulders. I want people to stop sniggering when they look at me.

FRANCIS: I don't snigger when I look at you.

RANDY: (*Seriously.*) You're my friend.

(FRANCIS *rises, uncomfortable.* RANDY *lights up a joint.*)

Is there a pool around here? I'd like to go swimming.

FRANCIS: That's a good way to get spinal meningitis. Look, Randy, don't you think I'm an unlikely choice for a jock buddy?

(JUDITH *comes out of the house, and joins them on the stoop.*)

JUDITH: Sorry that took so long, but Lucille didn't do anything, she just stood there and insisted I had to know her son. Hey, Francis, how are you going to entertain me? Is there a museum in walking distance of Philadelphia?

RANDY: That's low priority; we're going to the boat races.

JUDITH: Randy, why don't you simply realize you're pathetic, and stop boring intelligent people?

RANDY: And why don't you treat your hemorrhoids and stop acting like somebody out of Picasso's blue period . . .

(BUNNY *comes out of her house. She is wearing a very tight, white, crocheted suit, and carrying a plastic, flowered shopping bag. She is dressed for court.*)

BUNNY: (*Strikes a "stunning" pose.*) How do I look?

RANDY: Like you can win the case.

BUNNY: You're sweet. Give me a kiss for luck.

> (*Grabs and kisses him. Then yells.*)

Herschel! (*Back to* RANDY.) Look at his skin, look at his eyes; ain't anybody around here looks like you, honey. Like a fuckin' white sheik!

> (HERSCHEL *enters from his house. He is dressed for a visit with his father, in an enormous, ill-fitting brown suit. He is munching on something.*)

Oh, Herschel. Come on.

> (*Brushes his suit roughly.*)

And look you, don' you go havin' no asthma attacks wit your father, he blames me.

JUDITH: (*Suddenly.*) Herschel, Randy'll go with you; he wants to go to the park and study your subway books.

> (*She grabs one of the big books, and drops it in* RANDY's *hands.* RANDY *looks shocked.*)

HERSCHEL: (*Astounded and delighted.*) Really?

JUDITH: (*Before* RANDY *can speak.*) And do you happen to have, by any chance, a map of the subway system? Randy was just saying how much he wanted to study one.

HERSCHEL: Yes!

> (*Digs in his pockets.*)

I have three. This one is the most up to date. You're interested—really interested?

RANDY: Well—I . . .

HERSCHEL: (*Grabbing* RANDY's *arm.*) Come on, I'll walk you to the park!

> (*Drags* RANDY *off down the alley.*)

I know the way and everything . . .

BUNNY: (*Yelling after them.*) Don't fall down, Herschel, that suit costs a fortune to clean. (*To* JUDITH *and* FRANCIS.) Well, I'm off. Wish me luck.

JUDITH AND FRANCIS: (*Smoking a joint.*) Good luck.

BUNNY: (*Crosses to the gate.*) I'll see youse later. I mean I hope I see youse later.

> (*She exits, crossing her fingers for luck.* JUDITH *passes the joint to* FRANCIS. *She goes as if to kiss him, but instead, blows smoke in his mouth. He chokes.*)

FRANCIS: Did you come here to humiliate me?

JUDITH: What?

FRANCIS: What do you call coming here with your brother, climbing over the back fence, walking in on me, half-naked unannounced? And then, Bunny, Herschel—the house is a mess—

JUDITH: That doesn't bother me, really. You oughtn't to be ashamed.

FRANCIS: Oh, I wish you hadn't come, that's all, I wish you hadn't come, you or Randy . . .

JUDITH: But why? I took you seriously, I took—everything seriously and then I hadn't heard—

FRANCIS: I didn't want any more of either of you.

JUDITH: Francis!

FRANCIS: Have you looked at me? I'm fat!

JUDITH: You're not fat!

FRANCIS: Then what do you call this?

(*Makes two rolls of fat with his hands.*)

If I try I can make three—

JUDITH: You're crazy! What does that have to do with anything?

FRANCIS: No attractive person has ever been interested in me . . .

JUDITH: Well, maybe they thought you were a bore.

FRANCIS: "Love enters through the eyes," that's Dante . . .

JUDITH: And he liked little girls.

FRANCIS: Look, I don't know what you see when you look at me. I've made myself a monster—and tomorrow I'm to be twenty-one and all I can feel is myself sinking.

JUDITH: But Francis . . .

FRANCIS: Look, I don't want to discuss it now, not here, not with my father around the corner. Now I'm going into my room and play some music. Then I'm going for a walk. I would appreciate it if you'd strike your tent and gather up your things and your brother and leave before I return.

(*He goes into his room, and puts on some quiet music.* JUDITH *is left alone. Suddenly,* RANDY *appears over the fence.*)

RANDY: This is very mysterious.

(*Blackout.*)

Scene 2

(*Scene the same. Later that day. It is early evening. During the scene night falls.*

FRAN *is cooking spaghetti in his kitchen. He is singing "Strangers in the Night."*

RANDY *is inside the tent.*

FRANCIS *enters through the gate. Sees the tent. He slams the gate.*)

FRANCIS: They're still here.

FRAN: (*From inside house.*) Yo, Francis, is that you?

FRANCIS: Yes.

FRAN: I'm in the kitchen.

(FRANCIS *goes inside.*)

Where have you been?

FRANCIS: Where is she now?

FRAN: In your room. Why don't you go in to see her?

FRANCIS: Didn't it ever occur to you that I don' want you to interfere . . .

FRAN: (*Smiles.*) "Strangers in the night . . ."

(FRANCIS *goes into his room.* HERSCHEL *comes bounding in from the alley.*)

HERSCHEL: (*To* FRAN.) Hi. Where's Randy?

FRAN: In his tent. (*Yells.*) Yo, Randy! You got company.

(RANDY *peeks out of the tent.* HERSCHEL *sits down by the tent.*)

HERSCHEL: Hi. I just got back from my father's. He wanted me to stay over but I faked a petit mal and he let me go.

RANDY: A petit mal?

HERSCHEL: You know, a fit. A little one. I stumbled around and I slobbered and I told him everything was black. He got worried. I told him I left my medicine back here, so he gave me money for a cab. I took the bus.

(FRANCIS *and* JUDITH *appear in window.*)

Like, I was wondering, would you like to come with me

to, like, see the engine? It's not far from here. It's alright if you don't want to come, like, I mean, I understand, you know? Everybody can't be interested in Public Transportation, it's not that interesting, you know? So, like, I understand if you aren't interested but would you like to come?

RANDY: (*Who has gotten a towel and toilet case out of his knapsack.*) Can we have dinner first?

HERSCHEL: You mean you'll come? How about that! I'll go and change—I'll be right back.

(*He starts to run, trips over his own feet, falls, picks himself up, and runs into his house.*)

JUDITH: (*From window.*) I see you're about to be broadened.

RANDY: What could I do? (*To* FRAN *in kitchen.*) Mr. Geminiani!

FRAN: (*Appears in kitchen window.*) Fran, it's Fran!

RANDY: Fran. Can I take a shower?

FRAN: Be my guest. You got a towel?

RANDY: Yes.

(*He goes into the house.*)

FRAN: (*Comes out, yelling.*) Yo, Francis!

FRANCIS: (*He and* JUDITH *are right behind him.*) Jesus Christ, I'm right here.

FRAN: That's my Ivy League son. Look, once in a while when your lips get tired, go in and stir the spaghettis, hanh? I'm going to get Lucille.

FRANCIS: She lives around the corner, why can't she come over herself?

FRAN: Don' get smart and show some respect. She believes in the boogie man.

(*He throws the kitchen towel in through the window, like he was making a jump shot.*)

Yes! Two points!

(*Holds up two fingers like cuckold's horns.*)

"Strangers in the night . . ."

(*He exits through the gate.*)

JUDITH: Lucille and your father are—well, you know, aren't they?

FRANCIS: I don't know, they drink an awful lot of coffee.

JUDITH: Stimulates the gonads—

(*She embraces* FRANCIS *and kisses him. He looks uncomfortable.*)

What's the matter?

FRANCIS: I'm sorry.

JUDITH: Sorry about what?

(*He looks away.*)

You know, I think you are an eternal adolescent, a German Adolescent, a German Romantic Adolescent. You were born out of context, you'd have been much happier in the forties of the last century when it was eternally twilight.

FRANCIS: Do I detect a veiled reference to *Zwielicht* by Eichendorf?

JUDITH: I took Basic European Literature also, and did better than you did.

FRANCIS: You did not.

JUDITH: I got the highest mark on the objective test: 98! What did you get?

(*She laughs.*)

FRANCIS: (*Bantering with her.*) My SAT verbal and achievement tests were higher than yours.

JUDITH: How do you know?

FRANCIS: I looked them up in the office. I pretended to go faint, and while the registrar ran for water, I looked at your file.

JUDITH: (*Entering into his game.*) I find that hard to believe; I had the highest score in the verbal at St. Paul's and also in the English Achievement Test.

FRANCIS: That's what it said alongside your IQ.

JUDITH: (*Taken aback in spite of herself.*) My IQ?

FRANCIS: Very interesting that IQ. It was recorded in bright red ink. There was also a parenthesis, in which someone had written: "Poor girl, but she had great determination."

JUDITH: I find jokes about IQ's in poor taste.

FRANCIS: Then you are an adolescent, a German Adolescent, a German Romantic Adolescent.

JUDITH: And before this edifying discussion you were about to say: "Fuck you, Judith."

FRANCIS: Don't put it that way . . .

JUDITH: But more or less it was get lost, see you later, oh yes, have a nice summer—and maybe, just maybe, I'll tell you why later. You seem to want to skip that part, the why.

(*She picks up the end of a garden hose, and points it at* FRANCIS *like a machine gun, and with a Humphrey Bogart voice, says:*)

Look, I came to see you, that's ballsy, now you've got to reciprocate and tell me why . . .

(*She puts down the hose, and the accent.*)

Do I bore you? Do you think I'm ugly? Do I have bad breath?

FRANCIS: Oh, come on!

JUDITH: Hey, Francis, we're just alike, can't you see that?

FRANCIS: (*Indicates the house and yard.*) Oh yeah.

JUDITH: Two overachievers. Really. I know my family is better off than yours; but we're just alike, and there was something last winter and now you're telling me . . .

FRANCIS: Look, I'm going to be twenty-one tomorrow. Well . . . I don't know what to say.

JUDITH: Is there a reason?

FRANCIS: I don't think I can say.

JUDITH: That doesn't make any sense.

FRANCIS: I think I'm queer.

JUDITH: Why don't we back up a bit. I said: "We're just alike et cetera," and you said you were going to be twenty-one tomorrow, and I looked at you with deep-set, sea-blue eyes, and you said . . .

FRANCIS: I think I'm queer.

JUDITH: (*Laughs.*) Well, I guess we can't get around it. Do you want to amplify? I mean this seems like quite a leap from what I remember of those long, sweet, ecstatic nights, naked in each other's young arms, clinging to . . .

FRANCIS: We fucked. Big deal. That's what kids are supposed to do. And be serious.

JUDITH: I am serious. Is there a particular boy?

FRANCIS: Yes.

JUDITH: An adolescent, a German Adolescent . . .

FRANCIS: Not German, no.

JUDITH: Do I know him?

(FRANCIS *doesn't answer.*)

Reciprocal?

FRANCIS: It was just this spring. He began to haunt me. We became friends. We talked a lot—late in my room when you were studying. Well, I don't know, and you see— I've had, well, crushes before. I dreamed of him. It's not reciprocal, no, he doesn't know, but it became more and more obvious to me. I mean, I'd look at him, and then some other boy would catch my eye and I'd think—you see?

JUDITH: Well. I suppose I could start teaching you the secrets of makeup.

(FRANCIS *turns away, annoyed.*)

Well, how do you expect me to react? You seem to think I ought to leap out the window because of it. But it's like you're suddenly turning to me and saying you are from Mars. Well, you might be, but I don't see much evidence and I can't see what difference it makes. I'm talking about you and me, I and thou and all that. Alright, maybe you do have an eye for the boys, well so do I, but you . . . you are special to me. I wouldn't throw you over just because a hockey player looked good, why do you have to give me up?

FRANCIS: I don't think that makes any sense, Judith. I mean, if I were from Mars, it would make a difference, I'd have seven legs and talk a different language and that's how I feel now.

(JUDITH *embraces him.*)

Don't touch me so much, Judith, and don't look at me . . .

JUDITH: Then you're afraid. That explains that fat and ugly nonsense and this sudden homosexual panic. You're afraid that anyone who responds to you will make demands you can't meet. You're afraid you'll fail . . .

FRANCIS: Good Evening Ladies and Gentlemen, Texaco Presents: "Banality on Parade!"

JUDITH: You're afraid to venture. That's why you've enshrined someone who doesn't respond to you, probably doesn't even know you're interested. If the relationship never happens, you are never put to the test and can't fail. The Overachiever's Great Nightmare!

FRANCIS: That's crazy!

JUDITH: I bet this boy who draws you is some Harvard sprite, a dew-touched freshman . . .

FRANCIS: He was a freshman.

JUDITH: In Randy's class and that proves it. Look at Randy—what kind of response could someone like that have but the giggles? And you know that. You're afraid of commitment. And remember what Dante says about those who refuse to make commitments. They're not even in Hell, but are condemned to run about the outskirts for eternity.

(FRANCIS, *who has heard enough, has stuck his head inside* BUNNY's *kitchen window, and brought it down over his neck like a guillotine.* JUDITH *now runs over to the fence, and starts climbing to the top.*)

Ed io che reguardai vidi una insegna che girando correva tanta ratta, che d'ogni posa me parea indegna . . . !

(*She leaps off the fence.* FRANCIS *runs to her aid.*)

FRANCIS: Judith! Jesus Christ!

JUDITH: (*As he helps her up.*) You see? I ventured, I made the great leap and remained unscathed.

(HERSCHEL *runs out of his house, dressed in his old pants and torn sweat shirt, carrying one sneaker.*)

HERSCHEL: I heard a noise. Is Randy alright?

FRANCIS: Judith, you're alright?

JUDITH: Good as nude!

(*Limps over to stoop and sits.*)

FRANCIS: Oh shit! I forgot to stir the spaghetti. Now they'll all stick together . . .

(*Runs into the kitchen, runs out again.*)

You're sure you're alright?

JUDITH: Stir the spaghetti. We don't want them sticking together.

(FRANCIS *goes into the kitchen.*)

HERSCHEL: You're the one who fell?

JUDITH: You might put it that way.

HERSCHEL: (*Sits down beside* JUDITH. *Puts on his other sneaker.*) I do that. One time I fell while I was having an asthma attack. My mother called the ambulance. She has, like, an uncle who's a driver. They rushed me to the hospital. Like, you know, the siren screaming? That was two years ago, right before I went to high school. It was St. Agnes Hospital over Track 37 on the A, the AA, the AA 1 through 7 and the B express lines, maybe you passed it? I didn't get, like, hurt falling, you know. Still, my mother asked me what I wanted most in the whole world, you know? I told her and she let me ride the subway for twelve whole hours. Like, she rode them with me. She had to stay home from work for two days.

JUDITH: (*Crosses to tent, and gets a bandana out of her knapsack. She sits down, and starts cleaning her knee, which she'd hurt in leaping off the fence.*) Why are you so interested in the subways?

HERSCHEL: (*Joins her on the ground.*) Oh, not just the subways. I love buses too, you know? And my favorites are, well, you won't laugh? The trolleys. They are very beautiful. There's a trolley graveyard about two blocks from here. I was thinking, like maybe Randy would like to see that, you know? I could go see the engine any time. The trolley graveyard is well, like, I guess, beautiful, you know? Really. They're just there, like old creatures everyone's forgotten, some of them rusted out, and some of them on their sides, and one, the old thirty-two, is like standing straight up as though sayin', like, I'm going to stand here and be myself, no matter what. I talk to them. Oh, I shouldn't have said that. Don't tell my mother, please? It's, you know, like people who go to castles and look for, for, well, like, knights in shining armor, you know? That past was beautiful and somehow, like, pure. The same is true of the trolleys. I follow the old thirty-two route all the time. It leads right to the graveyard where the thirty-two is buried, you know? It's like, well, fate. The tracks are half-covered with filth and pitch, new pitch like the city pours on. It oozes in the summer and people walk on it, but you can see the tracks and you see, like, it's true, like, old things last,

good things last, like, you know? The trolleys are all
filthy and half-covered and rusted out and laughed at,
and even though they're not much use to anybody and
kind of ugly like, by most standards, they're, like,
they're, well, I guess, beautiful, you know?

(RANDY *enters, having finished his shower. He flicks
his towel at* HERSCHEL.)

RANDY: Hey, that shower is a trip. I should have taken my
surfboard.

HERSCHEL: Like, you should have used our shower, it's in
much better shape, you know? Next time you want to
take a shower, let me know.

JUDITH: Well, there's one cosmic issue settled.

RANDY: (*Crosses to kitchen window.*) Mmmmm. That
sauce smells good.

FRANCIS: (*Appears in kitchen window.*) We call it gravy.

RANDY: When will it be ready?

FRANCIS: Soon. (*Disappears inside house.*)

HERSCHEL: (*To* RANDY.) Then we can go to the graveyard.
(RANDY *looks surprised.*)
See, like, I decided it might be, well, more fun, if we saw
all the dead trolleys, you know, and leave the engine for
later.

RANDY: Whatever you say. (*Back to the window.*) Francis,
look—is there something wrong?

FRAN: (*Offstage yelling.*) Yo, Francis! We're here.
(*Comes in from gate.*)
Hi, kids.
(*Going into house.*)
You stir that stuff?

FRANCIS: (*From inside.*) Yeah.
(RANDY *gets a shirt out of his knapsack and crawls
into the tent.* HERSCHEL *starts crawling into the tent.*)

RANDY: Herschel . . . careful!

HERSCHEL: (*Inside the tent.*) I'm careful.

LUCILLE: (*Offstage.*) Judith!

RANDY: Well, sit over there.
(HERSCHEL *plops down, blocking the entire entrance
with his back.* LUCILLE *comes into yard with a
sweater and jacket. She approaches* JUDITH.)

LUCILLE: Judy, I brought you a sweater. I thought you might be chilly later tonight and I didn't know if you brought one with you.

JUDITH: Thank you.

LUCILLE: (*Puts sweater around* JUDITH's *shoulders.*) It's real sheep's wool. My friend, Diane, gave it to me. Her daughter, Joann, is a model for KYZ-TV in Center City—special shift. She's a Cancer, so am I, that's why Fran says I'm a disease. My son, Donny, he's at Yale in pre-med, Branford Scholarship. I think he'll make a wonderful doctor, don't Yale make wonderful doctors?

JUDITH: I'm sure I don't know.

(FRAN *comes out with* FRANCIS. *He is carrying a large fold-up metal table.*)

FRAN: Make yourself useful, Lucille. I got the table, go get the plates.

RANDY: (*Getting away from* HERSCHEL, *who is hovering around him.*) I'll help set up.

(LUCILLE *goes into the house, and returns with a tray, with plates, napkins, cutlery, glasses, bug spray, and a "plastic lace" tablecloth.*)

FRAN: How was your shower?

RANDY: I expected to see seals and Eskimos any minute.

FRAN: At least you got out of the bathroom alive. There are beach chairs in the cellar, why don't you get them? Francis, show this young man where the beach chairs is in the cellar.

(FRAN *goes back into house,* FRANCIS, RANDY, *and* HERSCHEL *go past the house to the cellar, and* LUCILLE *starts setting the table.*)

LUCILLE: You know Judy, my daughter, she's a dental technician at The Graduate Hospital—special shift. She wanted to go to Yale, but she couldn't get in. She thought it was her teeth. They're buck. She said the woman looked at her funny the whole time at the interview. Now I told her she should just carry herself with poise and forget her teeth. Y'know what she said to me: how can I forget my teeth; they're in my mouth! Not a very poised thing to say. That's why she didn't get into Yale: No poise. That's why she ain't got no husband, either. Do the people at Yale think teeth are important?

JUDITH: I don't know anything about Yale.

LUCILLE: But what do you think?

JUDITH: Yes, I think teeth are very important for success in life.

(*She is setting out cutlery.*)

At the prep school I attended they had us practice our bite three times a day.

LUCILLE: (*Politely, taken in.*) Oh?

JUDITH: We would bite off a poised bite, and chew with poise, and then sing a C major scale whilst we swilled the food in our mouths. I could even sing songs whilst swilling food with poise. In fact, I once sang the first aria of the Queen of the Night while swilling half a hamburger and a bucket of french fries. . . . Of course, remaining utterly poised, or "pwased," as we say at Harvard.

LUCILLE: Oh.

(*She walks around the table spraying insect repellant.*)

It kills them very quickly.

(FRANCIS, RANDY, *and* HERSCHEL *enter the yard with beach chairs and old kitchen chairs, which they proceed to set up.*)

RANDY: (*To* FRANCIS, *continuing a conversation.*) C'mon, Francis, what's going on?

FRAN: (*From the kitchen.*) Yo, Lucille, give me a hand!

JUDITH: I'll be glad to help.

(*Runs into the kitchen.*)

RANDY: Come on, Francis, I mean I'm three years younger than you—so tell me . . .

(*Simultaneously,* LUCILLE *and* HERSCHEL *approach* RANDY.)

HERSCHEL: Would you like to see my models of the trolley fleet of 1926?

LUCILLE: (*Giving* RANDY *a jacket.*) I brought you one of my son's jackets, because I thought you might get cold later and I didn't know if you brought one wit you. My son's girl friend bought it for him at Wanamaker's.

(FRAN *and* JUDITH *come back out.*)

BUNNY: (*Calling from inside her house.*) Yo! Where is everybody?

FRAN: Yo, Bun! We're out here.

(BUNNY *comes stumbling out of her house. She has been drinking. She never stops moving, constantly dancing and leaping about, she cries out in war hoops and screams of victory.*)

BUNNY: I won! I won! I wanna kiss from everybody but Lucille!

(*She goes around kissing everyone, except* LUCILLE. *She gets to* RANDY.)

Oh, you're such a honeybun, I could eat you.

(*She kisses him, then grabs his crotch.*)

I'll skip Francis too.

RANDY: Wanna smoke, Herschel?

HERSCHEL: Sure.

(*They sit down by the tent,* HERSCHEL *sitting as far away from* BUNNY *as possible.*)

BUNNY: Break out the horsepiss, Fran!

(FRAN *goes into the kitchen for liquor.*)

Jesus Christ in heaven, I won!

FRAN: (*Returns with bottle of Scotch.*) How do you want it?

BUNNY: Straight up the dark and narrow path, honey.

(*She takes a swig from the bottle.*)

You shoulda seen me in that courtroom, I told them all about it, that bitch didn't even have the decency to fart before throwin' herself on top a me. I coulda been ruptured for life, I says, and she's a Catholic, I couldn't believe it. Catholics got self-control.

LUCILLE: (*To* JUDITH.) Well, good Catholics have self-control. Sister Mary Emaryd, my friend, she used to work at Wanamaker's before she married Christ. She . . .

BUNNY: (*To* RANDY.) That judge looked at me, let me tell you.

LUCILLE: She would allow herself to go to the bathroom only twice a day.

BUNNY: (*To* FRAN.) I felt twenty again.

LUCILLE: (*To* JUDITH.) She said: Urgency is all in the mind.

BUNNY: (*To* RANDY.) I felt like a fuckin' young filly in heat. Look, honey, you ever see my boobies swayin'?

(*She sways them for* RANDY. *He giggles.*)

LUCILLE: (*To* FRANCIS.) I go to the bathroom more than that, yet I go to Mass every Sunday . . .

BUNNY: (*To* RANDY.) You smokin' that killer weed, hon?

RANDY: Sure. You want some?

BUNNY: Don' need that shit. Don' need nothin' to get high, I'm high naturally. I was born floatin'.

(*She leans on table, almost knocking everything over.*)

Come and dance with me, baby.

(*She grabs a very reluctant* RANDY.)

C'mon! "Flat foot floozie with the floy, floy . . ."

(*They start doing the jitterbug, and* RANDY *bumps into* BUNNY, *knocking the breath out of her.*)

Fuck you, world! Fuck you, Mary O'Donnel! Fuck you, Sam the Jew! Fuck you, Catholic Church! Fuck you, Mom, I won! You shoulda seen them look at me, I felt like a fuckin' starlit. My boobies swayin', and when I walked to the stand I did my strut; my fuckin' bitch-in-heat strut. Come on, Lucille, can you strut like this?

(*She comes up behind* LUCILLE, *and "bumps" her.* LUCILLE *starts swearing in Italian.* BUNNY *turns to* JUDITH.)

Come on, honey, what's your name, can you strut like this? I can fuckin' strut up a storm. My hips have made many a wave in their time, honey, many a wave! I sent out hurricanes, I sent out earthquakes, I sent out tidal waves from my fuckin' hips. Yo, Fran!

FRAN: Yo, Bun!

BUNNY: Remember when I was in that fuckin' community theatre down at Gruen Recreation Center?

FRAN: Seventeenth Street.

LUCILLE: Sixteenth and Wolf!

BUNNY: I played Sadie Thompson in that play. I let my hair grow down long. It was real long then, not dyed shit yellow like it is now. I fuckin' got hair like hepatitis now. I played that part! I hadda sheer slip on and my legs, Jesus Christ, my legs! I fuckin' felt the earth tremble when I walked, I played that bitch like Mount Vesuvius and the clappin', honey, the clappin'!

FRAN: You were a big hit, yep.

BUNNY: At the curtain call, I held my boobs out like this: (*She sticks out her chest.*) . . . and they screamed, honey, those fuckin' grown men screamed! (*To* RANDY.) Feel 'em, honey, feel these grapes of mine. *She puts* RANDY's *hand on her boobs.*)

RANDY: Mrs. Weinberger!

BUNNY: They're still nice, hanh? I fuckin' won that case! (*She has to sit down.*)
Then I married Sam the Jew and bore Herschel. Look at the fruit of my loins, look, this is one of the earthquakes I sent out of my hips. Boom! Boom! When he walks you can hear him around the corner, but he's a fuckin' genius at least. He's got an IQ of 187 or 172, dependin' on which test you use, despite his father!

LUCILLE: (*This has been building up.*) Che disgraziat'! (*She runs into the house followed by* FRAN.)

BUNNY: (*Looking after* FRAN.) I coulda had . . . well, almost anybody, more or less. I coulda been a chorus girl, then I met Sam the Kike and that was that. He had the evil eye, that Hebe, them little pointy eyes. He'd screw them up like he was lookin' for blackheads, then, suddenly, they'd go real soft and get big. I was a sucker for them fuckin' eyes. He's a jeweller, called me his jewel. Sam the Jew. I smell like old peanuts!

RANDY: (*Offering her the joint.*) Sure you don't want some?

BUNNY: No, honey, I got me some coke for a giddy sniff. I get it from my uncle on the force; he gives me a discount, he's a captain.
(*She suddenly sees* HERSCHEL *smoking behind the tent.*)
Hey, wait a minute! You been smokin' that shit? Herschel! Have you been smokin' that shit?

HERSCHEL: (*Butts the point quickly.*) No . . .

BUNNY: Don' you lie to me. Didn't I tell you never to smoke that shit? It'll fuckin' rot your brain and you'll be more of a vegetable than you already are. God damn you, I'll beat the shit outta you!

> (*She lunges for him.*)

HERSCHEL: (*Scurrying out of her way.*) Come on!

BUNNY: Come on???? Come on??? I'll come on, you fuckin' four-eyed fat-assed creep, I'll come on!

> (*She grabs the bottle of Scotch, and chases* HERSCHEL *into the house. We see them in their kitchen window. She is beating the shit out of* HERSCHEL.)

Twelve fuckin' hours! Twelve fuckin' hours I was in labor wit you, screamin' on that table and for what? To fuckin' find you smokin' dope?

> (*His asthma attack is starting.*)

That's right! Go ahead! Have a fuckin' asthma attack, cough your fuckin' head off! See if I care!

> (*She disappears inside the house.* HERSCHEL *is at the window, gasping for air, until he realizes that she has gone. His asthma attack miraculously stops. He disappears. During* HERSCHEL's *attack everyone on stage stares at him, horrified.* RANDY *passes* JUDITH *the joint. She refuses it.* FRANCIS *takes a toke, and passes it back to* RANDY. BUNNY, *inside her house, is heard singing at the out-of-tune piano. Offstage.*)

"Moon river, wider than a mile
I'm screwing up in style some day . . ."

> (*FRAN and* LUCILLE *come in from the house. He has a big bowl of spaghetti, and she is carrying a very elaborate antipasto.*)

FRAN: (*Sitting down at the head of the table.*) Well, I hope everybody's gotta appetite, 'cause there's enough to feed the Chinee army and ain't no room to keep it either.

LUCILLE: (*Sniffing the air.*) I think the Delassandroes down the alley are burning their children's clothing again. That smell!

> (*RANDY and* FRANCIS *break up, and put out the joint.*)

FRAN: You all got plates, I'll serve. Francis, you get the gravy pot, I'll pass the macs, we also got antipast'; made special by Lucille Pompi . . .

(LUCILLE *simpers.*)

and Lucille Pompi's antipast' is a delicacy.

(*He gives* LUCILLE *a hug.* FRANCIS *arrives with the gravy pot.* FRAN *is serving.*)

And here we got the gravy meat: Veal, sausage, lamb, meatballs, and brasiole.

(*He passes plate to* JUDITH.)

JUDITH: Oh, that's too much!

FRAN: Your stomach's bigger than your eyes. We also got wine. Francis!

(RANDY *snaps his fingers at* FRANCIS, *as if to say: Hop to it.* FRANCIS *goes into house for wine.* FRAN *passes plate to* LUCILLE.)

Lucille?

LUCILLE: No thank you, Fran, I'll just pick.

(*He passes the plate to* RANDY.)

Randy?

(LUCILLE *is busy making sure everyone is taken care of.* FRANCIS *has returned and is going around the table pouring wine.* FRAN *serves a plate to* FRANCIS.)

Francis?

FRANCIS: I'm not so hungry tonight.

FRAN: (*Keeping the plate for himself.*) Oh, we better get down on our knees, we've just witnessed a miracle.

LUCILLE: Oh, Fran, don't blaspheme.

FRAN: (*Everyone is eating but* LUCILLE.) Sure you don' wan' none, Lucille?

LUCILLE: I'll just pick out of your plate.

(*She then proceeds to pick a large piece of lettuce from* FRAN's *plate and stuffs it in her mouth.*)

FRAN: (*To* RANDY *and* JUDITH.) You kids enjoying your stay?

(LUCILLE *now gets a forkful of spaghetti from* FRAN's *plate and proceeds to eat that.*)

This is your first time in South Philly, I bet. You ought to get Francis to take you around tomorrow and see the sights. Them sights'll make you nearsighted, that's how pretty South Philly is.

(LUCILLE *has speared more lettuce from* FRAN, *and he grabs her wrist.*)

Yo, Lucille, I'll get you a plate.

LUCILLE: (*She frees her hand, stuffs the lettuce in her mouth, and says:*) No, thank you, Fran, I'm not hungry.

(*She notices something on* JUDITH's *plate, picks it, and eats it.* JUDITH *and* RANDY *are amazed.*)

FRAN: Lucille! Let that kid alone and fill your own plate.

LUCILLE: (*With a full mouth.*) Fran, I'm not hungry!

(*She sees a tomato wedge on* RANDY's *plate. She picks up her fork, and pounces on the tomato.*)

FRAN: Lucille!

LUCILLE: He wasn't going to eat that.

FRAN: How do you know?

LUCILLE: Look how skinny he is.

(HERSCHEL *appears in his doorway.*)

FRAN: Hi ya, Herschel.

(*Everyone greets him.*)

You feel better?

HERSCHEL: I guess.

FRAN: Well, get a plate and sit down!

HERSCHEL: You don't mind?

FRAN: You're the guest of honor.

(HERSCHEL *comes down to the table, to the empty chair, and starts pulling it around the table, making* FRANCIS *get out of the way, until he is next to* RANDY. RANDY, JUDITH, *and* LUCILLE, *who are all sitting on the long side of the table have to scoot over to make room for* HERSCHEL. *He sits down next to* RANDY.)

HERSCHEL: (*To* RANDY.) Can we still . . .

RANDY: Yeah, yeah, sure.

(FRAN *has piled spaghetti and sauce for* HERSCHEL. *He is trying to pass the plate to* HERSCHEL, *but* LUCILLE *snatches it, gets a forkful of pasta, and then passes the plate on. Everyone, except* FRANCIS, *is eating.*)

FRAN: Gonna be night soon. And tomorrow's my son's birthday. Seems like yesterday he was my little buddy, on the chubby side, but cute all the same, and tomorrow he's gonna be—what? Six? Gonna be a man tomorrow. Looka him squirm. Everybody hits twenty-one sooner or later, 'cept me, I'm still nineteen. *Salute!*

(*They all lift their glasses in a toast and drink, except* HERSCHEL, *who keeps shoveling it down.*)

Judith, look, you can see that fig tree wave in the wind if you squint. Francis, remember the day I planted it? I got the sledgehammer out of the cellar, people that was here before us left it, and I broke that concrete. His mother, she'd had enough of both of us, and took off headin' down south. She was like a bird had too much of winter. Met a nice Southern man.

LUCILLE: Protestant.

FRAN: They're married. Can't have kids though; she had a hysterectomy just before she left. It's a shame. She's good people and so's this man, she shoulda had kids wit him. He's real normal, nice lookin', don' cough like I do, don' get rashes neither, and to him, horses is for ridin'!

(*He breaks himself up. Then starts to cough.* LUCILLE *is picking out of* JUDITH's *plate. Big forkful of spaghetti.*)

They'd have had nice kids. The kind that woulda made her happy. She's one of them people that like to fade inna the air. Don' wanna stand out. Francis and me, well, we stand out. Don't wanna, understand, but we talk too loud, cough, scratch ourselves, get rashes, are kinda big. You have to notice us. Don' have to like us but you gotta see us.

(LUCILLE *pats* FRAN's *cheek lovingly.*)

Well, his mother, she was good people and meant well, but she wasn't too easy wit us, she wanted a home in the suburbs, all the Sears and Roebuck catalogs lined up against the wall, and two white kids, just like her, white like the fog, kids you hadda squint to see. Well, this one day, she packed her bags, see, rented a big truck and took everything, even my portable TV. (*He laughs at the "joke."*) I guess it'll be cool tonight. She left me, you see, she left me. So I come out here and smash that concrete. Next day I planted the fig tree. I went to the one guy in the neighborhood would give me the time of

day, borrowed thirty dollars and bought this tree, the
dirt, some fertilizer . . .

(LUCILLE's *hand is in his plate again.*)

Jesus Christ in Heaven! Lucille! Would you fill your
own plate and stop actin' like the poor relative??!

LUCILLE: (*She quickly stuffs food in her mouth.*) Stop
pickin' on me! I ain't actin' like the poor relative!

FRAN: Whataya call pickin' at his plate, then pickin' at my
plate, then pickin' at his plate, then pickin' at her plate,
for Christ' sake, hanh? Stop pickin'! Take! Take wit
both hands, it's there, why you act like there ain't plenty
when there is, hanh? What's the matter you???!!!!

(*He has taken two enormous handfuls of spaghetti out
of the bowl and dropped them into* LUCILLE's *plate.*)

LUCILLE: (*Screaming.*) Eh! Sta'zit'!

FRAN: (*Shaking her plate under her nose.*) Mangi taci' o—

LUCILLE: (*Stands up and screams at him.*) Fongoul!

(*She runs out of the yard.*)

FRAN: Jesus Christ! See you kids later. (*Yells.*) Lucille, I
was only kidding!

(*Runs off after her.*)

HERSCHEL: (*Rising, to* RANDY.) I'm finished.

RANDY: (*With a sigh.*) Alright. (*To* JUDITH *and* FRANCIS.)
See you later.

(HERSCHEL *and* RANDY *exit through the alley.*)

JUDITH: (*Rises, starts stacking.*) I'll put the dishes in the
sink.

(*She suddenly drops the plates on the table.*)

It's Randy, isn't it?

BUNNY: (*Stumbles out of her house. She is in her robe and
nightgown again.*) Hi, you two. You got some more
horsepiss? I'm out.

FRANCIS: I'll look, Bunny.

(*Runs into his kitchen.*)

BUNNY: You look sort of peaked, hon, upset over somethin'? A man, maybe?

JUDITH: Maybe.

BUNNY: Well, take my advice and heat up the coke bottle;
men ain't worth shit, not shit.

FRANCIS: (*Coming out with a bottle.*) Here, Bunny.

BUNNY: (*Takes a slug of whiskey.*) You're a saint, just a fuckin' saint.

> (*She collapses in a heap, completely out.* FRANCIS *gets her under each arm, and* JUDITH *holds the door open.* FRANCIS *starts dragging her back in.* BUNNY, *coming to for a moment:*)

Shit! Why am I such a whale? Why ain't I a porpoise or a dolphin? Why do I gotta be a whale wit hepatitis hair?

FRANCIS: Come on, Bunny, I'll help you inside . . .

BUNNY: You're a saint, a fuckin' saint.

> (*They disappear inside* BUNNY's *house.* FRANCIS *returns immediately.*)

JUDITH: You and Randy . . . !

FRANCIS: Me and Randy nothing. He doesn't know a thing about it. He's been following me around all day asking why I won't look at him. What can I say? We were friends, and he can't understand . . .

> (RANDY *and* HERSCHEL *have reentered from the alley.*)

Well, who can understand . . .

JUDITH: What about the trolleys?

HERSCHEL: A different guard was there. We can go tomorrow though, my friend'll be there.

RANDY: (*To* JUDITH.) What's the matter?

JUDITH: (*To* FRANCIS, *indicating* RANDY.) Just look at him. (*Peals of laughter.*) And look at you.

HERSCHEL: (*To* RANDY.) It's early yet, would you like to see my books on ornamental tiles . . .

RANDY: Good night, Herschel.

HERSCHEL: I guess everybody can't be interested in . . .

RANDY: (*Pushes him inside, and closes the door behind him.*) Good night, Herschel!

HERSCHEL: Good night, Randy.

> (*Disappears inside his house.*)

RANDY: (*To* FRANCIS *and* JUDITH.) Now, what's going on?

> (JUDITH *continues laughing.*)

Francis?

FRANCIS: Alright, Judith, why don't you just tell him?

JUDITH: And you don't want him told? What future is there for you if he doesn't even know? Happiness begins with knowledge, doesn't it?

FRANCIS: If it does, you are in a lot of trouble!
 (*Runs into his house, slamming the door.*)
RANDY: Hey look, this is unfair. What's going on?
JUDITH: I have discovered this fine day that I have a rival
 for the affections of one Francis Geminiani.
RANDY: Oh yeah? I'm not surprised.
JUDITH: What?
RANDY: Well, Judy, you're kind of a bitch, you know. I
 mean, talking in Italian to his father and Lucille—
 nothing personal, I mean . . .
JUDITH: Well, you are a creep, aren't you?
RANDY: And I mean like forcing me to look at those sub-
 way books with Herschel, just so you could be alone
 with Francis. So who's this rival? Somebody from the
 neighborhood who can make good gravy?
 (*He is laughing, and crawling inside the tent.*)
JUDITH: (*Starts rubbing her hands together gleefully.*)
 Well, the person in question is in the yard right now,
 under the fig tree, and it isn't me.
RANDY: (*Pops his head out.*) What?
 (*Blackout.*)

ACT TWO

Scene 1

(*Scene the same. The next morning, about nine o'clock.*

As the lights come up, FRANCIS *is seen in his window, staring at the tent.* JUDITH *is asleep in a sleeping bag outside the tent, and* RANDY *is inside.*

BUNNY *comes out of her house, dressed in her ragged housecoat, she is disoriented and mumbles to herself.* FRANCIS *sees her but says nothing.*

She is carrying a brown paper bag. She disappears into the alley, and is next seen climbing up the telephone pole behind the alley wall. She has to stop every few rungs and almost falls off once or twice. Finally she gets to the top of the alley wall, still clutching the bag, shakes her fist at the heavens and prepares to jump.

A dog is heard barking in the distance.)

FRANCIS: (*Yelling from his window.*) Hey, Bunny! What are you doing?

BUNNY: (*Peering in his direction, trying to bring him into focus.*) Hanh?

FRANCIS: What are you doing?

BUNNY: Who's 'at?

FRANCIS: Francis next door. Come down, you'll hurt yourself.

BUNNY: What are ya, blind? You go to Harvard and can't tell I'm gonna jump?

FRANCIS: Bunny!

BUNNY: Shut up, Francis, I'm gonna splatter my fuckin' body on the concrete down there and don' wan' no interference. I thought it all out. My uncle's an undertaker, he'll do it cheap.

(HERSCHEL *sticks his head out the second-story window of* BUNNY'S *house*.)

HERSCHEL: Mom! What are you doing?

BUNNY: Herschel, don' look, it'll give you asthma.

HERSCHEL: Don't jump, Mom!

BUNNY: Herschel, I gotta favor to ask of you. If I don' die in jumpin', I want you to finish me off wit this. (*Waves the bag.*) It's rat poison. Was Uncle Eddie's Christmas present.

HERSCHEL: Mom, please!

BUNNY: You didn't scratch them new mosquito bites, did you?

HERSCHEL: No. And I took my medicine and I used my atomizer and brushed my teeth, please don't jump.

BUNNY: Good, you keep it up. Don' wan' to be a mess at my funeral.

HERSCHEL: Funeral!

(*Pulls his head in, and runs out into the yard.* JUDITH *is awake and getting dressed.* RANDY *comes out of the tent, a little confused by the noise.* FRANCIS *has come out, and is trying to coax her down.*)

RANDY: What's going on

HERSCHEL: (*Arrives, puffing, in the yard. His pajamas are disgracefully dirty, as is his robe which is much too small for him.*) Please, Mom, I'm sorry, I didn't mean to do it . . .

BUNNY: What?

HERSCHEL: I don't know, it must be something I did. I'll never have asthma again, I'll stop having seizures, I'll take gym class. Don't jump!

BUNNY: (*Starts climbing higher, till she is about the height of the second-story window.*) Herschel, is that any way to act, hanh? Was you raised in the jungle? Show some dignity, you want the neighbors to talk?

HERSCHEL: I'll burn my transfer collection, I'll give up the subways . . .

BUNNY: Nah, that's alright, Herschel. You'll be better off in a home.

HERSCHEL: A home??!!!

> (*He can hardly get the word out. He starts having an asthma attack.*)

BUNNY: Jesus Christ in heaven, he's havin' an attack! Can't I even commit suicide in peace?

JUDITH: Should I call the police?

FRANCIS: Call Lucille. DE 6-1567.

JUDITH: DE 6-1567.

> (*She runs into* FRANCIS's *house.*)

RANDY: What about Herschel?

BUNNY: Get his fuckin' atomizer—it's in the third room on the second floor.

> (RANDY *runs into* BUNNY's *house.*)

Jesus Christ in Heaven! And it's all for attention.

BUNNY: His fuckin' attacks! I read them books! It's all for attention, that all these kids want nowadays. I didn't get no attention when I was a kid and look at me! Am I weird? Nah! I didn't get no asthma, I didn't even get pimples.

JUDITH: (*Appears in the kitchen window.*) I get a busy signal.

FRANCIS: Busy? This time of day?

BUNNY: They think because they can fart and blink at the same time they got the world conquered.

FRANCIS: Did you get the number right?

BUNNY: That's all they want: attention!

JUDITH: DE 6-1567.

FRANCIS: Jesus! That's our number. It's DE 6-1656.

> (JUDITH *disappears inside the house.* RANDY *appears in the second-story window of Bunny's house.*)

RANDY: I can't find the atomizer!

HERSCHEL: (*Gasping, on the ground at the foot of the wall.*) By the bed, under all that Kleenex!

> (RANDY *continues looking for it.*)

FRANCIS: Come on, Bunny, climb down!

BUNNY: (*Climbing down to the top of the wall.*) Education! That's these kids' problems! Look at him—a fuckin' genius; and he looks like some live turd some fuckin' giant laid. Huff some more, Herschel . . .

RANDY: (*Running out of house.*) I got it! I got it.

(HERSCHEL *grabs the atomizer. His attack subsides.*)

BUNNY: They all oughta be put to work! That's what happened to me. Yeah! My mom put me to work when I was ten, singin' songs for pennies in the Franciscan monastery on Wolf Street!

(JUDITH *comes back into the yard.*)

I hadda sing for everybody—them bums, them old ladies. Once some crazy old lady made me sing "Mein Yiddische Mama" six times—then gave me a five-dollar bill. Well, even though it's a Catholic place I figured, shit, make the money. So I learned "Bci Mir Bist du Shoen" for the next week and sang it—and they beat the shit outta me. If that wasn't a birth trauma, what was! I read them books, know all about it. I've hadda shit-filled life; feel like some turd stuck in the pipe so Herschel get your fat ass outta the way, you too, hon, or I'll crush youse!

FRAN: (*Offstage, yelling.*) What's goin' on out here?

BUNNY: Yo, Fran!

FRAN: Yo, Bun!

BUNNY: I'm gonna jump!

LUCILLE: (*Running into the yard from gate, in hair curlers.*) *Che disgraziat!* Who's gonna clean it up, hanh?

FRAN: (*Follows* LUCILLE *in.*) Whataya mean you're gonna jump?

BUNNY: Whataya mean, whataya mean? I'm gonna leap off this fuckin' wall and if that don' finish me, I'm takin' this rat poison and Herschel better move or I'm takin' him with me. Jesus Christ, can't even die without his havin' a attack.

(FRAN *and* FRANCIS *half-carry, half-drag* HERSCHEL *away from the wall, and lay him down on the stoop. He is screaming and kicking.*)

You mean I gotta listen to that in Heaven?

LUCILLE: You ain't going to Heaven!

FRAN: Come on, be good and get down. You don't got no reason to jump!

BUNNY: I got reason, I got reason!

FRAN: Yeah, what?

BUNNY: Got nobody in the whole fuckin' world, I turned ugly, I got no money, I ain't got no prospects . . .

FRAN: That's been true of my whole life and you don' see me jumpin' off alley walls and takin' rat poison. Besides, it's Francis' twenty-first birthday today.

BUNNY: You mean there's gonna be a party?

FRAN: A big one!

BUNNY: Why didn't you say so, hanh? Get that friggin' ladder, I'm comin' down!

(FRANCIS *and* RANDY *run to get the ladder that has been leaning against the fence. They set it up under the wall, and help* BUNNY *climb down.* BUNNY, *to* RANDY.)

You're so strong, hon, give me a kiss!

(*Kisses him. Then she turns on* HERSCHEL, *who is still wheezing and crying.*)

You! Get in that fuckin' house! Makin' a spectacle of yourself wit them pajamas!

(*She chases* HERSCHEL *into their house. Much shaking of heads from the others. Everyone is very tense.* FRANCIS *takes the ladder back to the fence.*)

HERSCHEL: (*As he is running inside.*) What the fuck do you want me to do?

BUNNY: (*In her house continuing a diatribe against* HERSCHEL.) And what's this I hear from your no-good father? You had a fuckin' petit mal yesterday?!

HERSCHEL: (*In the house.*) No, I didn't!

BUNNY: Liar! Didn't I tell you to behave wit him?

(*Sounds of her beating him.*)

I told you to act normal.

HERSCHEL: Who could act normal with you for a mother?

(*A sound like a piano falling over is heard from* BUNNY's *house. A silence. Then suddenly, long surprised screams of pain from* HERSCHEL. FRAN *tries to hug*

FRANCIS. FRANCIS *gets away.* BUNNY *comes running
out of her house to the stoop.*)

BUNNY: You guys wanna get a piano offa Herschel?

FRAN: What's the piano doin' on Herschel?

BUNNY: He gave me some lip and I threw it on him.

FRAN: Oh, alright.

(*Kisses* FRANCIS.)

Happy birthday, my son.

(FRAN *and* FRANCIS *run into* BUNNY'*s house.*)

BUNNY: Do you think I ruptured him for life?

(BUNNY *and* RANDY *run into the house.* JUDITH *begins
to follow, but* LUCILLE *stops her.*)

LUCILLE: Ain't ladylike to go in there.

JUDITH: Herschel might be hurt.

LUCILLE: If that kid ain't dead yet, he's indestructible.

(*From inside the house, noises of the piano being
lifted.*)

He's always fallin' down stairs, gettin' hit by cars, gettin'
beat up, havin' fits, gettin' asthma, throwin' up, comin'
down with pneumonia. A piano ain't gonna hurt him.

(*She sets a garden chair next to the tent.*)

Besides, that piano's out of tune, how much damage
could it do?

JUDITH: This is crazy! All that noise and Bunny on the
wall . . .

LUCILLE: (*Sits in chair.*) Happens alla the time. That's
why no neighbors stuck their heads out. We're used to it
around here. Tessie across the street come back from the
shore last Sunday and found this burglar in her cellar.

(JUDITH *has gone in the tent to finish dressing.*)

Judy, she ties him to an old sofa, then, wit her sister, she
shoves it down the front steps. Then she sets it on fire.
We come back from church and there is this sofa on the
front steps wit a scream' man on it and flames everywhere. We call the fire engine. They hose the poor bastard down and rush him to the hospital. So this mornin'
was mild, believe me.

(JUDITH *is now sitting by the tent, putting on her
sneakers.*)

Do you wanna come wit me to Wanamaker's and buy

Francis a present? I have a employee's discount so you
can buy him somethin' real nice for less. Or did you get
somethin' already?

JUDITH: Not really—a few joke things. I don't think he's
gonna think they're funny.

(*She gets a brush and mirror out of her knapsack.
Music is heard from* BUNNY'S *house.* BUNNY *appears
in her window, brushing her hair.*)

BUNNY: Yo, Lucille! We got the piano up. You wanna
come in and sing?

LUCILLE: No, Bunny.

BUNNY: Well, I'm cookin' breakfast. You wan' some?

LUCILLE AND JUDITH: No thanks.

JUDITH: How is Herschel?

BUNNY: A little purple about the shins, but he'll survive.
You sure you don' wan' some breakfast?

JUDITH: No thank you!

BUNNY: You should take some lessons from your brother.

(*She disappears inside her house.*)

LUCILLE: What did she mean about your brother?

JUDITH: Everybody loves Randy—EVERYBODY it
seems!

LUCILLE: Well, he's nice lookin', that's for sure. But I'm
not crazy about him. I never warm up to white people
much. You're an exception. You got poise. You have
lovely teeth.

(*From inside the house we hear:*)

"I want a girl

Just like the girl

That married dear old dad

She was a pearl

And the only girl

That daddy ever had . . ."

(*Dialogue continues over this.*)

JUDITH: They got Francis to play the piano, all those
wrong notes.

LUCILLE: Why are you interested in Francis when you're
so beautiful?

JUDITH: If I hear that once more, I'm going to stick my
face in acid!

LUCILLE: But why? *Perchè?* What do you see in him?

JUDITH: Why are you interested in his father

LUCILLE: I ain't got much choice. I'm not pretty. I'm a widow. Nobody wants a widow. It's like bein' an old sheet. I might be clean and kept nice but people can't help noticin' it's been used.

> (BUNNY *is heard singing.*)

"When Irish eyes are smilin'."

> (LUCILLE *continues over song.*)

So I put up wit Fran. He's good people, he means well. But you know, he coughs alla the time, eats too much, makes noises, you know he's got the colitis, and them rashes! Between coughin', scratchin' and runnin' to the bathroom, I'm surprised he's got so much weight on him. Oh, well, that's my life.

> (JUDITH *offers her the brush. She is about to use it, then discretely pulls* JUDITH's *hair out of the bristles.*)

But, Francis? Like father like son, remember.

JUDITH: Oh, I don't know. We talked yesterday and I was up most of the night, thinking: why? All the possible bad reasons started cramming themselves into my head. Perhaps I have sensed it all along and I was attracted to Francis because he was . . . (*Stops herself.*) Well, just because he's the way he is.

> (*From inside the house we hear:*)

"For it was Mary, Mary

Plain as any name can be

For in society, propriety

Will say, Marie."

> (LUCILLE *speaks over this.*)

LUCILLE: You mean queer? Don' be shocked, I know what queer is.

> (*She turns her chair toward* JUDITH.)

I had a long talk wit my son, Donny, about it before he went off. He's at Yale, pre-med, Branford Scholarship. I warned him to be careful. My friend, Diane's husband, he's a foot doctor, they met in a singles bar, then got married because he had corns real bad, well, he told me, Yale puts out a lot of queers along wit the doctors and the lawyers. But Donny's got a girl friend, and though I think she's a pig, I guess it proves he's got some interest in the girls. But Francis? Well, Fran and me had a long talk. He's afraid for Francis. Well, I think Francis is. There ain't been no girls around here except to sell cookies. That's why Fran was so happy to see you, and wanted you to stay, even though you wanted to go. It's hard on a man to have a queer for a son. I mean, I guess Fran would rather he was queer than humpbacked or dead, still it's hard.

JUDITH: Well, I thought that might be why I was interested. He'd be safe then. But I don't think so. He and I are really alike, you see. Neither of us makes contact with people. We both goof a lot, but most of the time, that's all there is.

BUNNY: (*From inside her house.*) Alright, I'm slingin' this shit on the table!

JUDITH: And there are other reasons. Just where I am, you know? I'm a romantic, I guess, and I assume there is something worth doing, that active is better than passive. But I feel on the edge of falling, or freezing.

LUCILLE: (*Shakes her head.*) When I was your age— *madone* . . . !

JUDITH: Maybe it's harder for us, now. The war's over, no one much is ethnic anymore, there aren't many jobs. When there were marches and strikes and moratoriums, people didn't think much about the future, they were distracted, sort of a hippie bread and circuses idea.

LUCILLE: (*Nods her head, but she doesn't understand one word.*) Yeah.

JUDITH: No one had time to worry about how they'd live five years from now—it was all now. Everybody could be a hero, occupy a dean's office, publish his memoirs, have them serialized in *The New York Times*—

LUCILLE: Wit the small print!

JUDITH: And you have to wonder, all that energy, and that courage, was it just adolescence? Sometimes I'm afraid. Just afraid. Maybe we're at the end of the spiral which people once thought endless. Maybe it's running out. I don't want it to be over. Francis is afraid too. But together . . . I'm sorry, I'm not making any sense, I didn't sleep much.

LUCILLE: But you didn't buy him a birthday present.

JUDITH: Is that important?

LUCILLE: Vital. It's the gesture. Don' matter what it is but you got to make the gesture. It shows respect. It shows you're serious. No birthday present and he' gotta right to wonder if you mean it. It's like an outward sign. You just can't go around sayin': I need you, or I love you, and then ignorin' them on special occasions. That don' make no sense. So you buy them the birthday present, you send them the card, you go visit them inna hospital, you bake them the cake—you show them respect. *Cabisce?* Respect!

JUDITH: *Si.*

LUCILLE: *Bene.* All you can do is try and hope. That's how I got my husband, may God forgive him, and may he rest in peace. You really like Francis? Come on, you come wit me to Wanamaker's we buy Francis a present we cheer ourselves up.

(FRAN *comes out of* BUNNY'S *house.*)

FRAN: Yo, Lucille!

LUCILLE: Judith and me's goin' ta Wanamaker's to buy Francis a present.

FRAN: See youse later, be good and be careful.

(LUCILLE *and* JUDITH *exit through the gate.* FRANCIS *comes racing out of* BUNNY'S *house.*)

Yo, where you goin'?

FRANCIS: Nowhere.

FRAN: You got company.

FRANCIS: I didn't invite them.

FRAN: (*Embraces* FRANCIS.) Happy birthday, son.

FRANCIS: Don't hang on me so much.

FRAN: What are you afraid of? You got somewhere to go you take some coin.

(*Offers him some money.*)

FRANCIS: I don't need any money.

FRAN: Well, take some more.

FRANCIS: I don't need any more.

FRAN: Take!

FRANCIS: I don't need it!!

FRAN: Look, my son, I'm gonna give you a piece of advice
I learned from the army, from dealin' wit your mother
and from twenty years in the Printers' Union: Take!
Take wit both hands, both feet and your mouth too. If
your ass is flexible enough take wit that, use your knees
and your elbows, train your balls and take! *Prend'—
cabisce?* Somebody offers you somethin', you take it,
then run . . .

(*Puts the money in* FRANCIS's *shirt pocket.*)

. . . but always say thank you first. And look, if there's
ever anything, well, that conventional people, not like us
Geminiani Italians—but other people might be ashamed
of, don't ever be afraid to come to me, no matter how
hard it is, I'll understand—understand?

FRANCIS: I don't understand.

(*Suddenly embraces his father.*)

But I understand, okay?

(*Runs out through the gate.*)

FRAN: Where you goin'?

FRANCIS: To buy some diet soda.

FRAN: That diet crap is gonna kill ya.

(RANDY *comes out of* BUNNY's *house, trailed by* HER-
SCHEL.)

RANDY: Where's Francis?

FRAN: He went to buy diet crap.

HERSCHEL: (*Grabs* RANDY's *arm, and starts pulling him toward the alley.*) Maybe we'll pass him, you know, like
on our way to the trolleys . . .

RANDY: (*Freeing himself.*) Is there a pool around here? I'd
like to go swimming.

FRAN: Yeah.

HERSCHEL: You promised!

FRAN: There's a Community Center about four blocks
from here, Herschel can go with you. You can change
here.

RANDY: Great.

(RANDY *crawls into the tent to change.* BUNNY *comes
out of her house, eating a sandwich.*)

BUNNY: Hey, Herschel, I thought you was draggin' Beau Brummel to the trolleys—

HERSCHEL: He wants to go swimming.

BUNNY: Why don't you go wit him?

HERSCHEL: (*Under his breath.*) Fuck!

BUNNY: Where's the birthday boy?

FRAN: He took off.

BUNNY: Helluva way to treat company. Prob'ly went to buy a opera record.

RANDY: (*Still inside the tent.*) He already has thousands.

FRAN: (*To* BUNNY.) Look, I got stuff to do, gotta buy Francis a birthday cake. Bun, you wanna come?

BUNNY: Sure, I could use a donut or two.

> (*They exit through the gate.* HERSCHEL *picks up his tricycle.*)

HERSCHEL: Randy, Randy!

RANDY: (*From inside the tent.*) What?

HERSCHEL: Would you like to play trolley?

RANDY: How?

HERSCHEL: Just call ding, when I ask you to. Like . . . (*Pipes out.*) Ding!

RANDY: Okay.

HERSCHEL: (*Careening around the yard like a trolley, making a lot of noise.*) Ritner! . . . Now.

RANDY: Ding!

HERSCHEL: Good. (*Careens.*) Tasker! . . . Now.

RANDY: Ding!

HERSCHEL: Dickinson! . . . Now. (*Silence.*) Now. Oh, you missed that one.

> (RANDY *comes out of the tent, in a T-shirt and shorts.*)

RANDY: Ding!

> (HERSCHEL *is gaping at him.*)

Do you think I look weird?

> (HERSCHEL *shakes his head "No".*)

I mean, skinny.

HERSCHEL: I think you look, like, you know—

RANDY: Yeah, yeah. But do you think my legs are too thin?

HERSCHEL: Oh, no!

RANDY: Boy, it's rough being this thin, you know, I've tried to put on at least ten pounds. I bought two quarts of this stuff called "Wate-On."

HERSCHEL: (*Points to his stomach.*) Oh yeah, like "weight on"—

RANDY: Putrid stuff. I drank a quart of it, tastes like milk of magnesia, I got sick for a week and lost ten pounds.

HERSCHEL: I tried to kill myself by drinking a quart of milk of magnesia once; but I didn't lose any weight.

(FRANCIS *enters through the gate, drinking a diet soda. A tense moment between* FRANCIS *and* RANDY.)

RANDY: We're going swimming.

FRANCIS: I'll stay here.

RANDY: Okay, Herschel, let's go . . .

(*They start off, suddenly* RANDY *staggers, clutches the air, twists about, acts dizzy, and falls to the ground. He is faking a petit mal.*)

HERSCHEL: (*Very alarmed.*) Randy, what is it?

FRANCIS: (*Catching on.*) Looks like a petit mal, Herschel.

HERSCHEL: No, no, that's epilepsy. Take your belt off!

FRANCIS: Why?

HERSCHEL: So he won't bite his tongue off. Give it to me!

(*Sticks belt in* RANDY's *mouth.*)

I'll get my medicine!

(*Rushes into his house.*)

RANDY: (*Who has been writhing on the ground until now, suddenly sits up.*) Are you a faggot?

(HERSCHEL *comes running out with a bottle of medicine.* RANDY *starts writhing again.*)

HERSCHEL: Here—you have to shake it first!

FRANCIS: (*Shaking the bottle.*) I think he'll need some Valium too—

HERSCHEL: Good idea!

(*Runs into house, and reappears almost instantly.*) Fives or tens?

FRANCIS: Fives should do it.

(HERSCHEL *races into house.*)

RANDY: (*Sits up, dropping the fit.*) I mean homosexual—I mean, gay person—

HERSCHEL: (*Racing back out.*) We're out!

(RANDY *fakes the fit again.*)

FRANCIS: Do you have any aspirin?

RANDY: (*Mumbling unintelligibly.*) Aspirin upsets my stomach!

FRANCIS: Aspirin upsets his stomach.

HERSCHEL: Tylenol?

FRANCIS: Tylenol?

RANDY: Tylenol!

HERSCHEL AND FRANCIS: Tylenol!

HERSCHEL: I'll go get some!

(*Races off through the alley.*)

RANDY: (*He stands, dusts himself off, awkward pause.*) When we talked and all that, you know in your room, were you just trying to make me?

FRANCIS: I don't know.

RANDY: I don't care that much, but it's worse being treated like you were laying a trap for me. And I didn't think you were gay—odd maybe. Have there . . .

(*He realizes how silly this is going to sound.*)

. . . been many before me?

FRANCIS: Well, starting in high school there was Max. He was a poet, a Libra, on the fencing team, short and dark, compact you might say, very dashing with his épées. Then there were George and Eliot, they were twins. Then, Sheldon Gold, briefly.

RANDY: How many did you sleep with?

FRANCIS: Sleep with? They didn't even talk to me.

RANDY: You never told them how you felt?

FRANCIS: Well, that's it, you see. I'm never sure how I feel, really.

RANDY: Have you ever had sex with a man?

(FRANCIS *shakes his head "No."*)

Were there girls before Judith?

FRANCIS: Well, there was Elaine Hoffenburg. She had braces.

RANDY: Braces on her teeth?

FRANCIS: Legs. I took her to the Senior Prom.

(RANDY *looks incredulous.*)

Well, I was no catch, either. I was very fat then. It wasn't too bad. Once she got enough momentum going, she could do a passable waltz. Then there was Luise

Morely. Slightly pockmarked but pretty in a plain sort
of way. We held hands through *The Sandpiper,* then we
did it afterwards. It was my first time. Elaine had been
willing, but it was a little hard getting her legs apart.

RANDY: Gross! I worked for months to get Nancy Simmons
to go to the prom with me, then I got car sick on the
way and threw up all over her; and you remember Rob-
erta Hasserfluth. I broke up with her just as you and
Judith got together, well, we decided we would do it, so
we went to the drive-in movie in Waltham. It was *The
Four Stewardesses*—

FRANCIS: Wasn't that in 3-D?

RANDY: Oh, was it ever, we had to wear goggles and everything. Well, I bought this bottle of Mateus, see, and
since I'd never bought wine before I forgot you needed a
corkscrew. So I couldn't get it open, so there we are
watching this dirty movie in the dead of winter, with this
bottle of Mateus between my legs, trying to get it open
with my car key—

FRANCIS: Well, did you ever do it?

RANDY: Too cold! I'm sort of a jerk with girls, but I like
them. I like you too, you're my friend. But I don't think
I'm in love with you. Does that mean you were in love
with me?

   (FRANCIS *shrugs.*)

I mean, Francis, has it ever occurred to you you might
be suffering from homosexual panic.

FRANCIS: (*Snaps his fingers.*) I knew I should have taken
Psych. 101.

RANDY: I mean, it's true. It's really common in a competi-
tive society.

FRANCIS: (*Shakes his head, irritated at being put on.*) Oh,
really.

RANDY: I'm serious. I mean, if you've never slept with a
man, never laid a hand on me . . .

FRANCIS: Are you saying that if you were to strip right
now and lie down inside that tent, I couldn't—well, do
anything?

RANDY: Well, there's only one way to find out.
   (*Starts to strip.*)

FRANCIS: What are you doing? Randy, what are you doing?

RANDY: I'm stripping.

FRANCIS: Are you crazy? In front of me? Here?

> (FRANCIS *makes a dash for his door, but* RANDY *intercepts him.* RANDY *stands in front of the door, blocking it. He looks around the yard, up at the windows, then unzips his fly.*)

Jesus Christ!

RANDY: (*Walks over to the tent.*) I'll save the rest for inside the tent.

> (*Crawls inside.*)

FRANCIS: Jesus Christ! Oh Jesus . . .

> (*Holding his chin.*)

I didn't shave this morning.

> (FRANCIS *is about to crawl into the tent, as* HERSCHEL *comes bounding in from the alley.*)

HERSCHEL: How's Randy

FRANCIS: (*Exasperated.*) Jesus Christ, Herschel, he's dead!

HERSCHEL: (*Horror-struck.*) He is??!!

FRANCIS: Ten minutes ago; heart failure.

HERSCHEL: Are you sure? I mean, I faked a heart attack in gym class last month. Maybe he's faking. Call an ambulance!

FRANCIS: Damn it, Herschel, he's dead, now go away!

HERSCHEL: Can I see the body?

RANDY: (*Sticks his head out of the tent.*) Hello, Herschel.

HERSCHEL: Randy! He said . . .

RANDY: I heard. Look, Herschel, Francis and I . . .

FRANCIS: (*Trying to stop him.*) Randy!

RANDY: . . . are involved in a very serious ritual. We will both be drummed out of our exclusive clubs at Harvard if we don't do this.

HERSCHEL: Oh, heavy.

RANDY: Very. So, Herschel, would you please go away and come back a little later?

HERSCHEL: Sure.

> (*He sets a little bottle of Tylenol in front of the tent, and starts for the alley.* RANDY *throws the shorts out at*

FRANCIS. HERSCHEL *turns back*.)

Like five minutes?

FRANCIS: (*Grabs the shorts, hides them behind his back*.) Herschel, take a long walk!

(HERSCHEL, *dejected, exits out the alley.* FRANCIS *hesitates, peers into the tent, and finally crawls inside. There is no movement for a few seconds, then* RANDY, *wrapped in the sleeping bag, comes bounding out of the tent, followed by* FRANCIS.)

Randy, what's the matter? What's the matter? Why did you strip if you didn't mean it? Were you bringing me on?

RANDY: No!

(*Runs back into the tent*.)

FRANCIS: Is that what was going on this spring? Perhaps somewhere in some subconscious avenue of that boy-man mind of yours you sensed I had a vulnerable point and decided to make the most of it?

RANDY: (*From inside the tent*.) I was seventeen fucking years old this spring—what's your excuse?

FRANCIS: Well, you're eighteen now.

RANDY: (*Coming out of tent, wearing jeans*.) I liked you!

FRANCIS: (*Sarcastic*.) Thanks!

RANDY: I really did.

FRANCIS: It's vicious of you.

RANDY: How?

FRANCIS: Because you did it all just to humiliate me—

RANDY: I really do like you. I mean, liking does exist, doesn't it? It doesn't have to include sex, or love, or deep need, does it?

FRANCIS: I don't know.

RANDY: I don't know either.

FRANCIS: I don't know either.

RANDY: Boy . . . you are really fucked up.

(*He embraces* FRANCIS.)

FRANCIS: I know.

(*He puts his arms around* RANDY. JUDITH *enters the yard from the gate carrying a large gaily wrapped box. She sees this embrace and lets out a surprised yell. The two jump apart, confused, and looking guilty.*)

RANDY: Judith!

JUDITH: You're disgusting!

RANDY: It's not my fault, he's older than I am!

JUDITH: He's younger than you are!

FRANCIS: Judith . . .

JUDITH: (*Turns on him.*) And you!

FRANCIS: Now, look, Judith, it didn't have anything to do with sex!

JUDITH: Oh, no! I'm sure! Nothing you do has anything to do with sex! It's all a bring on, isn't it? You get to that point, and then you're ugly, or you're fat, or you're gay! What did you use on him? That you were ugly, fat, and straight? Well, I'm on to you! Happy birthday!
(*She throws the box at* FRANCIS.)

FRANCIS: Act your age, Judith!

JUDITH: Oh ho, act my age, act my age says this paragon of maturity, this pristine sage now come of age!

FRANCIS: It's hard to explain . . .

RANDY: That's right!

JUDITH: Hard? Hard to explain? What is? You're going to fuck my brother, that's very simple, that's the birds and the bees, that's Biology 1A. I thought I loved you. I thought I loved you!
(*Starts hitting* RANDY.)
I thought I loved him!

FRANCIS: Judith, will you please calm down.

JUDITH: And my mother told me never to trust fatties, they're self-indulgent. Go have a banana split!

RANDY: For Christ' sake, calm down!

JUDITH: I knew there was something suspicious in your wanting to come along. I bet the two of you were laughing at me, comparing notes, carrying on behind my back the whole time. Why, Francis, why would you do this to me?

FRANCIS: He was bringing me on, standing here with no clothes on, hanging onto me, what would you do?

JUDITH: Puke!

RANDY: Do you think I enjoyed it? Huh, tubby?

JUDITH: (*To* RANDY.) So, you're a faggot too—won't the sophomore class be surprised?

RANDY: Why are you screaming at me, it's his fault!

FRANCIS: (*Shaking his finger at* RANDY.) It's your fault!

JUDITH: Oh, my God, it's love! M and M—mutual masturbation!

RANDY: (*Angry.*) I thought I could help him, I should have known better, I can't help you—
(*Shoves* FRANCIS. HERSCHEL *comes bounding in from alley.*)

HERSCHEL: Randy, your ceremony seems to be over, we can go see the . . .

RANDY: (*Screaming, runs into tent.*) And I can't help you either, Herschel!

HERSCHEL: Francis . . .

FRANCIS: God damn it, Herschel, go away!

HERSCHEL: Oh, no, I did it again!
(JUDITH *is on one side of the stage, talking to* FRANCIS, *and* HERSCHEL *is on the other side, talking to the tent.*)

JUDITH: And I was even out buying you a present!

HERSCHEL: I tried to be your friend, I don't know how . . .

JUDITH: And I was willing to be understanding.

HERSCHEL: I'm just stupid.

JUDITH: All those Callas records, and I hate her voice and her wobble!

FRANCIS: She only wobbles on the late recordings!

HERSCHEL: What did I do?

JUDITH: And that Toti dal Monte, for Christ' sake, she sounds like a broken steam engine!

FRANCIS: Her mad scene is still the best on records!

HERSCHEL: It's just me!

JUDITH: And what about my mad scene?

HERSCHEL: I'm just retarded like they all say!
(*He runs into his house.*)

RANDY: (*From inside the tent.*) Shut up, Judith!

JUDITH: Oh God, and I even came here bringing your beloved! And you kissed me, and you stroked me, and we held hands along the Charles River, and I thought: He's weird, he's pudgy, he likes Maria Callas, but he responds to me! What a laugh! That's funnier than *The Barber of Seville,* that's funnier than *The Girl of the Golden West*—

FRANCIS: Shut, shut up, Judith, God damn it, act your age! You're like a fucking six-year-old!

JUDITH: And you? How old are you?!

(*They are right in front of the* GEMINIANI *door.* BUNNY, FRAN, *and* LUCILLE *enter grandly from* FRAN's *house, carrying a huge birthday cake and singing. They are wearing party hats.* BUNNY *is running around, putting hats on* JUDITH *and* FRANCIS, *and* RANDY, *as he emerges from the tent.* FRAN *has the cake on the same typing table that was used for breakfast. He also has a camera.*)

BUNNY, FRAN, AND LUCILLE:
"Happy birthday to you,
Happy birthday to you,
Happy birthday, dear Francis,
Happy birthday to you!"

FRAN: Happy birthday, my son!

(*Snaps a picture.*)

LUCILLE: Come on, blow out the candles and cut the cake, it's too hot to wait.

BUNNY: There's only six candles, all we could find.

(FRANCIS *is about to blow them out.*)

LUCILLE: Come on, make a wish.

(*He does.* FRAN *takes another picture, and* FRANCIS *blows out the candles. They all cheer and applaud.* JUDITH *and* RANDY *are still stunned.*)

FRANCIS: Thank you. I would first like to thank my father, now that I am officially an adult, for teaching me how to dance and sing and cough and fart and scratch and above all how to treat a rash once it becomes visible to the general public, then I would like to thank my next-door neighbor Bunny . . .

(FRAN *snaps a photo of* BUNNY.)

for demonstrating once and for all that motherhood ought to be abolished, along with drunks and whores, Lucille, for teaching me how to ruin the happiest occasion with one glance and the cheapest insect spray, and Randy, for providing us with living proof of the vacuity of American Higher Education, and then Judith, our brilliant, bubbly, and let's not forget, mature Italian major from Radcliffe will recite to us in her main line Italian all the nonsense syllables of her upbringing and her recent reading. And I want you all to know precisely what I think of all this: this neighborhood, Bunny and Lucille, Randy and Judith!

(*He rips into the cake with his hands and tears it apart, hurling pieces at* JUDITH *and the others. All duck away. After* FRANCIS *has destroyed the cake, he runs off through the gate.* HERSCHEL *stumbles out of his house, holding the bag of rat poison, powder all over his mouth.*)

HERSCHEL: I swallowed Uncle Eddie's rat poison!

BUNNY: My baby!

FRAN: Holy shit!

BUNNY: (*On her knees by* HERSCHEL.) My baby!

LUCILLE: Who's gonna clean it up, hanh?

(*Blackout.*)

Scene 2

Evening. FRAN *has a huge trash bag and is cleaning up the yard.* LUCILLE *is sitting on the divider between the two houses.* RANDY *is finished ·packing. Their tent has been struck and is rolled up again.*

LUCILLE: Rum and chocolate sauce everywhere—did he know how much it cost?

FRAN: Well, it was his birthday cake, if he wanted a throw it around, it's his right I guess.

LUCILLE: But it ain't his right to clean it up, hanh? (*She points to a piece of cake.*) Over there. Jesus, I'm sick and tired of cleanin' up afta people. (*Points again.*) Over here. Cleanin' up afta my brothers . . .

FRAN: (*Under his breath, still picking up.*) Your brothers . . .

LUCILLE: Afta pop . . .

FRAN: Afta pop . . .

LUCILLE: Then my mom got senile . . .

FRAN: Then mom . . .

LUCILLE: Then my husband . . .

FRAN: Your husband . . .

LUCILLE: Then Donny . . .

FRAN: (*Joking*) Ain't he at Yale?

LUCILLE: Hanh? Of course he's at Yale, that's a stupid question, *ma stupidezza* . . .

RANDY: I'll see if Judith is ready.

(*Runs into* BUNNY's *house.*)

FRAN: I hope Francis gets back soon—I think his guests are gonna leave any minute—

LUCILLE: Well, I'm surprised they stayed as long as they did. Well, at least he didn't play so much opera music this weekend—all that screamin'—that's what I got against opera, Fran, ain't like real life.

(*She tries to clean up some whipped cream with a Kleenex.* BUNNY *enters from her house, depressed.*)

BUNNY: Yo, Fran.

FRAN: Yo, Bun. How's Herschel?

BUNNY: Better and better, just ate all my leftovers.

FRAN: I guess they're gettin' ready to leave.

BUNNY: Yep.

LUCILLE: (*About* BUNNY, *mean.*) *E questa si chiama una madre?*

FRAN: Lucille, take this bag in the house—tape up the top so nothin' gets in . . .

(LUCILLE *takes the bag, and goes into* FRAN's *house. He calls after her.*)

And put on the coffee!

BUNNY: (*Sits down on her stoop.*) She could use a enema, lye and hot pepper! (*Looks at* FRAN.) Remember way back when, when we did it?

FRAN: Oh, Bun.

BUNNY: Oh, Fran! 'Sbeen a long time. I think it's time we did it again. Don't say it, you got Lucille! What's Lucille? Shit, she gotta get on the subway to get her hips movin'.

FRAN: You don' need me, Bun.

BUNNY: We was good together.

FRAN: How often? Five times the most? I remember the first time.

> (*He sits down beside her.*)

You remember? We forced Francis to take Herschel to the movies; it was *Lady and the Tramp*. They was that young, we could force them. Can you see the two of them together?

BUNNY: They was both so fat they probably took up a whole row between them.

FRAN: Didn't they have rashes too?

BUNNY: Nah, that was the third time. We forced Francis to take Herschel into Center City to buy calamine lotion.

> (*She puts her head on his shoulder. He looks up to his window, checking for* LUCILLE.)

FRAN: Why don't you give Sam a call?

BUNNY: He ain't interested.

FRAN: I bet you still like him.

BUNNY: You still like your wife?

FRAN: Sure, I married her, didn't I! We went together two years and were pretty happy until Francis came along. She wasn't the same after that. Oh well, she's gone. And now there's Lucille—at least she bakes good fiadone. And she's good people, even if she schives too much. I mean, what kinda choice I got? Hanh? Women today, they look at you, they see a man wheezin', coughin', goin' to the bathroom, scratchin', gettin' rashes, they take off. But Sam ain't attached yet—give him a call, fix yourself up, grow up a little—

BUNNY: Grow up a little? Like that was easy. Jesus, if only I didn't still act and feel nineteen. I look in the mirror and I know there's fat and wrinkles there; Jesus Christ do I know there's fat and wrinkles! Yet, I'll be damned if I don't still, somewhere in there, see this nineteen-year-old filly hot to trot and on fire for some kind of success in life! (*Looks at house, tricycle.*) And look what I got—

FRAN: So Herschel's a little crazy, but he's gonna do wonders—

BUNNY: He's a fuckin' genius! Grow up a little. And what about Francis?

FRAN: Don' know, this Judith girl—

BUNNY: She seems to like him, hard as that is to believe, but I don't see much evidence of his liking her.

FRAN: No, I guess not, but kids nowadays, maybe they act different when they're goin' together—and maybe she isn't his last chance.

BUNNY: Don't kid yourself. Look, why don't you just ask him and save yourself years of wonderin' and never bein' sure . . . ?

FRAN: It's the hardest thing for a father to ask his son. Don' know why it should be, I know guys who . . . like . . . other guys who are regular, you know, in every other way. But you know, it's his life now, he's gonna pay the consequences for whatever he does . . . but still, I hope.

BUNNY: Well, I worry about Herschel too. But Jesus, I figure we're lucky if he lives to be twenty-one—

LUCILLE: (*Appears in the doorway.*) Yo, Fran!

FRAN: (*Gets away from* BUNNY.) Yo, Lucille!

LUCILLE: I see the monster comin' down the street—(*She goes back in.*)

FRAN: Bunny, let's go inside, he won't want to see us right off—

> (*They go into* BUNNY'S *house.* FRANCIS *enters from the gate. He sees the packed knapsacks under the fig tree. After a moment,* JUDITH *enters from* BUNNY'S *house. She is wearing a skirt and blouse.*)

JUDITH: Well . . . Azael has returned.

FRANCIS: Who?

JUDITH: Who else? The Prodigal!

> (LUCILLE *comes out of* FRAN'S *house, carrying a coffeepot, and a new robe for* HERSCHEL. *She sees* FRANCIS.)

LUCILLE: *Ma Sporcacione!* (*She slams the door, and goes into* BUNNY'S *house.*)

FRANCIS: Is everyone furious at me?

JUDITH: We have Bunny's uncle on the force waiting inside with handcuffs.

FRANCIS: Oh Jesus, you're at it again—

JUDITH: Well, to be serious, Lucille is making a novena to Saint Jude the Obscure, Patron Saint of the Hopeless and Pudgy who spoil their own birthday parties.

(*She gets a sweater out of her knapsack.*)

Herschel took rat poison.

FRANCIS: Is he dead?

JUDITH: No more than ever. Bunny called her uncle on the ambulance squad and he was rushed to St. Agnes Hospital, across Track 37 on the A, the AA 1 through 7, and the B express lines, perhaps you've passed it? They cleaned up the yard as best they could, but you'll probably be finding birthday cake here and there for the next few months. Still the fall rains and the march of time should wash away all stains from your yard, your life, and these, the Days of our Youth! Thank you.

FRANCIS: And you're leaving.

JUDITH: You noticed! Maybe you aren't autistic. Yes, we're walking over to Broad Street, where we will get a cab to 30th Street Station, where we will take the 9:05 train to Boston, from there we're going to our summer home. We are not hitching, you'll notice, we've lost the stomach for it. Oh, by the way, happy birthday.

FRANCIS: Thank you.

JUDITH: I'm sorry.

FRANCIS: So am I.

(*They are about to go to each other, when* RANDY *comes out of* BUNNY's *house.*)

RANDY: C'mon Judith. We have nineteen minutes to catch that train.

(FRAN *and* LUCILLE *come out of* BUNNY's *house.*)

FRAN: So, Igor's back, hanh? I guess you kids is off.

(RANDY *and* JUDITH *are putting on their knapsacks and collecting their belongings.*)

RANDY: We're off!

LUCILLE: Good-bye!

FRAN: The way I see it, life is made up of hellos and goodbyes and forgivin' and forgettin'. So you two forgive and forget and come back, hanh? Even if Frankenstein ain't here, you're always welcome.

(BUNNY *comes out of her house with* HERSCHEL. *He is wearing clean pajamas and a new bathrobe.*)

BUNNY: (*Sees* FRANCIS.) So, Igor's back, hanh? (*To* RANDY *and* JUDITH.) We wanted to see youse off, you're good people, you kids.

LUCILLE: (*To* JUDITH.) If I give you Donny's number at Yale, maybe you could get in touch with him this fall, he's nice, real good-looking and athletic, and he ain't no party pooper neither.

(*She gives* JUDITH *a slip of paper.*)

I have somethin' in the house for you.

(*She goes inside.*)

HERSCHEL: (*To* RANDY, *shyly.*) Like, if I promise to lose weight and get less weird, can we be friends?

RANDY: Sure, even if you gain and get weirder.

HERSCHEL: Like, don't lie to me, you know? Like, I understand if you aren't interested. But can I, like, you know, write you letters?

RANDY: Oh sure. I'll give you our summer address, otherwise, just write me at Harvard.

(*He writes address on a little piece of paper that* HERSCHEL *had ready.* LUCILLE *returns with a plate wrapped in tinfoil. The following three lines are said at about the same time.*)

JUDITH: C'mon, Randy, let's go!

LUCILLE: C'mon, Randy, you're gonna miss the train.

RANDY: See you, Herschel.

JUDITH, FRAN, *and* LUCILLE *go out through the gate. They stand in the entrance saying final good-byes.* RANDY, *about to say good-bye to* FRANCIS, *is grabbed by* BUNNY.)

BUNNY: Oh, honeybun, I feel like I've known you for years. Maybe I'm gettin' funny in the head, but I know a promising hunk when I see one.

RANDY: Thank you.

BUNNY: I'm gonna miss you.

(RANDY *smiles and tries to get away but she hangs on.*)

JUDITH: (*Calling from the gate.*) C'mon, Randy!

BUNNY: Be careful when you sit down on toilets, put paper

there, you hear? And see that some people may be
pretty, even if they got strange faces, and mean well,
even if they act weird, and think of me once in a while,
hanh?

(*She kisses him.*)

Good-bye!

(*She goes into her house.* HERSCHEL *and* RANDY *shake
hands, then* HERSCHEL, *looking back sadly, blinking
back tears, follows his mother into the house.*)

RANDY: (*Goes to* FRANCIS.) In the fall, right?

FRANCIS: Right.

(*They shake hands.*)

JUDITH: Randy!

RANDY: Listen, I was just trying to help, okay?

(RANDY *leaves. The good-byes are heard from behind
the fence.* FRANCIS *is left alone.*)

FRAN: Come back soon! Please!

(FRANCIS *goes into his room, and puts on a quiet, sad
piece of music.* FRAN *and* LUCILLE *come back into the
yard.*)

Let's go to your place, hanh? Need some coffee.

LUCILLE: I got some nice cheesecake for you, Fran.

FRAN: Yeah? Sounds good. (*Yells to* FRANCIS.) Yo, Francis! We're goin' a Lucille's for coffee and cake. Wanna
come?

(*There is no answer.*)

Yo, Francis!

FRANCIS: (*From his room.*) God damn it, no!

FRAN: That's my Ivy League son.

(FRAN *and* LUCILLE *exit through the gate.* FRANCIS *appears in his window. He is very agitated. The music is
playing.*)

FRANCIS: Jesus Christ, what am I doing? (*Calls out.*) Dad!
Dad! Yo, Dad!

(*He runs out of the house to the gate.*)

FRAN: (*Heard from offstage.*) What is it?

FRANCIS: Give me some coin, I'm going to Boston! (*Runs
back into his room.*)

FRAN: (*Running into yard.*) Jesus Christ in Heaven! Yo,
Bun!

(BUNNY's *lights go on.* FRANCIS *turns off the music.*)

BUNNY: (*At her window.*) Yo, Fran!

FRAN: Call your uncle on the ambulance service. We gotta get Francis to the train!

BUNNY: Holy shit!

(*She goes to her telephone in the kitchen.*)

LUCILLE: (*Running into house.*) I'll help you pack.

BUNNY: (*On the phone.*) Hello, Uncle Marty, bring your fuckin' ambulance down, we gotta make a train!

HERSCHEL: (*Coming out of his house.*) What's going on?

FRAN: Francis is going to Boston.

HERSCHEL: To see Randy?

BUNNY: (*Still on the phone.*) Hello, Uncle Jimmy, send a fuckin' squad car down, we gotta make a train.

FRAN: Hey, Herschel! Catch them kids.

(*Pushes him to the gate.*)

HERSCHEL: This way's quicker!

(*Runs out through alley behind his house.*)

FRAN: (*Yelling after him.*) And bring them back! I'm fuckin' outta money. Lucille!

LUCILLE: (*In* FRANCIS's *room, with a large laundry bag.*) There ain't no clean clothes in here!

FRAN: You got some money? I'm out.

LUCILLE: (*Hurling coin purse out the window.*) Look!

FRANCIS: Oh, I want to take my new records—Callas in *Parsifal,* 1950, and the 1955 *Norma!*

(*Runs into his room.*)

FRAN: (*Going through change purse.*) Jesus Christ, Lucille, all these pennies!

LUCILLE: For the tax!

FRAN: Yo, Bun!

BUNNY: Yo, Fran!

FRAN: We need some more money!

(BUNNY *comes out of her house, reaches into her bosom, and removes wad.*)

BUNNY: Here's the house money, take what you need. (*Sirens are heard in the distance, getting closer.*) They're comin'!

(FRANCIS *runs out of the house, holding record albums.*)

You stick wit me, kid, I got connections!

(*Hugs* FRANCIS, *as* FRAN *counts money.*)

Where's Gargantua?

FRAN: He went to get the kids. (*To* FRANCIS.) I think this is enough—

(*Gives him money.*)

BUNNY: I hope he doesn't frighten them away!

LUCILLE: (*Runs out of the house with the laundry bag.*) This is the best I could do—go to a laundromat when you get there!

(FRANCIS *takes bag, hugs her.*)

FRANCIS: Thanks everybody, I mean, thanks . . .

FRAN: Well, it's your birthday.

(*Sirens increase.* HERSCHEL *comes running in from the alley with* JUDITH *and* RANDY.)

HERSCHEL: I got 'em! I got 'em!

FRAN: They're back!

(FRANCIS *embraces* JUDITH. *Sirens much louder.*)

BUNNY: (*At gate.*) My uncles is here!

(*The kids run out. The others watch at the gate.*)

FRAN: (*Checks his watch, then puts his arm around* LUCILLE *and* BUNNY.) I think they're gonna make it!

(*Blackout.*)

BURIED CHILD

by Sam Shepard

PULITZER PRIZE 1979

While the rain of your fingertips falls,
while the rain of your bones falls,
and your laughter and marrow fall down,
you come flying.

Pablo Neruda

Characters:

DODGE	In his seventies.
HALIE	His wife. Midsixties.
TILDEN	Their oldest son.
BRADLEY	Their next oldest son, an amputee.
VINCE	Tilden's son.
SHELLY	Vince's girl friend.
FATHER DEWIS	A Protestant minister

Buried Child was first produced at the Magic Theatre, San Francisco, on June 27, 1978. It was directed by Robert Woodruff with the following cast:

DODGE	*Joseph Gistirak*
HALIE	*Catherine Willis*
TILDEN	*Dennis Ludlow*
BRADLEY	*William M. Carr*
SHELLY	*Betsy Scott*
VINCE	*Barry Lane*
FATHER DEWIS	*Rj Frank*

The New York premiere was directed by Robert Woodruff with the following cast:

DODGE	*Richard Hamilton*
HALIE	*Jacqueline Brookes*
TILDEN	*Tom Noonan*
BRADLEY	*Jay O. Sanders*
SHELLY	*Mary McDonnell*
VINCE	*Christopher McCann*
FATHER DEWIS	*Bill Wiley*

ACT ONE

SCENE: *Day. Old wooden staircase down left with pale, frayed carpet laid down on the steps. The stairs lead offstage left up into the wings with no landing. Up right is an old, dark green sofa with the stuffing coming out in spots. Stage right of the sofa is an upright lamp with a faded yellow shade and a small night table with several small bottles of pills on it. Down right of the sofa, with the screen facing the sofa, is a large, old-fashioned brown TV. A flickering blue light comes from the screen, but no image, no sound. In the dark, the light of the lamp and the TV slowly brighten in the black space. The space behind the sofa, upstage, is a large, screened-in porch with a board floor. A solid interior door to stage right of the sofa, leading into the room on stage; and another screen door up left, leading from the porch to the outside. Beyond that are the shapes of dark elm trees.*

Gradually the form of DODGE *is made out, sitting on the couch, facing the TV, the blue light flickering on his face. He wears a well-worn T-shirt, suspenders, khaki work pants and brown slippers. He's covered himself in an old brown blanket. He's very thin and sickly looking, in his late seventies. He just stares at the TV. More light fills the stage softly. The sound of light rain.* DODGE *slowly tilts his head back and stares*

*at the ceiling for a while, listening to the rain. He
lowers his head again and stares at the TV. He turns
his head slowly to the left and stares at the cushion of
the sofa next to the one he's sitting on. He pulls his
left arm out from under the blanket, slides his hand
under the cushion, and pulls out a bottle of whiskey.
He looks down left toward the staircase, listens, then
uncaps the bottle, takes a long swig and caps it again.
He puts the bottle back under the cushion and stares
at the TV. He starts to cough slowly and softly. The
coughing gradually builds. He holds one hand to his
mouth and tries to stifle it. The coughing gets louder,
then suddenly stops when he hears the sound of his
wife's voice coming from the top of the staircase.*

HALIE'S VOICE: Dodge?
    (DODGE *just stares at the TV. Long pause. He stifles
    two short coughs.*)
HALIE'S VOICE: Dodge! You want a pill, Dodge?
    (*He doesn't answer. Takes the bottle out again and
    takes another long swig. Puts the bottle back stares at
    TV, pulls blanket up around his neck.*)
HALIE'S VOICE: You know what it is, don't you? It's the
rain! Weather. That's it. Every time. Every time you get
like this, it's the rain. No sooner does the rain start then
you start. (*Pause.*) Dodge?
    (*He makes no reply. Pulls a pack of cigarettes out
    from his sweater and lights one. Stares at TV. (Pause.)*
HALIE'S VOICE: You should see it coming down up here.
Just coming down in sheets. Blue sheets. The bridge is
pretty near flooded. What's it like down there? Dodge?
    (DODGE *turns his head back over his left shoulder and
    takes a look out through the porch. He turns back to
    the TV.*)
DODGE: (*To himself.*) Catastrophic.
HALIE'S VOICE: What? What'd you say, Dodge?
DODGE: (*Louder.*) It looks like rain to me! Plain old rain!
HALIE'S VOICE: Rain? Of course it's rain! Are you having a
seizure or something! Dodge? (*Pause.*) I'm coming

down there in about five minutes if you don't answer
me!

DODGE: Don't come down.

HALIE'S VOICE: What!

DODGE: (*Louder.*) Don't come down!
  (*He has another coughing attack. Stops.*)

HALIE'S VOICE: You should take a pill for that! I don't see
why you just don't take a pill. Be done with it once and
for all. Put a stop to it.
  (*He takes bottle out again. Another swig. Returns
  bottle.*)

HALIE'S VOICE: It's not Christian, but it works. It's not nec-
essarily Christian, that is. We don't know. There's some
things the ministers can't even answer. I, personally,
can't see anything wrong with it. Pain is pain. Pure and
simple. Suffering is a different matter. That's entirely different. A pill seems as good an answer as any. Dodge?
(*Pause.*) Dodge, are you watching baseball?

DODGE: No.

HALIE'S VOICE: What?

DODGE: (*Louder.*) No!

HALIE'S VOICE: What're you watching? You shouldn't be
watching anything that'll get you excited! No horse racing!

DODGE: They don't race on Sundays.

HALIE'S VOICE: What?

DODGE: (*Louder.*) They don't race on Sundays!

HALIE'S VOICE: Well they shouldn't race on Sundays.

DODGE: Well they don't!

HALIE'S VOICE: Good. I'm amazed they still have that kind
of legislation. That's amazing.

DODGE: Yeah, it's amazing.

HALIE'S VOICE: What?

DODGE: (*Louder.*) It is amazing!

HALIE'S VOICE: It is. It truly is. I would've thought these
days they'd be racing on Christmas even. A big flashing
Christmas tree right down at the finish line.

DODGE: (*Shakes his head.*) No.

HALIE'S VOICE: They used to race on New Year's! I remember that.

DODGE: They never raced on New Year's!

HALIE'S VOICE. Sometimes they did.

DODGE: They never did!

HALIE'S VOICE: Before we were married they did!

> (DODGE *waves his hand in disgust at the staircase.*
> *Leans back in sofa. Stares at TV.*)

HALIE'S VOICE: I went once. With a man.

DODGE: (*Mimicking her.*) Oh, a "man."

HALIE'S VOICE: What?

DODGE: Nothing!

HALIE'S VOICE: A wonderful man. A breeder.

DODGE: A what?

HALIE'S VOICE: A breeder! A horse breeder! Thorough-breds.

DODGE: Oh, Thoroughbreds. Wonderful.

HALIE'S VOICE: That's right. He knew everything there was to know.

DODGE: I bet he taught you a thing or two huh? Gave you a good turn around the old stable!

HALIE'S VOICE: Knew everything there was to know about horses. We won bookoos of money that day.

DODGE: What?

HALIE'S VOICE: Money! We won every race I think.

DODGE: Bookoos?

HALIE'S VOICE: Every single race.

DODGE: Bookoos of money?

HALIE'S VOICE: It was one of those kind of days.

DODGE: New Year's!

HALIE'S VOICE: Yes! It might've been Florida. Or California! One of those two.

DODGE: Can I take my pick?

HALIE'S VOICE: It was Florida!

DODGE: Aha!

HALIE'S VOICE: Wonderful! Absolutely wonderful! The sun was just gleaming. Flamingos. Bougainvilleas. Palm trees.

DODGE: (*To himself, mimicking her.*) Bougainvilleas. Palm trees.

HALIE'S VOICE: Everything was dancing with life! There were all kinds of people from everywhere. Everyone was dressed to the nines. Not like today. Not like they dress today.

DODGE: When was this anyway?

HALIE'S VOICE: This was long before I knew you.

DODGE: Must've been.

HALIE'S VOICE: Long before. I was escorted.

DODGE: To Florida?

HALIE'S VOICE: Yes. Or it might've been California. I'm not sure which.

DODGE: All that way you were escorted?

HALIE'S VOICE: Yes.

DODGE: And he never laid a finger on you I suppose? (*Long silence.*) Halie?
  (*No answer. Long pause.*)

HALIE'S VOICE: Are you going out today?

DODGE: (*Gesturing toward rain.*) In this?

HALIE'S VOICE: I'm just asking a simple question.

DODGE: I rarely go out in the bright sunshine, why would I go out in this?

HALIE'S VOICE: I'm just asking because I'm not doing any shopping today. And if you need anything you should ask Tilden.

DODGE: Tilden's not here!

HALIE'S VOICE: He's in the kitchen.
  (DODGE *looks toward stage left, then back toward TV.*)

DODGE: All right.

HALIE'S VOICE: What?

DODGE: (*Louder.*) All right!

HALIE'S VOICE: Don't scream. It'll only get your coughing started.

DODGE: All right.

HALIE'S VOICE: Just tell Tilden what you want and he'll get it. (*Pause.*) Bradley should be over later.

DODGE: Bradley?

HALIE'S VOICE: Yes. To cut your hair.

DODGE: My hair? I don't need my hair cut!

HALIE'S VOICE: It won't hurt!

DODGE: I don't need it!

HALIE'S VOICE: It's been more than two weeks, Dodge.

DODGE: I don't need it!

HALIE'S VOICE: I have to meet Father Dewis for lunch.

DODGE: You tell Bradley that if he shows up here with those clippers, I'll kill him!

HALIE'S VOICE: I won't be very late. No later than four at the very latest.

DODGE: You tell him! Last time he left me almost bald! And I wasn't even awake! I was sleeping! I woke up and he'd already left!

HALIE'S VOICE: That's not my fault!

DODGE: You put him up to it!

HALIE'S VOICE: I never did!

DODGE: You did too! You had some fancy, stupid meeting planned! Time to dress up the corpse for company! Lower the ears a little! Put up a little front! Surprised you didn't tape a pipe to my mouth while you were at it! That woulda' looked nice! Huh? A pipe? Maybe a bowler hat! Maybe a copy of *The Wall Street Journal* casually placed on my lap!

HALIE'S VOICE: You always imagine the worst things of people!

DODGE: That's not the worst! That's the least of the worst!

HALIE'S VOICE: I don't need to hear it! All day long I hear things like that and I don't need to hear more.

DODGE: You better tell him!

HALIE'S VOICE: You tell him yourself! He's your own son. You should be able to talk to your own son.

DODGE: Not while I'm sleeping! He cut my hair while I was sleeping!

HALIE'S VOICE: Well he won't do it again.

DODGE: There's no guarantee.

HALIE'S VOICE: I promise he won't do it without your consent.

DODGE: (*After pause.*) There's no reason for him to even come over here.

HALIE'S VOICE: He feels responsible.

DODGE: For my hair?

HALIE'S VOICE: For your appearance.

DODGE: My appearance is out of his domain! It's even out of mine! In fact, it's disappeared! I'm an invisible man!

HALIE'S VOICE: Don't be ridiculous.

DODGE: He better not try it. That's all I've got to say.

HALIE'S VOICE: Tilden will watch out for you.

DODGE: Tilden won't protect me from Bradley!

HALIE'S VOICE: Tilden's the oldest. He'll protect you.

DODGE: Tilden can't even protect himself!

HALIE'S VOICE: Not so loud! He'll hear you. He's right in the kitchen.

DODGE: (*Yelling off left.*) Tilden!

HALIE'S VOICE: Dodge, what are you trying to do?

DODGE: (*Yelling off left.*) Tilden, get in here!

HALIE'S VOICE: Why do you enjoy stirring things up?

DODGE: I don't enjoy anything!

HALIE'S VOICE: That's a terrible thing to say.

DODGE: Tilden!

HALIE'S VOICE: That's the kind of statement that leads people right to the end of their rope.

DODGE: Tilden!

HALIE'S VOICE: It's no wonder people turn to Christ!

DODGE: TILDEN!!

HALIE'S VOICE: It's no wonder the messengers of God's word are shouted down in public places!

DODGE: TILDEN!!!!

(DODGE *goes into a violent, spasmodic coughing attack as* TILDEN *enters from stage left, his arms loaded with fresh ears of corn.* TILDEN *is* DODGE'S *oldest son, late forties, wears heavy construction boots, covered with mud, dark green work pants, a plaid shirt and a faded brown windbreaker. He has a butch haircut, wet from the rain. Something about him is profoundly burned out and displaced. He stops center stage with the ears of corn in his arms and just stares at* DODGE *until he slowly finishes his coughing attack.* DODGE *looks up at him slowly. He stares at the corn. Long pause as they watch each other.*)

HALIE'S VOICE: Dodge, if you don't take that pill nobody's going to force you.

(*The two men ignore the voice.*)

DODGE: (*To* TILDEN.) Where'd you get that?

TILDEN: Picked it.

DODGE: You picked all that?
  (TILDEN *nods.*)
DODGE: You expecting company?
TILDEN: No.
DODGE: Where'd you pick it from?
TILDEN: Right out back.
DODGE: Out back where!
TILDEN: Right out in back.
DODGE: There's nothing out there!
TILDEN: There's corn.
DODGE: There hasn't been corn out there since about nineteen thirty-five! That's the last time I planted corn out there!
TILDEN: It's out there now.
DODGE: (*Yelling at stairs.*) Halie!
HALIE'S VOICE: Yes dear!
DODGE: Tilden's brought a whole bunch of corn in here! There's no corn out in back is there?
TILDEN: (*To himself.*) There's tons of corn.
HALIE'S VOICE: Not that I know of!
DODGE: That's what I thought.
HALIE'S VOICE: Not since about nineteen thirty-five!
DODGE: (*To* TILDEN.) That's right. Nineteen thirty-five.
TILDEN: It's out there now.
DODGE: You go and take that corn back to wherever you got it from!
TILDEN: (*After pause, staring at* DODGE.) It's picked. I picked it all in the rain. Once it's picked you can't put it back.
DODGE: I haven't had trouble with neighbors here for fifty-seven years. I don't even know who the neighbors are! And I don't wanna know! Now go put that corn back where it came from!
  (TILDEN *stares at* DODGE *then walks slowly over to him and dumps all the corn on* DODGE'S *lap and steps back.* DODGE *stares at the corn then back to* TILDEN. *Long pause.*)
DODGE: Are you having trouble here, Tilden? Are you in some kind of trouble?
TILDEN: I'm not in any trouble.

DODGE: You can tell me if you are. I'm still your father.

TILDEN: I know you're still my father.

DODGE: I know you had a little trouble back in New Mexico. That's why you came out here.

TILDEN: I never had any trouble.

DODGE: Tilden, your mother told me all about it.

TILDEN: What'd she tell you?

(TILDEN *pulls some chewing tobacco out of his jacket and bites off a plug..*)

DODGE: I don't have to repeat what she told me! She told me all about it!

TILDEN: Can I bring my chair in from the kitchen?

DODGE: What?

TILDEN: Can I bring my chair from the kitchen?

DODGE: Sure. Bring your chair in.

(TILDEN *exits left.* DODGE *pushes all the corn off his lap onto the floor. He pulls the blanket off angrily and tosses it at one end of the sofa, pulls out the bottle and takes another swig.* TILDEN *enters again from left with a milking stool and a pail.* DODGE *hides the bottle quickly under the cushion before* TILDEN *sees it.* TILDEN *sets the stool down by the sofa, sits on it, puts the pail in front of him on the floor.* TILDEN *starts picking up the ears of corn one at a time and husking them. He throws the husks and silk in the center of the stage and drops the ears into the pail each time he cleans one. He repeats this process as they talk.*)

DODGE: (*After pause.*) Sure is nice looking corn.

TILDEN: It's the best.

DODGE: Hybrid?

TILDEN: What?

DODGE: Some kinda fancy hybrid?

TILDEN: You planted it. I don't know what it is.

DODGE: (*Pause.*) Tilden, look, you can't stay here forever. You know that, don't you?

TILDEN: (*Spits in spittoon.*) I'm not.

DODGE: I know you're not. I'm not worried about that. That's not the reason I brought it up.

TILDEN: What's the reason?

DODGE: The reason is I'm wondering what you're gonna do.

TILDEN: You're not worried about me, are you?

DODGE: I'm not worried about you.

TILDEN: You weren't worried about me when I wasn't here. When I was in New Mexico.

DODGE: No, I wasn't worried about you then either.

TILDEN: You shoulda worried about me then.

DODGE: Why's that? You didn't do anything down there, did you?

TILDEN: I didn't do anything.

DODGE: Then why should I have worried about you?

TILDEN: Because I was lonely.

DODGE: Because you were lonely?

TILDEN: Yeah. I was more lonely than I've ever been before.

DODGE: Why was that?

TILDEN: (*Pause.*) Could I have some of that whiskey you've got?

DODGE: What whiskey? I haven't got any whiskey.

TILDEN: You've got some under the sofa.

DODGE: I haven't got anything under the sofa! Now mind your own damn business! Jesus God, you come into the house outa the middle of nowhere, haven't heard or seen you in twenty years and suddenly you're making accusations.

TILDEN: I'm not making accusations.

DODGE: You're accusing me of hoarding whiskey under the sofa!

TILDEN: I'm not accusing you.

DODGE: You just got through telling me I had whiskey under the sofa!

HALIE'S VOICE: Dodge?

DODGE: (*To* TILDEN.) Now she knows about it!

TILDEN: She doesn't know about it.

HALIE'S VOICE: Dodge, are you talking to yourself down there?

DODGE: I'm talking to Tilden!

HALIE'S VOICE: Tilden's down there?

DODGE: He's right here!

HALIE'S VOICE: What?

DODGE: (*Louder.*) He's right here!

HALIE'S VOICE: What's he doing?

DODGE: (*To* TILDEN.) Don't answer her.

TILDEN: (*To* DODGE.) I'm not doing anything wrong.

DODGE: I know you're not.

HALIE'S VOICE: What's he doing down there!

DODGE: (*To* TILDEN.) Don't answer.

TILDEN: I'm not.

HALIE'S VOICE: Dodge!

> (*The men sit in silence.* DODGE *lights a cigarette.* TIL-
> DEN *keeps husking corn, spits tobacco now and then
> in spittoon.*)

HALIE'S VOICE: Dodge! He's not drinking anything, is he?
You see to it that he doesn't drink anything! You've
gotta watch out for him. It's our responsibility. He can't
look after himself anymore, so we have to do it. Nobody
else will do it. We can't just send him away somewhere.
If we had lots of money we could send him away. But
we don't. We never will. That's why we have to stay
healthy. You and me. Nobody's going to look after us.
Bradley can't look after us. Bradley can hardly look
after himself. I was always hoping that Tilden would
look out for Bradley when they got older. After Bradley
lost his leg. Tilden's the oldest. I always thought he'd be
the one to take responsibility. I had no idea in the world
that Tilden would be so much trouble. Who would've
dreamed. Tilden was an all-American, don't forget. Don't
forget that. Fullback. Or quarterback. I forget which.

TILDEN: (*To himself.*) Fullback. (*Still husking.*)

HALIE'S VOICE: Then when Tilden turned out to be so
much trouble, I put all my hopes on Ansel. Of course
Ansel wasn't as handsome, but he was smart. He was the
smartest probably. I think he probably was. Smarter
than Bradley, that's for sure. Didn't go and chop his leg
off with a chain saw. Smart enough not to go and do
that. I think he was smarter than Tilden too. Especially
after Tilden got in all that trouble. Doesn't take brains to
go to jail. Anybody knows that. Course then when Ansel
died that left us all alone. Same as being alone. No different. Same as if they'd all died. He was the smartest.
He could've earned lots of money. Lots and lots of
money.

(HALIE *enters slowly from the top of the staircase as she continues talking. Just her feet are seen at first as she makes her way down the stairs, a step at a time. She appears dressed completely in black, as though in mourning. Black handbag, hat with a veil, and pulling on elbow-length black gloves. She is about sixty-five with pure white hair. She remains absorbed in what she's saying as she descends the stairs and doesn't really notice the two men who continue sitting there as they were before she came down, smoking and husking.*)

HALIE: He would've took care of us, too. He would've seen to it that we were repaid. He was like that. He was a hero. Don't forget that. A genuine hero. Brave. Strong. And very intelligent. Ansel could've been a great man. One of the greatest. I only regret that he didn't die in action. It's not fitting for a man like that to die in a motel room. A soldier. He could've won a medal. He could've been decorated for valor. I've talked to Father Dewis about putting up a plaque for Ansel. He thinks it's a good idea. He agrees. He knew Ansel when he used to play basketball. Went to every game. Ansel was his favorite player. He even recommended to the City Council that they put up a statue of Ansel. A big, tall statue with a basketball in one hand and a rifle in the other. That's how much he thinks of Ansel.

(HALIE *reaches the stage and begins to wander around, still absorbed in pulling on her gloves, brushing lint off her dress and continuously talking to herself as the men just sit.*)

HALIE: Of course, he'd still be alive today if he hadn't married into the Catholics. The Mob. How in the world he never opened his eyes to that is beyond me. Just beyond me. Everyone around him could see the truth. Even Tilden. Tilden told him time and again. Catholic women are the Devil incarnate. He wouldn't listen. He was blind with love. Blind. I knew. Everyone knew. The wedding was more like a funeral. You remember? All those Italians. All that horrible black, greasy hair. The smell of cheap cologne. I think even the priest was wearing a pistol. When he gave her the ring I knew he was a dead man. I knew it. As soon as he gave her the ring. But then it was the honeymoon that killed him. The honeymoon. I knew he'd never come back from the honeymoon. I kissed him and he felt like a corpse. All white. Cold. Icy blue lips. He never used to kiss like that. Never before. I knew then that she'd cursed him. Taken his soul. I saw it in her eyes. She smiled at me with that Catholic sneer of hers. She told me with her eyes that she'd murder him in his bed. Murder my son. She told me. And there was nothing I could do. Absolutely nothing. He was going with her, thinking he was free. Thinking it was love. What could I do? I couldn't tell him she was a witch. I couldn't tell him that. He'd have turned on me. Hated me. I couldn't stand him hating me and then dying before he ever saw me again. Hating me in his deathbed. Hating me and loving her! How could I do that? I had to let him go. I had to. I watched him leave. I watched him throw gardenias as he helped her into the limousine. I watched his face disappear behind the glass.

(*She stops abruptly and stares at the cornhusks. She looks around the space as though just waking up. She turns and looks hard at* TILDEN *and* DODGE *who continue sitting calmly. She looks again at the cornhusks.*)

HALIE: (*Pointing to the husks.*) What's this in my house! (*Kicks husks.*) What's all this!

(TILDEN *stops husking and stares at her.*)

HALIE: (*To* DODGE.) And you encourage him!

(DODGE *pulls blanket over him again.*)

DODGE: You're going out in the rain?

HALIE: It's not raining.

(TILDEN *starts husking again.*)

DODGE: Not in Florida it's not.

HALIE: We're not in Florida!

DODGE: It's not raining at the racetrack.

HALIE: Have you been taking those pills? Those pills always make you talk crazy. Tilden, has he been taking those pills?

TILDEN: He hasn't took anything.

HALIE: (*To* DODGE.) What've you been taking?

DODGE: It's not raining in California or Florida or the race-track. Only in Illinois. This is the only place it's raining. All over the rest of the world it's bright golden sunshine. (HALIE *goes to the night table next to the sofa and checks the bottle of pills.*)

HALIE: Which ones did you take? Tilden, you must've seen him take something.

TILDEN: He never took a thing.

HALIE: Then why's he talking crazy?

TILDEN: I've been here the whole time.

HALIE: Then you've both been taking something!

TILDEN: I've just been husking the corn.

HALIE: Where'd you get that corn anyway? Why is the house suddenly full of corn?

DODGE: Bumper crop!

HALIE: (*Moving center.*) We haven't had corn here for over thirty years.

TILDEN: The whole back lot's full of corn. Far as the eye can see.

DODGE: (*To* HALIE.) Things keep happening while you're upstairs, ya' know. The world doesn't stop just because you're upstairs. Corn keeps growing. Rain keeps raining.

HALIE: I'm not unaware of the world around me! Thank you very much. It so happens that I have an overall view from the upstairs. The backyard's in plain view of my window. And there's no corn to speak of. Absolutely none!

DODGE: Tilden wouldn't lie. If he says there's corn, there's corn.

HALIE: What's the meaning of this corn, Tilden!

TILDEN: It's a mystery to me. I was out in back there. And the rain was coming down. And I didn't feel like coming back inside. I didn't feel the cold so much. I didn't mind the wet. So I was just walking. I was muddy but I didn't mind the mud so much. And I looked up. And I saw this stand of corn. In fact I was standing in it. So, I was standing in it.

HALIE: There isn't any corn outside, Tilden! There's no

corn! Now, you must've either stolen this corn or you bought it.

DODGE: He doesn't have any money.

HALIE: (*To* TILDEN.) So you stole it!

TILDEN: I didn't steal it. I don't want to get kicked out of Illinois. I was kicked out of New Mexico and I don't want to get kicked out of Illinois.

HALIE: You're going to get kicked out of this house, Tilden, if you don't tell me where you got that corn!

(TILDEN *starts crying softly to himself but keeps husking corn. Pause.*)

DODGE: (*To* HALIE.) Why'd you have to tell him that? Who cares where he got the corn? Why'd you have to go and tell him that?

HALIE: (*To* DODGE.) It's your fault you know! You're the one that's behind all this! I suppose you thought it'd be funny! Some joke! Cover the house with cornhusks. You better get this cleaned up before Bradley sees it.

DODGE: Bradley's not getting in the front door!

HALIE: (*Kicking husks, striding back and forth.*) Bradley's going to be very upset when he sees this. He doesn't like to see the house in disarray. He can't stand it when one thing is out of place. The slightest thing. You know how he gets.

DODGE: Bradley doesn't even live here!

HALIE: It's his home as much as ours. He was born in this house!

DODGE: He was born in a hog wallow.

HALIE: Don't you say that! Don't you ever say that!

DODGE: He was born in a goddamn hog wallow! That's where he was born and that's where he belongs! He doesn't belong in this house!

HALIE: (*She stops.*) I don't know what's come over you, Dodge. I don't know what in the world's come over you. You've become an evil man. You used to be a good man.

DODGE: Six of one, a half dozen of another.

HALIE: You sit here day and night, festering away! Decomposing! Smelling up the house with your putrid body! Hacking your head off til all hours of the morning!

Thinking up mean, evil, stupid things to say about your own flesh and blood!

DODGE: He's not my flesh and blood! My flesh and blood's buried in the backyard!

(*They freeze. Long pause. The men stare at her.*)

HALIE: (*Quietly.*) That's enough, Dodge. That's quite enough. I'm going out now. I'm going to have lunch with Father Dewis. I'm going to ask him about a monument. A statue. At least a plaque.

(*She crosses to the door up right. She stops.*)

HALIE: If you need anything, ask Tilden. He's the oldest. I've left some money on the kitchen table.

DODGE: I don't need anything.

HALIE: No, I suppose not. (*She opens the door and looks out through porch.*) Still raining. I love the smell just after it stops. The ground. I won't be too late.

(*She goes out door and closes it. She's still visible on the porch as she crosses toward stage left screen door. She stops in the middle of the porch, speaks to* DODGE *but doesn't turn to him.*)

HALIE: Dodge, tell Tilden not to go out in the back lot anymore. I don't want him back there in the rain.

DODGE: You tell him. He's sitting right here.

HALIE: He never listens to me, Dodge. He's never listened to me in the past.

DODGE: I'll tell him.

HALIE: We have to watch him just like we used to now. Just like we always have. He's still a child.

DODGE: I'll watch him.

HALIE: Good.

(*She crosses to screen door, left, takes an umbrella off a hook and goes out the door. The door slams behind her. Long pause.* TILDEN *husks corn, stares at pail.* DODGE *lights a cigarette, stares at TV.*)

TILDEN: (*Still husking.*) You shouldn't a told her that.

DODGE: (*Staring at TV.*) What?

TILDEN: What you told her. You know.

DODGE: What do you know about it?

TILDEN: I know. I know all about it. We all know.

DODGE: So what difference does it make? Everybody knows, everybody's forgot.

TILDEN: She hasn't forgot.

DODGE: She should've forgot.

TILDEN: It's different for a woman. She couldn't forget that. How could she forget that?

DODGE: I don't want to talk about it!

TILDEN: What do you want to talk about it!

DODGE: I don't want to talk about anything! I don't want to talk about troubles or what happened fifty years ago or thirty years ago or the racetrack or Florida or the last time I seeded the corn! I don't want to talk!

TILDEN: You don't wanna die do you?

DODGE: No, I don't wanna die either.

TILDEN: Well, you gotta talk or you'll die.

DODGE: Who told you that?

TILDEN: That's what I know. I found that out in New Mexico. I thought I was dying but I just lost my voice.

DODGE: Were you with somebody?

TILDEN: I was alone. I thought I was dead.

DODGE: Might as well have been. What'd you come back here for?

TILDEN: I didn't know where to go.

DODGE: You're a grown man. You shouldn't be needing your parents at your age. It's unnatural. There's nothing we can do for you now anyway. Couldn't you make a living down there? Couldn't you find some way to make a living? Support yourself? What'd'ya come back here for? You expect us to feed you forever?

TILDEN: I didn't know where else to go.

DODGE: I never went back to my parents. Never. Never even had the urge. I was independent. Always independent. Always found a way.

TILDEN: I didn't know what to do. I couldn't figure anything out.

DODGE: There's nothing to figure out. You just forge ahead. What's there to figure out?

(TILDEN *stands*.)

TILDEN: I don't know.

DODGE: Where are you going?

TILDEN: Out back.

DODGE: You're not supposed to go out there. You heard what she said. Don't play deaf with me!

TILDEN: I like it out there.

DODGE: In the rain?

TILDEN: Especially in the rain. I like the feeling of it. Feels like it always did.

DODGE: You're supposed to watch out for me. Get me things when I need them.

TILDEN: What do you need?

DODGE: I don't need anything! But I might. I might need something any second. Any second now. I can't be left alone for a minute!

(DODGE *starts to cough.*)

TILDEN: I'll be right outside. You can just yell.

DODGE: (*Between coughs.*) No! It's too far! You can't go out there! It's too far! You might not ever hear me!

TILDEN: (*Moving to pills.*) Why don't you take a pill? You want a pill?

(DODGE *coughs more violently, throws himself back against sofa, clutches his throat.* TILDEN *stands by helplessly.*)

DODGE: Water! Get me some water!

(TILDEN *rushes off left.* DODGE *reaches out for the pills, knocking some bottles to the floor, coughing in spasms. He grabs a small bottle, takes out pills and swallows them.* TILDEN *rushes back on with a glass of water.* DODGE *takes it and drinks, his coughing subsides.*)

TILDEN: You all right now?

(DODGE *nods. Drinks more water.* TILDEN *moves in closer to him.* DODGE *sets glass of water on the night table. His coughing is almost gone.*)

TILDEN: Why don't you lay down for a while? Just rest a little.

(TILDEN *helps* DODGE *lay down on the sofa. Covers him with blanket.*)

DODGE: You're not going outside are you?

TILDEN: No.

DODGE: I don't want to wake up and find you not here.

TILDEN: I'll be here.

(TILDEN *tucks blanket around* DODGE.)

DODGE: You'll stay right here?

TILDEN: I'll stay in my chair.

DODGE: That's not a chair. That's my old milking stool.

TILDEN: I know.

DODGE: Don't call it a chair.

TILDEN: I won't.

(TILDEN *tries to take* DODGE'S *baseball cap off.*)

DODGE: What're you doing! Leave that on me! Don't take that offa me! That's my cap!

(TILDEN *leaves the cap on* DODGE.)

TILDEN: I know.

DODGE: Bradley'll shave my head if I don't have that on. That's my cap.

TILDEN: I know it is.

DODGE: Don't take my cap off.

TILDEN: I won't.

DODGE: You stay right here now.

TILDEN: (*Sits on stool.*) I will.

DODGE: Don't go outside. There's nothing out there.

TILDEN: I won't.

DODGE: Everything's in here. Everything you need. Money's on the table. TV. Is the TV on?

TILDEN: Yeah.

DODGE: Turn it off! Turn the damn thing off! What's it doing on?

TILDEN: (*Shuts off TV, light goes out.*) You left it on.

DODGE: Well turn it off.

TILDEN: (*Sits on stool again.*) It's off.

DODGE: Leave it off.

TILDEN: I will.

DODGE: When I fall asleep you can turn it on.

TILDEN: Okay.

DODGE: You can watch the ball game. Red Sox. You like the Red Sox don't you?

TILDEN: Yeah.

DODGE: You can watch the Red Sox. Pee Wee Reese. Pee Wee Reese. You rememeber Pee Wee Reese?

TILDEN: No.

DODGE: Was he with the Red Sox?

TILDEN: I don't know.

DODGE: Pee Wee Reese. (*Falling asleep.*) You can watch the Cardinals. You remember Stan Musial.

TILDEN: No.

DODGE: Stan Musial. (*Falling into sleep.*) Bases loaded. Top a' the sixth. Bases loaded. Runner on first and third. Big fat knuckle ball. Floater. Big as a blimp. Cracko! Ball just took off like a rocket. Just pulverized. I marked it. Marked it with my eyes. Straight between the clock and the Burma Shave ad. I was the first kid out there. First kid. I had to fight hard for that ball. I wouldn't give it up. They almost tore the ears right off me. But I wouldn't give it up.

> (DODGE *falls into deep sleep.* TILDEN *just sits staring at him for a while. Slowly he leans toward the sofa, checking to see if* DODGE *is well asleep. He reaches slowly under the cushion and pulls out the bottle of booze.* DODGE *sleeps soundly.* TILDEN *stands quietly, staring at* DODGE *as he uncaps the bottle and takes a long drink. He caps the bottle and sticks it in his hip pocket. He looks around at the husks on the floor and then back to* DODGE. *He moves center stage and gathers an armload of cornhusks then crosses back to the sofa. He stands holding the husks over* DODGE *and looking down at him he gently spreads the cornhusks over the whole length of* DODGE'S *body. He stands back and looks at* DODGE. *Pulls out bottle, takes another drink, returns bottle to his hip pocket. He gathers more husks and repeats the procedure until the floor is clean of cornhusks and* DODGE *is completely covered in them except for his head.* TILDEN *takes another long drink, stares at* DODGE *sleeping then quietly exits stage left. Long pause as the sound of rain continues.* DODGE *sleeps on. The figure of* BRADLEY *appears up left, outside the screen porch door. He holds a wet newspaper over his head as a protection from the rain. He seems to be struggling with the door then slips and almost falls to the ground.* DODGE *sleeps on, undisturbed.*)

BRADLEY: Sonuvabitch! Sonuvagoddamnbitch!

(BRADLEY *recovers his footing and makes it through the screen door onto the porch. He throws the newspaper down, shakes the water out of his hair, and brushes the rain off of his shoulders. He is a big man dressed in a gray sweat shirt, black suspenders, baggy dark blue pants and black janitor's shoes. His left leg is wooden, having been amputated above the knee. He moves with an exaggerated, almost mechanical limp. The squeaking sounds of leather and metal accompany his walk coming from the harness and hinges of the false leg. His arms and shoulders are extremely powerful and muscular due to a lifetime dependency on the upper torso doing all the work for the legs. He is about five years younger than* TILDEN. *He moves laboriously to the stage right door and enters, closing the door behind him. He doesn't notice* DODGE *at first. He moves toward the staircase.*)

BRADLEY: (*Calling to upstairs.*) Mom!

(*He stops and listens. Turns upstage and sees* DODGE *sleeping. Notices cornhusks. He moves slowly toward sofa. Stops next to pail and looks into it. Looks at husks.* DODGE *stays asleep. Talks to himself.*)

BRADLEY: What in the hell is this?

(*He looks at* DODGE's *sleeping face and shakes his head in disgust. He pulls out a pair of black electric hair clippers from his pocket. Unwinds the cord and crosses to the lamp. He jabs his wooden leg behind the knee, causing it to bend at the joint and awkwardly kneels to plug the cord into a floor outlet. He pulls himself to his feet again by using the sofa as leverage. He moves to* DODGE's *head and again jabs his false leg. Goes down on one knee. He violently knocks away some of the cornhusks then jerks off* DODGE's *baseball cap and throws it down center stage.* DODGE *stays asleep.* BRADLEY *switches on the clippers. Lights start dimming.* BRADLEY *cuts* DODGE's *hair while he sleeps. Lights dim slowly to black with the sound of clippers and rain.*)

ACT TWO

SCENE: *Same as Act 1. Night. Sound of rain.* DODGE *still asleep on sofa. His hair is cut extremely short and in places the scalp is cut and bleeding. His cap is still center stage. All the corn and husks, pail and milking stool have been cleared away. The lights come up to the sound of a young girl laughing off stage left.* DODGE *remains asleep.* SHELLY *and* VINCE *appear up left outside the screen porch door sharing the shelter of* VINCE'S *overcoat above their heads.* SHELLY *is about nineteen, black hair, very beautiful. She wears tight jeans, high heels, purple T-shirt and a short rabbit fur coat. Her makeup is exaggerated and her hair has been curled.* VINCE *is* TILDEN'S *son, about twenty-two, wears a plaid shirt, jeans, dark glasses, cowboy boots and carries a black saxophone case. They shake the rain off themselves as they enter the porch through the screen door.*

SHELLY: (*Laughing, gesturing to house.*) This is it? I don't believe this is it!

VINCE: This is it.

SHELLY: This is the house?

VINCE: This is the house.

SHELLY: I don't believe it!

VINCE: How come?

SHELLY: It's like a Norman Rockwell cover or something.

VINCE: What's a' matter with that? It's American.

SHELLY: Where's the milkman and the little dog? What's the little dog's name? Spot. Spot and Jane. Dick and Jane and Spot.

VINCE: Knock it off.

SHELLY: Dick and Jane and Spot and Mom and Dad and Junior and Sissy!

(*She laughs. Slaps her knee.*)

VINCE: Come on! It's my heritage. What dya' expect?

(*She laughs more hysterically, out of control.*)

SHELLY: "And Tuffy and Toto and Dooda and Bonzo all went down one day to the corner grocery store to buy a big bag of licorice for Mr. Marshall's pussycat!"

(*She laughs so hard she falls to her knees holding her stomach.* VINCE *stands there looking at her.*)

VINCE: Shelly will you get up!

(*She keeps laughing. Staggers to her feet. Turning in circles holding her stomach.*)

SHELLY: (*Continuing her story in kid's voice.*) "Mr. Marshall was on vacation. He had no idea that the four little boys had taken such a liking to his little kitty cat."

VINCE: Have some respect would ya'!

SHELLY: (*Trying to control herself.*) I'm sorry.

VINCE: Pull yourself together.

SHELLY: (*Salutes him.*) Yes sir.

(*She giggles.*)

VINCE: Jesus Christ, Shelly.

SHELLY: (*Pause, smiling.*) And Mr. Marshall—

VINCE: Cut it out.

(*She stops. Stands there staring at him. Stifles a giggle.*)

VINCE: (*After pause.*) Are you finished?

SHELLY: Oh brother!

VINCE: I don't wanna go in there with you acting like an idiot.

SHELLY: Thanks.

VINCE: Well, I don't.

SHELLY: I won't embarrass you. Don't worry.

VINCE: I'm not worried.

SHELLY: You are too.

VINCE: Shelly look, I just don't wanna go in there with you giggling your head off. They might think something's wrong with you.

SHELLY: There is.

VINCE: There is not!

SHELLY: Something's definitely wrong with me.

VINCE: There is not!

SHELLY: There's something wrong with you too.

VINCE: There's nothing wrong with me either!

SHELLY: You wanna know what's wrong with you?

VINCE: What?

(SHELLY *laughs.*)

VINCE: (*Crosses back left toward screen door.*) I'm leaving!

SHELLY: (*Stops laughing.*) Wait! Stop. Stop! (VINCE *stops.*) What's wrong with you is that you take the situation too seriously.

VINCE: I just don't want to have them think that I've suddenly arrived out of the middle of nowhere completely deranged.

SHELLY: What do you want them to think then?

VINCE: (*Pause.*) Nothing. Let's go in.

(*He crosses porch toward stage right interior door.* SHELLY *follows him. The stage right door opens slowly.* VINCE *sticks his head in, doesn't notice* DODGE *sleeping. Calls out toward staircase.*)

VINCE: Grandma!

(SHELLY *breaks into laughter, unseen behind* VINCE. VINCE *pulls his head back outside and pulls door shut. We hear their voices again without seeing them.*)

SHELLEY'S VOICE: (*Stops laughing.*) I'm sorry. I'm sorry, Vince. I really am. I really am sorry. I won't do it again. I couldn't help it.

VINCE'S VOICE: It's not all that funny.

SHELLY'S VOICE: I know it's not. I'm sorry.

VINCE'S VOICE: I mean this is a tense situation for me! I haven't seen them for over six years. I don't know what to expect.

SHELLY'S VOICE: I know. I won't do it again.

VINCE'S VOICE: Can't you bite your tongue or something?

SHELLY'S VOICE: Just don't say "Grandma," okay? (*She giggles, stops.*) I mean if you say "Grandma" I don't know if I can stop myself.

VINCE'S VOICE: Well try!

SHELLY'S VOICE: Okay. Sorry.

(*Door opens again.* VINCE *sticks his head in then enters.* SHELLY *follows behind him.* VINCE *crosses to staircase, sets down saxophone case and overcoat, looks up staircase.* SHELLY *notices* DODGE's *baseball cap. Crosses to it. Picks it up and puts it on her head.* VINCE *goes up the stairs and disappears at the top.* SHELLY *watches him then turns and sees* DODGE *on the sofa. She takes off the baseball cap.*)

VINCE'S VOICE: (*From above stairs.*) Grandma!

(SHELLY *crosses over to* DODGE *slowly and stands next to him. She stands at his head, reaches out slowly and touches one of the cuts. The second she touches his head,* DODGE *jerks up to a sitting position on the sofa, eyes open.* SHELLY *gasps.* DODGE *looks at her, sees his cap in her hands, quickly puts his hand to his bare head. He glares at* SHELLY *then whips the cap out of her hands and puts it on.* SHELLY *backs away from him.* DODGE *stares at her.*)

SHELLY: I'm uh, with Vince.

(DODGE *just glares at her.*)

SHELLY: He's upstairs.

(DODGE *looks at the staircase then back to* SHELLY.)

SHELLY: (*Calling upstairs.*) Vince!

VINCE'S VOICE: Just a second!

SHELLY: You better get down here!

VINCE'S VOICE: Just a minute! I'm looking at the pictures.

(DODGE *keeps staring at her.*)

SHELLY: (*To* DODGE.) We just got here. Pouring rain on the freeway so we thought we'd stop by. I mean Vince was planning on stopping anyway. He wanted to see you. He said he hadn't seen you in a long time.

(*Pause.* DODGE *just keeps staring at her.*)

SHELLY: We were going all the way through to New Mexico. To see his father. I guess his father lives out there. We thought we'd stop by and see you on the way. Kill two birds with one stone, you know? (*She laughs,* DODGE *stares, she stops laughing.*) I mean Vince has this thing about his family now. I guess it's a new thing with him I kind of find it hard to relate to. But he feels it's important. You know. I mean he feels he wants to get to know you all again. After all this time.

(*Pause.* DODGE *just stares at her. She moves nervously to staircase and yells up to* VINCE.)

SHELLY: Vince will you come down here please!

(VINCE *comes halfway down the stairs.*)

VINCE: I guess they went out for a while.

(SHELLY *points to sofa and* DODGE. VINCE *turns and sees* DODGE. *He comes all the way down staircase and crosses to* DODGE. SHELLY *stays behind near staircase, keeping her distance.*)

VINCE: Grandpa?

(DODGE *looks up at him, not recognizing him.*)

DODGE: Did you bring the whiskey?

(VINCE *looks back at* SHELLY *then back to* DODGE.)

VINCE: Grandpa, it's Vince. I'm Vince. Tilden's son. You remember?

(DODGE *stares at him.*)

DODGE: You didn't do what you told me. You didn't stay here with me.

VINCE: Grandpa, I haven't been here until just now. I just got here.

DODGE: You left. You went outside like we told you not to do. You went out there in back. In the rain.

(VINCE *looks back at* SHELLY. *She moves slowly toward sofa.*)

SHELLY: Is he okay?

VINCE: I don't know. (*Takes off his shades.*) Look, Grandpa, don't you remember me? Vince. Your Grandson.

(DODGE *stares at him then takes off his baseball cap.*)

DODGE: (*Points to his head.*) See what happens when you leave me alone? See that? That's what happens.

(VINCE *looks at his head.* VINCE *reaches out to touch his head.* DODGE *slaps his hand away with the cap and puts it back on his head.*)

VINCE: What's going on, Grandpa? Where's Halie?

DODGE: Don't worry about her. She won't be back for days. She says she'll be back but she won't be. (*He starts laughing.*) There's life in the old girl yet! (*Stops laughing.*)

VINCE: How did you do that to your head?

DODGE: I didn't do it! Don't be ridiculous!

VINCE: Well who did then?

    (*Pause.* DODGE *stares at* VINCE.)

DODGE: Who do you think did it? Who do you think?

    (SHELLY *moves toward* VINCE.)

SHELLY: Vince, maybe we oughta' go. I don't like this. I mean this isn't my idea of a good time.

VINCE: (*To* SHELLY). Just a second. (*To* DODGE.) Grandpa, look, I just got here. I just now got here. I haven't been here for six years. I don't know anything that's happened.

    (*Pause.* DODGE *stares at him.*)

DODGE: You don't know anything?

VINCE: No.

DODGE: Well that's good. That's good. It's much better not to know anything. Much, much better.

VINCE: Isn't there anybody here with you?

    (DODGE *turns slowly and looks off to stage left.*)

DODGE: Tilden's here.

VINCE: No, Grandpa, Tilden's in New Mexico. That's where I was going. I'm going out there to see him.

    (DODGE *turns slowly back to* VINCE.)

DODGE: Tilden's here.

    (VINCE *backs away and joins* SHELLY. DODGE *stares at them.*)

SHELLY: Vince, why don't we spend the night in a motel and come back in the morning? We could have breakfast. Maybe everything would be different.

VINCE: Don't be scared. There's nothing to be scared of. He's just old.

SHELLY: I'm not scared!

DODGE: You two are not my idea of the perfect couple!

SHELLY: (*After pause.*) Oh really? Why's that?

VINCE: Shh! Don't aggravate him.

DODGE: There's something wrong between the two of you. Something not compatible.

VINCE: Grandpa, where did Halie go? Maybe we should call her.

DODGE: What are you talking about? Do you know what you're talking about? Are you just talking for the sake of talking? Lubricating the gums?

VINCE: I'm trying to figure out what's going on here!

DODGE: Is that it?

VINCE: Yes. I mean I expected everything to be different.

DODGE: Who are you to expect anything? Who are you supposed to be?

VINCE: I'm Vince! Your Grandson!

DODGE: Vince. My Grandson.

VINCE: Tilden's son.

DODGE: Tilden's son, Vince.

VINCE: You haven't seen me for a long time.

DODGE: When was the last time?

VINCE: I don't remember.

DODGE: You don't remember?

VINCE: No.

DODGE: You don't remember. How am I supposed to remember if you don't remember?

SHELLY: Vince, come on. This isn't going to work out.

VINCE: (*To* SHELLY). Just take it easy.

SHELLY: I'm taking it easy! He doesn't even know who you are!

VINCE: (*Crossing toward* DODGE.) Grandpa, look—

DODGE: Stay where you are! Keep your distance!

(VINCE *stops. Looks back at* SHELLY *then to* DODGE.)

SHELLY: Vince, this is really making me nervous. I mean he doesn't even want us here. He doesn't even like us.

DODGE: She's a beautiful girl.

VINCE: Thanks.

DODGE: Very Beautiful Girl.

SHELLY: Oh my God.

DODGE: (*To* SHELLY.) What's your name?

SHELLY: Shelly.

DODGE: Shelly. That's a man's name isn't it?

SHELLY: Not in this case.

DODGE: (*To* VINCE.) She's a smart-ass too.

SHELLY: Vince! Can we go?

DODGE: She wants to go. She just got here and she wants to go.

VINCE: This is kind of strange for her.

DODGE: She'll get used to it. (*To* SHELLY.) What part of the country do you come from?

SHELLY: Originally?

DODGE: That's right. Originally. At the very start.

SHELLY: L.A.

DODGE: L.A. Stupid country.

SHELLY: I can't stand this, Vince! This is really unbelievable!

DODGE: It's stupid! L.A. is stupid! So is Florida! All those Sunshine States. They're all stupid! Do you know why they're stupid?

SHELLY: Illuminate me.

DODGE: I'll tell you why. Because they're full of smartasses! That's why.

(SHELLY *turns her back to* DODGE, *crosses to staircase and sits on bottom step.*)

DODGE: (*To* VINCE.) Now she's insulted.

VINCE: Well you weren't very polite.

DODGE: She's insulted! Look at her! In my house she's insulted! She's over there sulking because I insulted her!

SHELLY: (*To* VINCE.) This is really terrific. This is wonderful. And you were worried about me making the right first impression!

DODGE: (*To* VINCE.) She's a fireball isn't she? Regular fireball. I had some a' them in my day. Temporary stuff. Never lasted more than a week.

VINCE: Grandpa—

DODGE: Stop calling me Grandpa will ya'! It's sickening. "Grandpa." I'm nobody's Grandpa!

(DODGE *starts feeling around under the cushion for the bottle of whiskey.* SHELLY *gets up from the staircase.*)

SHELLY: (*To* VINCE.) Maybe you've got the wrong house. Did you ever think of that? Maybe this is the wrong address!

VINCE: It's not the wrong address! I recognize the yard.

SHELLY: Yeah but do you recognize the people? He says he's not your Grandfather.

DODGE: (*Digging for bottle.*) Where's that bottle!

VINCE: He's just sick or something. I don't know what's happened to him.

DODGE: Where's my goddamn bottle!

(DODGE *gets up from sofa and starts tearing the cushions off it and throwing them downstage, looking for the whiskey.*)

SHELLY: Can't we just drive on to New Mexico? This is terrible, Vince! I don't want to stay here. In this house. I thought it was going to be turkey dinners and apple pie and all that kinda stuff.

VINCE: Well I hate to disappoint you!

SHELLY: I'm not disappointed! I'm fuckin' terrified! I wanna' go!

(DODGE *yells toward stage left.*)

DODGE: Tilden! Tilden!

(DODGE *keeps ripping away at the sofa looking for his bottle, he knocks over the nightstand with the bottles.* VINCE *and* SHELLY *watch as he starts ripping the stuffing out of the sofa.*)

VINCE: (*To* SHELLY.) He's lost his mind or something. I've got to try to help him.

SHELLY: You help him! I'm leaving!

(SHELLY *starts to leave.* VINCE *grabs her. They struggle as* DODGE *keeps ripping away at the sofa and yelling.*)

DODGE: Tilden! Tilden get your ass in here! Tilden!

SHELLY: Let go of me!

VINCE: You're not going anywhere! You're going to stay right here!

SHELLY: Let go of me you sonuvabitch! I'm not your property!

(*Suddenly* TILDEN *walks on from stage left just as he did before. This time his arms are full of carrots.* DODGE, VINCE *and* SHELLY *stop suddenly when they see him. They all stare at* TILDEN *as he crosses slowly center stage with the carrots and stops.* DODGE *sits on sofa, exhausted.*)

DODGE: (*Panting, to* TILDEN.) Where in the hell have you been?

TILDEN: Out back.

DODGE: Where's my bottle?

TILDEN: Gone.

(TILDEN *and* VINCE *stare at each other.* SHELLY *backs away.*)

DODGE: (*To* TILDEN.) You stole my bottle!

VINCE: (*To* TILDEN.) Dad?

(TILDEN *just stares at* VINCE.)

DODGE: You had no right to steal my bottle! No right at all!

VINCE: (*To* TILDEN.) It's Vince. I'm Vince.

(TILDEN *stares at* VINCE *then looks at* DODGE *then turns to* SHELLY.)

TILDEN: (*After pause.*) I picked these carrots. If anybody wants any carrots, I picked 'em.

SHELLY: (*To* VINCE.) This is your father?

VINCE: (*To* TILDEN.) Dad, what're you doing here?

(TILDEN *just stares at* VINCE, *holding carrots,* DODGE *pulls the blanket back over himself.*)

DODGE: (*To* TILDEN.) You're going to have to get me another bottle! You gotta get me a bottle before Halie comes back! There's money on the table. (*Points to stage left kitchen.*)

TILDEN: (*Shaking his head.*) I'm not going down there. Into town.

(SHELLY *crosses to* TILDEN. TILDEN *stares at her.*)

SHELLY: (*To* TILDEN.) Are you Vince's father?

TILDEN: (*To* SHELLY.) Vince?

SHELLY: (*Pointing to* VINCE.) This is supposed to be your son! Is he your son? Do you recognize him? I'm just along for the ride here. I thought everybody knew each other!

(TILDEN *stares at* VINCE. DODGE *wraps himself up in the blanket and sits on sofa staring at the floor.*)

TILDEN: I had a son once but we buried him.

(DODGE *quickly looks at* TILDEN. SHELLY *looks to* VINCE.)

DODGE: You shut up about that! You don't know anything about that!

VINCE: Dad, I thought you were in New Mexico. We were going to drive down there and see you.

TILDEN: Long way to drive.

DODGE: (*To* TILDEN.) You don't know anything about that! That happened before you were born! Long before!

VINCE: What's happened, Dad? What's going on here? I thought everything was all right. What's happened to Halie?

TILDEN: She left.

SHELLY: (*To* TILDEN.) Do you want me to take those carrots for you?

(TILDEN *stares at her. She moves in close to him. Holds out her arms.* TILDEN *stares at her arms then slowly dumps the carrots into her arms.* SHELLY *stands there holding the carrots.*)

TILDEN: (*To* SHELLY.) You like carrots?

SHELLY: Sure. I like all kinds of vegetables.

DODGE: (*To* TILDEN.) You gotta get me a bottle before Halie comes back!

(DODGE *hits sofa with his fist.* VINCE *crosses up to* DODGE *and tries to console him.* SHELLY *and* TILDEN *stay facing each other.*)

TILDEN: (*To* SHELLY.) Backyard's full of carrots. Corn. Potatoes.

SHELLY: You're Vince's father, right?

TILDEN: All kinds of vegetables. You like vegetables?

SHELLY: (*Laughs.*) Yeah. I love vegetables.

TILDEN: We could cook these carrots ya' know. You could cut 'em up and we could cook 'em.

SHELLY: All right.

TILDEN: I'll get you a pail and a knife.

SHELLY: Okay.

TILDEN: I'll be right back. Don't go.

(TILDEN *exits off stage left.* SHELLY *stands center, arms full of carrots.* VINCE *stands next to* DODGE. SHELLY *looks toward* VINCE *then down at the carrots.*)

DODGE: (*To* VINCE.) You could get me a bottle. (*Pointing off left.*) There's money on the table.

VINCE: Grandpa why don't you lay down for a while?

DODGE: I don't wanna lay down for a while! Every time I lay down something happens! (*Whips off his cap, points at his head.*) Look what happens! That's what happens! (*Pulls his cap back on.*) You go lie down and see what happens to you! See how you like it! They'll steal your bottle! They'll cut your hair! They murder your children! That's what'll happen.

VINCE: Just relax for a while.

DODGE: (*Pause.*) You could get me a bottle ya' know. There's nothing stopping you from getting me a bottle.

SHELLY: Why don't you get him a bottle Vince? Maybe it would help everybody identify each other.

DODGE: (*Pointing to* SHELLY.) There, see? She thinks you should get me a bottle.

(VINCE *crosses to* SHELLY.)

VINCE: What're you doing with those carrots.

SHELLY: I'm waiting for your father.

DODGE: She thinks you should get me a bottle!

VINCE: Shelly put the carrots down will ya'! We gotta deal with the situation here! I'm gonna need your help.

SHELLY: I'm helping.

VINCE: You're only adding to the problem! You're making things worse! Put the carrots down!

(VINCE *tries to knock the carrots out of her arms. She turns away from him, protecting the carrots.*)

SHELLY: Get away from me! Stop it!

(VINCE *stands back from her. She turns to him still holding the carrots.*)

VINCE: (*To* SHELLY.) Why are you doing this! Are you trying to make fun of me? This is my family you know!

SHELLY: You coulda' fooled me! I'd just as soon not be here myself. I'd just as soon be a thousand miles from here. I'd rather be anywhere but here. You're the one who wants to stay. So I'll stay. I'll stay and I'll cut the carrots. And I'll cook the carrots. And I'll do whatever I have to do to survive. Just to make it through this.

VINCE: Put the carrots down, Shelly.

(TILDEN *enters from left with pail, milking stool and a knife. He sets the stool and pail center stage for* SHELLY. SHELLY *looks at* VINCE *then sits down on stool, sets the carrots on the floor and takes the knife from* TILDEN. *She looks at* VINCE *again then picks up a carrot, cuts the ends off, scrapes it and drops it in pail. She repeats this,* VINCE *glares at her. She smiles.*)

DODGE: She could get me a bottle. She's the type a' girl that could get me a bottle. Easy. She'd go down there. Slink up to the counter. They'd probably give her two bottles for the price of one. She could do that.

(SHELLY *laughs. Keeps cutting carrots.* VINCE *crosses up to* DODGE, *looks at him.* TILDEN *watches* SHELLY'*s hands. Long pause.*)

VINCE: (*To* DODGE.) I haven't changed that much. I mean physically. Physically I'm just about the same. Same size. Same weight. Everything's the same.

(DODGE *keeps staring at* SHELLY *while* VINCE *talks to him.*)

DODGE: She's a beautiful girl. Exceptional.

(VINCE *moves in front of* DODGE *to block his view of* SHELLY. DODGE *keeps craning his head around to see her as* VINCE *demonstrates tricks from his past.*)

VINCE: Look. Look at this. Do you remember this? I used to bend my thumb behind my knuckles. You remember? I used to do it at the dinner table.

(VINCE *bends a thumb behind his knuckles for* DODGE *and holds it out to him.* DODGE *takes a short glance then looks back at* SHELLY. VINCE *shifts position and shows him something else.*)

VINCE: What about this?

(VINCE *curls his lips back and starts drumming on his teeth with his fingernails making little tapping sounds.* DODGE *watches awhile.* TILDEN *turns toward the sound.* VINCE *keeps it up. He sees* TILDEN *taking notice and crosses to* TILDEN *as he drums on his teeth.* DODGE *turns TV on, watches it.*)

VINCE: You remember this, Dad?

(VINCE *keeps on drumming for* TILDEN. TILDEN *watches a while, fascinated, then turns back to*

SHELLY. VINCE *keeps up the drumming on his teeth, crosses back to* DODGE *doing it.* SHELLY *keeps working on carrots, talking to* TILDEN.)

SHELLY: (*To* TILDEN.) He drives me crazy with that sometimes.

VINCE: (*To* DODGE.) I Know! Here's one you'll remember. You used to kick me out of the house for this one.

(VINCE *pulls his shirt out of his belt and holds it tucked under his chin with his stomach exposed. He grabs the flesh on either side of his belly button and pushes it in and out to make it look like a mouth talking. He watches his belly button and makes a deep sounding cartoon voice to synchronize with the movement. He demonstrates it to* DODGE *then crosses down to* TILDEN *doing it. Both* DODGE *and* TILDEN *take short, uninterested glances then ignore him.*)

VINCE: (*Deep cartoon voice.*) "Hello. How are you? I'm fine. Thank you very much. It's so good to see you looking well this fine Sunday morning. I was going down to the hardware store to fetch a pail of water."

SHELLY: Vince, don't be pathetic will ya'!

(VINCE *stops. Tucks his shirt back in.*)

SHELLY: Jesus Christ. They're not gonna play. Can't you see that?

(SHELLY *keeps cutting carrots.* VINCE *slowly moves toward* TILDEN. TILDEN *keeps watching* SHELLY. DODGE *watches TV.*)

VINCE: (*To* SHELLY.) I don't get it. I really don't get it. Maybe it's me. Maybe I forgot something.

DODGE: (*From sofa.*) You forgot to get me a bottle! That's what you forgot. Anybody in this house could get me a bottle. Anybody! But nobody will. Nobody understands the urgency! Peelin carrots is more important. Playin piano on your teeth! Well I hope you all remember this when you get up in years. When you find yourself immobilized. Dependent on the whims of others.

(VINCE *moves up toward* DODGE. *Pause as he looks at him.*)

VINCE: I'll get you a bottle.

DODGE: You will?

VINCE: Sure.

(SHELLY *stands holding knife and carrot.*)

SHELLY: You're not going to leave me here are you?

VINCE: (*Moving to her.*) You suggested it! You said, "why don't I go get him a bottle." So I'll go get him a bottle!

SHELLY: But I can't stay here.

VINCE: What is going on! A minute ago you were ready to cut carrots all night!

SHELLY: That was only if you stayed. Something to keep me busy, so I wouldn't be so nervous. I don't want to stay here alone.

DODGE: Don't let her talk you out of it! She's a bad influence. I could see it the minute she stepped in here.

SHELLY: (*To* DODGE.) You were asleep!

TILDEN: (*To* SHELLY.) Don't you want to cut carrots anymore?

SHELLY: Sure. Sure I do.

(SHELLY *sits back down on stool and continues cutting carrots. Pause.* VINCE *moves around, stroking his hair, staring at* DODGE *and* TILDEN. VINCE *and* SHELLY *exchange glances.* DODGE *watches TV.*)

VINCE: Boy! This is amazing. This is truly amazing. (*Keeps moving around.*) What is this anyway? Am I in a time warp or something? Have I committed an unpardonable offence? It's true, I'm not married. (SHELLY *looks at him, then back to carrots.*) But I'm also not divorced. I have been known to plunge into sinful infatuation with the Alto Saxophone. Sucking on number five reeds deep into the wee wee hours.

SHELLY: Vince, what are you doing that for? They don't care about any of that. They just don't recognize you, that's all.

VINCE: How could they not recognize me! How in the hell could they not recognize me? I'm their son!

DODGE: (*Watching TV.*) You're no son of mine. I've had sons in my time and you're not one of 'em.

(*Long pause.* VINCE *stares at* DODGE *then looks at* TILDEN. *He turns to* SHELLY.)

VINCE: Shelly, I gotta go out for a while. I just gotta go

out. I'll get a bottle and I'll come right back. You'll be okay here. Really.

SHELLY: I don't know if I can handle this Vince.

VINCE: I just gotta think or something. I don't know. I gotta put this all together.

SHELLY: Can't we just go?

VINCE: No! I gotta find out what's going on.

SHELLY: Look, you think you're bad off, what about me? Not only don't they recognize me but I've never seen them before in my life. I don't know who these guys are. They could be anybody!

VINCE: They're not anybody!

SHELLY: That's what you say.

VINCE: They're my family for Christ's sake! I should know who my own family is! Now give me a break. It won't take that long. I'll just go out and I'll come right back. Nothing'll happen. I promise.

(SHELLY *stares at him. Pause.*)

SHELLY: All right.

VINCE: Thanks. (*He crosses up to* DODGE.) I'm gonna go out now, Grandpa, and I'll pick up a bottle. Okay?

DODGE: Change of heart huh? (*Pointing off left.*) Money's on the table. In the kitchen.

(VINCE *moves toward* SHELLY.)

VINCE: (*To* SHELLY.) You be all right?

SHELLY: (*Cutting carrots.*) Sure. I'm fine. I'll just keep real busy while you're gone.

(VINCE *looks at* TILDEN *who keeps staring down at* SHELLY'S *hands.*)

DODGE: Persistence see? That's what it takes. Persistence. Persistence, fortitude and determination. Those are the three virtues. You stick with those three and you can't go wrong.

VINCE: (*To* TILDEN.) You want anything, Dad?

TILDEN: (*Looks up at* VINCE.) Mc?

VINCE: From the store? I'm gonna get grandpa a bottle.

TILDEN: He's not supposed to drink. Halie wouldn't like it.

VINCE: He wants a bottle.

TILDEN: He's not supposed to drink.

DODGE: (*To* VINCE.) Don't negotiate with him! Don't make any transactions until you've spoken to me first! He'll steal you blind!

VINCE: (*To* DODGE.) Tilden says you're not supposed to drink.

DODGE: Tilden lost his marbles! Look at him! He's around the bend. Take a look at him.

(VINCE *stares at* TILDEN. TILDEN *watches* SHELLY's *hands as she keeps cutting carrots.*)

DODGE: Now look at me. Look here at me!

(VINCE *looks back to* DODGE.)

DODGE: Now, between the two of us, who do you think is more trustworthy? Him or me? Can you trust a man who keeps bringing in vegetables from out of nowhere? Take a look at him.

(VINCE *looks back at* TILDEN.)

SHELLY: Go get the bottle, Vince.

VINCE: (*To* SHELLY.) You sure you'll be all right?

SHELLY: I'll be fine. I feel right at home now.

VINCE: You do?

SHELLY: I'm fine. Now that I've got the carrots everything is all right.

VINCE: I'll be right back.

(VINCE *crosses stage left.*)

DODGE: Where are you going?

VINCE: I'm going to get the money.

DODGE: Then where are you going?

VINCE: Liquor store.

DODGE: Don't go anyplace else. Don't go off someplace and drink. Come right back here.

VINCE: I will.

(VINCE *exits stage left.*)

DODGE: (*Calling after* VINCE.) You've got responsibility now! And don't go out the back way either! Come out through this way! I wanna' see you when you leave! Don't go out the back!

VINCE'S VOICE: (*Off left.*) I won't!

(DODGE *turns and looks at* TILDEN *and* SHELLY.)

DODGE: Untrustworthy. Probably drown himself if he went

out the back. Fall right in a hole. I'd never get my bottle.

SHELLY: I wouldn't worry about Vince. He can take care of himself.

DODGE: Oh he can, huh? Independent.

(VINCE *comes on again from stage left with two dollars in his hand. He crosses stage right past* DODGE.)

DODGE: (*To* VINCE.) You got the money?

VINCE: Yeah. Two bucks.

DODGE: Two bucks. Two bucks is two bucks. Don't sneer.

VINCE: What kind do you want?

DODGE: Whiskey! Gold Star Sour Mash. Use your own discretion.

VINCE: Okay.

(VINCE *crosses to stage right door. Opens it. Stops when he hears* TILDEN.)

TILDEN: (*To* VINCE.) You drove all the way from New Mexico?

(VINCE *turns and looks at* TILDEN. *They stare at each other.* VINCE *shakes his head, goes out the door, crosses porch and exits out screen door.* TILDEN *watches him go. Pause.*)

SHELLY: You really don't recognize him? Either one of you?

(TILDEN *turns again and stares at* SHELLY'S *hands as she cuts carrots.*)

DODGE: (*Watching TV.*) Recognize who?

SHELLY: Vince.

DODGE: What's to recognize?

(DODGE *lights a cigarette, coughs slightly and stares at TV.*)

SHELLY: It'd be cruel if you recognized him and didn't tell him. Wouldn't be fair.

(DODGE *just stares at TV, smoking.*)

TILDEN: I thought I recognized him. I thought I recognized something about him?

SHELLY: You did?

TILDEN: I thought I saw a face inside his face.

SHELLY: Well it was probably that you saw what he used to look like. You haven't seen him for six years.

TILDEN: I haven't?

SHELLY: That's what he says.

(TILDEN *moves around in front of her as she contin-ues with carrots.*)

TILDEN: Where was it I saw him last?

SHELLY: I don't know. I've only known him for a few months. He doesn't tell me everything.

TILDEN: He doesn't?

SHELLY: Not stuff like that.

TILDEN: What does he tell you?

SHELLY: You mean in general?

TILDEN: Yeah.

(TILDEN *moves around behind her.*)

SHELLY: Well he tells me all kinds of things.

TILDEN: Like what?

SHELLY: I don't know! I mean I can't just come right out and tell you how he feels.

TILDEN: How come?

(TILDEN *keeps moving around her slowly in a circle.*)

SHELLY: Because it's stuff he told me privately!

TILDEN: And you can't tell me?

SHELLY: I don't even know you!

DODGE: Tilden, go out in the kitchen and make me some coffee! Leave the girl alone.

SHELLY: (*To* DODGE.) He's all right.

(TILDEN *ignores* DODGE, *keeps moving around* SHELLY. *He stares at her hair and coat.* DODGE *stares at* TV.)

TILDEN: You mean you can't tell me anything?

SHELLY: I can tell you some things. I mean we can have a conversation.

TILDEN: We can?

SHELLY: Sure. We're having a conversation right now.

TILDEN: We are?

SHELLY: Yes. That's what we're doing.

TILDEN: But there's certain things you can't tell me, right?

SHELLY: Right.

TILDEN: There's certain things I can't tell you either.

SHELLY: How come?

TILDEN: I don't know. Nobody's supposed to hear it.

SHELLY: Well, you can tell me anything you want to.

TILDEN: I can?

SHELLY: Sure.

TILDEN: It might not be very nice.

SHELLY: That's all right. I've been around.

TILDEN: It might be awful.

SHELLY: Well, can't you tell me anything nice?

(TILDEN *stops in front of her and stares at her coat.* SHELLY *looks back at him. Long pause.*)

TILDEN: (*After pause.*) Can I touch your coat?

SHELLY: My coat? (*She looks at her coat then back to* TILDEN.) Sure.

TILDEN: You don't mind?

SHELLY: No. Go ahead.

(SHELLY *holds her arm out for* TILDEN *to touch.* DODGE *stays fixed on TV.* TILDEN *moves in slowly toward* SHELLY, *staring at her arm. He reaches out very slowly and touches her arm, feels the fur gently then draws his hand back.* SHELLY *keeps her arm out.*)

SHELLY: It's rabbit.

TILDEN: Rabbit.

(*He reaches out again very slowly and touches the fur on her arm then pulls back his hand again.* SHELLY *drops her arm.*)

SHELLY: My arm was getting tired.

TILDEN: Can I hold it?

SHELLY: (*Pause.*) The coat? Sure.

(SHELLY *takes off her coat and hands it to* TILDEN. TILDEN *takes it slowly, feels the fur then puts it on.* SHELLY *watches as* TILDEN *strokes the fur slowly. He smiles at her. She goes back to cutting carrots.*)

SHELLY: You can have it if you want.

TILDEN: I can?

SHELLY: Yeah. I've got a raincoat in the car. That's all I need.

TILDEN: You've got a car?

SHELLY: Vince does.

(TILDEN *walks around stroking the fur and smiling at the coat.* SHELLY *watches him when he's not looking.* DODGE *sticks with TV, stretches out on sofa wrapped in blanket.*)

TILDEN: (*As he walks around.*) I had a car once! I had a white car! I drove. I went everywhere. I went to the mountains. I drove in the snow.

SHELLY: That must've been fun.

TILDEN: (*Still moving, feeling coat.*) I drove all day long sometimes. Across the desert. Way out across the desert. I drove past towns. Anywhere. Past Palm trees. Lightning. Anything. I would drive through it. I would drive through it and I would stop and I would look around and I would drive on. I would get back in and drive! I loved to drive. There was nothing I loved more. Nothing I dreamed of was better than driving.

DODGE: (*Eyes on TV.*) Pipe down would ya'!
   (TILDEN *stops. Stares at* SHELLY.)

SHELLY: Do you do much driving now?

TILDEN: Now? Now? I don't drive now.

SHELLY: How come?

TILDEN: I'm grown up now.

SHELLY: Grown up?

TILDEN: I'm not a kid.

SHELLY: You don't have to be a kid to drive.

TILDEN: It wasn't driving then.

SHELLY: What was it?

TILDEN: Adventure. I went everywhere.

SHELLY: Well you can still do that.

TILDEN: Not now.

SHELLY: Why not?

TILDEN: I just told you. You don't understand anything. If I told you something you wouldn't understand it.

SHELLY: Told me what?

TILDEN: Told you something that's true.

SHELLY: Like what?

TILDEN: Like a baby. Like a little tiny baby.

SHELLY: Like when you were little?

TILDEN: If I told you you'd make me give your coat back.

SHELLY: I won't. I promise. Tell me.

TILDEN: I can't. Dodge won't let me.

SHELLY: He won't hear you. It's okay.
   (*Pause.* TILDEN *stares at her. Moves slightly toward her.*)

TILDEN: We had a baby. (*Motioning to* DODGE.) He did. Dodge did. Could pick it up with one hand. Put it in the other. Little baby. Dodge killed it.

(SHELLY *stands.*)

TILDEN: Don't stand up. Don't stand up!

(SHELLY *sits again.* DODGE *sits up on sofa and looks at them.*)

TILDEN: Dodge drowned it.

SHELLY: Don't tell me anymore! Okay?

(TILDEN *moves closer to her.* DODGE *takes more interest.*)

DODGE: Tilden? You leave that girl alone!

TILDEN: (*Pays no attention.*) Never told Halie. Never told anybody. Just drowned it.

DODGE: (*Shuts off TV.*) Tilden!

TILDEN: Nobody could find it. Just disappeared. Cops looked for it. Neighbors. Nobody could find it.

(DODGE *struggles to get up from sofa.*)

DODGE: Tilden, what're you telling her! Tilden!

(DODGE *keeps struggling until he's standing.*)

TILDEN: Finally everybody just gave up. Just stopped looking. Everybody had a different answer. Kidnap. Murder. Accident. Some kind of accident.

(DODGE *struggles to walk toward* TILDEN *and falls.* TILDEN *ignores him.*)

DODGE: Tilden you shut up! You shut up about it!

(DODGE *starts coughing on the floor.* SHELLY *watches him from the stool.*)

TILDEN: Little tiny baby just disappeared. It's not hard. It's so small. Almost invisible.

(SHELLY *makes a move to help* DODGE. TILDEN *firmly pushes her back down on the stool.* DODGE *keeps coughing.*)

TILDEN: He said he had his reasons. Said it went a long way back. But he wouldn't tell anybody.

DODGE: Tilden! Don't tell her anything! Don't tell her!

TILDEN: He's the only one who knows where it's buried. The only one. Like a secret buried treasure. Won't tell any of us. Won't tell me or Mother or even Bradley. Especially Bradley. Bradley tried to force it out of him

but he wouldn't tell. Wouldn't even tell why he did it.
One night he just did it.

(DODGE's *coughing subsides.* SHELLY *stays on stool
staring at* DODGE. TILDEN *slowly takes* SHELLY's *coat
off and holds it out to her. Long pause.* SHELLY *sits
there trembling.*)

TILDEN: You probably want your coat back now.

(SHELLY *stares at coat but doesn't move to take it.
The sound of* BRADLEY's *leg squeaking is heard off left.
The others on stage remain still.* BRADLEY *appears up
left outside the screen door wearing a yellow rain
slicker. He enters through screen door, crosses porch
to stage right door and enters stage. Closes door.
Takes off rain slicker and shakes it out. He sees all the
others and stops.* TILDEN *turns to him.* BRADLEY *stares
at* SHELLY. DODGE *remains on floor.*)

BRADLEY: What's going on here? (*Motioning to* SHELLY.)
Who's that?

(SHELLY *stands, moves back away from* BRADLEY *as
he crosses toward her. He stops next to* TILDEN. *He
sees coat in* TILDEN's *hand and grabs it away from
him.*)

BRADLEY: Who's she supposed to be?

TILDEN: She's driving to New Mexico.

(BRADLEY *stares at her.* SHELLY *is frozen.* BRADLEY
*limps over to her with the coat in his fist. He stops in
front of her.*)

BRADLEY: (*To* SHELLY, *after pause.*) Vacation?

(SHELLY *shakes her head "no," trembling.*)

BRADLEY: (*To* SHELLY, *motioning to* TILDEN.) You taking
him with you?

(SHELLY *shakes her head "no."* BRADLEY *crosses back
to* TILDEN.)

BRADLEY: You oughta'. No use leaving him here. Doesn't
do a lick a' work. Doesn't raise a finger. (*Stopping, to*
TILDEN.) Do ya' (*To* SHELLY.) 'Course he used to be an
all-American. Quarterback or fullback or somethin'. He
tell you that?

(SHELLY *shakes her nead "no."*)

BRADLEY: Yeah, he used to be a big deal. Wore lettermen's

sweaters. Had medals hanging all around his neck. Real purty. Big deal. (*He laughs to himself, notices* DODGE *on floor, crosses to him, stops.*) This one too. (*To* SHELLY.) You'd never think it to look at him would ya'? All bony and wasted away.

    (SHELLY *shakes her head again.* BRADLEY *stares at her, crosses back to her, clenching the coat in his fist. He stops in front of* SHELLY.)

BRADLEY: Women like that kinda' thing don't they?

SHELLY: What?

BRADLEY: Importance. Importance in a man?

SHELLY: I don't know.

BRADLEY: Yeah. You know, you know. Don't give me that. (*Moves closer to* SHELLY.) You're with Tilden?

SHELLY: No.

BRADLEY: (*Turning to* TILDEN.) Tilden! She with you?

    (TILDEN *doesn't answer. Stares at floor.*)

BRADLEY: Tilden!

    (TILDEN *suddenly bolts and runs off up stage left.* BRADLEY *laughs. Talks to* SHELLY. DODGE *starts moving his lips silently as though talking to someone invisible on the floor.*)

BRADLEY: (*Laughing.*) Scared to death! He was always scared!

    (BRADLEY *stops laughing. Stares at* SHELLY.)

BRADLEY: You're scared too, right? (*Laughs again.*) You're scared and you don't even know me. (*Stops laughing.*) You don't gotta be scared.

    (SHELLY *looks at* DODGE *on the floor.*)

SHELLY: Can't we do something for him?

BRADLEY: (*Looking at* DODGE.) We could shoot him. (*Laughs.*) We could drown him! What about drowning him?

SHELLY: Shut up!

    (BRADLEY *stops laughing. Moves in closer to* SHELLY. *She freezes.* BRADLEY *speaks slowly and deliberately.*)

BRADLEY: Hey! Missus. Don't talk to me like that. Don't talk to me in that tone a' voice. There was a time when I had to take that tone a' voice from pretty near everyone. (*Motioning to* DODGE.) Him, for one! Him and that half brain that just ran outa' here. They don't talk to me like that now. Not anymore. Everything's turned around now. Full circle. Isn't that funny?

SHELLY: I'm sorry.

BRADLEY: Open your mouth.

SHELLY: What?

BRADLEY: (*Motioning for her to open her mouth.*) Open up.

(*She opens her mouth slightly.*)

BRADLEY: Wider.

(*She opens her mouth wider.*)

BRADLEY: Keep it like that.

(*She does. Stares at* BRADLEY. *With his free hand he puts his fingers into her mouth. She tries to pull away.*)

BRADLEY: Just stay put!

(*She freezes. He keeps his fingers in her mouth. Stares at her. Pause. He pulls his hand out. She closes her mouth, keeps her eyes on him.* BRADLEY *smiles. He looks at* DODGE *on the floor and crosses over to him.* SHELLY *watches him closely.* BRADLEY *stands over* DODGE *and smiles at* SHELLY. *He holds her coat up in both hands over* DODGE, *keeps smiling at* SHELLY. *He looks down at* DODGE *then drops the coat so that it lands on* DODGE *and covers his head.* BRADLEY *keeps his hands up in the position of holding the coat, looks over at* SHELLY *and smiles. The lights black out.*)

ACT THREE

SCENE: *Same set. Morning. Bright sun. No sound of rain. Everything has been cleared up again. No sign of carrots. No pail. No stool.* VINCE's *saxophone case and overcoat are still at the foot of the staircase.* BRADLEY *is asleep on the sofa under* DODGE's *blanket. His head toward stage left.* BRADLEY's *wooden leg is leaning against the sofa right by his head. The shoe is left on it. The harness hangs down.* DODGE *is sitting on the floor, propped up against the TV set facing stage left wearing his baseball cap.* SHELLY's *rabbit fur coat covers his chest and shoulders. He stares off toward stage left. He seems weaker and more disoriented. The lights rise slowly to the sound of birds and remain for a while in silence on the two men.* BRADLEY *sleeps very soundly.* DODGE *hardly moves.* SHELLY *appears from stage left with a big smile, slowly crossing toward* DODGE *balancing a steaming cup of broth in a saucer.* DODGE *just stares at her as she gets close to him.*

SHELLY: (*As she crosses.*) This is going to make all the difference in the world, Grandpa. You don't mind me calling you Grandpa do you? I mean I know you minded when Vince called you that but you don't even know him.

DODGE: He skipped town with my money ya' know. I'm gonna hold you as collateral.

SHELLY: He'll be back. Don't you worry.

(*She kneels down next to* DODGE *and puts the cup and saucer in his lap.*)

DODGE: It's morning already! Not only didn't I get my bottle but he's got my two bucks!

SHELLY: Try to drink this, okay? Don't spill it.

DODGE: What is it?

SHELLY: Beef bouillon. It'll warm you up.

DODGE: Bouillon! I don't want any goddamn bouillon! Get that stuff away from me!

SHELLY: I just got through making it.

DODGE: I don't care if you just spent all week making it! I ain't drinking it!

SHELLY: Well, what am I supposed to do with it then? I'm trying to help you out. Besides, it's good for you.

DODGE: Get it away from me!

(SHELLY *stands up with cup and saucer.*)

DODGE: What do you know what's good for me anyway?

(*She looks at* DODGE *then turns away from him, crossing to staircase, sits on bottom step and drinks the bouillon.* DODGE *stares at her.*)

DODGE: You know what'd be good for me?

SHELLY: What?

DODGE: A little massage. A little contact.

SHELLY: Oh no. I've had enough contact for a while. Thanks anyway.

(*She keeps sipping bouillon, stays sitting. Pause as* DODGE *stares at her.*)

DODGE: Why not? You got nothing better to do. That fella's not gonna be back here. You're not expecting him to show up again are you?

SHELLY: Sure. He'll show up. He left his horn here.

DODGE: His horn? (*Laughs.*) You're his horn?

SHELLY: Very funny.

DODGE: He's run off with my money! He's not coming back here.

SHELLY: He'll be back.

DODGE: You're a funny chicken, you know that?

SHELLY: Thanks.

DODGE: Full of faith. Hope. Faith and hope. You're all alike you hopers. If it's not God then it's a man. If it's not a man then it's a woman. If its not a woman then its the land or the future of some kind. Some kind of future. (*Pause.*)

SHELLY: (*Looking toward porch.*) I'm glad it stopped raining.

DODGE: (*Looks toward porch then back to her.*) That's what I mean. See, you're glad it stopped raining. Now you think everything's gonna be different. Just 'cause the sun comes out.

SHELLY: It's already different. Last night I was scared.

DODGE: Scared a' what?

SHELLY: Just scared.

DODGE: Bradley? (*Looks at* BRADLEY.) He's a pushover. 'Specially now. All ya' gotta' do is take his leg and throw it out the back door. Helpless. Totally helpless.

(SHELLY *turns and stares at* BRADLEY'*s wooden leg, then looks at* DODGE. *She sips bouillon.*)

SHELLY: You'd do that?

DODGE: Me? I've hardly got the strength to breathe.

SHELLY: But you'd actually do it if you could?

DODGE: Don't be so easily shocked, girlie. There's nothing a man can't do. You dream it up and he can do it. Anything.

SHELLY: You've tried I guess.

DODGE: Don't sit there sippin' your bouillon and judging me! This is my house!

SHELLY: I forgot.

DODGE: You forgot? Whose house did you think it was?

SHELLY: Mine.

(DODGE *just stares at her. Long pause. She sips from cup.*)

SHELLY: I know it's not mine but I had that feeling.

DODGE: What feeling?

SHELLY: The feeling that nobody lives here but me. I mean everybody's gone. You're here, but it doesn't seem like you're supposed to be. (*Pointing to* BRADLEY.) Doesn't seem like he's supposed to be here either. I don't know what it is. It's the house or something. Something familiar. Like I know my way around here. Did you ever get that feeling?

(DODGE *stares at her in silence. Pause.*)

DODGE: No. No, I never did.

(SHELLY *gets up. Moves around space holding cup.*)

SHELLY: Last night I went to sleep up there in that room.

DODGE: What room?

SHELLY: That room up there with all the pictures. All the crosses on the wall.

DODGE: Halie's room?

SHELLY: Yeah. Whoever "Halie" is.

DODGE: She's my wife.

SHELLY: So you remember her?

DODGE: Whad'ya mean! 'Course I remember her! She's only been gone for a day, half a day. However long it's been.

SHELLY: Do you remember her when her hair was bright red? Standing in front of an apple tree?

DODGE: What is this, the third degree or something! Who're you to be askin' me personal questions about my wife!

SHELLY: You never look at those pictures up there?

DODGE: What pictures!

SHELLY: You're whole life's up there hanging on the wall. Somebody who looks just like you. Somebody who looks just like you used to look.

DODGE: That isn't me! That never was me! This is me. Right here. This is it. The whole shootin' match, sittin' right in front of you.

SHELLY: So the past never happened as far as you're concerned?

DODGE: The past? Jesus Christ. The past. What do you know about the past?

SHELLY: Not much. I know there was a farm.

(*Pause.*)

DODGE: A farm?

SHELLY: There's a picture of a farm. A big farm. A bull. Wheat. Corn.

DODGE: Corn?

SHELLY: All the kids are standing out in the corn. They're

all waving these big straw hats. One of them doesn't have a hat.

DODGE: Which one was that?

SHELLY: There's a baby. A baby in a woman's arms. The same woman with the red hair. She looks lost standing out there. Like she doesn't know how she got there.

DODGE: She knows! I told her a hundred times it wasn't gonna' be the city! I gave her plenty a' warning.

SHELLY: She's looking down at the baby like it was somebody's else's. Like it didn't even belong to her.

DODGE: That's about enough outa' you! You got some funny ideas. Some damn funny ideas. You think just because people propagate they have to love their offspring? You never seen a bitch eat her puppies? Where are you from anyway?

SHELLY: L. A. We already went through that.

DODGE: That's right, L.A. I remember.

SHELLY: Stupid country.

DODGE: That's right! No wonder.

(*Pause.*)

SHELLY: What's happened to this family anyway?

DODGE: You're in no position to ask! What do you care? You some kinda' Social Worker?

SHELLY: I'm Vince's friend.

DODGE: Vince's friend! That's rich. That's really rich. "Vince"! "Mr. Vince"! "Mr. Thief" is more like it! His name doesn't mean a hoot in hell to me. Not a tinkle in the well. You know how many kids I've spawned? Not to mention Grand kids and Great Grand kids and Great Great Grand kids after them?

SHELLY: And you don't remember any of them?

DODGE: What's to remember? Halie's the one with the family album. She's the one you should talk to. She'll set you straight on the heritage if that's what you're interested in. She's traced it all the way back to the grave.

SHELLY: What do you mean?

DODGE: What do you think I mean? How far back can you go? A long line of corpses! There's not a living soul behind me. Not a one. Who's holding me in their memory Who gives a damn about bones in the ground?

SHELLY: Was Tilden telling the truth?
  (DODGE *stops short. Stares at* SHELLY. *Shakes his head.
  He looks off stage left.*)
SHELLY: Was he?
  (DODGE's *tone changes drastically.*)
DODGE: TILDEN? (*Turns to* SHELLY, *calmly.*) Where is
  Tilden?
SHELLY: Last night. Was he telling the truth about the baby?
  (*Pause.*)
DODGE: (*Turns toward stage left.*) What's happened to Til-
  den? Why isn't Tilden here?
SHELLY: Bradley chased him out.
DODGE: (*Looking at* BRADLEY *asleep.*) Bradley? Why is he
  on my sofa? (*Turns back to* SHELLY.) Have I been here
  all night? On the floor?
SHELLY: He wouldn't leave. I hid outside until he fell
  asleep.
DODGE: Outside? Is Tilden outside? He shouldn't be out
  there in the rain. He'll get himself into trouble. He
  doesn't know his way around here anymore. Not like he
  used to. He went out West and got himself into trouble.
  Got himself into bad trouble. We don't want any of that
  around here.
SHELLY: What did he do?
  (*Pause.*)
DODGE: (*Quietly stares at* SHELLY.) Tilden? He got mixed
  up. That's what he did. We can't afford to leave him
  alone. Not now.
  (*Sound of* HALIE *laughing comes from off left.* SHELLY
  *stands, looking in direction of voice, holding cup and
  saucer, doesn't know whether to stay or run.*)
DODGE: (*Motioning to* SHELLY.) Sit down! Sit back down!
  (SHELLY *sits. Sound of* HALIE's *laughter again.*)
DODGE: (*To* SHELLY *in a heavy whisper, pulling coat up
  around him.*) Don't leave me alone now! Promise me?
  Don't go off and leave me alone. I need somebody here
  with me. Tilden's gone now and I need someone. Don't
  leave me! Promise!
SHELLY: (*Sitting.*) I won't.
  (HALIE *appears outside the screen porch door, up left*

with FATHER DEWIS. *She is wearing a bright yellow dress, no hat, white gloves and her arms are full of yellow roses.* FATHER DEWIS *is dressed in traditional black suit, white clerical collar and shirt. He is a very distinguished gray-haired man in his sixties. They are both slightly drunk and feeling giddy. As they enter the porch through the screen door,* DODGE *pulls the rabbit fur coat over his head and hides.* SHELLY *stands again.* DODGE *drops the coat and whispers intensely to* SHELLY. *Neither* HALIE *nor* FATHER DEWIS *are aware of the people inside the house.*)

DODGE: (*To* SHELLY *in a strong whisper.*) You promised! (SHELLY *sits on stairs again.* DODGE *pulls coat back over his head.* HALIE *and* FATHER DEWIS *talk on the porch as they cross toward stage right interior door.*)

HALIE: Oh Father! That's terrible! That's absolutely terrible. Aren't you afraid of being punished?
(*She giggles.*)

DEWIS: Not by the Italians. They're too busy punishing each other.
(*The both break out in giggles.*)

HALIE: What about God?

DEWIS: Well, prayerfully, God only hears what he wants to. That's just between you and me of course. In our heart of hearts we know we're every bit as wicked as the Catholics.
(*They giggle again and reach the stage right door.*)

HALIE: Father, I never heard you talk like this in Sunday sermon.

DEWIS: Well, I save all my best jokes for private company. Pearls before swine you know.
(*They enter the room laughing and stop when they see* SHELLY. SHELLY *stands.* HALIE *closes the door behind* FATHER DEWIS. DODGE's *voice is heard under the coat, talking to* SHELLY.)

DODGE: (*Under coat, to* SHELLY.) Sit down, sit down! Don't let 'em buffalo you!
(SHELLY *sits on stair again.* HALIE *looks at* DODGE *on the floor then looks at* BRADLEY *asleep on sofa and*

sees his wooden leg. She lets out a shriek of embar-
rassment for FATHER DEWIS.)

HALIE: Oh my gracious! What in the name of Judas Priest
is going on in this house!

(*She hands over the roses to* FATHER DEWIS.)

HALIE: Excuse me, Father.

(HALIE *crosses to* DODGE, *whips the coat off him and*
covers the wooden leg with it. BRADLEY *stays asleep.*)

HALIE: You can't leave this house for a second without the
devil blowing in through the front door!

DODGE: Gimme back that coat! Gimme back that goddamn
coat before I freeze to death!

HALIE: You're not going to freeze! The sun's out in case
you hadn't noticed!

DODGE: Gimme back that coat! That coat's for live flesh
not dead wood!

(HALIE *whips the blanket off* BRADLEY *and throws it*
on DODGE. DODGE *covers his head again with blanket.*
BRADLEY's *amputated leg can be faked by having half*
of it under a cushion of the sofa. He's fully clothed.
BRADLEY *sits up with a jerk when the blanket comes*
off him.)

HALIE: (*As she tosses blanket.*) Here! Use this! It's yours
anyway! Can't you take care of yourself for once!

BRADLEY: (*Yelling at* HALIE.) Gimme that blanket! Gimme
back that blanket! That's my blanket!

(HALIE *crosses back toward* FATHER DEWIS *who just*
stands there with the roses. BRADLEY *thrashes help-*
lessly on the sofa trying to reach blanket. DODGE *hides*
himself deeper in blanket. SHELLY *looks on from stair-*
case, still holding cup and saucer.)

HALIE: Believe me, Father, this is not what I had in mind
when I invited you in.

DEWIS: Oh, no apologies please. I wouldn't be in the minis-
try if I couldn't face real life.

(*He laughs self-consciously.* HALIE *notices* SHELLY
again and crosses over to her. SHELLY *stays sitting.*
HALIE *stops and stares at her.*)

BRADLEY: I want my blanket back! Gimme my blanket!

(HALIE *turns toward* BRADLEY *and silences him.*)

HALIE: Shut up, Bradley! Right this minute! I've had enough!

> (BRADLEY *slowly recoils, lies back down on sofa, turns his back toward* HALIE *and whimpers softly.* HALIE *directs her attention to* SHELLY *again. Pause.*)

HALIE: (*To* SHELLY.) What're you doing with my cup and saucer?

SHELLY: (*Looking at cup, back to* HALIE.) I made some bouillon for Dodge.

HALIE: For Dodge?

SHELLY: Yeah.

HALIE: Well, did he drink it?

SHELLY: No.

HALIE: Did you drink it?

SHELLY: Yes.

> (HALIE *stares at her. Long pause. She turns abruptly away from* SHELLY *and crosses back to* FATHER DEWIS.)

HALIE: Father, there's a stranger in my house. What would you advise? What would be the Christian thing?

DEWIS: (*Squirming.*) Oh, well. . . . I. . . . I really—

HALIE: We still have some whiskey, don't we?

> (DODGE *slowly pulls the blanket down off his head and looks toward* FATHER DEWIS. SHELLY *stands.*)

SHELLY: Listen, I don't drink or anything. I just—

> (HALIE *turns toward* SHELLY *viciously.*)

HALIE: You sit back down!

> (SHELLY *sits again on stair.* HALIE *turns again to* DEWIS.)

HALIE: I think we have plenty of whiskey left! Don't we Father?

DEWIS: Well, yes. I think so. You'll have to get it. My hands are full.

> (HALIE *giggles. Reaches into* DEWIS's *pockets, searching for bottle. She smells the roses as she searches.* DEWIS *stands stiffly.* DODGE *watches* HALIE *closely as she looks for bottle.*)

HALIE: The most incredible things, roses! Aren't they incredible, Father?

DEWIS: Yes. Yes they are.

HALIE: They almost cover the stench of sin in this house. Just magnificent! The smell. We'll have to put some at the foot of Ansel's statue. One the day of the unveiling.

(HALIE *finds a silver flask of whiskey in* DEWIS's *vest pocket. She pulls it out.* DODGE *looks on eagerly.* HALIE *crosses to* DODGE, *opens the flask and takes a sip.*)

HALIE: (*To* DODGE.) Ansel's getting a statue, Dodge. Did you know that? Not a plaque but a real live statue. A full bronze. Tip to toe. A basketball in one hand a rifle in the other.

BRADLEY: (*His back to* HALIE.) He never played basketball!

HALIE: You shut up, Bradley! You shut up about Ansel! Ansel played basketball better than anyone! And you know it! He was an all-American! There's no reason to take the glory away from others.

(HALIE *turns away from* BRADLEY, *crosses back toward* DEWIS *sipping on the flask and smiling.*)

HALIE: (*To* DEWIS.) Ansel was a great basketball player. One of the greatest.

DEWIS: I remember Ansel.

HALIE: Of course! You remember. You remember how he could play. (*She turns toward* SHELLY.) Of course, nowadays they play a different brand of basketball. More vicious. Isn't that right, dear?

SHELLY: I don't know.

(HALIE *crosses to* SHELLY, *sipping on flask. She stops in front of* SHELLY.)

HALIE: Much, much more vicious. They smash into each other. They knock each other's teeth out. There's blood all over the court. Savages.

(HALIE *takes the cup from* SHELLY *and pours whiskey into it.*)

HALIE: They don't train like they used to. Not at all. They allow themselves to run amuck. Drugs and women. Women mostly.

(HALIE *hands the cup of whiskey back to* SHELLY *slowly.* SHELLY *takes it.*)

HALIE: Mostly women. Girls. Sad, pathetic little girls. (*She crosses back to* FATHER DEWIS.) It's just a reflection of the times, don't you think, Father? An indication of where we stand?

DEWIS: I suppose so, yes.

HALIE: Yes. A sort of a bad omen. Our youth becoming monsters.

DEWIS: Well, I uh—

HALIE: Oh you can disagree with me if you want to, Father. I'm open to debate. I think argument only enriches both sides of the question don't you? (*She moves toward* DODGE.) I suppose, in the long run, it doesn't matter. When you see the way things deteriorate before your very eyes. Everything running downhill. It's kind of silly to even think about youth.

DEWIS: No, I don't think so. I think it's important to believe in certain things.

HALIE: Yes. Yes, I know what you mean. I think that's right. I think that's true. (*She looks at* DODGE.) Certain basic things. We can't shake certain basic things. We might end up crazy. Like my husband. You can see it in his eyes. You can see how mad he is.

(DODGE *covers his head with the blanket again.* HALIE *takes a single rose from* DEWIS *and moves slowly over to* DODGE.)

HALIE: We can't not believe in something. We can't stop believing. We just end up dying if we stop. Just end up dead.

(HALIE *throws the rose gently onto* DODGE's *blanket. It lands between his knees and stays there! Long pause as* HALIE *stares at the rose.* SHELLY *stands suddenly.* HALIE *doesn't turn to her but keeps staring at rose.*)

SHELLY: (*To* HALIE.) Don't you wanna' know who I am! Don't you wanna know what I'm doing here! I'm not dead!

(SHELLY *crosses toward* HALIE. HALIE *turns slowly toward her.*)

HALIE: Did you drink your whiskey?

SHELLY: No! And I'm not going to either!

HALIE: Well that's a firm stand. It's good to have a firm stand.

SHELLY: I don't have any stand at all. I'm just trying to put all this together.

(HALIE *laughs and crosses back to* DEWIS.)

HALIE: (*To* DEWIS.) Surprises, surprises! Did you have any idea we'd be returning to this?

SHELLY: I came here with your Grandson for a little visit! A little innocent friendly visit.

HALIE: My Grandson?

SHELLY: Yes! That's right. The one no one remembers.

HALIE: (*To* DEWIS.) This is getting a little farfetched.

SHELLY: I told him it was stupid to come back here. To try to pick up from where he left off.

HALIE: Where was that?

SHELLY: Wherever he was when he left here! Six years ago! Ten years ago! Whenever it was. I told him nobody cares.

HALIE: Didn't he listen?

SHELLY: No! No he didn't. We had to stop off at every tiny little meatball town that he remembered from his boyhood! Every stupid little doughnut shop he ever kissed a girl in. Every drive-in. Every drag strip. Every football field he ever broke a bone on.

HALIE: (*Suddenly alarmed, to* DODGE.) Where's Tilden?

SHELLY: Don't ignore me!

HALIE: Dodge! Where's Tilden gone?

(SHELLY *moves violently toward* HALIE.)

SHELLY: (*To* HALIE.) I'm talking to you!

(BRADLEY *sits up fast on the sofa,* SHELLY *backs away.*)

BRADLEY: (*To* SHELLY.) Don't you yell at my mother!

HALIE: Dodge! (*She kicks* DODGE.) I told you not to let Tilden out of your sight! Where's he gone to?

DODGE: Gimme a drink and I'll tell ya'.

DEWIS: Halie, maybe this isn't the right time for a visit.

(HALIE *crosses back to* DEWIS.)

HALIE: (*To* DEWIS.) I never should've left. I never, never should've left! Tilden could be anywhere by now! Anywhere! He's not in control of his faculties. Dodge knew that. I told him when I left here. I told him specifically to watch out for Tilden.

(BRADLEY *reaches down, grabs* DODGE's *blanket and yanks it off him. He lays down on sofa and pulls the blanket over his head.*)

DODGE: He's got my blanket again! He's got my blanket!

HALIE: (*Turning to* BRADLEY.) Bradley! Bradley, put that blanket back!

(HALIE *moves toward* BRADLEY. SHELLY *suddenly throws the cup and saucer against the stage right door.* DEWIS *ducks. The cup and saucer smash into pieces.* HALIE *stops, turns toward* SHELLY. *Everyone freezes.* BRADLEY *slowly pulls his head out from under blanket, looks toward stage right door, then to* SHELLY. SHELLY *stares at* HALIE. DEWIS *cowers with roses.* SHELLY *moves slowly toward* HALIE. *Long pause.* SHELLY *speaks softly.*)

SHELLY: (*To* HALIE.) I don't like being ignored. I don't like being treated like I'm not here. I didn't like it when I was a kid and I still don't like it.

BRADLEY: (*Sitting up on sofa.*) We don't have to tell you anything, girl. Not a thing. You're not the police are you? You're not the government. You're just some prostitute that Tilden brought in here.

HALIE: Language! I won't have that language in my house!

SHELLY: (*To* BRADLEY.) You stuck your hand in my mouth and you call me a prostitute!

HALIE: Bradley! Did you put your hand in her mouth? I'm ashamed of you. I can't leave you alone for a minute.

BRADLEY: I never did. She's lying!

DEWIS: Halie, I think I'll be running along now. I'll just put the roses in the kitchen.

(DEWIS *moves toward stage left.* HALIE *stops him.*)

HALIE: Don't go now, Father! Not now.

BRADLEY: I never did anything, Mom! I never touched her! She propositioned me! And I turned her down. I turned her down flat!

(SHELLY *suddenly grabs her coat off the wooden leg and takes both the leg and coat down stage, away from* BRADLEY.)

BRADLEY: Mom! Mom! She's got my leg! She's taken my leg! I never did anything to her! She's stolen my leg!

(BRADLEY *reaches pathetically in the air for his leg.* SHELLY *sets it down for a second, puts on her coat fast and picks the leg up again.* DODGE *starts coughing softly.*)

HALIE: (*To* SHELLY.) I think we've had about enough of you, young lady. Just about enough. I don't know where you came from or what you're doing here but you're no longer welcome in this house.

SHELLY: (*Laughs, holds leg.*) No longer welcome!

BRADLEY: Mom! That's my leg! Get my leg back! I can't do anything without my leg.

(BRADLEY *keeps making whimpering sounds and reaching for his leg.*)

HALIE: Give my son back his leg. Right this very minute!

(DODGE *starts laughing softly to himself in between coughs.*)

HALIE: (*To* DEWIS.) Father, do something about this would you! I'm not about to be terrorized in my own house!

BRADLEY: Gimme back my leg!

HALIE: Oh, shut up, Bradley! Just shut up! You don't need your leg now! Just lay down and shut up!

(BRADLEY *whimpers. Lays down and pulls blanket around him. He keeps one arm outside blanket, reaching out toward his wooden leg.* DEWIS *cautiously approaches* SHELLY *with the roses in his arms.* SHELLY *clutches the wooden leg to her chest as though she's kidnapped it.*)

DEWIS: (*To* SHELLY.) Now, honestly dear, wouldn't it be better to try to talk things out? To try to use some reason?

SHELLY: There isn't any reason here! I can't find a reason for anything.

DEWIS: There's nothing to be afraid of. These are all good people. All righteous people.

SHELLY: I'm not afraid!

DEWIS: But this isn't your house. You have to have some respect.

SHELLY: You're the strangers here, not me.

HALIE: This has gone far enough!

DEWIS: Halie, please. Let me handle this.

SHELLY: Don't come near me! Don't anyone come near me. I don't need any words from you. I'm not threatening anybody. I don't even know what I'm doing here. You all say you don't remember Vince, okay, maybe you don't. Maybe it's Vince that's crazy. Maybe he's made this whole family thing up. I don't even care anymore. I was just coming along for the ride. I thought it'd be a nice gesture. Besides, I was curious. He made all of you sound familiar to me. Every one of you. For every name, I had an image. Every time he'd tell me a name, I'd see the person. In fact, each of you was so clear in my mind that I actually believed it was you. I really believed when I walked through that door that the people who lived here would turn out to be the same people in my imagination. But I don't recognize any of you. Not one. Not even the slightest resemblance.

DEWIS: Well you can hardly blame others for not fulfilling your hallucination.

SHELLY: It was no hallucination! It was more like a prophecy. You believe in prophecy, don't you?

HALIE: Father, there's no point in talking to her any further. We're just going to have to call the police.

BRADLEY: No! Don't get the police in here. We don't want the police in here. This is our home.

SHELLY: That's right. Bradley's right. Don't you usually settle your affairs in private? Don't you usually take them out in the dark? Out in the back?

BRADLEY: You stay out of our lives! You have no business interfering!

SHELLY: I don't have any business period. I got nothing to lose.

(*She moves around, staring at each of them.*)

BRADLEY: You don't know what we've been through. You don't know anything!

SHELLY: I know you've got a secret. You've all got a secret. It's so secret in fact, you're all convinced it never happened.

(HALIE *moves to* DEWIS.)

HALIE: Oh, my God, Father!

DODGE: (*Laughing to himself.*) She thinks she's going to get it out of us. She thinks she's going to uncover the truth of the matter. Like a detective or something.

BRADLEY: I'm not telling her anything! Nothing's wrong here! Nothin's ever been wrong! Everything's the way it's supposed to be! Nothing ever happened that's bad! Everything is all right here! We're all good people!

DODGE: She thinks she's gonna suddenly bring everything out into the open after all these years.

DEWIS: (*To* SHELLY.) Can't you see that these people want to be left in peace! Don't you have any mercy? They haven't done anything to you.

DODGE: She wants to get to the bottom of it. (*To* SHELLY.) That's it, isn't it? You'd like to get right down to bedrock? You want me to tell ya'? You want me to tell you what happened! I'll tell ya'. I might as well.

BRADLEY: No! Don't listen to him. He doesn't remember anything!

DODGE: I remember the whole thing from start to finish. I remember the day he was born.

(*Pause.*)

HALIE: Dodge, if you tell this thing—if you tell this, you'll be dead to me. You'll be just as good as dead.

DODGE: That won't be such a big change, Halie. See this girl, this girl here, she wants to know. She wants to know something more. And I got this feeling that it doesn't make a bit a' difference. I'd sooner tell it to a stranger than anybody else.

BRADLEY: (*To* DODGE.) We made a pact! We made a pact between us! You can't break that now!

DODGE: I don't remember any pact.

BRADLEY: (*To* SHELLY.) See, he doesn't remember anything. I'm the only one in the family who remembers. The only one. And I'll never tell you!

SHELLY: I'm not so sure I want to find out now.

DODGE: (*Laughing to himself.*) Listen to her! Now she's runnin' scared!

SHELLY: I'm not scared!

(DODGE *stops laughing, long pause.* DODGE *stares at her.*)

DODGE: You're not huh! Well, that's good. Because I'm not either. See, we were a well established family once. Well established. All the boys were grown. The farm was producing enough milk to fill Lake Michigan twice over. Me and Halie here were pointed toward what looked like the middle part of our life. Everything was settled with us. All we had to do was ride it out. Then Halie got pregnant again. Outa' the middle a' nowhere, she got pregnant. We weren't planning on havin' any more boys. We had enough boys already. In fact, we hadn't been sleepin' in the same bed for about six years.

HALIE: (*Moving toward stairs.*) I'm not listening to this! I don't have to listen to this!

DODGE: (*Stops* HALIE.) Where are you going! Upstairs! You'll just be listenin' to it upstairs! You go outside, you'll be listenin' to it outside. Might as well stay here and listen to it.

(HALIE *stays by stairs.*)

BRADLEY: If I had my leg you wouldn't be saying this. You'd never get away with it if I had my leg.

DODGE: (*Pointing to* SHELLY.) She's got your leg. (*Laughs.*) She's gonna keep your leg too. (*To* SHELLY.) She wants to hear this. Don't you?

SHELLY: I don't know.

DODGE: Well even if ya' don't I'm gonna' tell ya'. (*Pause.*) Halie had this kid. This baby boy. She had it. I let her have it on her own. All the other boys I had had the best doctors, best nurses, everything. This one I let her have by herself. This one hurt real bad. Almost killed her, but she had it anyway. It lived, see. It lived. It wanted to grow up in this family. It wanted to be just like us. It wanted to be a part of us. It wanted to pretend that I was its father. She wanted me to believe in it. Even when everyone around us knew. Everyone. All our boys knew. Tilden knew.

HALIE: You shut up! Bradley, make him shut up!

BRADLEY: I can't.

DODGE: Tilden was the one who knew. Better than any of us. He'd walk for miles with that kid in his arms. Halie let him take it. All night sometimes. He'd walk all night

out there in the pasture with it. Talkin' to it. Singin' to
it. Used to hear him singing to it. He'd make up stories.
He'd tell that kid all kinds a' stories. Even when he
knew it couldn't understand him. Couldn't understand a
word he was sayin'. Never would understand him. We
couldn't let a thing like that continue. We couldn't allow
that to grow up right in the middle of our lives. It made
everything we'd accomplished look like it was nothin'.
Everything was cancelled out by this one mistake. This
one weakness.

SHELLY: So you killed him?

DODGE: I killed it. I drowned it. Just like the runt of a
litter. Just drowned it.

(HALIE *moves toward* BRADLEY.)

HALIE: (*To* BRADLEY.) Ansel would've stopped him! Ansel
would've stopped him from telling these lies! He was a
hero! A man! A whole man! What's happened to the
men in this family! Where are the men!

(*Suddenly* VINCE *comes crashing through the screen
porch door up left, tearing it off its hinges. Everyone
but* DODGE *and* BRADLEY *back away from the porch
and stare at* VINCE *who has landed on his stomach on
the porch in a drunken stupor. He is singing loudly to
himself and hauls himself slowly to his feet. He has a
paper shopping bag full of empty booze bottles. He
takes them out one at a time as he sings and smashes
them at the opposite end of the porch, behind the
solid interior door, stage right.* SHELLY *moves slowly
toward stage right, holding wooden leg and watching*
VINCE.)

VINCE: (*Singing loudly as he hurls bottles.*) "From the
Halls of Montezuma to the Shores to Tripoli. We will
fight our country's battles on the land and on the sea."
(*He punctuates the words "Montezuma," "Tripoli,"
"battles" and "sea" with a smashed bottle each. He
stops throwing for a second, stares toward stage right
of the porch, shades his eyes with his hand as though
looking across to a battlefield, then cups at his hands
around his mouth and yells across the space of the*

porch to an imaginary army. *The others watch in terror and expectation.*)

VINCE: (*To imagined army.*) Have you had enough over there, 'Cause there's a lot more here where that came from! (*Pointing to paper bag full of bottles.*) A helluva lot more! We got enough over here to blow ya' from here to kingdomcome!

(*He takes another bottle, makes high whistling sound of a bomb and throws it toward stage right porch. Sound of bottle smashing against wall. This should be the actual smashing of bottles and not tape sound. He keeps yelling and heaving bottles one after another.* VINCE *stops for a while, breathing heavily from exhaustion. Long silence as the others watch him.* SHELLY *approaches tentatively in* VINCE's *direction, still holding* BRADLEY's *wooden leg.*)

SHELLY: (*After silence.*) Vince?

(VINCE *turns toward her. Peers through screen.*)

VINCE: Who? What? Vince who? Who's that in there!

(VINCE *pushes his face against the screen from the porch and stares in at everyone.*)

DODGE: Where's my goddamn bottle!

VINCE: (*Looking in at* DODGE.) What! Who is that?

DODGE: It's me! Your Grandfather! Don't play stupid with me! Where's my two bucks!

VINCE: Your two bucks?

(HALIE *moves away from* DEWIS, *upstage, peers out at* VINCE, *trying to recognize him.*)

HALIE: Vincent? Is that you, Vincent?

(SHELLY *stares at* HALIE *then looks out at* VINCE.)

VINCE: (*From porch.*) Vincent who? What is this! Who are you people?

SHELLY: (*To* HALIE.) Hey, wait a minute. Wait a minute! What's going on?

HALIE: (*Moving closer to porch screen.*) We thought you were a murderer or something. Barging in through the door like that.

VINCE: I am a murderer! Don't underestimate me for a minute! I'm the Midnight Strangler! I devour whole families in a single gulp!

(VINCE *grabs another bottle and smashes it on the porch.* HALIE *backs away.*)

SHELLY: (*Approaching* HALIE.) You mean you know who he is?

HALIE: Of course I know who he is! That's more than I can say for you.

BRADLEY: (*Sitting up on sofa.*) You get off our front porch you creep! What're you doing out there breaking bottles? Who are these foreigners anyway! Where did they come from?

VINCE: Maybe I should come in there and break them!

HALIE: (*Moving toward porch.*) Don't you dare! Vincent, what's got into you! Why are you acting like this?

VINCE: Maybe I should come in there and usurp your territory!

(HALIE *turns back toward* DEWIS *and crosses to him.*)

HALIE: (*To* DEWIS.) Father, why are you just standing around here when everything's falling apart? Can't you rectify this situation?

(DODGE *laughs, coughs.*)

DEWIS: I'm just a guest here, Halie. I don't know what my position is exactly. This is outside my parish anyway.

(VINCE *starts throwing more bottles as things continue.*)

BRADLEY: If I had my leg I'd rectify it! I'd rectify him all over the goddamn highway! I'd pull his ears out if I could reach him!

(BRADLEY *sticks his fist through the screening of the porch and reaches out for* VINCE, *grabbing at him and missing.* VINCE *jumps away from* BRADLEY's *hand.*)

VINCE: Aaaah! Our lines have been penetrated! Tentacles animals! Beasts from the deep!

(VINCE *strikes out at* BRADLEY's *hand with a bottle.* BRADLEY *pulls his hand back inside.*)

SHELLY: Vince! Knock it off will ya'! I want to get out of here!

(VINCE *pushes his face against screen, looks in at* SHELLY.)

VINCE: (*To* SHELLY.) Have they got you prisoner in there,

dear? Such a sweet young thing too. All her life in front
of her. Nipped in the bud.

SHELLY: I'm coming out there, Vince! I'm coming out
there and I want us to get in the car and drive away
from here. Anywhere. Just away from here.

(SHELLY *moves toward* VINCE's *saxophone case and
overcoat. She sets down the wooden leg, downstage
left and picks up the saxophone case and overcoat.*
VINCE *watches her through the screen.*)

VINCE: (*To* SHELLY.) We'll have to negotiate. Make some
kind of a deal. Prisoner exchange or something. A few of
theirs for one of ours. Small price to pay if you ask me.

(SHELLY *crosses toward stage right door with overcoat and case.*)

SHELLY: Just go and get the car! I'm coming out there
now. We're going to leave.

VINCE: Don't come out here! Don't you dare come out
here!

(SHELLY *stops short of the door, stage right.*)

SHELLY: How come?

VINCE: Off limits! *Verboten!* This is taboo territory. No
man or woman has ever crossed the line and lived to tell
the tale!

SHELLY: I'll take my chances.

(SHELLY *moves to stage right door and opens it.*
VINCE *pulls out a big folding hunting knife and pulls
open the blade. He jabs the blade into the screen and
starts cutting a hole big enough to climb through.*
BRADLEY *cowers in a corner of the sofa as* VINCE *rips
at the screen.*)

VINCE: (*As he cuts screen.*) Don't come out here! I'm
warning you! You'll disintegrate!

(DEWIS *takes* HALIE *by the arm and pulls her toward
staircase.*)

DEWIS: Halie, maybe we should go upstairs until this blows
over.

HALIE: I don't understand it. I just don't understand it. He
was the sweetest little boy!

(DEWIS *drops the roses beside the wooden leg at the
foot of the staircase then escorts* HALIE *quickly up the*

stairs. HALIE *keeps looking back at* VINCE *as they climb the stairs.*)

HALIE: There wasn't a mean bone in his body. Everyone loved Vincent. Everyone. He was the perfect baby.

DEWIS: He'll be all right after a while. He's just had a few too many that's all.

HALIE: He used to sing in his sleep. He'd sing. In the middle of the night. The sweetest voice. Like an angel. (*She stops for a moment.*) I used to lie awake listening to it. I used to lie awake thinking it was all right if I died. Because Vincent was an angel. A guardian angel. He'd watch over us. He'd watch over all of us.

(DEWIS *takes her all the way up the stairs. They disappear above.* VINCE *is now climbing through the porch screen onto the sofa.* BRADLEY *crashes off the sofa, holding tight to his blanket, keeping it wrapped around him.* SHELLY *is outside on the porch.* VINCE *holds the knife in his teeth once he gets the hole wide enough to climb through.* BRADLEY *starts crawling slowly toward his wooden leg, reaching out for it.*)

DODGE: (*To* VINCE.) Go ahead! Take over the house! Take over the whole goddamn house! You can have it! It's yours. It's been a pain in the neck every since the very first mortgage. I'm gonna die any second now. Any second. You won't even notice. So I'll settle my affairs once and for all.

(*As* DODGE *proclaims his last will and testament,* VINCE *climbs into the room, knife in mouth and strides slowly around the space, inspecting his inheritance. He casually notices* BRADLEY *as he crawls toward his leg.* VINCE *moves to the leg and keeps pushing it with his foot so that it's out of* BRADLEY's *reach then goes on with his inspection. He picks up the roses and carries them around smelling them.* SHELLY *can be seen outside on the porch, moving slowly center and staring in at* VINCE. VINCE *ignores her.*)

DODGE: The house goes to my Grandson, Vincent. All the furnishings, accoutrements and paraphernalia therein. Everything tacked to the walls or otherwise resting under this roof. My tools—namely my band saw, my skill saw, my drill press, my chain saw, my lathe, my electric sander, all go to my eldest son, Tilden. That is, if he ever shows up again. My shed and gasoline powered equipment, namely my tractor, my dozer, my hand tiller plus all the attachments and riggings for the above mentioned machinery, namely my spring-tooth harrow, my deep plows, my disk plows, my automatic fertilizing equipment, my reaper, my swathe, my seeder, my John Deere Harvester, my post-hole digger, my jackhammer, my lathe—(*To himself.*) Did I mention my lathe? I already mentioned my lathe—my Benny Goodman records, my harnesses, my bits, my halters, my brace, my rough rasp, my forge, my welding equipment, my shoeing nails, my levels and bevels, my milking stool—no, not my milking stool—my hammers and chisels, my hinges, my cattle gates, my barbed wire, self-tapping augers, my horsehair ropes and all related materials are to be pushed into a gigantic heap and set ablaze in the very center of my fields. When the blaze is at its highest, preferably on a cold, windless night, my body is to be pitched into the middle of it and burned til nothing remains but ash.

(*Pause.* VINCE *takes the knife out of his mouth and smells the roses. He's facing toward audience and doesn't turn around to* SHELLY. *He folds up knife and pockets it.*)

SHELLY: (*From porch.*) I'm leaving, Vince. Whether you come or not, I'm leaving.

VINCE: (*Smelling roses.*) Just put my horn on the couch there before you take off.

SHELLY: (*Moving toward hole in screen.*) You're not coming?

(VINCE *stays downstage, turns and looks at her.*)

VINCE: I just inherited a house.

SHELLY: (*Through hole, from porch.*) You want to stay here?

VINCE: (*As he pushes* BRADLEY'S *leg out of reach.*) I've gotta carry on the line. I've gotta see to it that things keep rolling.

(BRADLEY *looks up at him from floor, keeps pulling himself toward his leg.* VINCE *keeps moving it.*)

SHELLY: What happened to you, Vince? You just disappeared.

VINCE: (*Pause, delivers speech front.*) I was gonna run last night. I was gonna run and keep right on running. I drove all night. Clear to the Iowa border. The old man's two bucks sitting right on the seat beside me. It never stopped raining the whole time. Never stopped once. I could see myself in the windshield. My face. My eyes. I studied my face. Studied everything about it. As though I was looking at another man. As though I could see his whole race behind him. Like a mummy's face. I saw him dead and alive at the same time. In the same breath. In the windshield, I watched him breathe as though he was frozen in time. And every breath marked him. Marked him forever without him knowing. And then his face changed. His face became his father's face. Same bones. Same eyes. Same nose. Same breath. And his father's face changed to his Grandfather's face. And it went on like that. Changing. Clear on back to faces I'd never seen before but still recognized. Still recognized the bones underneath. The eyes. The breath. The mouth. I followed my family clear into Iowa. Every last one. Straight into the Corn Belt and further. Straight back as far as they'd take me. Then it all dissolved. Everything dissolved.

(SHELLY *stares at him for a while then reaches through the hole in the screen and sets the saxophone case and* VINCE's *overcoat on the sofa. She looks at* VINCE *again.*)

SHELLY: Bye Vince.

(*She exits left off the porch.* VINCE *watches her go.* BRADLEY *tries to make a lunge for his wooden leg.* VINCE *quickly picks it up and dangles it over* BRADLEY's *head like a carrot.* BRADLEY *keeps making desperate grabs at the leg.* DEWIS *comes down the staircase and stops halfway, staring at* VINCE *and* BRADLEY. VINCE *looks up at* DEWIS *and smiles. He keeps moving*

backwards with the leg toward upstage left as BRADLEY
crawls after him.)

VINCE: (*To* DEWIS *as he continues torturing* BRADLEY.) Oh,
excuse me, Father. Just getting rid of some of the vermin
in the house. This is my house now, ya' know? All mine.
Everything. Except for the power tools and stuff. I'm
gonna get all new equipment anyway. New plows, new
tractor, everything. All brand-new. (VINCE *teases* BRAD-
LEY *closer to the up left corner of the stage.*) Start right
off on the ground floor.

(VINCE *throws* BRADLEY'S *wooden leg far off stage left.*
BRADLEY *follows his leg offstage, pulling himself along
on the ground, whimpering. As* BRADLEY *exits* VINCE
*pulls the blanket off him and throws it over his own
shoulder. He crosses toward* DEWIS *with the blanket
and smells the roses.* DEWIS *comes to the bottom of the
stairs.*)

DEWIS: You'd better go up and see your Grandmother.

VINCE: (*Looking upstairs, back to* DEWIS.) My Grandmother? There's nobody else in this house. Except for
you. And you're leaving aren't you?

(DEWIS *crosses toward stage right door. He turns back
to* VINCE.)

DEWIS: She's going to need someone. I can't help her. I
don't know what to do. I don't know what my position
is. I just came in for some tea. I had no idea there was
any trouble. No idea at all.

(VINCE *just stares at him.* DEWIS *goes out the door,
crosses porch and exits left.* VINCE *listens to him leaving. He smells roses, looks up the staircase then smells
roses again. He turns and looks upstage at* DODGE. *He
crosses up to him and bends over looking at* DODGE'S
open eyes. DODGE *is dead. His death should have come
completely unnoticed by the audience.* VINCE *covers*
DODGE'S *body with the blanket, then covers his head.
He sits on the sofa, smelling roses and staring at*
DODGE'S *body. Long pause.* VINCE *places the roses on*
DODGE'S *chest then lays down on the sofa, arms folded
behind his head, staring at the ceiling. His body is in*

the same relationship to DODGE'*s. After a while* HALIE'*s* VOICE *is heard coming from above the staircase. The lights start to dim almost imperceptibly as* HALIE *speaks.* VINCE *keeps staring at the ceiling.*)

HALIE'S VOICE: Dodge? Is that you, Dodge? Tilden was right about the corn you know. I've never seen such corn. Have you taken a look at it lately? Tall as a man already. This early in the year. Carrots too. Potatoes. Peas. It's like a paradise out there, Dodge. You oughta' take a look. A miracle. I've never seen it like this. Maybe the rain did something. Maybe it was the rain.

(*As* HALIE *keeps talking offstage,* TILDEN *appears from stage left, dripping with mud from the knees down. His arms and hands are covered with mud. In his hands he carries the corpse of a small child at chest level staring down at it. The corpse mainly consists of bones wrapped in muddy, rotten cloth. He moves slowly downstage toward the staircase, ignoring* VINCE *on the sofa.* VINCE *keeps staring at the ceiling as though* TILDEN *wasn't there. As* HALIE'*s* VOICE *continues,* TILDEN *slowly makes his way up the stairs. His eyes never leave the corpse of the child. The lights keep fading.*)

HALIE'S VOICE: Good hard rain. Takes everything straight down deep to the roots. The rest takes care of itself. You can't force a thing to grow. You can't interfere with it. It's all hidden. It's all unseen. You just gotta wait till it pops up out of the ground. Tiny little shoot. Tiny little white shoot. All hairy and fragile. Strong though. Strong enough to break the earth even. It's a miracle, Dodge. I've never seen a crop like this in my whole life. Maybe it's the sun. Maybe that's it. Maybe it's the sun.

(TILDEN *disappears above. Silence. Lights go to black.*)

THE PROSE POEM

Edited and with an Introduction
by **Michael Benedikt**

The prose poem, a genre of poetry self-consciously written in prose and characterized by intense usage of poetic devices, has enjoyed a rebirth in America recently. Surprisingly, however, its foundations trace back to the early literature of civilizations around the world. In researching those foundations, Michael Benedikt has collected more than 500 of the finest examples of this prose poetry, arranged them geographically and chronologically, and produced the first international anthology of its kind.

🌿 **A Laurel Edition** $2.50

Two Novels by

COLETTE

Translated from the French by Margaret Crosland

Duo A masterfully drawn portrait of the disintegration of a seemingly happy marriage, and **LeToutounier** A story which traces a woman's life after the demise of her marriage, as she seeks to bridge the gap that men have created between herself and her sisters.

Few writers have portrayed a woman's situation as powerfully or as precisely as Sidonie-Gabrielle Colette.

"She was a sentimentalist, perhaps, and a titillator, certainly—both out of sheer calculation; but she was also an artist. Colette had the intuition, the insight, that her successors so largely lack and that made the good novelist a good reader of souls as well." —*Saturday Review-World*

"A remarkable woman who was incapable of a badly written sentence." —*The Boston Globe*

"One reads her as one reads any other lyric poet. She was Colette, a magician."—John K. Hutchens, *Book-of-the-Month Club*

🌱 A LAUREL EDITION $1.95